AF538798

INDIAN KĀVYA LITERATURE

Volume One

LITERARY CRITICISM

Creators of abundant good
and of unfailing hospitality
Are common in the world,
but appreciators are rare.

—Bhāsa

'What are you sir?' 'I am a writer.' 'Friend, repeat
Somenew good saying.'
'Nowadays I have given up discussing literature.' 'Why?'
'Listen:
There is no appreciator here who is a good writer him-
self and rightly discriminates
the value of good qualities and faults—or if by chance
there is one, he is not unselfish.'

—Rājaśekhara

Sāhityasya sarvapārṣadatvāt.

—Bhoja

INDIAN KĀVYA LITERATURE

A.K. Warder

Volume One
LITERARY CRITICISM

MOTILAL BANARSIDASS
PUBLISHING HOUSE • DELHI
Email: naraina@mlbd.in • Website: www.mlbd.in
 *@mlbdofficial*
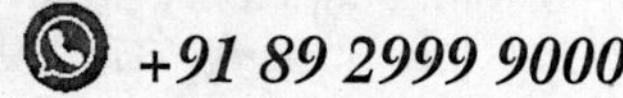 *+91 89 2999 9000*

*3rd Reprint: Delhi, **2024***
2nd Revised Edition: Delhi, 2009
1st Revised Edition: Delhi, 1989
First Edition: Delhi, 1972

ISBN: 978-93-5676-403-3 (Hardcover)
ISBN: 978-93-5676-388-3 (Paperback)
ISBN: 978-93-5966-191-9 (Hardcover set)
ISBN: 978-93-5966-694-5 (Paperback set)

Printed & Published by
Rajendra P Jain *for*
Motilal Banarsidass Publishing House
A-44, Naraina Industrial Area, Phase I,
New Delhi–110 028 (INDIA)
Email: naraina@mlbd.in Website: www.mlbd.in
Tel.: (+91-11)4751 1592
Showroom:
4637/20, F-2, Hari Sadan, First Floor, Ansari Road, Daryaganj
Delhi–110 002 (Opp. Fire Station) ***Tel.:*** (+91-11)4559 7999

The author records his grateful acknowledgments to the Canada Council for their research grants, which have enabled him to make the work more complete and may further enrich it through the discovery of 'lost' *kāvyas.*

PREFACE

The main purpose of this work is literary criticism, evaluating a great tradition of literature which recently has remained practically unknown to all but a few specialists in Sanskrit.

Previous publications on Indian literature in Western languages have at best sketched its history (i. e. attempted to clarify the chronology) and at worst given extremely misleading judgments on its nature. That such judgments have held the field should not be blamed on the incompetence of the scholars who invented them, or even simply on the prejudices which they shared with the fashionable thinkers of their times and countries. The scholars were most competent in their own field, which was philology, but literary criticism was not their profession. Western literary critics on the other hand had no access to original sources and left Indian literature to the 'specialists'. The scholars who tried to supply information on Indian literature applied whatever critical ideas they had picked up from their environment, accordingly taking Western (Greek, etc.) models as the only possible standard of good literature; unluckily they had picked up the Western tradition of criticism at its narrowest, as formulated during the +19. To them it appeared obvious that if Indian literature differed to any extent from the Greek or English models it must be inferior to precisely that extent. This cultural arrogance, accepted from their environment by scholars often most modest as individuals, was in some cases, especially in British writers, inflated to the most overweening proportions by the hot wind of colonialist and imperialist propaganda, this also docilely and dutifully accepted from their environment. It was an article of faith in British public opinion that Britain must rule India, hence anything that appeared to strengthen that faith, for example that the Indians were not competent to rule themselves or that Sanskrit literature was decadent, was readily believed.

The systematic disparagement of Indian culture during the +19 and +20 became a mighty industry with countless ramifications. It produced an impressive array of anti-textbooks, scholarly in outward manner and bearing the imprints of academic publishers. Its momentum has not yet entirely abated, although its political purpose disappeared in +1947, and on account of its influence it deserves detailed study and the publication of monographs making known its nature and extent. In our study of the literature here we shall ignore it, but it is necessary in a preface to warn the reader of the existence of these tenacious misrepresentations and of their continuing influence persisting among the secondary sources he may come across in libraries and bookshops (there are many reprints of older publications still in circulation, not yet superseded by more accurate and objective studies). It is particularly unfortunate that some recent Indian writers in English have followed their former British 'masters' and disparaged their own country's finest achievements, believing just this to be a 'modern', objective and broad-minded approach.

A new evaluation of Indian literature is long overdue. We may leave any anti-colonialist counterblast, and the criticism of prejudiced secondary sources, to those who are fond of polemic and political analysis. Our purpose here is the direct and positive enjoyment of literature. We shall regard it as axiomatic that the literature studied should be presented on its own terms, therefore we shall seek guidance from its creators and from the long and ancient Indian tradition of literary criticism which developed with it. No literature, least of all a highly sophisticated movement such as *kāvya*, can be understood unless we know what its creators were trying to achieve and what sort of contemporary criticism they may have hoped to satisfy.

If we are aiming to get closer to this literature and to understand its works in relation to contemporary influences, especially other works, we must try to improve our knowledge of its chronology. In preparing this book, a great deal of time has been spent on chronological problems, though their discussion has here been kept to the minimum in order not to interfere with the main purpose. Some of the problems have been studied in other publications (*Pali Metre*; *Indian Buddhism*; 'The Date of Bhāmaha'; 'The Possible Dates of Pārśva..') and the discussions need not be repeated, others must be treated briefly as they come up and the reasons for adopting a particular hypothesis indicated. Since our plan is to present the literature in chronological order, after preliminary chapters on criticism, some working hypothesis had to be adopted for each author. As the study proceeded and the works thought to belong to a given period were compared, various more or less subjective impressions grew in the present writer confirming or revising his ideas on chronological relationships. Where no other evidence seemed to be available he fell back on these impressions and makes no apology for doing so. Now that the fabric of his tentative chronological edifice is completed and each part can be surveyed in relation to the others, it will be easier for minute comparisons to be made of the details, which should lead to further constructive research and improvements in our knowledge. The day has not yet dawned when stylistic analysis by computer will illuminate the chronology of Indian literature.

It has been an important part of the critical purpose, here proposed, to study the positions of *kāvya* composers in the social and cultural history of India, a form of literary criticism which has not been seriously attempted before in the case of India. Besides having in mind the social milieu of each Indian author when reading his works, and visualising him as a real person in real situations of life, the present writer has set his literary panorama in his vision of Indian history as a whole. Here again one could not within the limits of a work such as this outline the political and social history of India, still less enter into full discussions of this highly controversial subject. This has been attempted in another work (see *An Introduction to Indian Historiography*). Suffice it to say here that the writer believes, having studied a mass of evidence, that India does indeed have a complex history of social change, development and conflict—contrary to widely received opinion. This view has been propounded in an article ('Desiderata in Indian Historiography') and as specific occasions arise below the evidence will be indicated for some of the social trends believed significant for the history of literature.

With the growing popularity of 'comparative literature', it should be useful to attempt to transpose into English the technical analysis, and its terminology, of the Indian critics. Indian literature ought to be available to students of world literature, as well as to specialists in Indian studies, on its own terms, moreover the critical theories of the Indians, such as those on the nature of the experience of the audience in the theatre, should be of wide interest. They are generally remarkable for their scientific, rather than subjective, character. Though Indian terminology is sometimes retained below, mainly for the sake of precision and for ease of reference to original sources by those who wish to make it, it is always explained in English.

The term *kāvya* means literature as a form of art. It excludes scriptures or religious writing (is therefore essentially secular), histories (except when history is made the subject of art, aiming at aesthetic rather than historical 'truth') and all technical writings on philosophy, science, the arts and so on. It includes poetry, drama and the novel, and history and biography when presented aesthetically. The term thus corresponds fairly well to 'literature' as used in the expressions 'English literature' or 'French literature', but it seemed preferable not to translate it in order to keep in mind that we are using it in its precise Indian sense. The West in fact seems to have no word for 'literature' in this strict sense. Thus the poetry of the *Veda* is excluded from our book, except in the discussion of origins, as 'scripture' *āgama*; and so is the ancient Epic (or 'Great Epic'), the *Mahābhārata*, since it is regarded as 'history' or 'tradition' *itihāsa*,—as a rich source of stories suitable for *kāvya* treatment, e. g. in dramas, but as not itself *kāvya*. Only the later 'epics', the artificial epics, of individual poets are properly *kāvya*, not the true traditional Epic, which we may conveniently distinguish with a capital letter in English. The *Rāmāyaṇa* on the other hand is regarded as *kāvya*, though in later times it has sometimes been invested with the authority of 'tradition'. In principle, *kāvya* may be written in any language, but it is associated especially with Sanskrit as the 'classical' language of India.

Our first eight chapters (Volume One) are introductory, presenting the Indian aesthetic and critical analysis and also the social milieu of the literature. This should provide a general idea of what Indian writers were aiming to achieve and may suggest to readers, especially Western or Westernised readers, how the literature was meant to be enjoyed.

The next eleven chapters (Volume Two) study the origins and formation of the style (or styles) and standard which came to be known as *kāvya*, with a survey of the early masterpieces which became classical models for many later writers (–400 to +200)

There follow ten chapters (Volume Three) on the next period (+200 to 600), when a 'feudal' type of social organisation was consolidated in India, suggesting or pursuing new ideals superimposed on Tradition and expressed in art. Most of our critics belong to the feudal period and seem more at home in this period than in early *kāvya*, which they neglected.

In principle all statements in our text are based on the original sources, i. e. the literary works in their original Indian languages. The editions used are shown in the Bibliography. Secondary sources and translations have been utilised as rapid preliminary guides through the literature as well as consulted for their opinions on chronology. It has been a rule, however, not to rely on them but to follow up their indications to the original sources and base our own statements only on these. There have been a very few exceptions to this rule in the case of unpublished manuscript *kāvyas* which are as yet inaccessible. All translations which appear in this book are original, in accordance with the above principle.

The author must here acknowledge his great debt to all the predecessors—editors of the original texts, translators and historians—who have pioneered the way, however frequently he may have disagreed with their views. Above all he was inspired as well as led by the *History of Classical Sanskrit Literature* of Dr. M. Krishnamachariar, in which for once he found a sympathetic pioneer and an extraordinarily persistent and devoted one. Operating in the Indian manuscript libraries over many years, Dr. Krishnamachariar succeeded in treating the unprinted literature on an equal basis with that in print and is therefore still up to date thirty years after publication, though happily many works known to him only in manuscript have since been printed. At times we could not follow his chronology, though his massive collection of chronological statements from original sources has continually guided us. In a sense our work is simply a commentary on his, using the rich materials he has assembled as a basis for an exercise in literary criticism on the originals. It is this *History* which first opened the eyes of the present writer, in +1949, to the unsuspected richness of *kāvya* and to the possibility of gleaning a far more complete history of the literature, from the numerous quotations of bibliographical and historical statements he had collected, than had seemed possible from the assertions made in other secondary sources.

The present book began simultaneously with *Pali Metre*, as a small card index of early *kavis* in chronological order, frequently rearranged, for reference while research for that study proceeded. After the completion of that work, which offered a basis for the chronology of the earliest period of *kāvya*, the card index grew into lecture notes for a course given first in +1955 to 56 in the University of Edinburgh. The idea of a book developed through the pursuit of the original sources to authenticate the lectures, along with the application to the literature of the appropriate analysis, which had meanwhile been studied from Bharata, Bhāmaha, Sāgaranandin, Śāradātanaya, Soḍḍhala, Rājaśekhara and the other old critics as they were gradually discovered.

It is to be hoped that readers of this book will be moved to learn Sanskrit and themselves tackle the originals of whatever here promises to be interesting. This book also is a secondary source, though the writer has done his best to make it as authentic as possible and to embody his subject in his book without interposing his own personality.

In the development of human consciousness India has played no small part. The student who has ventured into this vast field is indeed tempted to say that India's intellectual creation is to those of other lands as the Himālaya is to other mountains. It is because *kāvya* literature brings us, in the form of art, a great and characteristic part of this epic of human consciousness, that it should be read. Indian religion in its splendid variety can be studied through its proper texts, the scriptures *āgamas* and more systematic treatises *śāstras*. Philosophy also, of whatever kind, is systematically presented in its own treatises. *Kāvya* is distinguished from most scripture in that it is humanist, centred in man. As compared with philosophy, which also may be humanist in outlook, *kāvya* is an art, presenting its truths and its comments through images and individual characters. The humanism of *kāvya* differs from that of the critical and analytical schools of philosophy in its endless richness of concrete detail, which aims to present by examples the infinite variety of particular times, places, persons, situations and actions. Its subject matter is human experience of life, accumulated over thousands of years, an epic of humanity which is not available to us in any other form. This experience is presented in terms of the human emotions : the reactions of people to the situations of life.

In practice it was observed that the emotions could be grouped as a small number of basic ones, namely love, humour, energy, anger, fear, grief, disgust and astonishment (others, such as 'calm', seemed controversial), and a larger number of transient ones such as depression, envy, anxiety, bewilderment, shame, rashness, joy, pride, despair, indignation, reflection and so on. A theory was consequently worked out that a drama, and by extension any *kāvya* and even any work of art, will be most effective if it portrays one of the basic emotions as predominant in its subject matter, with other basic emotions in subordination to it and the appropriate transient emotions in the particular situations which occur. Thus the experience of life is reproduced in the form of a work of literary art.

But this effective presentation, which, we see from the *Nāṭyaśāstra*, was arrived at through the practical experience of actors in the ancient Indian theatre, led to the further consideration of the question why it was effective, in other words of the nature of the effect on the audience. Clearly the practical aim was to delight them, perhaps also to instruct them, but what was this delight ? It seems to be especially characteristic of the Indian theatre, and following it of *kāvya* generally, that the audience were found to 'taste' the emotions portrayed rather than to participate in them directly. This assumption that the spectator should remain separate from the hero he imagines to be present on the stage, that the experience of the spectator is different in kind from the emotions of the participant, may be essentially Indian. The true connoisseur of literature in India was by most critics taken to be engaged in a kind of contemplation of life as there presented, perhaps not unlike the meditation or reflection of a philosopher or even of a withdrawn ascetic. He adopted a higher and more objective standpoint, free from personal involvement, and in that relative detachment found a special delight and also the instruction of a wide view of the world extending far beyond his everyday experience. The 'taste' *rasa* he enjoyed, this aesthetic experience, was consequently described in terms other than those of direct emotion.

We may perhaps accurately explain the difference by distinguishing two 'levels' of experience (as suggested in a review in the *JRAS*, 1961) : (1) The 'aesthetic' level of the experience of the audience or readers; (2) the everyday 'psychological' level of the emotions portrayed in the characters on the stage or in the book. Thus when the basic emotion portrayed is love, the 'taste' enjoyed by the spectator, the aesthetic experience, is called the 'sensitive' (on this translation of *śṛṅgāra* see Chapter II [55]). When the emotion is grief, the aesthetic experience is the 'compassionate'. When the emotion is energy, the aesthetic experience is the 'heroic'. In this way the audience or readers are to be enriched in their experience through the portrayal, analysis, magnification and criticism of the human emotions, presented through their aesthetic understanding or appreciation. This enrichment is at the same time a form of education. On *śṛṅgāra* see Appendix to § 53.

The emotions appear through the actions of the subjects of *kāvya*. Human activity had been classified in India under four heads as directed towards either pleasure, or wealth and power, or moral ends ('virtue', 'justice', 'duty'), or renunciation of all worldly ends and seeking 'liberation' *mokṣa* or Nirvāṇa. *Kāvyas* were sometimes classified accordingly, but, if they incidentally provide instruction in these 'ends' of life (which should more properly be sought in the appropriate scientific, philosophical or religious treatises), their main educational function is to teach us humanity. Though we meet the gods in *kāvya*, and demons, as well as men, they are all human in their actions and emotions. By contemplating the strivings and passions of humanity we increase our sensitivity, our compassion, our sense of the comic and the marvellous, perhaps our 'heroism', even our fury at unjust acts and our apprehension (sense of danger) or abhorrence where appropriate. Here perhaps the purely aesthetic delight fuses with the practical educational expansion of the aesthetic understanding.

Man is still poor in humanity, a mere beginner as a social being. We have too little and too uncertain guidance. Let us then add to our common inheritance the experience of India, bequeathed to us by the several thousand poets, dramatists and story tellers who have reproduced it in their *kāvyas*.

Toronto, 1970 A. K. WARDER

NOTE TO THE SECOND EDITION

In the second edition a number of corrections have been made to the text and some cross-references added to vols. IV-VIII which have meanwhile been completed. An Appendix has been added of matter which could not be inserted without resetting, but keyed by paragraph number to the proper places.

1987 A. K. W.

NOTE TO THE READER ON TYPOGRAPHICAL DEVICES.

Dates.

The system of using '+' (plus) for 'A. D.' and '—' (minus) for 'B. C.' has been adopted, as being both convenient and secular. Dates are thus given as follows:

'–257' means '257 B. C.'

'+375' means 'A. D. 375'

The *centuries* have been abbreviated as follows :

'the—4' means 'the fourth century B. C.'

'the–4' means 'the fourth century B. C.'

'(+11)' means '(eleventh century A. D.)'

Since the dates in years contain three or four figures there should be no confusion between years and centuries. So far, no dates of years in the first century have been given. Should it be necessary to mention one, it will be clearly marked by the word 'year'.

Cross-references.

The entire work is divided into numbered paragraphs. This makes it possible to give precise cross-references, especially from Volume One (criticism, analysis) to later volumes (literature, practice) and from these back to Volume One. In this way unnecessary duplications of examples and explanations are avoided, along with undue prolixity in presenting either the criticism or the literature, yet the reader who wishes can easily find an example or the critical analysis by opening another volume. These cross-references are introduced in a fairly unobtrusive manner by simply enclosing the paragraph numbers referred to in square brackets, thus : [56], [1538], [341, 363, 379] and so on.

Sanskrit words.

Sanskrit and other Indian words which are the originals of English equivalents given immediately before them are as a rule simply italicised and not enclosed in brackets. For example :

'Literature *kāvya*, says Kuntaka, is the activity of the author *kavi*, aimed at beauty *vaicitrya*, which produces...' From the context it should be clear when a Sanskrit word is not translated, thus : 'drama being a form of *kāvya*'.

Footnotes and bibliography.

It seemed undesirable to clutter the pages of the work with footnotes and intolerable to interrupt the reader with demands to check something on another page, which might or might not turn out to be of interest to him, except for the substantial cross-references explained above. No serious objection could be found to including all essential information, and references to sources, in the text of the work itself. This provides much smoother reading than separated notes, which have therefore been avoided except in one or two cases where there seemed to be no satisfactory way of introducing the additional explanation into the text. Bibliographical information, on the other hand, is arranged systematically in the Bibliography, where it can easily be found both when reading the text and afterwards. Brief references to particular editions have naturally been incorporated where necessary in the text, with their page numbers.

A means see Appendix (1987).

CONTENTS OF VOLUME ONE

Page

PREFACE.................................... vii

Note on typographical devices xvi

CHAPTER

I. *Kāvya* and its languages 1

II. Indian Aesthetics 9

III. Indian Dramaturgy : the Construction of Plays 54

IV. Indian Poetics 77

V. The Literary Forms : The Drama...... 122

VI. The Literary Forms: Epic and Lyric Poetry 169

VII. The Literary Forms: Biography and the Novel (including the *campū* and Short Story).... 181

VIII. The Audience and the Readers of *Kāvya* and its Social Functions ' the Authors 200

BIBLIOGRAPHY 219

INDEX 261

APPENDIX 283

CHAPTER I

KĀVYA AND ITS LANGUAGES

1. *Kāvya*, as noted in the Preface, means literature as a form of art. This is distinguished from three other branches of composition : (1) scriptures or 'canonical' works *āgama*; (2) tradition or history *itihāsa*; (3) systematic treatises on any subject *śāstra*.

2. Canonical works include in the first place the *Veda*, the Canon of Brahmanism (or Vedism, *Vaidika*), but also the Canons of the Buddhists, Jainas and other schools (such as the Buddhist *Tripiṭaka* regarded as the words of the Buddha), though these might not be recognised by brahmans (*brāhmaṇas*: the priests of the Vedic tradition) as true canonical works, any more than these schools themselves recognised the *Veda*; lastly there are the Canons of Śaiva and Vaiṣṇava scriptures.

3. Tradition, which we may for our present purposes distinguish with a capital 'T', includes especially the great Epic, the *Mahābhārata*, handed down orally and probably largely extempore for many centuries before it became fixed in the form represented by the manuscript tradition. Associated with this are the *Purāṇas*, 'antiquities', or universal histories of the brahmans, numerous recensions of what was probably originally a single but again oral historical record. These records of antiquity begin, as perhaps the original did, with the evolution of the world and with mythology, and they have been rewritten from time to time as convenient media for all kinds of religious doctrines which could be tacked on to them, and even as encyclopaedic collections of miscellaneous information, secular as well as religious. In style they still resemble the *Mahābhārata*, though for the most part they are much later. In fact texts of this kind have been concocted even in quite recent times and passed off as the work of ancient sages. In principle, Tradition is the words of ancient sages, carrying great authority on account of the learning and virtue of the supposed authors, though inferior in this respect to a revelation of a transcendental text such as the *Veda*.

4. Under 'treatises' any technical or systematic work is included, along with commentaries of any kind. The term *śāstra*, which may be used either for a technical book or for a 'subject' thus expounded, was, however, sometimes used, for example by Rājaśekhara (*Kāvyamīmāṃsā* p. 2), as a general term for all literature other than *kāvya*; including therefore canonical works, Tradition and systematic treatises under the single head of learning, contrasted with art.

5. Since the various kinds of composition developed gradually over many centuries, it is not surprising if we find some overlapping between them, not to mention occasional deliberate infringements of the boundaries by later writers, some of which we shall have to mention in later chapters. The *Veda*, to begin with, represents all we now have of the earliest literature of India and is in fact very varied in content though eventually restricted to liturgical use. It certainly includes 'art' literature of its period, composed by poets. The Epic is indisputably poetry, at least in its more original parts, though it is regarded as primarily history. The distinctions we here use, in fact, arose gradually in the period between about the –5 and the –1, during which *kāvya* as we now understand it developed and became recognised as a special kind of literature. When we come to trace this development we shall have to look for the origin of 'literature as an art' in the *Veda*, in the *Tripiṭaka* and in the Epic.

6. *Kāvya* was (and is) composed by *kavis*. It is usual to translate *kavi* as 'poet', and *kāvya* is sometimes translated 'poetry', but this is imprecise. In India, prose *gadya* and verse *padya* are both used in *kāvya*, and they are both used in other branches of composition, including technical treatises. Verse is easier to memorise than prose, for the purposes of a handbook for students, but need not be at all poetic in a treatise on law or mathematics. On the other hand a novel, though in prose, may have all the necessary attributes of *kāvya*.

7. *Kāvya* is composed in various languages, although it is especially associated with Sanskrit *saṃskṛta*. In the strict sense Sanskrit, sometimes called 'Classical Sanskrit', is a refined and elevated form of the ancient language of northern India, which was described with extraordinary comprehensiveness by the renowned grammarian Pāṇini (–4). Sanskrit is thus con-

trasted with the more ancient 'Vedic' of the *Veda* and even with the dialect of the Epic. The perfection of Pāṇini's description was such as to have made possible the production of literature in fluent Sanskrit ever since, without any variation in grammar although the vocabulary has been continually enriched. The language as thus described and used is perfectly regular in its grammar, and even somewhat artificially polished and refined. It was based originally on the cultivated speech of educated *śiṣṭa* persons, especially the hereditary priesthood *brāhmaṇas*, in about the – 9, and kept up since then among the educated with little change until Pāṇini's codification fixed it for all time.

8. The language of the masses of the people had diverged from that of the educated before the – 9, and it also varied in the different regions of the Indo – Aryan community from the Hindu Kush, the historical frontier of India, to the delta of the Ganges. This language , or rather these dialects, naturally continued to change, passing through several phases down to the modern Indo-Aryan languages. The popular or vernacular languages of the period between about – 500 and + 500 are generally called Prakrits *prākṛtas*. At least a dozen of these were used in literature and particularly in *kāvya*. It is often presumed that all these forms of Indo-Aryan speech, Sanskrit and Prakrit, go back to a common ancestor in the – 2nd millennium. It appears, however , that this ancient language was already dialectally divided. Only the language of the *Veda* is preserved from this period, but it shows certain phonological features distinct from Sanskrit and from the easternmost Prakrit, Māgadhī, which lead us to infer the existence of at least three major dialects in the – 2nd millennium: Vedic in the North-West, the ancestor of Sanskrit in the centre, and the ancestor of Māgadhī in the East (then located in the upper rather than the lower basin of the Ganges).

9. The language of Tradition or of the Great Epic, usually called 'Epic Sanskrit', is in fact a rather free and irregular form of Sanskrit (thus not strictly 'Sanskrit') not always agreeing with the descriptions of the grammarians. In style it is somewhat rough and improvised, but enlivened by stock epithets, formulae and similes such as are the characteristics of traditional epic poetry in many languages. Though constantly interpolated, and enormously lengthened, by successive generations of minstrels down to about the +4, when it attained the form of the present vulgate (as established in the Critical Edition), the Great Epic is presumably based on the standard language of the Pañcāla Empire (capital Hastināpura on the upper Ganges) of North-Central and North-West India (under the Paurava Dynasty, *c.* -900 to -750, the descendants of the victors in the Bhārata War described in the Epic). It is thus closely related to Sanskrit, the language of the educated and especially priestly classes in the same Empire. The Epic bards of the court were not priests and were not 'educated' by the standards of the priesthood.

10. Māgadhī was the standard language of the great empire of Magadha, a state on the lower Ganges, which from the -5 to the -2 ruled over most of Northern India and for a shorter time over most of the South as well, with decisive consequences in the cultural unification of India which has endured ever since. Sanskrit was cultivated in this empire, though Māgadhī was the language of government and administration and of much, perhaps most, literature. The greatest Sanskrit grammarians, including Pāṇini, lived in this period and were patronised by some of the emperors. Sanskrit was used for the learned writings of the priesthood and to some extent for other literature, including *kāvya*, though it was probably restricted to a fairly narrow circle of educated connoisseurs.

11. Little literature has survived from the period of the Magadhan Empire. From the evidence extant, however, we can say with fair confidence that the *kāvya* movement originated in the Magadhan Empire and very probably in the Māgadhī language itself. Through changes in fashion, and in the Māgadhī language, the earliest *kāvya* literature was mostly neglected and lost in subsequent ages. The chief exception is the Sanskrit *Rāmāyaṇa*, traditionally revered as the first *kāvya*, though as preserved it contains interpolations and substantial additions later than the +1.

12. The earliest examples of *kāvya* now available and approximately datable are found in the Canon or *āgama* of the Sthaviravāda school of Buddhism in Pali (*pāḷi*), a Prakrit dialect very close to the old Māgadhī and strongly influenced by it. This appears to have been spoken in Western India (Avanti) during the period of the Magadhan Empire. On these problems see *Pali Metre*, especially pp. 7ff., 85, 103, 211. In these texts, which happened to be included in an *āgama* collection because they expressed Buddhist ideals, we are able to trace the development, and perhaps the origin, of *kāvya* between the -5 and the -2.

13. According to some later Indian Buddhist writers the Sthaviravāda Canon was in the Prakrit called Paiśācī, whence we might infer that Pali (a term used only later and meaning simply 'text', 'canonical text', and not properly the name of a language) is Paiśācī (see Lin Li-Kouang, 1949, 176ff. —Śākyaprabha and others, interpreted by Bu-ston). In Ceylon it was believed that Pali was Māgadhī, but this can be accepted only in the broadest sense of a language of the period of the ascendancy of Magadha, and certainly under Māgadhī influence, not in the sense of a regional dialect. Secular literature is known to have been written in a dialect called Paiśācī, which appears to have been current some time between the – 4 and the – 1 in the country of the Dakṣiṇāpatha (modern 'Deccan'), the 'Road to the South' which led from Avanti to the Godāvarī River. This country was an outpost of Indo-Aryan speech on the borders of the Dravidian South. Later it was called Mahārāṣṭra and its language came to be called Māhārāṣṭrī. The Māhārāṣṭrī of the +2 and +3 and later is very different from Paiśācī, and represents a new phase of Prakrit. As to Paiśācī, descriptions by grammarians, and especially the few fragments that survive from the original of the famous Paiśācī novel *Bṛhatkathā* (now available only in later paraphrases in other languages), show a language in many respects similar to Pali, though distinct from it in minor details. Since according to the grammatical writers there were eleven different varieties of 'Paiśācī', Pali may well be one of these and the *Bṛhatkathā* in another. Linguistically and historically Paiśācī, 'Pali' and the dialects of the inscriptions of the – 3 in the Magadhan Empire form a closely related group representing what may be called early Prakrit, current between the – 5 and the – 2. Early Māgadhī belonged to this group.

14. Prakrit languages continued in use as standard languages (in administration, inscriptions, etc.) in India until the +2, when they were superseded by Sanskrit in most regions. Beginning from the +1 we find also a period of the ascendancy of Sanskrit in literature. The early Prakrits had then become obsolete, as the vernaculars reached what may be called the intermediate phase of Prakrit. These intermediate Prakrits, especially Māhārāṣṭrī but also the intermediate phases of other Prakrits such as Śaurasenī and Māgadhī, occupied a now subordinate position alongside Sanskrit in *kāvya*. Śaurasenī is the basic Prakrit used in the drama, but not found elsewhere. Since it was the dialect of Mathurā, the eastern Kuṣāṇa capital, we may infer that the classical theatre of India became standardised there during the +1 and +2. This phase of Prakrit, representing roughly the vernaculars of the+1 to+4, became stereotyped as a group of subordinate dialects used in *kāvya*. In what may be called their 'classical' forms, of this period, these Prakrits were described by grammarians and continued to be used indefinitely according to the usages in literature of about the +4.

15. Māhārāṣṭrī was the most favoured by *kavis* among these intermediate standard literary Prakrits. It was the furthest removed from Sanskrit linguistically, hence most different in character, and also it was the last to give way to Sanskrit as the standard language of the country where it was spoken, as may be seen by studying the inscriptions through the +4.

16. Both Paiśācī and Māhārāṣṭrī literature are recorded to have been written in the Āndhra (Sātavāhana) Empire of Mahārāṣṭra, which flourished from about the -2 to the early +3. The known inscriptions of that empire, however, show a language intermediate between them. A tradition recorded in some Sanskrit versions of the *Bṛhatkathā* states that the Paiśācī language was despised by a Sātavāhana emperor, who criticised the language of the novel when it was first presented to him and thus delayed its publication and nearly caused its destruction. This suggests that Paiśācī was then an obsolete literary language, still used for prose fiction set in the past, perhaps because of its archaic character, but no longer a spoken or official standard. It seems to have been the same emperor in tradition, though probably a different one in fact, who enthusiastically patronised the earliest known Māhārāṣṭrī literature, a collection of lyric poems based on country lyrics and folk songs [769]. This collection was apparently made in the+2, though probably additions have been made to it since then. The administrative language of the empire was still the older standard dialect of the inscriptions, whilst Māhārāṣṭrī was never used in the empire for inscriptions, appearing only later in the successor states after the collapse of the Āndhras. From this some scholars have hastily concluded that Māhārāṣṭrī originated only later and that the traditional association of the language with a Sātavāhana emperor is false. In fact there is no reason why a country dialect admired as a medium for lyrics should at once be adopted as an imperial administrative language. Though it might later spread and become a standard, the superseding of an established, though archaic, standard would be a much more serious matter than the appearance of a new literary fashion at court.

17. By the middle of the +1st millennium the intermediate Prakrits had been replaced in speech by a later phase of vernacular dialects called Deśī ('country', 'provincial') or 'Apabhraṃśa'. The term Apabhraṃśa has two distinct meanings : (1) it is used by grammarians to denote any linguistic form not accepted by them as standard Sanskrit—this is its earlier use and would include all Prakrit forms, (2) it came to be used to denote the vernaculars of the mid +1st millennium and the following seven centuries or so as distinguished from the earlier Prakrits. Historically it is regarded as a late form of Prakrit, although it might be more natural linguistically to regard Apabhraṃśa as the early phase of the modern Indo-Aryan languages. The boundary between Apabhraṃśa and the modern languages is very arbitrary, the development from the +6 to the +16 being a gradual one with no sweeping changes at any point. Apabhraṃśa and in turn the modern languages were recognised in due course as media for *kāvya*. It appears that the Apabhraṃśa trend originated in Sindhu and spread from there, being thus known as 'Saindhava' [341, 357, 363, 377].

18. The *kavi* Rājaśekhara (*c*. +860 to 930) suggests that *kāvya* may be in any language (*Kāvyamīmāṃsā* pp. 19, 48ff.). Daṇḍin already (+7) had referred to novels in 'all languages' (*Kāvyalakṣaṇa* I. 38). *Kāvya* was not restricted in practice to any group of languages, and besides the Indo-Aryan languages (which of course include Sinhalese) *kāvyas* appear in the Dravidian languages, especially Tamil, and in languages as remote as Javanese, which has an extensive classical *kāvya* literature. It is not possible for one person to survey all these ramifications of *kāvya* in detail. The plan of a general study cannot conveniently embrace such a manifold history. On the other hand it is impossible to isolate any one language of *kāvya*, on account of the mutual interaction of the *kavis* as well as the mixture of languages usual in dramas and the broad view taken by even the earliest critics in their studies. If we attempt to follow the main line of development in India we must include Sanskrit, the Prakrits and Apabhraṃśa on an equal footing and we must also notice the developments in the modern languages and in the Dravidian languages. The literature of the many modern languages could not be fully treated in a book on *kāvya* even if the author were adequately qualified, but, if we follow the fortunes of *kāvya* down to modern times, though we concentrate mainly on Sanskrit we should observe those trends in the modern languages which are related to our theme. Dravidian *kāvya* in the earlier period may be regarded as outside the main stream flowing from North East India, and in fact examples of it appear only fairly late. In the +2nd millennium, when most of Northern India fell under an alien rule unsympathetic to *kāvya*, and regarding the suppression of drama in particular as a sacred duty, the stream was broken into several isolated fractions, of which the Southern was by far the largest and strongest. Though an adequate survey of Dravidian *kāvya* cannot be given in this book or by the present writer, it will be desirable at least in the later period to refer to *kāvyas* in Tamil [2063], Kannaḍa [3239], Telugu [5277] and Malayālam [8069 ff.]

CHAPTER II

INDIAN AESTHETICS

19. An extensive theoretical literature on *kāvya* has been preserved, which will serve as a guide to our exploration. Two main branches of this critical work are usually distinguished, as poetics and dramaturgy. The old name of poetics is *kriyākalpa* or *kāvyakriyākalpa*, 'procedure for composition (of *kāvya*)' (Raghavan, *Some Concepts of the Alaṅkāra Śāstra*, 264ff., cf. Ratnaśrījñāna p. 6), but the subject is now commonly known as *alaṅkāraśāstra*, referring to the figures of speech *alaṅkāras* regarded by some critics as the essential characteristic of *kāvya*. Dramaturgy is simply *nāṭyaśāstra*, 'the study of drama', which is also the title of the most ancient extant treatise on the subject. Naturally these two branches of study overlap, drama being a form of *kāvya* and using the same styles and figures, whilst poetics is actually treated in the *Nāṭyaśāstra* as a part of the techniques of the theatre. However, they have tended to be kept separate. The earliest discussions we know of on poetics are due to ancient grammarians, beginning with Yāska (his date is controversial, – 4 or earlier), and the subject tended to be treated as part of the enquiry into the nature of language. Dramaturgy on the other hand was in ancient times primarily the practical technique of the stage, leading only incidentally into theoretical considerations on the nature and purpose of the theatre.

20. A variety of aesthetic theories developed from these two branches of study, approaching the subject either through the consideration of what constitutes beauty in the language of *kāvya* or through the consideration of the effect of *kāvya* on its readers and audience. Thus in the former case the 'aesthetic experience' *rasa* is part of the meaning of the subject matter, brought effectively to the reader because the language expressing it is beautiful (see e.g. Bhāmaha [192, 194]), therefore presumably also one part of the overall 'delight' *prīti* which it is the function of a beautiful *kāvya* to produce. In the latter case (see e. g. the *Nāṭyaśāstra* [182]) the figures of speech and other beauties of expression are entirely subordinate to the purpose of producing 'aesthetic experience' *rasa*. At first sight this might seem to be just a difference of emphasis, but on further analysis it can be seen to lead to a fundamental divergence of conception. If beauty of language is the essential characteristic of *kāvya*, as Bhāmaha maintains (I.13ff., cf. II.85ff. and I.36), enabling it to produce delight, then the special aesthetic experience described by the dramaturgists might seem to be dispensable, although Bhāmaha himself (I. 21) requires it at least in an epic *kāvya*. On the other hand the *Nāṭyaśāstra* seems to restrict the delight produced by the drama (if not of all *kāvya*) to the specific aesthetic experience consisting in the tasting of human emotions. Later critics worked out various solutions of the problem thus posed.

21. In this Chapter we shall consider the dramatic theory of the aesthetic experience and matters related to it and in the following Chapter the theory of the construction of plays and certain other features of the Indian theatre. After that we can turn to the writers on poetics. To complete this preliminary statement on the theoretical resources of *kāvya*, we may note that treatises on metre form a bulky supplement to those on poetics, whilst the *kavi* was expected to have studied many other subjects, from grammar and logic to nature and love.

22. The history of the theory takes us back to the earliest period of *kāvya* (the Pali Canon contains remarks on poetic theory—see Chapter XI below). Indeed *kāvya* presupposes *kāvya* theory : if there were no conscious theory behind it a work would perhaps not be *kāvya*. A developing and highly controversial theory accompanied the practice of *kāvya* throughout its history, and this intellectual sophistication is an essential characteristic of the work of a *kavi*, it being not uncommon to announce the theoretical standpoint to be illustrated at the beginning of a poem or play and to make some critical observations at the beginning of a novel. A short but reasoned apology might be added at the end of a poem. The full appreciation of a *kāvya*, like that of a piece of 'classical' music, presupposes some acquaintance with theory and some familiarity with trends and controversies among creative and critical authors.

23. As part of the social background of *kāvya*, which may have a bearing on its aesthetics as well as being important for a part of its subject matter, we should notice the existence and influence of a theory of pleasure *kāma*. The works devoted to its exposition are concerned primarily with sex, but also with elegant living in general. Sex is, or was, a highly technical subject of infinite complexity and requiring great diligence to achieve a full command of its resources. In the treatises on pleasure its technicalities are elaborated after a general introduction on the life of pleasure. The standard textbook which is the earliest now available, the *Kāmasūtra*, in the course of this introduction makes reference to many other subjects regarded as subordinate branches of pleasure, which were dealt with in special treatises and accordingly are here merely listed in a statement that they are to be studied as parts of the science of pleasure. This list of the branches of pleasure enumerates sixty-four arts, crafts, sciences and amusements. They include the fine arts and *kāvya*, the decorative arts, health, games and sports, gambling, chemistry, geology, engineering, carpentry, toy-making, war and the study of languages (*Kāmasūtra* pp. 29f.).

24. The science of pleasure *kāmaśāstra* arose in the distant past, before the rise of *kāvya*, if not at the origin of the universe, as some have it. It appears to have developed first under the auspices of the materialist or naturalist (Lokāyata) school of philosophers, who maintained that pleasure was the highest object of human life and denounced the pretensions of religion, that enemy of human happiness. This rather advanced doctrine appeared impracticable to the rulers or ruling classes of ancient and medieval India, and the Lokāyata did not prosper.

25. The orthodox brahmans, however, recognised the importance and influence of pleasure, and, probably in the +3, one of them, Mallanāga Vātsyāyana, produced an orthodox and respectable manual of pleasure, the *Kāmasūtra* we now possess, in which pleasure is stated to be subordinate to virtue (*dharma*, in this case the Brahmanical religion) and the acquisition of wealth (p. 14). At the same time he offered his work as a convenient summary of the very extensive earlier literature on pleasure. He also outlines a history of the science, which in its earliest part is mythical. This orthodox compromise was generally accepted by the priesthood and the aristocracy, the theory being that pleasure is a proper end to pursue provided that it does not conflict with the higher ends of vistas and wealth, in which case it must give way.

26. No earlier literature on the subject appears to have been preserved, Mallanāga's work being generally referred to as authoritative by later writers. It may be worth noting from Mallanāga's own account that, discounting the mythological origins (Brahmā himself after creating living beings is said to have propounded detailed teachings on the three ends of life, *Kāmasūtra* p. 4, then Śiva's attendant Nandin composed a separate *Kāmasūtra*—these references make the science appear orthodox), Śvetaketu (*c.* —800?) is remembered as a famous teacher of *kāma*, then Bābhravya of Pāñcāla (between the – 8 and -5) prepared what long remained the standard work covering the whole subject; finally Dattaka, Cārāyaṇa, Ghoṭakamukha and others (from the —5 onwards, mostly in Magadha or its empire) composed seven separate monographs on the topics of the seven sections of Bābhravya's work (p. 5).

27. In the *Kāmasūtra* the wealthy but educated private citizen *nāgaraka* is recommended to pursue a life of refined pleasure, though without neglecting essential religious duties and his business (pp. 38ff.). He should live in a house and garden designed for the maximum aesthetic effect, with facilities for writing, painting, music, chess and carpentry as well as for lovemaking. His business should be despatched in the morning, after which he will have lunch and then amuse himself in various ways, including the practice of the arts. At this time he may receive such visitors as the 'parasite' *viṭa*, whom he commissions for important errands in connection with social and amorous affairs. Later in the afternoon he dresses up and joins his circle *goṣṭhī* of friends to sit and converse, especially about literature and art—though as an amateur he should not display a too severe learning. He has a second meal in the late afternoon or evening. The evening is the time for music, after which the art of love should be practised. A

28. The *goṣṭhī* is a semi-public gathering : though its members may meet at their own houses they meet also in public buildings or parks and in the houses of geisha[1] girls.

1. The word 'geisha', though not Indian, is familiar in English

Their aim is pleasure, including the amusement of the public, and the recitation and criticism of poetry—including the verses of the *nāgarakas* themselves – is a prominent feature of the entertainment. On festival days a special *goṣṭhī* may be arranged (which might on rare occasions be attended by the wives of members), and fortnightly or monthly there should be a festive assembly *samāja* at the local temple of Sarasvatī, the goddess of literature and the arts (p. 44). For this *samāja* the *nāgaraka* must engage players for dramatic performances to entertain the people. Many varieties of these parties and festivals are described, and it is clear that public entertainment as well as private amusement was a social obligation of the *nāgaraka* and perhaps the main justification for his way of life. The *Harivaṃśa* (II.88) describes a *goṣṭhī* by and on the sea. Literature and drama are conspicuous at most of these social and popular gatherings, which in their public aspect were perhaps a more sophisticated variation on the ancient (and modern) popular recitations of epic poems. A

29. The prologues of plays often name a festival for which they were performed, and it is clear that the primary function of the drama in ancient and medieval India, as long as Indian civilisation maintained its independence, was this social one, whether the patron were a local *nāgaraka* or a prince, and that on the frequent festival occasions every city in India and many towns and villages enjoyed performances of plays.

30. If the would-be *nāgaraka* were not wealthy, three careers in the service of *nāgarakas* and geishas were open to him, according to the *Kāmasūtra*. If married, he could be a parasite (p. 50), who is primarily a messenger and ambassador with wide experience of human nature, or he could be a 'jester' or 'fool' *vidūṣaka*. The parasite is expert in polite and quick-witted conversation and flattery and so lubricates social intercourse. It is his business to know everything that is going on in society. Though something of a rogue, he is on the whole a stickler for

---

and seems useful as an equivalent for *gaṇikā* and its many synonyms in Sanskrit. It suggests the sophistication and elegance, and skill in the fine arts including literature and music, of the Indian as of the Japanese girls, which seems quite foreign to the 'harlot', 'courtesan', etc., of English and most European tradition. The Greek *hetaira* might offer some parallel, but the Japanese geisha, being perhaps historically connected with the *gaṇikā* by cultural diffusion from India, probably represents her more accurately.

what he interprets as the proper social conventions and does not tolerate odd behaviour or what seems to him immoral, i. e. departures from the usual custom. The *nāgaraka* commissions him especially to help in temporary affairs with women, particularly geishas, to persuade them out of their jealousy which has produced a lovers' quarrel, arrange new introductions and so on. In *kāvya* he appears especially in the satirical monologue (see e. g. Ch. XIX below [1103]). A

31. The jester is a frivolous companion, often greedy and vain as depicted in *kāvyas*, but attempting to appear educated whilst in fact stupid and clumsy. If employed as a messenger he is sure to bungle the affair, but his antics may serve as a useful screen or diversion. Being always absolutely loyal to his patron and trying to serve his interests, he provides moral support in times of stress, not least by his unintentional absurdities. His patchy acquaintance with the arts makes him good entertainment in the *goṣṭhī*. In *kāvyas* he always claims to be a brahman, but the *Kāmasūtra* mentions simply his partial education, playfulness and trustworthiness (p. 50) [1086, 1187].

32. A bachelor too poor to be a *nāgaraka* could become a 'tutor' (*pīṭhamarda*—p. 50) [1221], teaching the arts regarded as the branches of pleasure, which we have mentioned above. His name derives from a peculiar kind of portable stool *pīṭha* on a stick which he traditionally carried everywhere with him, as it were a portable professorial 'chair' which he kept well polished *marda*—Yaśodhara's commentary. He could make a living by teaching but sometimes might become the companion and friend of a *nāgaraka*. Some later writers on drama (e.g. Dhanañjaya p. 40, Śiṅgabhūpāla, p. 21) are inclined to regard the secondary hero in some dramas, who is a friend of the main hero and the protagonist in the sub-plot which assists the main action, as a 'tutor', but it would surely be too much to make a generalisation of this. Bahurūpamiśra (on *Daśarūpaka* II. 8) has a good interpretation here restricting 'tutor' to its proper *Kāmasūtra* sense. These three characters could make a living in the circle of the *nāgarakas* and geishas, and the *Kāmasūtra* calls them the 'ministers' of these. [2266]

33. It is clear that *kāvya* in such a setting as this will be fundamentally secular in outlook, and this is in fact the impression given by the majority of *kāvyas* now available, beginning with the earliest examples extant. *Kāvya* in the service of religion, though occasionally found, is a secondary and sporadic phenomenon. The atmosphere of a court was similar to that of a *goṣṭhī*. The prince played the part of the leading *nāgaraka* and was expected to be, and aspired to be admired as, a sophisticated patron of all the arts and if possible a successful creative artist as well.

34. Just as *kāvya* is here regarded as a means to pleasure *kāma*, so in the theoretical works on *kāvya* (on dramaturgy and poetics) its primary function is generally stated to be to produce joy or delight (*harṣa* in *Nāṭyaśāstra* VI, p. 71; *prīti* in Bhāmaha [192], Vāmana, Abhinavagupta, etc.; *vinoda*, 'diversion', in *Nāṭyaśāstra* I, verse 117, along with solace *viśrāma*, verse 112, from unhappiness). In these works, however, a second function is discussed, namely education ('instruction' *upadeśa* in *Nāṭyaśāstra* I, verse 110, Kāśī; expertise *vaicakṣaṇya* in Bhāmaha I.2). The *Nāṭyaśāstra* in its account of the origin of the drama indeed describes it as a fifth *Veda* (along with the Epic—I.15), intended for all classes of society (the four *Vedas* proper being restricted to the Aryans, whose tradition it originally was). Since *veda* means 'knowledge', whilst the function of the *Veda* is to teach religion or virtue, this would suggest that the drama was intended to be religious as well as educational. However, the purpose of the account of the origin of the drama would appear to be to make it seem thoroughly respectable among the educated classes in India: in the last chapter of the *Nāṭyaśāstra* it is explained how the actors came to be regarded as of low social class, though originally they were descended from gods. In other words they were in fact looked upon as 'low' and so in their own handbook of the theatre they invented myths to glorify their calling and ancestry and set their art on a level with the most honoured and sacred literature. The true nature of their art is hinted at in the origin myth itself (*Nāṭyaśāstra* I.11), when the gods ask Brahmā for something that is playful or pleasant *krīḍanīyaka* as their 'fifth *veda*'. Though there were religious plays based on stories of the gods in the earliest period of the Indian theatre, alongside the heroic (from the Epic) and comic repertory, they do not seem to have become popular and were superseded in the effective repertory by plays of the other types.

35. The relationships between giving delight and giving instruction are perhaps not made as clear as they might be (particularly in the *Nāṭyaśāstra*, which is not given much to theorising but is simply a compilation of rather miscellaneous ideas handed down among the actors), but the impression is that both are to be effected simultaneously as far as possible, or in the best *kāvyas*, whilst giving delight should always predominate (is the essential, as Abhinavagupta says, *Dhvanyālokalocana* p. 40, Kāśī ed.). Without this we would have simply a treatise *śāstra*, not a work of art. The element of instruction nevertheless seems inevitable on the *Nāṭyaśāstra* view, since it is the nature of the drama that it is an 'imitation' (*anukaraṇa*—I. 109) of all actions, of the whole world, and therefore disseminates knowledge of the world. Finally it would seem to be the view which ultimately prevailed, in dramatic theory, that no subject matter (story, content) can be presented without the aesthetic experience *rasa* (*Nāṭyaśāstra* VI, prose after verse 31).

36. Before examining this *rasa* theory in detail it will be useful to summarise the account of the nature of drama given in the First Chapter of the *Nāṭyaśāstra*, to which we have referred already for its remarks on the functions of drama or *kāvya* ('drama' *nāṭya* and *kāvya* are almost interchangeable terms in the *Nāṭyaśāstra*; the *kāvya* referred to meaning usually the texts of the plays, as distinct from the acting *prayoga* of them, and 'drama' meaning the complete theatrical performance).

37. In describing the origin of the drama, in the first place, the *Nāṭyaśāstra* explains that this took place during the Tretā Yuga, the second age of the (present) evolution of the world, when society became divided by passion and greed, starting low habits, being deluded by envy and anger and experiencing happiness and unhappiness (I.8f.). The point is that in the first age, the Kṛta Yuga, society was perfectly harmonious and happy, as Abhinavagupta reminds us in his commentary, so that there were no conflicts and therefore no scope for drama.

38. We can learn more about the conception of the four ages of successive decadence of civilisation from Tradition (e.g. *Mahābhārata*, *Śānti*, 224; *Vāyu Purāṇa* 8) and also, with more exact details, from the Buddhist *Āgama* (*Tripiṭaka*—e.g. in the

Pali version, *Dīgha Nikāya*, *Suttantas* 27 and 26, corresponding to the Chinese version, Taishō No. 1, *Sūtras* 5 and 6), where we are told how the perfect ancient society, which was classless, had no priesthood, no aristocracy and no king but simply the harmonious assembly of all the people. Moreover there was no work (only food collecting from prolific wild plants), no violence (for which there was no occasion) and no evils or bad conduct of any other kind. This originally harmonious society gradually became divided into social classes and ruled by kings with violence, full of every kind of social evil, as a result of the operation of greed and of the invention of agriculture, private property, trading, theft, falsehood and every other kind of wickedness.

39. The *Nāṭyaśāstra* thus assumes that conflict is necessary for there to be drama, that it will exist in the world when there is unhappiness and happiness and the striving of people to attain happiness, also the struggle of good against evil. Evil is when people are under the control of pleasure and greed (instead of controlling them), led by envy and anger (i.e. deluded). Good is the self-control of the hero who understands how happiness can really be achieved and how a perfect society might be restored. In this assumption the Indian actors are in fact in general agreement with the European tradition of the drama, but it is important for us to adduce theoretical confirmation of the idea that conflict is essential, since at least one superficial Western writer on the Indian theatre has denied it in presenting his own romantic and exotic view. The fact of conflict should be clear enough from any attentive reading of the plays themselves; the theoretical working out of plot construction resulting from it will be discussed in our next chapter.

40. The new 'Fifth *Veda*' should therefore, in this time of social divisions, be designed for all social classes, including non-Aryans (Śūdras) as well as Aryans. It is understood that the original fourfold *Veda* had been for all members of society before it became divided (before there were any Śūdras, these and all barbarians having originated as depraved Aryans), but now fell short of its purpose since it was taught only to Aryans. This *Nāṭyaveda* was created by Brahmā, through taking the essential features from each of the old Four *Vedas* and combining them: recitation from the *Ṛc*, song from the *Sāman*, acting (i.e. from the ritual) from the *Yajus* and 'tastes' *rasas* from the *Atharvan*. He added the *Upavedas* (Archery, Music and Medicine) and made it playful *lalita*. It was connected with (meaning instructive in, according to Abhinavagupta) virtue [1362], wealth [1619] and fame [1606]. It showed all actions and contained the matter of all branches of knowledge (I.11ff.). A

41. Later in the First Chapter the first performance of a play is described, in Heaven before the assembled gods and demons. The occasion was the Festival of Indra (the King of the Gods) and the play appropriately showed a victory of the gods over the demons (in this corrupt age the society of Heaven, as of Earth, had become divided, hence conflict and the possibility of drama had developed there; drama was brought down to Earth only later). The gods are pleased with the play, but the demons are enraged at seeing their defeat represented and interrupt the performance. Indra himself restores order, laying about him with his staff, and since that day his staff or standard has been honoured as the protector of the theatre before the beginning of any performance.

42. Brahmā then explains the nature of the drama in order to pacify the demons, who complain that his *Nāṭyaveda* is partial to the gods and that he ought not to have made it so, since he was the creator of gods and demons alike and should not favour the gods only. He argues that his drama represents (*vikalpaka*—I. 102) the good and bad actions of both the gods and the demons, in agreement with their real actions and emotions (including dispositions and intentions). It is not one-sided, as between the gods and demons, but retells the emotions of the whole universe. He has created it as an imitation of the actions of the world, containing the various emotions and situations. Sometimes it shows virtue, people engaged in virtuous actions [1033], sometimes play [1445], sometimes those who pursue wealth [331], sometimes weariness [1593] (alternative reading: 'calm'), sometimes humour [1086], sometimes war [950], sometimes pleasure *kāma* and those attached to it [1404], sometimes killing [1044]. It shows killing by those who are ill-behaved [1048] and the restraint of those who are well behaved [946]. It shows the arrogance of the impotent and the energy of proud heroes [948]. It shows the enlightening of the ignorant and the wisdom of wise men [958]. It shows the play (amusements) of the rich [1383], the fortitude of those afflicted by unhappiness and the courage of those whose minds are agitated (who are in trouble) [955] (I.54ff. and especially 102ff.). A

43. Brahmā then continues, having in fact suggested that he is not impartial as between good and bad principles but only as between persons, that his drama will be productive of advantageous instruction, depending on the actions of high, low and middling characters. It appears then that his objectivity is far from being an absolute detachment and that his art is intended to have a critical function : it will display evil actions and intentions and their results, and with them contrast what is good, thus educating and changing his audience for the advantage of the world, attacking the evils of a corrupt age and upholding the higher ideals or ends of life as recognised in the Indian tradition. The ancient society which was happy and free from conflict has disappeared, and its *Veda* or religion has lost its effectiveness, but we can try to make a happier world by studying the experience of various actions and intentions through the delightful medium of the theatre, which in future will show us how we should act.

44. Concluding his discourse to the demons Brahmā remarks that his drama will produce solace for unfortunate persons afflicted by unhappiness, weariness and grief. It will be connected with virtue, fame, long life, will be advantageous, will increase intelligence and produce instruction about the world. There is no knowledge, no craft, science, art, no combination of subjects (so Abhinavagupta interprets *yoga*, however it may have meant 'reasoning', 'logic', when the text was originally composed, as formerly applied to the Vaiśeṣika school of philosophy and its antecedents), no action which is not seen in this drama. Representing knowledge of the *Veda*, Tradition and histories, it will produce diversion (I.111ff. in Kāśī, 114ff. Baroda ed.).

45. It is possible that this First Chapter of the *Nāṭyaśāstra* was composed later than the Sixth Chapter, which expounds the *rasa* theory, and the rest of the central part of the work which follows that. The entire book is supposed to have been recited by the sage Bharata, who heard it from Brahmā and was commissioned by him, when he created drama, to produce plays in heaven. The word *bharata*, however, means 'actor', and the text is evidently the final stage of development of the *sūtras* of the actors (*naṭas*, a synonym for *bharata*) mentioned by Pāṇini (IV. 3. 110) in the—4. These were probably handed down by oral tradition among the actors for many centuries. What we now have is not the work of one author but the outcome of a long period of practical stagecraft. There are references (e.g. Abhinavagupta in his commentary, Vol. I p. 9) to three main recensions of the *Nāṭyaśāstra*, of varying lengths, of which only one, regarded as the most authoritative, has come down to us in two versions, differing in arrangement rather than in actual text although there are numerous variant readings of individual words.

46. That this text is composite appears at once from the Sixth Chapter, which begins with a table of contents as if it were the first and also says that the theory will be expounded in concise statements from the *sūtras*, with detailed explanations from the commentary *bhāṣya*, mentioning further *kārikās* (versified *sūtras*) and etymologies as other categories of texts used. It continues in alternate prose and verse, where the prose is largely in *sūtra* form but sometimes takes the form of disquisitions more suitably described as 'commentary', whilst the verses are mostly more or less paraphrases of the prose, in other words another recension of the text. Dissentient views are quoted also. A few of the following chapters have this mixed form but the majority are in verse only.

47. One may conjecture that the earliest stratum of text was in prose *sūtras*. Prose commentary was in due course added to it. Then a parallel version in verse *kārikās* was made. The etymologies, perhaps once a separate lexicon of the technical terminology, were incorporated in the mixed *sūtra* and commentary text. At this stage someone made a synthetic handbook by selecting parts of the prose and verse versions, with a summary or table of contents (in verse) at the beginning, which we now have at the beginning of Chapter Six. Such a synthetic text perhaps extended almost to the end of the subject matter of our present recension, including the chapters on music (as indicated by the summary). For the most part, in that case, the original prose text was afterwards eliminated and only the verse paraphrase retained and probably extended. Finally the first five chapters, which are entirely in verse, were added, along with the concluding chapters. It is thus hard to delimit the date of any part of the final text and still harder to trace the origin of particular ideas in it. From the actual early plays now available it appears that the principles of the present *Nāṭyaśāstra* were in practice by the +1. The present text might be a century or so later than that. There seem to be no means of telling whether the *sūtras* referred to by Pāṇini included any of those in our present text, such as those on the *rasa* theory. The practice and theory may have changed or been extended in scope. Perhaps the prose commentary text was composed about the –2, followed by the verse *kārikās* a century later and the synthetic handbook in about the +1, but this is very speculative. A

48. Turning now to Chapter VI of the *Nāṭyaśāstra* for the exposition of *raso*, we find the topic introduced by the statement already mentioned, that no subject matter can be presented without *rasa* (prose after verse 31). This means that the audience will not accept the story, and other content of a play, unless it produces *rasa* in them, i.e. unless it produces in them a certain kind of enjoyment.

49. The term *rasa* has been variously translated by Western writers on the subject, and by modern Indian writers in Western languages. There has been considerable confusion through the widespread failure to distinguish between *rasa* and *bhāva* ('emotion'), stemming from the Aristotelian assumption that the audience at the theatre has a simple emotional experience and overlooking the Indian distinction of a specific aesthetic experience. This distinction has been briefly stated in our Preface. We must now study it more closely.

50. Our point of departure in understanding the term *rasa* is that its original meaning, and its current everyday meaning, is 'taste', i.e. as in the 'taste' of food. Some translators have used this literal equivalent, or synonyms such as 'flavour' and 'relish', but most have felt it to be unsuitable in the context of the theatre and have substituted 'feeling', 'sentiment', 'mood' and the like, in effect 'emotion'. Finally Gnoli (*The Aesthetic Experience according to Abhinavagupta*) has proposed 'the aesthetic experience' and Kunhan Rāja (*Survey of Sanskrit Literature*) has used 'beauty'. If *rasa* meant some kind of emotion, then it has to be explained whether and how it differs from *bhāva* and also why such an unsuitable word as one meaning 'taste' came to be used for it. In fact Gnoli and Kunhan Rāja seem to be on the right track by keeping the term in the realm of aesthetic experience, as indicated by its original meaning.

51. There being no specific term for 'aesthetic experience' in general in ancient India, but only terms relating to the particular senses, it was natural to use one of the latter metaphorically for it. Neither 'sound' nor 'sight' would be adequate, since drama uses both, not one only, and the distinction from everyday hearing and seeing would not be properly stressed. 'Taste' was presumably chosen as obviously metaphorical in this context and as indicating some special meaning not expressible by any word in its literal sense. Since we speak of 'taste' in connection with art criticism in European languages, though not quite in the sense of *rasa* (it is a qualification of a connoisseur rather than his experience), there should be no difficulty in accepting the metaphor. The relationship to emotion has to be explained, along with the fact that it was emotions which were supposed to be 'tasted', but it appears most accurate to adopt 'aesthetic experience' as our equivalent for *rasa* in this book. 'Taste' would be more literal and equally correct, but less clear.

52. The *Nāṭyaśāstra* after introducing the subject actually uses the analogy of cookery for the art of the theatre. Just as from the conjunction of various food substances with spices and herbs the taste arises, so from the conjunction of causes of emotion, effects of emotion and transient emotions the 'taste' arises. As the 'six tastes' are produced by the substances, sugar and so on, with spices and herbs, so the basic emotions compounded with various emotions attain the state of being 'tastes' (the eight 'tastes' of the drama). The text continues that the word 'taste' *rasa* is used in the sense of 'tasting' (*āsvādyatva*, a synonym). Just as a gourmet enjoying food prepared with various spices tastes *ā-svad* the tastes *rasas* and finds joy *harṣa*, etc. ('etc.' = refreshment, life, nourishment, strength and health—Abhinavagupta), so a connoisseur of the theatre tastes the basic emotions compounded with speech, gesture and expressions and spiced with the acting of various emotions and finds joy, etc. ('etc.' = instruction in virtue, etc., sophistication and so on—Abhinavagupta).

53. The taste or aesthetic experience thus enjoyed is classified as of eight kinds corresponding to the eight basic emotions *sthāyibhāvas* tasted. These are as follows (the corresponding basic emotion being given in brackets after each one): sensitive *śṛṅgāra* (love *rati* [999]), comic *hāsya* (humour *hāsa* [1086]), compassionate *karuna* (grief *śoka* [953]), furious *raudra* (anger *krodha* [1144, 1349]), heroic *vīra* (energy *utsāha* [948, 1519]), apprehensive *bhayānaka* (fear *bhaya* [701, 1631]), horrific *bībhatsa* (disgust *jugupsā* [1199]) and marvellous *adbhuta* (astonishment *vismaya* [104, 1048, 1285]) (VI.15ff.). A

54. The fundamental statement of the practice of the actors made in this *Nāṭyaśāstra* exposition is known as the *rasa sūtra* (in the same prose passage after VI. 31). It is as follows: 'The aesthetic experience arises from the conjunction of causes of emotion, effects of emotion and transient emotions'. The causes of emotion *vibhāvas* are the appropriate causes drawn from real life, which would produce the basic emotions in the characters represented on the stage. These causes are indicated to the audience as the situation in which the characters find themselves : the scene will be described by them, other characters act as causes of emotion in a particular hero, and prior events have been either represented or reported in building up the situation. The effects of emotion *anubhāvas* are shown by the actors through speech, gestures and expressions. The 'transient emotions' (*vyabhicārins* or *vyabhicāribhāvas*) are also effects shown by the actors, but they are distinguished as indicating emotions which are transient as opposed to the eight basic emotions [56]. They are regarded as subsidiary to the basic emotions : other emotions as side effects of the main ones.

55. The basic emotions are not mentioned in this statement. The reason for this seems clear : they do not actually exist in the theatre. The actors cannot act the actual emotions but only their visible and audible effects, in relation to a representation of their causes. As actors they are not experiencing themselves the emotions imagined to be present in the characters. The characters with their emotions are of course present only in imagination. The audience imagine the emotions thus suggested and taste them, but what they actually experience is not the emotions but their *rasa*, their taste, the aesthetic experience. For example if the emotion imagined is love the actors act as if they were in love (naturally the drama is not concerned with their private affairs) ; the audience should then experience the 'sensitive' taste, which does not mean that they are supposed to fall in love with the actors or actresses, or with the imagined characters. As a matter of fact they enjoy the taste of emotions which, if actually experienced, would be very unpleasant, as later Indian writers on the drama point out (see below [85]). Moreover it is clear from the list of corresponding basic emotions and aesthetic experiences that the relationship between these pairs varies: thus grief is not transferred directly as a 'grievous' experience but produces the compassionate; a hero performing some great action is imagined to feel energy, the audience experience the heroic (a real hero does not feel 'heroic', we may note). This again shows that the audience are not supposed to have direct psychological experience of emotions in the theatre, but an indirect transfer to another level from which they are contemplated, the level of the aesthetic experience.

56. The transient emotions are : indifference *nirveda* [1307], depression *glāni* [732, 1475], alarm *śaṅkā* [1480], envy *asūyā* (including especially jealousy [1270, 1471: A18], for which no distinct term seems to be used in Sanskrit), intoxication *mada* [1504], weariness *śrama* [1502], lassitude *ālasya* [1136], misery *dainya* [1470, 1482], anxiety *cintā* [1561], bewilderment *moha* [732], remembrance *smṛti* [650], contentment *dhṛti* [1341], shame *vrīḍā* [1474], vanity *capalatā* [1602], joy *harṣa* [1400], agitation *āvega* [807, 986], stupidity *jaḍatā* [733], pride *garva* [947 (24)], despair *viṣāda* [980, 1439], eagerness *autsukya* [1476, 1483], drowsiness *nidrā* [975], forgetfulness *apasmāra* (being 'possessed' [cf. 1170]), sleeping *supta* (this includes dreaming as an effect) [1048], awaking *vibodha* [1048], indignation *amarṣa* [806], dissimulation *avahittha* [1471 : A18], ferocity *ugratā* [948], reflection *mati* [1421, 1519], sickness *vyādhi* [805], madness *unmāda* [1407], dying *maraṇa* [952], terror *trāsa* [1404, 1527] and doubt *vitarka* [1404]—thirty three in all (VI. 18-21).

57. The *Nāṭyaśāstra* outlines typical causes and effects for each of the aesthetic experiences and lists the appropriate transient emotions which may occur in connection with them. For example (prose after VI.45) in the sensitive the causes will be the desired person (from the point of view of the character in whom love is supposed to be present [1404]) and such things as the season (e.g. spring [1426]), flowers, cosmetics [740], jewellery, objects of pleasure (e.g. music [1172]), enjoying excellent buildings, enjoying going to a park, hearing and seeing amusements, and play and so on. The effects will be movements of the eyes and eyebrows, sidelong glances, wandering about, playful and gentle gestures and speech, and so on. All the transient emotions may occur except terror, lassitude, ferocity and disgust. The mention of this last reminds us that with each basic emotion other 'basic' emotions may be introduced as subordinate to it : from this mention of disgust as transient it appears they may then lose their basic status and be treated like other transients. This outline applies to the case of 'union' *sambhoga,* when the lovers come together or when they meet for the first time. The sensitive, however, has another state, that of 'frustration' *vipralambha* when the lovers are not yet united, or are separated, which of course will be acted differently [803, 1468]. The *Nāṭyaśāstra* states that when there is hope of reunion the aesthetic experience is sensitive. If there is no hope it will instead be compassionate.

58. There are still further points here which may be noted briefly. The four aesthetic experiences sensitive, furious, heroic and horrific are said to be primary and to serve as causes of the other four, respectively of the comic, compassionate, marvellous and apprehensive (VI. 39—41). This seems rather restrictive and artificial, though these relationships may sometimes occur : later writers, such as Abhinavagupta in his commentary on this, point out other possible relationships between the experiences. [3836]

59. Then in addition to the various sorts of emotion so far referred to there are eight 'expressive' *sāttvika* emotions: paralysis (and choking [1037]), perspiring [808], horripilation ('thrilling' is a possible equivalent) [828], change of voice, trembling [808], change of colour, tears [807] and fainting (VI.22). The point about these is that they are shown directly; otherwise they count as transients and are noted as appropriate under the various aesthetic experiences.

60. The heroic experience may be of three kinds, relating to magnanimity *dāna* [1277], justice *dharma* [1516] (virtue) and war *yuddha* [1026, 1433] (VI.79).

61. In any drama one of the aesthetic experiences must predominate, but several others should be brought in as auxiliaries subordinate to it and helping to bring it to full development (*Nāṭyaśāstra* XXII.68; the point is stressed e.g. by Ānandavardhana, pp. 378ff. = III.21ff., and Sāgaranandin, 1965, among later critics).

62. The discussion in Chapter VI of the *Nāṭyaśāstra* suggests an almost entirely empirical origin for the *rasa* theory. In fact it is presented as a practice rather than as a theory, and it would seem to have arisen among the actors through trial and error. Only later did it begin to assume the appearance of a system. The *Nāṭyaśāstra* makes no attempt to explain why there should be just eight aesthetic experiences : this apparently was taken simply as a fact of observation. Only later do theorists discuss how many *rasas* there are and argue about which should be recognised and what the relationships are between them. The *Nāṭyaśāstra* frequently refers to the 'world' *loka* as the source of further information for the actors and dramatists, whence the causes and effects of emotion should be studied and gestures should be imitated. In general, as we have seen, it is the 'world' whose actions are to be imitated in drama. Though the drama has a mass of conventions of its own *nāṭyadharma*, these are everywhere to be supported and supplemented by drawing on the ways of the world *lokadharma*. The art has its special devices and methods but its aim is realism. A

63. It is clear from the *Nāṭyaśāstra* (though almost taken for granted) that the ending of a play should be auspicious. A famous hero ought not to be killed in a *nāṭaka* (the main type of play, XX.22 Kāśī ed.) A play should show the attainment of virtue (justice), wealth and pleasure (XXI.8), although it will contain a mixture of happiness and unhappiness (XX.12). At the conclusion the marvellous aesthetic experience should always be produced (XX.47). The conclusion should also contain the offering of a boon (of further happiness for the hero) and a panegyric (XXI.105), the latter in practice a benediction on the audience and on the whole country. The attaining of the main objective at the end of a play means gaining the fruits of action corresponding to the complete original desire (XXI.14). These indications of auspicious ending are abundantly confirmed by the practice of the available dramas; they no doubt fitted well with the custom of festive performances which we noted earlier. The final benedictions ask for such blessings as peace, abundance and freedom from all kinds of natural and political disasters. In our next Chapter we shall see that the construction of dramas is fitted to an auspicious ending, whatever obstacles and appearances of tragedy may threaten to prevent it. The idea of tragedy, deriving from Greek religion in the European tradition, does not occur in its strict sense in India, if only because the religious milieu was different—a point worth examining in a moment,—although in the Epic the dominant experience is compassionate, in effect tragic. [cf. 3132 ff.]

64. In the ancient traditions preserved in the Great Epic one may speak in a sense of stories which are tragic. The good things which are sought being of this world and the ideas of another world or of transmigration being shadowy, the death of the hero is a tragic conclusion. Later the outlook changes and becomes more complex. Even in the Epic itself there supervenes the idea of renunciation of a world which is fundamentally unsatisfactory and in which a good man cannot find happiness and peace. This outlook is even characteristic of the Epic tradition in later times and affects some *kavis* who studied the Great Epic deeply in its final form.

65. Such an outlook grew powerfully in India from the time of the Buddha (-566 to -486), the greatest advocate of the renunciation of worldly ends, and provided a completely different, non-tragic, type of conclusion to a superficially tragic story and a different attitude to death. If this type of conclusion seemed to many inappropriate for the theatre, there developed, in opposition to the ascetic trend towards renunciation, other conceptions about the nature of the universe, especially characteristic of orthodox Brahmanism. Here the world was a place of struggle between good and evil; part of a universe in which the gods strove to hold their own against the demons. The hero in the service of good served cosmic ends and was assured of divine support though also of demoniacal opposition. Transmigration, which included translation to heaven, provided for the hero's future happiness and reward even if he were killed, so that such a disaster was merely a temporary setback in the cosmic advance of good, a minor and transient event or a glorious apotheosis rather than a tragedy. The doctrine of moral causation, common to Buddhism and Brahmanism and most other Indian philosophical and religious systems, provided for absolute fairness in the ultimate working out of human affairs: everyone would reap the reward of his actions and any 'tragedy' was transformed into its opposite by the consoling belief in the inevitable eventual production of the fruits of virtue. This doctrine of an absolutely just universal order gradually transformed the old conception of a struggle between good and evil spirits.It was a form of compromise between Buddhism and Brahmanism.

66. There were of course many variations on this doctrine. It can be moral or purely ritualistic, atheist or theist, polytheist or monotheist, pluralist or monist. For example in monotheist Śaivism God (Śiva) is omnipotent and hence there can be no real evil (everything comes from God) : it follows that the universe is created merely for sport, thus for aesthetic and not moral purposes, also that the individual soul can, if so disposed, retire from the game and return to the bliss of union with Śiva. In atheist orthodox Brahmanism (Mīmāṃsā tradition) the meticulous observance of the duties of one's station and the due performance of rituals leads to rebirth in heaven. The intermediate moralist variations need no further comment.

67. Thus death is not tragic but a phase in the grand development of the universe. It leads to a just reincarnation or to divine happiness. Moreover, since a play deals with some episode and should be auspicious, the (main) hero is finally triumphant and his death cannot take place unless as an apotheosis (which in fact is a rare ending). It is a rule that the death of any character should not be represented on the stage. It must be reported to a character on the stage, or may be observed and described by those on the stage (e.g. watching a battle from a point of vantage). On the stage an apotheosis may be represented, and in this manner mortal death may be shown (the dying hero sees a divine chariot descending towards him, surrounded by celestial nymphs, for example, then 'goes to heaven' [954]). Besides this the only apparent exceptions are a metamorphosis in which a dying character reverts to another form [1048], an attempted murder whose victim recovers [1197] or an illusory and temporary death due to a mistake in the underworld, subsequently rectified [1087].

68. As in the case of death, it was an established convention that fighting (except in a *ḍima* [333]), eating, kissing, taking a bath and certain other actions should not be represented. Fighting is frequently described by onlookers on stage: for example a group of soldiers excitedly watching a battle and giving a running commentary [951] (NŚ XXIV.285ff., XX. 21).

69. In other forms of *kāvya* the entire life of a hero may be narrated, ending with death and apotheosis (or Nirvāṇa) [714].

70. It may be appropriate to add a further note about the religions of India, in relation to the philosophy of aesthetics. This may explain the absence of serious antagonism in India between religion and ethics on the one hand and art on the other, and the harmony of a civilisation in which a powerful ascetic tradition and a refined cultivation of pleasure could flourish side by side.

71. Fundamentally Indian religion is not ascetic and hostile to this world. Certainly it regards asceticism as a natural and admirable practice for some people, who have a vocation for it, and for most people when temporarily engaged in very serious business. But it was accepted by almost all schools of thought that the natural and entirely praiseworthy aim of all living beings was happiness. Opinion then differed chiefly over the question as to which kinds of happiness were best, or real, or attainable. Some found happiness in asceticism itself, in the peace of mind they attained by renouncing worldly concerns. Others believed that ascetic practices would lead to future happiness in another life in this world or in heaven or in attaining Nirvāṇa. As to which, if any, was a true, or the true, account of the nature of the universe, Indian philosophers and theologians have always contented themselves with experience, argument and exhortation as the only possible means to establish truth and spread it. Hence India has always been a society of many religions and a profusion of philosophies, not of a state dogma (except temporarily when foreign rulers, fortunately restricted to part of India only and strenuously resisted by Indian rivals, have attempted to impose alien dogma on India).

72. Among the major movements in Indian thought Buddhism has been conspicuously world renouncing and seeking a higher happiness. Yet its propagandists have always assumed that most people would not, or not for long ages, wish to withdraw from the world to devote their lives to ascetic meditation, despite their exhortations. Buddhism includes another moment in its teaching, inextricably bound up with the Way to Nirvāṇa itself, namely compassion, sympathy and love (in the sense of loving kindness), which follows from its principle of 'all-self-ness' *sarvātmatā*, of considering all beings as like oneself, putting oneself in the place of others. The avoidance of all actions harmful to others, and activity for their welfare, are an essential part of the practice of the Way. It followed from this doctrine that Buddhism had a social programme for the improvement of life in this world and always urged rulers to seek the welfare of their countries in economic as well as religious matters. The Buddhists firmly believed, moreover, that a peaceful and prosperous society was the best setting for the propagation of their doctrine, because people must have leisure to be able to think about their true wellbeing and must not be always and urgently concerned with merely securing the means of existence.

73. If the quest for happiness in this world, as well as in some higher form, were regarded as natural and legitimate by the more ascetic Buddhists, the orthodox Brahmans, who allowed asceticism a much more restricted place in their scheme for human wellbeing, accepted the material as well as the spiritual world as natural and moreover good. According to Mallanāga Vātsyāyana, God (Brahmā) created the science of pleasure along with the world, and according to the first chapter of the *Nāṭyaśāstra* Brahmā created drama as a fifth *Veda*, to save the world from evil passions by a means accessible to everyone (unlike the other four *Vedas*). Thus drama is held to be socially essential as providing a kind of 'aesthetic education'. (There is however an older claim that Tradition, primarily the Great Epic, is the fifth and universal *Veda*.) There is thus no conflict between art and ethics or religion. The Brahmanical ideal is not renunciation (except for a few specialists) but a perfectly harmonious society in which all the aims of man, religion or spiritual wellbeing ('virtue'), wealth and pleasure, are attained by everyone.

74. Theoretical writing on aesthetics generally agreed with the basic position of 'Bharata' in the *Nāṭyaśāstra*. K. C. Pandey has suggested (*Indian Aesthetics*, pp. ix, 1, 603ff. of the second edition, 1959) that three 'primary' arts were recognised in India: *kāvya*, music and architecture. Painting and sculpture would be subordinate to architecture. Such a conception does not seem to be clearly formulated anywhere in the old texts available and the views expressed in any case vary. Thus writers on painting *citra* (or *citrasūtra*) claim their own art is primary (e.g. *Viṣṇudharmottara* III *adhyāya* 35 : independent origin of painting; Pandey himself admits, p. 605, that Bhoja makes the same claim). Nevertheless, the same text (*Viṣṇudharmottara* III *adhyāya* 2) says that knowledge of painting is dependent on that of dancing (meaning of the movements, gestures, expressions, etc., studied in that art). The knowledge of dancing itself is dependent on that of instrumental music and that of the latter on singing. This then leads to an exposition in several *adhyāyas* of metres, poetics, *kāvya*, the *rasa* theory, drama, etc. Thus we would have a hierarchy of arts, with *kāvya* (including drama and its aesthetic theories) supreme, music subordinate to it and painting subordinate to music. After discussing these, the *Viṣṇudharmottara* takes up in turn sculpture *pratimā* (or *pratimālakṣaṇa*, *adhyāyas* 44ff.) and architecture *prāsāda* (or *prāsādalakṣaṇa*, 86ff.), which appears to imply that these two are subordinate to painting and that architecture is subordinate to sculpture (the art on which it is dependent has to be understood first, then the subordinate art is expounded). [3729]

75. The mutual relationships of all the arts would seem to be more important for aesthetics than traditions of the independent origin of some of them. Here all are shown as interconnected: in essence, art is art, there is only one. The fundamental theory of all art in India is in fact that of the aesthetic experience *rasa*. Pandey seems to draw his ideas from three main sources: Śārṅgadeva's *Saṅgītaratnākara* on music, Bhoja's *Samarāṅgaṇasūtradhāra* on architecture and the *Nāṭyaśāstra*, with Abhinavagupta's commentary, on drama or *kāvya*. He argues that in music sound *nāda* is identified with *brahman*, ultimate reality (*Saṅgītaratnākara* I. 2, cf. Bhartṛhari's speech *śabda* identified with *brahman* in *Vākyapadīya* I). This *brahman* is delight and is a stage attained through the art. As a matter of fact Abhinavagupta (*Tantrāloka* II.200) also says that music produces delight *ānanda*. Śiṅgabhūpāla in his commentary on the *Saṅgītaratnākara* here quotes Mataṅga's *Bṛhaddeśī*, an earlier work on music, for the identification of sound with *brahman* and with the whole universe. Then in architecture building *vāstu* is identified with *brahman* and pervades the whole universe (*Samarāṅgaṇasūtradhāra* II.4). An ancient Vedic idea probably underlies this, namely that the universe is the dwelling of the gods, built by them as their house (*Ṛgvedasaṃhitā* X. 81, cf. II. 15, X.149, VI.49, etc.; the *Taittirīya Brāhmaṇa* 2, 8, 9, 6 explains that they built Heaven and Earth out of *brahman*). Bhoja later (XXXI.18—9) says that a (beautiful) house arouses astonishment *vismaya* or wonder *āścarya*, which might suggest that it produces the 'marvellous' *adbhuta* aesthetic experience in the beholder, and also love *rati*, suggesting the 'sensitive'. Collecting such hints, one can suppose that architecture could produce all the aesthetic experiences, depending on the various types of buildings and their functions suggesting various emotions as the basis for them. Finally, the *Nāṭyaśāstra* and Abhinavagupta commenting on it make all the other arts auxiliary to drama, producing the aesthetic experience. Here Pandey supposes that 'aesthetic experience' *rasa* is to be identified with *brahman* (an idea derived from the *Taittirīya Upaniṣad*) and he could quote Abhinavagupta (I p. 267) to the effect that drama is *rasa*.

76. What one should surely conclude from all this is that each of these arts was thought to work in a similar way and to produce, for those who enjoyed it, the highest delight or aesthetic experience. The differences of media or materials are not as important as this essential unity in the experience produced. Now it appeared that all the arts were contained in drama. Besides the text or *kāvya*, it makes much use of music and is presented in a beautiful theatre embodying architecture, sculpture and painting. The visual nature of the acting seems to embody, and by its movement to surpass, sculpture and painting. With its supreme capacity for expression, it would seem natural enough that the aesthetics of the theatre, whose foundations were laid in the *Nāṭyaśāstra*, should become a general aesthetics for all the arts. We have suggested elsewhere (*Pali Metre* § 195) that the drama very early became the unifying goal of all the arts in India. Its aesthetics in turn became the theory of all of them. The *Nāṭyaśāstra* (XXIX, Kāśī) discussing modes *jātis* brings music proper under the dominating *rasa* theory, Śārṅgadeva also (e.g. VII. 1361-2) discusses music in relation to the *rasas*. The *Viṣṇudharmottara* discusses paintings producing nine *rasas* (III. 41-3), in temples, palaces and houses, i.e. in the context of architecture. Bhoja (*Samarāṅgaṇasūtradhāra* LXXXII) has eleven *rasas* in painting (unless the text is corrupt and we should read twelve : these *rasas* are the original eight and certain additional ones, which we shall discuss below [99]). The same aesthetic theory is valid for all *kāvya,* though originally proper to the drama and extended from it. It is not surprising that we find drama called the highest form of *kāvya* (Vāmana I.3.30-1).

77. The greatest of the philosophers who wrote on aesthetics was perhaps Abhinavagupta (*fl.* beginning of the +11). He followed in the main Bharata for the drama and Ānandavardhana for *kāvya* in general (whose theories we shall be discussing later [247]), but elaborated an overall doctrine of the nature of the aesthetic experience, supplying theoretical principles to underlie the practical account of the theatre given by Bharata. It is noteworthy that Abhinavagupta was one of the monistic Śaiva philosophers of the Kaśmīra or Pratyabhijñā ('Recognition') school, and accepted neither orthodox Brahmanism nor Buddhism. It is equally noteworthy that his doctrines have been found perfectly congenial by the majority of Brahmanical writers on *kāvya* since his time. In Śaivism, an independent and extremely ancient religion with its own scriptures, Śiva is of course God, not the Vedic Brahmā, though, in accordance with the prevailing toleration of Indian theologians, writers on both sides generally regarded Śiva and Brahmā as aspects of one another. In the *Nāṭyaśāstra*

Brahmā and Śiva collaborate in the perfecting of the drama. In monistic Śaivism the creation of the universe by Śiva is accounted for as pure sport. Śiva being perfect in himself, and also the unique being, there could be no other purpose. Eventually He will draw the whole creation back into the blissful condition of being again united with Him. It is clear that such a religion is in the highest degree propitious for the cultivation of the arts and the study of aesthetics. Śiva was always specially associated with the dance and with drama. He who created the universe for pleasure is essentially an aesthetic God.

78. For Abhinavagupta the aesthetic experience is not merely of educational value, it is identical with the highest religious experience and leads to the greatest good for the spectator or connoisseur, especially for the audience in the theatre. It is superior to the practice of asceticism for spiritual uplift, and is much easier and more widely accessible. The operation of the aesthetic experience is as it were to sublimate emotion from the psychological to the aesthetic plane. In this process individual emotion is transformed into, or replaced by, an aesthetic experience *rasa*, which is non-individual, universal, transcending space, time and particular circumstances. The individual forgets himself and attains a universality of outlook, which also brings him the highest happiness (Vol. I pp. 36 and 279).

79. Explaining his idea of literary and dramatic appreciation, Abhinavagupta argues (pp. 278 ff. of Vol. I of the Baroda second ed., 14ff. in Gnoli's) that in simple unpoetic statements one may have first the understanding of just the particular event mentioned, followed by a second understanding, transcending time, of the generality of such actions, including the suggested possibility that one could perform them oneself. In *kāvya*, similarly, when an emotional experience is described there is an implied meaning, transcending space, time, the individual person, etc., of that emotion in general; but this is different from the real life situation of emotional involvement, where one would be preoccupied with the matter of taking appropriate action in the situation, and in the absence of such a reaction the experience seems to be simply perceived, entering the appreciative mind as the corresponding aesthetic experience *rasa*. This generalisation has no limits but embraces all possible cases like a universal proposition (in logic). The various members of an audience in the theatre respond to it according to the traces of their own varied past experiences, which are innumerable ('beginningless', following the theory of beginningless transmigration through which they have accumulated these traces). This experience, free from the reactions of everyday life with its involvement, is 'admiration' (*camatkāra*, 'admiration', 'delight', another term used for aesthetic experience by the later critics). The aesthetic experience *rasa* thus differs from the basic emotion (corresponding to it) in that it is not actually accomplished in the natural way (is not the experience of the emotion itself) but its one essential is that it is 'tasted' (*carv*, 'chew', 'relish', 'enjoy'), it does not go beyond tasting (p. 284, Gnoli 24). To underline his idea of the detachment of the audience, Abhinavagupta elsewhere in his commentary on the *Nāṭyaśāstra* (Vol. I p. 27, Gnoli p. 79, footnote) says that a play should not imitate contemporary events, because these would arouse the passions and aversions, even the neutrality, of the audience (i.e. their emotions) instead of delight *prīti*. It would in any case be futile to show particular contemporary actions and their results on the stage when they were actually observed in real life (by the audience when outside the theatre).

80. Among earlier interpretations of the *rasa* theory of the *Nāṭyaśāstra*, now known to us, one old view was that *rasa* was simply the basic emotion much increased or intensified. The philosophers who held this perhaps followed the Mīmāṃsā school or that of the grammarians (Bhartṛhari); Daṇḍin (late +7), who starts his work on poetics (*Kāvyalakṣaṇa* I.4) with the concept of 'speech' *śabda* as the 'light of the universe', remarks that love, when multiplied (*bāhulya*, made abundant), becomes the sensitive (II.279, Darbhanga ed.).

81. Lollaṭa (early+9), in a commentary on the *Nāṭyaśāstra* known to us only from a few quotations, held similarly that *rasa* is the basic emotion increased *upacita*. This increase is effected by its conjunction with the causes and effects of emotion, i.e. in the *rasa sūtra* of the *Nāṭyaśāstra* we are to understand that the basic emotion is included in the conjunction, though it is not listed there with the other ingredients producing *rasa*. This *rasa* is produced in the character represented and in the actor; presumably it is then perceived by the audience (discussed by Abhinavagupta, I p. 272). Abhinavagupta rejects this interpretation, though he afterwards (p. 280) allows that the aesthetic experience is a kind of 'increase' in the sense that it is unlimited in space, etc.

82. Śaṅkuka (mid+9) already had criticised Lollaṭa, especially on account of the difficulty of explaining the distinctive character of *rasa* if it was merely a different degree of intensity. His philosophical standpoint appears to have been that of the Nyāya school (again his work is known only from quotations). According to him, *rasa* is so called because it is an imitation *anukaraṇa* of the basic emotion. The basic emotion is not mentioned in the *rasa sūtra* because it is not in question, does not occur in this situation; only its imitation is there and that is mentioned and called *rasa*. To the audience, its presence is implied through the power of its 'characteristics' (*liṅgas*, the 'middle terms' of logic), namely the causes and effects of emotion and the transients. It thus seems to them to be present in the actor (the imitator) (Abhinavagupta I pp. 272f.). Later (p. 284), Abhinavagupta seems to apply the term 'inference' *anumiti* to Śaṅkuka's theory, i.e. it is a theory that the audience 'infer' the *rasa* by a logical process. A

83. Abhinavagupta objects to this idea that *rasa* is only an imitation: to him it is something real, even the actor may use his own real feelings and real past experiences in his acting. However, he then gets into difficulties over the *Nāṭyaśāstra's* very clear statements that the drama as a whole is an 'imitation' of life. In fact he allows there is imitation in the sense of 'following'. As to the theory of inference, he objects that only the basic emotion could be inferred from its characteristics, not *rasa*.

84. Mahiman (late +11) followed a similar theory of inference, that *rasa* is communicated to the audience by inference, and set out a general theory of the enjoyment of *kāvya* as something produced by inference (*Vyaktiviveka*—on *rasa* see pp. 58f., 62, 66 ff., 83, 101ff., 111, 142, 165, 179ff., 466, etc., Kashi ed.). In literature everything must be subordinate to this inferring of *rasa*, must be appropriate for the *rasa* intended. He accepts a definition of *kāvya* (source unknown, perhaps

Nāyaka) as the description of the causes and effects of emotion; drama being the same when acted and also enhanced by song, etc. (pp. 101-2).

85. Nāyaka (late +9) criticised the theories of Lollaṭa and Śaṅkuka on the ground that the audience would actually experience emotions, including unpleasant emotions, if they were true, whereas *rasa* is in the highest degree enjoyable *bhuj*, *ānanda*, and is also generalised, is not like individual experience. His own theory is based on the Sāṃkhya philosophy and the enjoyment of the aesthetic experience is for him similar to the enlightenment and joy attained when 'goodness' *sattva* preponderates. The aesthetic experience is 'developed' by a certain activity called 'development' (*bhāvanā* or *bhāvakatva*). The use of this term suggests meditation and moral training as practised by the Sāṃkhya and Buddhist schools, but it also suggests the power of the 'emotions' represented in drama, as explained at the beginning of the Seventh Chapter of the *Nāṭyaśāstra* (··*bhāvayantīti bhāvāḥ*). This development of the aesthetic experience stops delusion (again as in Sāṃkhya training). It may be relevant here to recall the usual Sāṃkhya doctrine (Īśvarakṛṣṇa) that the souls are entirely passive: they contemplate the differentiations of the physical universe as the audience in a theatre watch an actress, or they may cease to contemplate the physical universe and revert to their proper state of liberation. Nāyaka does not in fact follow Īśvarakṛṣṇa (he may have belonged to another school of Sāṃkhya): his audience do not cease to contemplate but gain the highest joy, with release from the ignorance and limitation of individual incarnate existence, through the generalising aesthetic experience. Nāyaka's monograph on aesthetics (the *Hṛdayadarpaṇa*) seems to have been lost and his views are now known only from quotations (particularly Abhinavagupta I pp. 276f.). He exerted very great influence for several centuries, particularly on Dhanañjaya and Bhoja. Abhinavagupta does not accept Nāyaka's formulations, though his own theory is very similar in general conception.

86. The Buddhist schools had their own theories, apparently rather similar to those of Nāyaka and Abhinavagupta (the latter seems to have had very little disagreement with them on aesthetics and even epistemology, his references to

Dharmakīrti and to Vijñānavāda being appreciative, but of course he could not have approved of their atheism), but their works seem to be lost and little is known of their aesthetics. A

87. The Jaina school is represented by the joint work of Rāmacandra and Guṇacandra (+12: the *Nāṭyadarpaṇa*, fortunately extant). This develops (III. 7 with the authors' commentary on it) a view which seems generally to resemble Lollaṭa's and Daṇḍin's, and may go back in a less elaborated form to one of the lost early commentaries on the *Nāṭyaśāstra*. Following the conception that the basic emotion when enhanced or increased, *utkarṣa* or *upacaya*, becomes *rasa*, the authors accept the implication that the latter may have the nature of either happiness or unhappiness (*sukhaduḥkhātmako rasaḥ*). At the same time they admit that the audience may experience 'admiration' *camatkāra*, through the skill of the author or actor : but in this case the tasting of the *rasa* itself is interrupted *virāma* so that even when the unhappy *rasas* are present an intelligent audience will experience the highest delight *ānanda*. This appears to be a kind of compromise. The authors appeal to the actual experience in the theatre that audiences become disturbed (*ud-vij*, troubled, afflicted) by the unhappy *rasas* and not by the happy ones, despite which they show admiration. They also propose the analogy of drinks being enjoyed more when they have a sharp (*tīkṣṇa*, pungent, dry) taste. Authors interweave happiness and unhappiness in their works, corresponding to the nature of real life in the world of transmigration, which is both happy and unhappy. The imitation of something unhappy must be unhappy, otherwise it would not be a proper imitation. The aesthetic experiences having the nature of happiness are the sensitive, comic, heroic, marvellous and calmed (*śānta*, a ninth *rasa* added by several of the later authors : see below). Those having the the nature of unhappiness are the compassionate, furious, horrific and apprehensive.

88. These Jaina writers reflect logical views like those of Śaṅkuka, in holding that the effects of emotion are characteristics through which the *rasa* is ascertained, the latter being itself unseen (*parokṣa*—a Jaina logical term). The aesthetic experience, however, has its locus in the audience: if the actor experiences it that is inessential. The experience of the audience does not relate to the individual characters represented but is generalised: it relates to all characters of that class; for example, if the sensitive is being imitated of Rāma with respect to Sītā, the audience experience the sensitive not with respect to Sītā but with respect to all women. The tasting of the aesthetic experience is, further, common to all connoisseurs, whether it is found in *kāvya* or in everyday life, but not in all cases with the same basis, since it is a mental activity (*citta-vṛtti*, 'thought-activity') independent of the basis (presumably the character, etc.) depicted. The *rasa* being in the connoisseur, it is not correct to say that a *kāvya* is *rasa*, though since it produces *rasa* it may be said to have *rasa*-ness or to be the basis when there is *rasa*.

89. Along with these studies of the nature of the aesthetic experience there naturally developed investigations as to whether the number of *rasas* should be fixed at eight, as laid down in the *Nāṭyaśāstra*, or whether there could be more, or whether, following the suggestion in the *Nāṭyaśāstra* itself that there were interconnections between the *rasas*, they might all be reduced to one basic type of aesthetic experience with its derivatives.

90. The first problem which arose here, as far as we now know, was whether the 'calmed' *śānta* should be recognised as a ninth variety of aesthetic experience. This would correspond to 'liberation' *mokṣa* from the universe of transmigration, sometimes distinguished from 'virtue' *dharma* as a fourth end of life. A number of early Buddhist *kāvyas*, of which the best known are those of Aśvaghoṣa (+1), represent a hero attaining liberation (or *nirvāṇa*, 'extinction') as the highest end [607, 714]. For example the life of the Buddha himself was narrated in *kāvya* epics. The Great Epic *Mahābhārata* was by some later writers (e.g. Ānandavardhana, p. 530) held to produce the calmed experience, and although as Tradition it was not usually regarded as *kāvya* (some writers, exceptionally, do regard it as being *kāvya* as well as Tradition, when treating it as poetry) it would at least exemplify the possibility of a 'calmed' aesthetic experience. In the Epic as we now have it the hero, Yudhiṣṭhira, though generally depicted as pursuing virtue or justice *dharma*, does in the end renounce the world and his empire, as a consummation of the experience developed throughout the story that life is full of unhappiness and tragedy and even the great victory a disaster in human terms, since so many lives were lost on both sides.

91. It was probably some Buddhist writers on aesthetics who first maintained, following their great poet Aśvaghoṣa, that the calmed was a distinct *rasa*, possible as the main aesthetic experience produced by a *kāvya*. Śāradātanaya in fact names one Vāsuki as having proposed it (p. 46), but practically nothing seems to be known of such a writer and this may be a piece of mythology giving respectable antiquity to a controversial idea. The real first formulator of the calmed *rasa* may have been the Buddhist writer on drama, Rāhula, whose work is known only from a few references (e.g. Sāgaranandin 2873). Controversy developed around the significance of such plays on Buddhist themes as the *Lokānanda* [1285] and the *Nāgānanda*, where the heroes sacrifice everything and abandon their lives to help others but are eventually restored to a state of worldly happiness. One can stress their attitude of renunciation and regard the main experience as the calmed, despite the conclusions, which are 'auspicious' in the ordinary worldly sense. On the other hand the experience can be enjoyed as the heroic, of the magnanimous variety. Abhinavagupta (I p. 339) appears to take the former view, and certainly accepts the calmed as a ninth aesthetic experience. He moreover regards it as the highest *rasa*, being transcendent, in which view he is really following his religious assumptions.

92. Abhinavagupta reads a text of the *Nāṭyaśāstra* which actually gives the calmed in its list of *rasas*, and a brief description of it, with 'calm' *śama* as the basic emotion. He claims to have found this in some 'old' manuscripts. It seems clear, however, that it was a relatively late interpolation, perhaps introduced by one of the earlier commentators. The earliest critic, whose work is extant, to accept the calmed *rasa* is Udbhaṭa (late +8), in his *Kāvyālaṅkārasārasaṅgraha* on poetics, though his commentary on the *Nāṭyaśāstra* seems to have been lost. Earlier than this a Jaina canonical work, the *Anuyogadvāra Sūtra* (*c.* +300 according to its critical edition, p. 71), gives a list of nine *kāvya rasas*, including the calmed (*pasaṃta* in Prakrit = *śānta*, pp. 121-24). It also gives a 'shameful' (*velaṇaa*=*vrīḍanaka*) experience in place of the usual 'apprehensive', a new *rasa* not known to have found recognition elsewhere.

93. Dhanañjaya and Dhanika, contemporaries of Abhinavagupta (but living in a different part of India and generally following Nāyaka), do not accept the calmed fully on the ground that the calm emotion is not in fact developed in dramas (IV.35 and *Vyākhyā*, Nirṇayasāgar ed.) and cannot be a 'basic emotion'. Instead, however, they hold (IV.45) that the connoisseurs (of drama), though they do not taste a calmed aesthetic experience, corresponding to liberation and free from happiness and unhappiness and from all passions, may be moved by the representation of sympathetic joy (*muditā*, i.e. rejoicing in another's success), benevolence *maitrī*, compassion and equanimity *upekṣā* to a kind of tasting of the calmed. These four qualities mentioned are derived from an ancient Buddhist practice of compassionate meditation, for both monks and layman, in order to pervade the universe with thoughts charged with them [567]. It was held conducive to liberation but it also referred to the fundamental ethical principle of considering all living beings as like oneself and was required 'in the world' also by the Buddhist social programme. [72]

94. In the later Middle Ages religion seems to have exerted much more influence on Indian society than in earlier periods and we find more *kāvyas* serving the purpose of religious teaching. The calmed experience was then fairly widely recognised (Mammaṭa in the +11 followed Abhinavagupta and exerted wide influence), although a series of major writers on the drama rejected it (Sāgaranandin, Śāradātanaya, Śiṅgabhūpāla).

95. In mentioning that some *rasas* can be subdivided into different kinds, the *Nāṭyaśāstra* (VI.77 Kāśī) says that the sensitive, comic and furious can each be of three kinds: having the nature of, or else simply 'with', speech, costume or action (gesture). On the strength of this, Mātṛgupta (+400), a poet and critic whose works unfortunately are known only from quotations [1306], says that *rasas* are of three kinds, produced by speech, costume or 'nature' *svabhāva*, namely 'speech *rasa*', 'costume *rasa*' and 'natural *rasa*', the last through such qualities as beauty, youth, firmness, etc. (quoted by

Rāghavabhaṭṭa in his *Arthadyotanikā* on the *Abhijñānaśākuntala*, p. 7 Nirṇayasāgar 11th ed.). In fact these would seem to be causes and effects of emotion which can produce the aesthetic experience. However, such expressions probably tended to open the way to speaking of *rasas* more loosely: one might 'taste' the speech, costume, etc., or indeed any of the causes and effects of emotion represented. This would appear to be destructive of the *rasa* theory. Nevertheless Lollaṭa (quoted by Abhinavagupta, I p. 298) said that *rasas* were endless in fact, though traditionally restricted in number. The suggestion was further considered by Bhoja (see below [110]).

96. Rudraṭa (+9) in his *Kāvyālaṅkāra* (XII. 3 and XV. 17ff.) is the first known writer to put forward a tenth *rasa*, the 'affectionate' *preyas*, with reference to friendship and paternal, filial and brotherly love, as distinguished from sexual love in the sensitive. Earlier writers, such as Bhāmaha, are known to mention the 'affectionate' as a kind of figure of speech, but they list it next to the 'having *rasa*' *rasavant* figure, which means an expression specially productive of one of the eight *rasas*. The basic emotion for it is affection *sneha*. The affectionate (and the synonymous *vātsalya*, or *sneha* itself called *rasa*) seems never to have been widely accepted. In addition, and perhaps in the same way as Lollaṭa, Rudraṭa held (XII.4) that any emotion, including the transients, could be enjoyed, giving rise to a specific *rasa*. [214 f.]

97. Abhinavagupta (I p. 341) mentions, in order to reject, besides the affectionate, some other *rasas* proposed by critics unknown to us : 'devotion' (*bhakti* : taken up much later by Rūpa [118]) and 'greediness' (*laulya*, especially unlimited sexual ambition). Dhanañjaya (IV.83) rejects 'hunting' *mṛgayā* and 'gambling' *akṣa* as *rasas*.

98. From different points of view Bhoja (+11) considered *rasa* as many or as one, as we shall see below, but in pointing out that it could be many at a certain level, at least as many as there are emotions (including transients), he sometimes particularly stresses twelve *rasas* as of special importance (*Sarasvatīkaṇṭhābharaṇa* V.163ff. = pp. 595ff. Nirṇayasāgar 2nd ed.; *Śṛṅgāraprakāśa* Vol. II p. 441 Josyer's ed.). These are the ten of Rudraṭa (including the calmed and affectionate) plus two others which he found in other earlier writers whose names are not known to us. As in the case of the affectionate, however, there is a figure of speech familiar in earlier poetics, the 'exalted' *ūrjasvin* [216], corresponding to one or even both of them.

99. According to Bhoja the four *rasas* additional to the usual eight are based on the four kinds of hero found among characters of intermediate or high quality. These are mentioned already in the *Nāṭyaśāstra* (XXXIV.16 ff. Kāśī) and distinguished as 'calmed' *śānta*, 'playful' *lalita*, 'exalted' *udātta* or 'proud' *uddhata*. They are all 'firm' (*dhīra*, 'steadfast'). The affectionate corresponds to the playful hero. In the *Nāṭyaśāstra* the 'calmed' hero is not connected with liberation from the world, though he is in a sense 'unworldly': he may be a priest (brahman) or a merchant. For the remaining two Bhoja gives the 'exalted' (*udātta* or *ūrjasvin*) and 'proud' *uddhata rasas*. The basic emotion for the exalted is reflection (usually a transient) or (in the *Śṛṅgāraprakāśa*—see below) 'egoism' *ahaṃkāra*. That for the proud is pride (usually a transient). The 'egoism' of the exalted may be presumed to be the Sāṃkhya principle of self-consciousness as first differentiated according to the theory of evolution of that school, which Bhoja followed. In practice it will be the self-respect, and resultant concern for good or proper conduct, of an exalted hero.

100. Rāmacandra and Guṇacandra considered nine *rasas* (including the calmed) useful in practice though they thought others theoretically possible (p. 145). Besides the affectionate and 'greediness', they here mention three more which do not seem to be discussed elsewhere in the extant sources : 'vice' *vyasana*, 'unhappiness' *duḥkha* and 'happiness' *sukha* The corresponding basic emotions would be 'addiction' *āsakti*, 'discontent' *arati* and 'contentment' *santoṣa*.

101. Bhānudatta (+15), followed by Kṛṣṇaśarman (+17 ?), proposed an 'illusion' *māyā rasa* for worldly attachment as opposed to the calmed of renunciation (*Rasataraṅgiṇī* VII, *Mandāramaranda* p. 106). The basic emotion is 'wrong cognition' (*mithyājñāna*, 'misapprehension'). Bhānudatta examines but rejects 'miserliness' *kārpaṇya*, with 'yearning' *spṛhā* as basic emotion : if developed this would in fact be the comic.

102. Finally we may note that Haripāla (+12 ?) divided the sensitive into two, 'union' and 'frustration', as additional *rasas* besides the sensitive itself, and further distinguished from the calmed a 'supreme' *brāhma rasa*. The last is connected with realising the absolute eternal reality, the Vedānta version of liberation, with joy *ānanda* as basic emotion. The basic emotion for the calmed, on the other hand, is here given as 'indifference' *nirveda*, emphasising that it is connected with the simple renunciation of worldly aims, the revulsion against an unsatisfactory world. (Information from the unpublished *Saṅgītasudhākara* given by Raghavan in *The Number of Rasas*, pp. 144ff. and 54ff.)

103. The dramatist Bhavabhūti (+8) seems to suggest in his *Uttararāmacarita* (Act III verse 47) that there is really only one *rasa*, the compassionate, which is divided by different causes and evolves into many forms. The ultimate inspiration for this suggestion comes from the *Rāmāyaṇa*, the 'First *Kāvya*', itself, on the tragic (but probably apocryphal) conclusion of which this play is based, with the addition of an auspicious ending. Some later critics (e.g. Ānandavardhana, p. 529) give the compassionate as the *rasa* of the *Rāmāyaṇa*, although in its original version the heroic may ultimately have prevailed, despite grievous episodes. There is further the old tradition that the original author, Vālmīki, was inspired to create the new *vaktra* metre, in which his epic is composed, by a tragic scene, the killing of one of a pair of birds. Of course a play is not (as a rule) a theoretical work and Bhavabhūti does not positively exclude the independent existence of other *rasas* here, simply stressing the pervasive nature of the compassionate. One could interpret the suggestion as hyperbole *atiśayokti*, perfectly appropriate in the situation represented. Yet a conviction of pervasive tragedy in life and an all-embracing compassion are in fact suggested throughout Bhavabhūti's works, not just here, and so it seems probable that it was really his view that the ultimate aesthetic experience is the compassionate, all other *rasas* being secondary. The commentator Vīrarāghava (+1800), explaining the verse, holds that it is Bhavabhūti's view that there is only one all-pervasive *rasa*, the compassionate. Even the sensitive in 'union' is mixed with pain. Audiences enjoy the compassionate because of its varied forms.

104. Śaktibhadra (probably +9) on the other hand, also in a play on Rāma, the *Āścaryacūḍāmaṇi*, Wonderful Crest Jewel, is generally supposed to have made the marvellous the prevailing *rasa* in his play, which is thus differentiated sharply from all known earlier Indian dramas (even so the *Naṭāṅkuśa*, an anonymous work on dramatic criticism, notes its *rasa* as the heroic—Kunjunni Raja, *The Contribution of Kerala to Sanskrit Literature*, p. 210). There is no actual statement by the dramatist himself that there is only one *rasa*, however, but simply the example of a 'marvellous' play. Some later writers took up the implication [117]. For Śaktibhadra's inspiration we may look to Guṇāḍhya's *Bṛhatkathā* [690] and to Daṇḍin, who emulated Guṇāḍhya in his own novel, the *Avantisundarī*, and seems fond of the marvellous in his theoretical *Kāvyalakṣaṇa* (I.38), though not to the exclusion of the other *rasas*. Even Bhavabhūti mentions the marvellous in the last act of his *Uttararāmacarita*, along with the compassionate, without insisting that it is only a modification of the latter (first speech of the producer in the play within the play *antarnāṭaka*). [2113]

105. The dramatist Bodhāyana (+2 ?), in the prologue to his comedy *Bhagavadajjukīya* [1085], maintains that the comic is the best *rasa*, therefore one should act a comedy in preference to other types of play.

106. Abhinavagupta (I pp. 339f.) is the first critic known to us to argue categorically for one *rasa* being the highest and dominating all the others. Accepting the calmed, as we saw above, he says it is superior to the other eight. His idea is that during the aesthetic experience in the theatre the thoughts of the audience are withdrawn from everyday worldly objects, are therefore calmed in the sense of being detached and ready to transcend their limited individuality in a higher experience. In this connection, however, he gives a verse as what appears to be a quotation from an unknown author, who would therefore be an earlier protagonist of the view of the calmed as the highest *rasa*. It is very likely that this author was Nāyaka, quoted earlier by Abhinavagupta (I p. 5) as speaking very highly of the calmed. That quotation itself quotes a half verse from the interpolated text on the calmed in the *Nāṭyaśāstra*, but with a wording different from that read by Abhinavagupta and saying that *rasa* arises from the calmed

(Abhinavagupta has instead that the basic emotion arises). Buddhist critics, however, probably spoke highly of their new calmed aesthetic experience long before Nāyaka and Abhinavagupta.

107. Dhanañjaya, though following Nāyaka in some respects, rejects the calmed and proposes a different kind of theory concerning the interrelations of the aesthetic experiences. No one among them is ultimate or highest, but all form parts, or zones, in a range of thought (IV.43ff., cf. Dhanika's explanation). There are four zones or phases : opening (*vikāsa*, a word used of the opening of flowers), extension (*vistara*, full expansion), agitation (*kṣobha*, shaking) and scattering (*vikṣepa*, confusion, falling). We are probably to conceive this range of thought-types through the metaphor of the blossoming of a flower : the aesthetic experience has an eager inceptive phase, a steadier fully expanded phase, an unsteady phase when it begins to fade and to seem too frail to stand the buffeting of the causes and effects of emotion, finally the phase in which it wilts and is scattered. These mental phases occur in the four aesthetic experiences sensitive, heroic, horrific and furious respectively. Then when these four primary *rasas* have occurred, as stated in the *Nāṭyaśāstra* (see above [58]) the four secondary aesthetic experiences, comic, marvellous, apprehensive and compassionate, are produced (through the proper causes and effects of emotion) respectively with the same mental phases. Through this analysis the number of *rasas* is fixed at eight. Dhanañjaya has here propounded a remarkable aesthetic theory (partly anticipated by Nāyaka, who has only three phases, with 'melting' *druti* in place of agitation plus scattering—see Abhinavagupta, I p. 277), of aesthetic experience as a single type of thought activity, but having these eight aspects, which are not arbitrary divisions but a regular classification of the data of experience, showing their basis in the attitude to an environment ranging from favourable (conditions conducive to opening and expansion) to unfavourable. Dhanika and Nṛsiṃha in their commentaries have somewhat modified his position.

108. Bhoja took some ideas from Nāyaka and Dhanañjaya, whilst representing himself usually as a follower of Daṇḍin. In fact he follows Daṇḍin in words rather than meanings, reading his own system into the work of an orthodox Brahmanical predecessor. Within Daṇḍin's framework he stored a vast assemblage of ideas collected from many other earlier writers, especially Bhāmaha, also Vāmana, Rudraṭa, Lollaṭa and Rājaśekhara. In part he aimed at a synthesis of all previous work on literary criticism and aesthetics, in part at crowning this synthesis with his own comprehensive aesthetic theory. His theory is that ultimately there is only one *rasa*, the sensitive.

109. In what is believed to be the earlier of the two works in which Bhoja elaborates his aesthetics, the *Sarasvatīkaṇṭhābharaṇa*, he says (V.1) that the aesthetic experience is the sensitive, which is also 'egoism' (*ahaṃkāra*, self-consciousness, self-respect) and 'self-assertion' (*abhimāna*, consciousness of self, especially in satisfying a desire). Clearly this conception is quite opposite to Abhinavagupta's, in which the individual forgets himself and rises to universality. It is based on Bhoja's fundamentally Sāṃkhya outlook, according to which the souls are absolutely and eternally separate from one another and have experiences only by being entangled in the evolving physical world, where 'self-consciousness' *ahaṃkāra* is an intangible, only slightly evolved, state of matter which makes experience possible.

110. According to Bhoja (ibid. pp. 704f.) this aesthetic experience has three levels. At the fundamental or 'ultimate point' *parā koṭiḥ* it is the one sensitive *rasa*, for which 'egoism' and 'self-assertion' are merely different names. In the 'intermediate state' *madhyamāvasthā* it produces many emotions which can become as many distinct aesthetic experiences. At this level Bhoja mentions particularly the twelve *rasas* we discussed above (as a matter of fact he is especially fond of having sets of twelve in a class), but he makes it clear that he considers that in the intermediate state any emotion whatsoever can become a *rasa* if suitably developed. Many of these are noted subsequently in the same book (p. 719 and later : many transients and various others, e.g. p. 724) by way of example and without attempting a complete list, which would presumably not be possible [1527]. Thirdly there is the 'highest point' *uttarā koṭiḥ*, at which 'love' *rati*, the 'queen' of all these emotions, developed to the highest degree and ceasing to be an emotion, absorbing into itself all other emotions in the form of love of these, takes the form of the *rasa* 'egoism'. The other emotions are absorbed because each is a kind of 'love', i.e. love for its specific thought-activity (one can love humour, one can also love being indignant, says Bhoja).

111. From its title *Śṛṅgāraprakāśa* the other work should be entirely devoted to the exposition of the sensitive. Under this aegis it in fact elaborates the entire field of poetics and dramaturgy as subservient to the purposes of this aesthetic experience. Its Eleventh Chapter deals more particularly with the theory of *rasas*. On the whole it agrees with the presumed earlier work. The Eleventh Chapter begins its discussion (p. 429) by taking up the point we have just noted from the other work : since there is love of fighting, love of indignation and love of humour, as well as love of love, the development of all the emotions ends in love *preman*. From this we proceed to the statement that the aesthetic experience *rasa* is self-assertion *abhimāna*, defined as the cause of the experience of the consciousness of joy, etc., through whatever is agreeable to the mind. The person who is 'sensitive' has all the emotions, not one who is not sensitive. These are developed by 'development' (*bhāvanā*, as in Nāyaka's theory) until they become *rasa*. The same emotions are sometimes 'basic' and sometimes 'transient', depending on the situation. The basic emotions do not all become (separate) *rasas*, however, for only the sensitive is *rasa*, but when the sensitive appears with the causes and effects of these emotions it is especially relished. (The result of the 'development', as we saw in the *Sarasvatīkaṇṭhābharaṇa*, is not several *rasas* but one, since all the emotions are absorbed in 'love', they all give rise to the same *rasa*, but the experience is enjoyed more when a variety of causes and effects of emotion have contributed to it.)

112. Bhoja calls *rasa* a kind of quality of the egoism (*ahaṃkāra*, self-consciousness) of the soul *ātman*. It is the sensitive and self-assertion *abhimāna* as well as *rasa* . From it, all the emotions, love, etc., are born (p. 431). This is perhaps a slight modification of the theory of the other work, since here *rasa* is not egoism but a quality of it, and what is now being stressed is that *rasa* is 'self-assertion' (which relates particularly to satisfying desires). If *rasa* is a quality of the egoism of the soul (of the reader or audience, and of the author) it is not a quality of the *kāvya*, a kind of figure of speech or ornament, though the *kāvya* produces it (or conveys it) (435f.). On the contrary it is the 'figures of speech' *alaṅkāras*, which include the 'qualities' of style, the dramatic 'modes', etc., which are strictly subordinate to *rasa*, along with the causes and effects of emotion (p. 433).

113. There follows (p. 436) a slightly different version of the three levels of *rasa*. The first is here called the 'former point' *pūrvā koṭiḥ* instead of the 'ultimate point'. Here it is simply *rasa*, for which egoism (correct the text to *ahaṃkāra*), self-assertion and the sensitive are other names. That it is 'made of pride', i.e. self-respect, noted in the other work, is further elaborated here : for example when a man is pleased with himself because a pretty girl looks at him, it is a case of *rasa* in this sense. The second level seems unchanged, though in the light of the preceding discussion we should perhaps understand the production of many *rasas*, which is implied here, as being really of the sensitive diversified by the variety of causes and effects of many emotions. Here it is called the sensitive. The 'highest point', where it is 'egoism', is unchanged (except for a variant *uttamā* for *uttarā*), but later on (p. 444) it is called the 'utmost limit' *paramā kāṣṭhā* of *rasa*. In connection with the possibility of understanding many *rasas* at the second level, this work, like the other, mentions various *rasas* by name as such on pp. 439ff., with some new *rasas* on p. 451, for instance.

114. Bhoja then demonstrates that what is generally understood to be expression of the basic emotions (producing *rasa*) is 'egoism (being) grown', i.e. that it is development of the egoism *ahaṃkāra*, the self-consçiousness or self-respect, of the characters represented, taking well known examples from the literature (p. 444). The first of the three levels is thus the original, undeveloped egoism in the soul, its primaeval involvement in the physical universe. This has nothing to do with art, it is to be regarded as simply a physical fact in the nature of living beings, but it makes art possible. In the first place it makes the emotions possible, and then, on the basis of the development of these, art and the strictly aesthetic experience become possible.

115. In the latter part of the Eleventh Chapter Bhoja

considers the various *kāvya* forms and types in relation to the aesthetic experience. Some forms, such as the novel [679], are dominated by 'pleasure' *kāma*, i.e. their characters are engaged mainly in the pursuit of pleasure, and there it is immediately clear that Bhoja's sensitive aesthetic experience is to be developed. In other forms other ends of life may be primarily pursued, thus in epics 'wealth' *artha* is the usual or main end, though all the ends may properly appear [1516] (p. 480, last verse but one : probably *caturvarga* should be read for *caturvarṇa*, as on the preceding page). In these forms, according to Bhoja, the experience is still 'sensitive', just as all emotions involve 'love' (as we saw above) and their very possibility is a development of the original egoism. No further explanation is needed to show how all the ends of life, all human activity, are understood to develop the sensitive aesthetic experience. However, Bhoja actually writes of the sensitive in each of the four ends of life (liberation, virtue, wealth and pleasure). Thus the self-assertion *abhimāna* of a person desiring liberation is the 'sensitive' with reference to liberation (p. 547). Afterwards a chapter is devoted to each of these varieties of the sensitive. In each case the idea of 'self-assertion' is the basis of the discussion. As far as the three worldly ends are concerned, finally, it is said that the sensitive with respect to pleasure is the dominant one, since it is the final result which is aimed at even in the cases of the sensitive in virtue and wealth : virtue and wealth according to Bhoja are only pursued as causes of, i.e. means to, pleasure (beginning of Chapter XXII, p. 1 of Yadugiriyati's ed.).

116. Maladhārin Hemacandra (*c*. +1100, not the most famous Hemacandra), in his commentary on the *Anuyogadvāra Sūtra* (p. 134), maintains that the heroic is the first and best of the *rasas*, particularly when it relates to magnanimity and asceticism (this latter is a new view in aesthetics, as far as we know, but heroic asceticism is an ancient idea in Jainism), though he does not suggest that it is in any sense the only *rasa*. The *Sūtra* itself places the heroic first in its enumeration, so the primacy of the heroic may have been an early contribution to aesthetics by the Jaina tradition.

117. The idea that the marvellous is the only *rasa* was taken up by Nārāyaṇa and Dharmadatta (+14). Unfortunately their work does not seem to have been preserved, but Dharmadatta's book is quoted by Viśvanātha (*Sāhityadarpaṇa*, *Vṛtti* on III.3, p. 73 of Nirṇayasāgar 3rd ed.), who seems inclined to follow the view himself. Dharmadatta had studied Bhoja's theory (Raghavan, *The Number of Rasas*, p. 173) but disagreed with it. He says in the quotation that the essence of the aesthetic experience is always 'admiration' *camatkāra* (contrast the *Nāṭyadarpaṇa* view [87] and cf. Abhinavagupta [79]). This being the case, the aesthetic experience is always the marvellous, as stated by the learned Nārāyaṇa : 'Only the marvellous is *rasa*'. Viśvanātha himself (+15) explains that 'admiration' is a synonym for astonishment *vismaya*, the basic emotion for the marvellous. He sums up the view in his *kārikā* (III.3): the aesthetic experience is essentially ('its life is') transcendent *lokottara* admiration, it is tasted by connoisseurs in its undivided own feature *svākāra*. (In other words *rasa* is one, and by implication the marvellous.) Bhānudatta (*Rasataraṅgiṇī* I) accepts that the marvellous is the dominant *rasa*, since there is admiration in the experience of the sensitive and the others. The dramatist Mahādeva (+17), in his play which has the significant title *Adbhutadarpaṇa*, The Marvellous Mirror, suggests (Act IV verse 8) that the marvellous is the only *rasa*. In practice he has emphasised this by writing a play full of surprises, based mostly on deception.

118. Rūpa Gosvāmin (+16), inspired by the revival of the Kṛṣṇa cult, worked out a theory of 'devotion' *bhakti*, with various aspects, as the supreme *rasa*. The sensitive is a prominent aspect of this 'devotion', which in effect is a reworking of the theory of the sensitive as only *rasa*, on a religious basis. Rūpa has expounded his ideas in two theoretical works, the *Bhaktirasāmṛtasindhu* and its supplement *Ujjvalanīlamaṇi*, and put them into practice in his plays on the life of Kṛṣṇa. The purpose of the plays is to excite devotion to Kṛṣṇa (the chief 'cause of emotion'). In his theory he puts forward a seemingly new view on the aesthetic experience, that the audience should identify themselves with the characters in the play. A great part of his theoretical discussions is concerned with the actual characters in the Kṛṣṇa story, which alone, it appears, is a proper subject for dramas.

119. The *Nāṭyaśāstra* itself uses the term *rasa* in the singular number as if in some sense it is one kind (or class ?) of experience. The critics whose works we have just reviewed have interpreted this in various ways, mostly taking one of the several distinct *rasas* as fundamental and the others as derivatives from it. Dhanañjaya, however, takes *rasa* as such and explains the eight separate *rasas* as phases or zones within its range. Kavikarṇapūra (+16) also studied *rasa* as such in his *Alaṅkārakaustubha*, Chapter V. It has a kind of basic emotion, namely 'joy' *ānanda* or the 'root (bulb) of the shoot of tasting' *āsvādāṅkurakanda*. This basic emotion is one and is an essential quality *dharma* of the mind *cetas* (p. 121). Lokanātha's commentary says it is like a crystal which takes on many different colours, for example of flowers, when in contact with those flowers. In the same way this 'joy' takes on the different (separate) basic emotions, energy, astonishment, grief, etc., when in contact with the several causes of these emotions (p. 122). Kavikarṇapura continues that good people have this root of the shoot of tasting when 'goodness' *sattva* prevails in them to the exclusion of passion and darkness (unnumbered verse, apparently text and not commentary, on p. 121: the edition is very confused). He thus follows Sāṃkhya theory in some respects. The aesthetic experience, he continues (p. 129), is happiness *sukha*, which is admiring *camatkārin*, which is joined to its own causes (of emotion), etc., and which checks other activities of the mind and the senses. The aesthetic experience is one (literally 'has singleness'—*aikadhya*), because it has the essential quality of 'joy' (which is one, and it has no other essential quality, therefore it can be only of one kind) (p. 130). Emotion on the other hand is various, because of the differences among its variable qualities *upādhis*, love and the other basic emotions being these variable qualities. At the beginning of his book (p.5) Kavikarṇapūra has said that *rasa* is the 'essence' or 'soul' *ātman* of *kāvya*. This could be understood much as Abhinavagupta's remark on drama above [75], or it may be no more than a figure of speech. If it is more, it is possible that it is also supposed to be the soul of the connoisseur, which has the essential quality of joy, and so on. In Chapter V, however, this joy is called an essential quality of the mind. It is called simply 'emotion' and the root of the aesthetic experience (tasting), whilst the old 'basic emotions' are now variable qualities of it, in that they are not essential but are capable of being imposed on it.

120. The writers on poetics, as distinct from dramaturgy, start out from the question of the nature of the language of *kāvya* and are therefore in principle concerned with *kāvya* itself rather than with its effect on the reader. Obviously the two questions are related, and in this chapter we have inevitably overlapped a little into some critics who wrote primarily from the point of view of poetics. Several of the later writers (particularly Abhinavagupta) dealt equally with both and attempted a synthesis between the two methods of analysing language and studying its effects. Before we turn to the question of what it is that constitutes the beauty of the language of *kāvya*, in our fourth chapter, there is another major aspect of the theory of drama to be considered, namely the construction of plays, and this we may conveniently take up in the next chapter.

Chapter III

INDIAN DRAMATURGY : THE CONSTRUCTION OF PLAYS

121. The *Nāṭyaśāstra* calls the story *itivṛtta* the 'body' of *kāvya*, implying that this is what is to be adorned by the art. It devotes a chapter (XXI in Kāśī ed., XIX in Baroda) to the story and how it should be adapted to the requirements of drama. As usual its approach is practical, it sets out a method used by the old actors and producers. The companies of actors in ancient times had playwrights attached to them to prepare plays as needed, or the producer himself might have arranged plays on stories well known to the actors. The early productions were probably ephemeral and it was presumably only later that fixed texts began to be handed down and to be permanently recorded in book form. In constructing a play, the method sets out the 'elements' *prakṛtis* of the 'matter' *artha*, constituting the story, and the stages of the action, together with the essential 'conjunctions' *sandhis* in the development of the plot and numerous secondary devices used in this.

122. The most important 'element' is the 'objective' *kārya*, the gaining of which brings the activities of the characters to a state of relative rest and the play to an end. In other words the playwright must select, or invent, one main action to be accomplished and then construct his play accordingly : there must be unity of action and everything included in the presentation must serve the main action [1617]. Subordinate to the main action or story *ādhikārika itivṛtta* there will frequently be a 'subsidiary' *prāsaṅgika* one which assists it, such as the story of a friend or ally of the main hero. This subsidiary action sets events in motion which contribute decisively to the success of the main action, it is thus shown as necessary for the play. Under the name 'sub-plot' *patākā* this decisive subsidiary action is another 'element' of the matter, dealing with a friend who gains his own end whilst helping the main hero [1209, 1359]. A third element is the 'intervention' *pra-*

karī, a subsidiary action restricted to a single incident without development, involving another character but again a necessary factor in the story of the main hero. For example it could result in his gaining essential information. The other character may gain nothing for himself [1133] and his helpful action may be tragic [1357].

123. There are two other 'elements' of the matter. Given the 'objective', there must be a starting point where this is first proposed. At this starting point, at the beginning of the play, there must be the 'seed' *bīja*, the potential of the objective, a small beginning which will ramify and end as the accomplishment of the final result or fruit of the main action [1629]. At the starting point the seed is the mere desire for the final fruit, without any definite plan of action being in sight. Afterwards it will sometimes be seen and sometimes apparently lost and the matter even given up, but it will have 'sprouted' and will grow in fact until it bears fruit.

124. Lastly there is the 'impulse' or 'continuity' (*bindu*, literally 'drop', variously explained later as the metaphor of a drop of oil spreading out on water or of dripping water feeding the 'seed'). The 'continuity' prevents the actual interruption of the matter even when the 'seed' seems to have been lost. It pervades the whole subject matter up to the completion of the action (see also *Nāṭyaśāstra* XX.15, Kāśī) [980, 1588]. The later writers on dramaturgy generally explain the 'continuity' in terms of the consciousness of various characters leading to continuing action; the *Nāṭyaśāstra* does not elaborate on it but notes (XX.16) its connection with the division of the matter into acts *aṅkas*, all of which must be in contact with it.

125. The acts must show various characters in a variety of situations, productive of several 'aesthetic experiences'. The division into acts is determined simply by the exit of all the characters from the stage: this constitutes a pause in the *kāvya* but not the completion of the growth of the 'seed'. During an act the characters shown attain various immediate objectives and so maintain the continuity. The events of an act should not occupy more than a day. Between acts a month or even as much as a year may elapse (XX.14ff.). [160]

126. The intervening events may be reported (instead of shown) in several kinds of 'introductory scene' or scenes 'hinting at the matter' (*arthopakṣepaka*, called *praveśaka* in XX) prefixed to an act, inserted in it or attached at the end (XXI. 108ff.). These may also be used to report actions regarded as unsuitable for representation, such as fighting in most (not all) kinds of drama, the fall of a kingdom, death, the siege of a city. The *Nāṭyaśāstra* gives five varieties of scenes 'hinting at the matter', namely the 'introductory scene' (proper) *praveśaka*, 'supporting scene' *viṣkambhaka*, 'crest' *cūlikā*, 'introduction to the (next) act' *aṅkāvatāra* and 'opening to the act' *aṅkamukha*. An 'introductory scene' is played by 'low' characters speaking Prakrit and serves to report (directly) a lot of action in a few words [1164]. A 'supporting scene', which, like the preceding, stands at the beginning of an act, differs from this in admitting 'middle' as well as low characters (e.g. a chamberlain, ministers, etc.), speaking Sanskrit [978]. According to Cārāyaṇa (reported by Sāgaranandin 362ff.) it differs from an introductory scene principally in that it bears on the main action only indirectly. A 'crest' is a voice from behind the curtain held across the stage, for example a character declares his intentions [1587] or a court bard recites something significant from 'off stage' [1628]. Alone among these scenes the crest can occur in the middle of an act. An 'introduction to the (next) act' is a scene at the end of the preceding act which prepares for the next by hinting at the action to take place in it. For example the jester speaks of a dancing competition about to be held and of hearing the drum already [367, 1384]. The 'opening to the act' is obscure because the *Nāṭyaśāstra* describes it too briefly and the later writers offer two or three different interpretations. It tends to be confused with either the supporting scene or the introduction to the act. The *Nāṭyaśāstra* states simply that it is given by one character only and briefly indicates what has happened [1046]. Of these five, only the introductory scene and crest are fairly common, the supporting scene less common but not rare. The others being less well established in practice were liable to reinterpretation. A

127. The action has five 'stages' or 'situations' *avasthās*, which are said (XXI.6, 121, 15) to be based on real life. In a drama these have no necessary connection with the division into acts, which arises from less essential features of the matter, namely the accidents of the span of time covered, the nature of certain events and the convenience of representing the activities of the characters. The first stage, the 'commencement' (*ārambha* or *prārambha*), depends on the 'seed' and consists of the simple desire for attaining its fruit (which will be the 'objective'). The second is the 'undertaking' *prayatna*, when actual action towards the fruit is begun, though the character undertaking it cannot see as yet the precise means by which it could be attained. The third is the 'possibility of attainment' *prāptisambhava*, when there has been some success in the matter and a means to the final attainment can be imagined (only). The fourth, the 'certainty of attainment of the fruit' *niyatā phalaprāpti*, is when the means is actually seen, and through it the attainment. The fifth is the final 'attaining the fruit' *phalayoga* at the end of the action, when the complete fruit as originally desired is attained [1584].

128. In a drama on the largest scale (either of the two types *nāṭaka* and *prakaraṇa*, which will be discussed in our fifth chapter), the playwright should develop his plot with five 'conjunctions' (*sandhis*, XXI. 36ff.). This refers to the main action, and the conjunctions of subsidiary actions will be dependent on these. Following the plot, the 'opening' *mukha*, in the *kāvya*, is where the 'seed' is produced, with the arising of aesthetic experiences from various matters. This is the first conjunction [1404, 1586].

129. As usual the *Nāṭyaśāstra* is very laconic, and in this case the later writers are not agreed about the interpretation of the system of conjunctions or of the individual items in it. It is in fact possible that the seemingly different approaches to the analysis of construction, the elements, stages and conjunctions, were really independent doctrines in origin, afterwards combined in the *Nāṭyaśāstra*. Be this as it may, it seems possible to interpret it as a harmonious system without reducing the conjunctions to nothing more than the rigid combinations of the elements with the stages, as some of the later theorists would have it (see on Mātṛgupta below [166], and Dhanañjaya [169]). This view seems to be an oversimplification: it hardly agrees with the practice, it requires revision of the *Nāṭyaśāstra* text on substantial matters to produce a consistent theory for all types of play and other writers allow the conjunctions and stages to be at least partly independent and the elements to be handled freely (*Nāṭyadarpaṇa* p. 37).

130. The proper conclusion seems to be that the conjunctions are independent of the stages in conception and may either coincide or not in particular plays. The first and last are obviously more closely linked than the others, being necessarily at the beginning and end of the play. Otherwise, the stages represent the natural and progressive accomplishment of any successful action, according to the *Nāṭyaśāstra*, whereas the conjunctions represent the artistic development of a plot, as art rather than in a naturalistic manner, or at any rate with 'ups and downs' which are common enough in life but are regarded as essential to art in order to engage the interest of the audience. All the writers agree that a conjunction is a combination or collision of two (or more) things, involving the main action: the proper interpretation seems to be that what was meant is conjunctions between the actions, and activating emotions, of different characters in the plot as arranged by the playwright. The opening will thus be when the actions of two (or more) characters cross in such a way as to produce the seed. At the same time the 'element' seed is necessarily conjoined here, but not only here. Naturally the commencement stage, which depends on the seed, will cover this conjunction.

131. The second conjunction is the 're-opening' *pratimukha*, described as the 'sprouting' *udghāṭana* of the seed, when it is as if 'seen and lost'. In other words the seed begins to develop, but then through some action between the characters it looks as if it will come to nothing: the opposition is too strong or one of the protagonists fails in some way. From the point of view of the art, the audience is kept in suspense. There is hope and then a setback [1405, 1589-90].

132. The third conjunction is the 'embryo' *garbha*, implying that there has been a clear development. The seed has germinated *udbheda* and there is both success and lack of success, with 'searching' (presumably for some means to attain the fruit). Here evidently there is a major but not yet decisive conflict between the two parties: according to Abhinavagupta (III p. 25) the 'success' is on the part of the hero, the 'lack of success' in the action of the opponent, the 'searching' common to both. If Abhinavagupta means that the hero succeeds and the opponent fails, that seems unwarranted by the *Nāṭyaśāstra* text and makes the second expression redundant; perhaps he means, what is surely the natural original meaning, that through the action of the opponent the hero is checked after his initial success (and then seeks the means to decisive success) [1406, 1591, 1612].

133. The fourth conjunction is read as either 'obstacle' *avamarśa* or 'pause' *vimarśa*, both readings being noted by Abhinavagupta (III p. 26). The pause is in the 'matter' (of the story), namely of the seed which had been 'germinated' in the 'embryo', caused by beguiling [1585] or anger [1407] or a disaster (so what seems to be the better text, followed by Abhinavagupta) [1352, 1373]. This refers to the decisive obstacle to final success, a calamity or threat of calamity which momentarily seems to bring the growth of the seed to nothing and to cause the fruit to be given up as unattainable. There was more controversy on this conjunction than on any other. The main problems concerned the relation to the stages, especially as the fourth stage was the 'certainty of attainment', which would imply that the obstacle had already been overcome, and the proper conclusion would seem to be that those, for example Udbhaṭa, who maintained that there should be no fixed relation were right (Abhinavagupta III p. 28). The playwright could arrange things to suit his own presentation of the story.

134. The last conjunction is the 'conclusion' *nirvahaṇa*, which is the accomplishment (reading *samānayanam*) of the matter, of the main story, with the seed and joined with the fruit (for the last term Abhinavagupta reads with excess of various emotions—III p. 29) [1202-5, 1369, 1408, 1594].

135. As regards subsidiary actions, it is noted (*Nāṭyaśāstra* XXI.30) that that of the sub-plot *patākā* may extend as far as either the 'embryo' or the 'obstacle' in the main action, but must then stop (it may not continue into the conclusion).

136. In plays of lesser scale, the obstacle, embryo and re-opening (in that order) should be omitted. Thus a one act comedy will have only the opening and conclusion, a one act heroic play will have these plus the re-opening, a three act cooperation (a kind of mythical play: these types will be discussed in Chapter V) will have these three plus the embryo (XXI.45-7).

137. As a further point of construction in relation to the emotions, the *Nāṭyaśāstra* notes (XX.46) that those which are 'exalted' *udātta* should be reserved for the latter part of a play, whilst the 'marvellous' aesthetic experience should always be created at the conclusion (XX.47). [1752, 2421]

138. It should be clear from what the *Nāṭyaśāstra* says that the conjunctions do not necessarily match the stages of the action. These latter apply to any action and presumably to any kind of play, including those in which there are only two conjunctions. The stages are regarded as inevitable, even in real life. The conjunctions are not inevitable, but some or all of them should be used by the playwright in his art, depending on the scale, especially the length, of his presentation. The conjunctions are all related to the seed of the objective and its development, in other words to the plot as devised by the playwright out of his original story material. They are largely concerned with impediments to this development, with the dramatic conflict. The stages on the other hand are distinguished in a straightforward manner in relation to the 'fruit' and the means to attain it. We may conclude that a straightforward narration (without a 'plot') is to be transformed into a work of art by the introduction of the conjunctions. 'The story is to be divided by the five conjunctions..' (XXI.1).

139. The art of the playwright in dramatic construction is not limited to these few conjunctions. We may leave the opening proceedings or prologue until we discuss the details of the dramatic forms in Chapter V [310]. There are five rhetorical devices for leading into the play proper from the prologue. Thus the words of the producer, who invariably appears in the prologue to announce the play, may be overheard and misunderstood by a character, who, provoked, at once enters and acts accordingly, beginning the play *udghātyaka* [1583]. Or there is leading in by parallelism *avalagita* of action between the producer and a character, as when guards arrive to make way for a royal personage and he is forced to retreat (exit), and likewise a character appears (but enters) also forced to move aside [965, 1355]. Or a character takes up the producer's words in their actual meaning, but of course applied to himself *kathodghāta* [1629]. Or the producer simply introduces a character announcing his approach *prayogātiśaya* [1103]. Or, finally, the producer mentions some action appropriate to the occasion of the performance, and a character enters engaged in just that *pravṛttaka* [cf. 1581] (XXII.30ff., and XX.121f.).

140. The first two of these can be used elsewhere in a play, and are consequently given with the thirteen rhetorical devices proper to the street play (hence called *vīthyaṅgas*, 'limbs of the street play'—see Chapter V [325] below), but recommended by the *Nāṭyaśāstra* for use in comedies too, and regarded by later critics as suitable for use on occasion in any kind of play. Most of these devices depend on equivocation.

141. For general use anywhere in a drama the *Nāṭyaśāstra* lists twenty-one 'other conjunctions' *sandhyantaras* : conciliation *sāman* [946], split *bheda* [1628], gift *pradāna* [955, 1195], coercion *daṇḍa* [1628], slaying *vadha* [1027], presence of mind *pratyutpannamati* [1384], blunder in names *gotraskhalita* [1406, 1580], boldness *sāhasa* [1612], fear *bhaya* [1404], understanding *dhī* [1628], illusion *māyā* [1614], anger *krodha* [1608], strength *ojas* [1610], concealment *saṃvaraṇa* [1076], error *bhrānti* [1192], ascertaining the cause *hetvavadhāraṇa* [1628], messenger *dūta* (envoy) [946, 1360], letter *lekha* [1405], dream *svapna* [1163], painting *citra* [1280], intoxication *mada* (with pride [1356] or liquor [1383]) (XXI.48ff.; Baroda XIX.107ff.).

142. The theory of the ten stages of love, borrowed from the science of pleasure, should be applied where appropriate (XXIV.159 ff.) [803, 806, 1586].

143. There are four varieties of injection of subsidiary matter *patākāsthānaka* into the main action, not bringing in other (episodic) characters but consisting either of an unexpected new situation between the main characters or of an exchange of equivocal words which foreshadows future events and so stimulates a character to new action [1590, 1610, 1628] (XXI.31ff.).

144. We may here pass over the endless resources for the Indian playwright provided by the arts of poetics (elevated or figurative language, style, etc.) and music, including song and dance, which the *Nāṭyaśāstra* offers him with profusion of detail [183, 306].

145. But the *Nāṭyaśāstra*, having set out the five conjunctions, prescribes for each of these a dozen or more 'limbs' *aṅgas* to make them complete. For our present purpose we need not enter into all the limbs in detail, but the *Nāṭyaśāstra* and the later writers attach great importance to them (though disagreeing about the details), so that it is necessary for us to seek clarification of a somewhat embroiled topic. The *Nāṭyaśāstra* is most laconic here and assumes knowledge of the terms by the reader, giving merely sufficient hints to remind the producer or playwright of the devices of the art. Let us first simply list the 'limbs' in translation, getting as close to their probable technical meanings as these hints and the traditions recorded by the commentators and other writers may allow.

146. In the opening there may be : hint *upakṣepa* [1586], extension *parikara* [1421], fixing *parinyāsa*, beguiling *vilobhana* [1404], judgment *yukti* (this and the next four should be found in the Dream Vāsavadattā [967-8, 987]), attainment *prāpti*, concentrating *samādhāna*, performing *vidhāna*, surprise *paribhāvanā* [1404], germination *udbheda*, action *karaṇa* and split *bheda*. A

147. In the re-opening there may be: play *vilāsa* [1589], tracing *parisarpa* [1589], spurning *vidhūta*, remorse *tāpana*, joke *narman*, laughing off *narmadyuti*, explanation *praśamana*, check *nirodha* [1589, 1611], apology *paryupāsana* [1589], thunderbolt (outspoken statement) *vajra* [1356, 1363], flowery speech *puṣpa* [1589], proposal *upanyāsa* [1590] and assembly *varṇasaṃkara* [1788]. A

148. In the embryo there may be : deception *abhūtāharaṇa*, declaration of truth *mārga* [1591, 1629], appearance *rūpa* [1357], extolling *udāharaṇa*, progress *krama* [1612], favour *saṅgraha*, inference *anumāna* [972, 1591], wish *prārthanā* [1613], exposure *ākṣipti*, outburst *toṭaka*, outwitting *adhibala*, alarm *udvega* [1206] and panic *vidrava* [1360]. A

149. In the obstacle there may be : reproach *apavāda* [1369, 1592], altercation *sampheṭa* [1419], desperation *drava* [1360], ability *śakti* [1352, 1419], perseverance *vyavasāya*, ancestral pride *prasaṅga* [1199], derision *dyuti* [1360], fatigue *kheda* [1358, 1593], prevention *niṣedhana*, contradiction *virodhana* [1352], resumption *ādāna* [1419], forbearance *chādana* [1373] and anticipation *prarocanā* [1593]. A

150. In the conclusion there may be : conjunction (reconnection with the 'seed') *sandhi* [1369], investigating *virodha* [1364], knotting (getting the problem 'tied up') *grathana* [1594], decision *nirṇaya* [1369], censure *paribhāṣaṇa* [1369], derision *dyuti* [1629], grace *prasāda* [1369], delight *ānanda* [1369], agreement *samaya* [1202], marvelling *upagūhana* [1369], conversation *bhāṣaṇa* [1203], reminding *pūrvavākya* [1629], consummation of the *kāvya kāvyasaṃhāra* [1353] and panegyric (the final benediction) *praśasti* [943, 1353], of which the last should perhaps not be reckoned an actual limb of one of the conjunctions. A

151. The *Nāṭyaśāstra* states that there are sixty four limbs but enumerates and defines sixty five. The later writers agree that there are sixty four and some of them have omitted one (besides revising the list in other ways) to obtain the stated number, but there is no general agreement as to which one ('wish' : Dhanañjaya, Vidyānātha, Śiṅgabhūpāla; cf. Rāmacandra and Viśvanātha—in the embryo). It seems that as just suggested we should regard the last, which is not really part of the play (an actor addresses the audience as actor, not as character), as outside the scheme of conjunctions. There are minor discrepancies of reading in the text of the *Nāṭyaśāstra* which we here disregard.

152. The *Nāṭyaśāstra* strongly recommends (XXI.52ff) the use of these limbs, saying that a *kāvya* cannot be acted if it is deficient in them. Some later writers (e.g. Udbhaṭa, Sāgaranandin) seem to think that this means that every single one should occur in a full scale play, whilst others (e.g. Dhanika) hold that only five or six in each conjunction are essential and the rest optional, though desirable if it is possible to include them. Abhinavagupta describes them as 'possible', not as 'necessary' (III pp. 36-7). There have been attempts to find all of them in various classical plays. Recently it has even been proposed to divide plays exhaustively into these sixty four as parts. A mechanical construction with all limbs seems contrary to the practical spirit of the *Nāṭyaśāstra*, whilst the attempts to find every limb in certain classical plays have led to artificial interpretations widening the meaning of the limbs until some of them seem to have hardly any definite significance. As to the idea that the limbs are sections of text, apart from the above difficulties it seems to conflict with the use of the other devices such as the 'limbs of the street play', the 'other conjunctions', the 'injections of subsidiary matter', etc. The *Nāṭyaśāstra* (Baroda ed. XIX.105) recommends the use of these limbs mixed in twos and threes and depending on the emotions and aesthetic experiences. Abhinavagupta explaining this (III p. 62) says that they need not be confined to a fixed order or to their proper conjunctions but can be used in others also: thus 'judgment' can be used in the embryo as well as in the opening. We may conclude that the limbs are dramatic devices particularly appropriate for developing the conjunctions to which they are assigned, their actual arrangement to be determined by this development in relation to the plot and its emotions, with an eye also to the artistic effect of concentration (twos and threes) and climax rather than to mechanical routine.

153. The *Nāṭyaśāstra* mentions six purposes served by the limbs (XXI.53-4). Arrangement of the selected matter. Provision of incidents. Making the play attractive *rāgaprāpti*. Keeping hidden what should be hidden. Displaying what should be displayed. A wonderful presentation. Abhinavagupta suggests (III p. 37) that the limbs are needed to prevent the matter from being too short, a point developed further in the *Nāṭyadarpaṇa* (p. 53)—even the story of Rāma would not be interesting if reduced to the bare five conjunctions.

154. On the arrangement by acts and the total length of a play the *Nāṭyaśāstra* gives only a little help. The statement (XX.46) that the composition is to be made *gopucchāgra* has been interpreted in various ways, of which the most convincing is that in general the acts should be successively shorter: in effect the action is gradually speeded up towards the end of the play. The extant plays on the whole agree with this interpretation, but with a good deal of irregularity. The total length of a performance is specified in connection with only one type of play, the 'cooperation', one of the rarest types in the extant repertory and one of the most archaic. It has three acts, of which the first should last twelve *nāḍikās*, the second four and the third two, where the time of a *nāḍikā* is stated to be half a *muhūrta*. A *muhūrta* is 48 minutes, one thirtieth of a day, and a *nāḍikā* therefore 24 minutes (the giving of a definition in terms of another measure in the text might indicate that it was already obsolete when the present recension was redacted)(XX.70-2). From this we can calculate that the first act should last 4 hours and 48 minutes, the second an hour and 36 minutes and the third 48 minutes, a total of 7 hours and 12 minutes, not allowing for intervals between the acts. We have no such precise statement for any other type of play except much later for the *durmallikā* (see Chapter V [349])—10 hours for four acts. A

155. In fact the acts of the extant plays of other types seem almost indefinitely variable in length, and the total duration of plays very variable. We have very few examples of cooperations, the earliest being Vatsarāja's *Samudramathana* (end of the +12). In case Vatsarāja approximately followed the specifications of the *Nāṭyaśāstra*, which is quite likely though not certain, we may note that as published (Baroda, 1918) it occupies 42 pp. of text, of which 28 pp. constitute Act I, 8 pp. Act II and 6 pp. Act III. Almost two pp. of Act I in fact belong to the Prologue and probably should not be counted in it. The general proportions are thus roughly followed and perhaps the actual time of performance also roughly followed the specification, at the rate of about two and a quarter of our pages per *nāḍikā* on the average, or roughly ten minutes per page. Given that the verses with which the dialogue is interspersed were often sung (there are 70 of them in Act I, of which four are in the Prologue, 16 in Act II and 14 in Act III), and that time might be required for other musical effects (entry and exit of a character, etc.), this seems likely enough.

156. In order now to estimate the duration of the full length plays with up to ten acts, particularly *nāṭakas*, we can bring to bear various considerations. A five act *nāṭaka*, the *Hammīramadamardana* of Jayasiṃha (*c.* +1225), printed in similar type to the *Samudramathana* (Baroda, 1920) occupies 57 pp., of which 3 belong to the Prologue. On the other hand Someśvara's *Ullāgharāghava* (*c.* +1240), a *nāṭaka* in eight acts, is almost three times as long as Jayasiṃha's play (Baroda, 1961, but different type). Most *nāṭakas* extant fall between these two in length, though a few fall outside their limits. On the whole there is a tendency for more recent plays to be longer.

157. A second consideration is the dramatic construction by conjunctions and their limbs, which might be more relevant to the acting time than the number of acts. A cooperation should have four conjunctions (with 51 limbs) as against the *nāṭaka's* five (with 64); it is thus quite a substantial type of play, not much inferior to the *nāṭaka* despite the fewness of its acts.

158. A third consideration is the recent practice of the Indian theatre, as it has survived in Kerala. Here we find (see K. Kunjunni Raja, 'Kūṭiyāṭṭam...', pp. 17ff.) that the performance of a play takes many nights and that even a single act cannot be presented in less than three nights, plus several nights' preliminaries, including presentation of the earlier histories of the characters and other explanatory matter. [1096]

159. This last, however, represents the outcome of several reforms of the stage in Kerala, including the intercalation of Malayālam translations of the original Sanskrit and Prakrit texts, many comic interludes by the jester and the elaborate enactment of the words of the text in gesture language: thus it can take up to two hours to present a single verse to the audience. In short, it appears to represent an extreme development which can tell us little about the ancient theatre, although it is applied to some of the earliest Indian plays now extant.

160. The *Nāṭyaśāstra* (Kāśī XX.24 and 28, Baroda XVIII.21 and 25) says both that an act is to be performed in a day and that its content ought not to exceed the events of one day. Abhinavagupta (II p. 419) explains that an act should not last more than 12 hours (actually 15 *muhūrtas*, half a day), so as not to interfere with meals, etc. Thus festival holidays seem to be in question, not just an evening's entertainment. For the latter a short one act play would suffice.

161. It follows that a play in several acts lasts a week or more if performed continuously. We would have presumably a play in several acts in as many successive days, since it would normally be undesirable to separate the acts of a performance by a longer interval. Such a performance would have to take place on the occasion of a festival lasting a week or so. A seven act play (a rather common length for a *nāṭaka*) would thus take exactly a week. In the Commentary to the Pali *Jātaka* (V 279), referring to practices of unknown date (which might be as early as the—2), performances of 'seven-day' plays *nāṭakas* are mentioned, supposedly in the time of King Ikṣvāku and for a ritual purpose (such a play is called 'small' *culla*, and there were middling and superior ones possibly longer). This seems conclusive. The practice would then develop of performing single favourite acts on other occasions, prefaced by the presentation of a brief synopsis of the preceding part of the play (a kind of extended introductory scene) and foreshadowing later trends in Kerala. It appears that the chapters of a biography or a *campū*, likewise the cantos of an epic, were also units to be recited or 'performed' on one day, in other words equivalent to 'acts' in a play [435, cf. 423, 436]. The recent practice of spreading an act over several days would seem to destroy its unity for the audience, but might be encouraged by those who took the plot for granted and concentrated on details, especially the virtuosity of the actors in surface appearances such as mime, including miming another character.

162. The length of an act as stated by Abhinavagupta is further specified and confirmed by the *Nāṭyadarpaṇa* of Rāmacandra and Guṇacandra (+12). This treatise recommends (pp. 30f.) that an act should not be longer than twelve hours (4 *yāmas* or 'watches', =30 *ghaṭikās* or *nāḍikās*) nor shorter than 48 minutes (one *muhūrta*, =2 *ghaṭikās* or *nāḍikās*), otherwise it would either interfere with essential activities or seem incomplete, at the expense of the aesthetic experience. This implies that a full length play (5 to 10 acts) was definitely not expected to acted in a day and confirms our interpretation above that an act constituted what was performed during one day. The available evidence thus indicates that in origin the act was simply a day's performance, which was a complete play in one act or part of a longer one.

163. The *Nāṭyaśāstra* has some additional recommendations concerning the proper time for performance (*adhyāya* XXVII). The use of water clocks for checking the time is mentioned (verse 29, Kāśī, 34 Baroda, see Abhinavagupta III p. 316). The times suitable for drama include the day and the night, but noon, midnight, sunrise, sunset and meal times should be avoided (XXVII.85ff./87ff.). The morning is suitable for the presentation of virtue *dharma*, the afternoon for goodness *sattva*, with much music, the evening for the sensitive aesthetic experience, with dancing as well as music, dawn (presumably between midnight and sunrise) for the compassionate (one variant reading adds the comic here). These times may be infringed on the command of the patron. This suggests that the successive acts of a *nāṭaka* or *prakaraṇa* would run at the same time of day, which seems natural in any case, depending on the aesthetic experience. Thus normally a performance continuing through several evenings, if the sensitive were the main aesthetic experience, for example, would seem more agreeable to these recommendations than one spanning more than one of the six-hour periods into which the day was divided.

164. The structural theory of the *Nāṭyaśāstra* has not been seriously modified by later writers. There has been much controversy over the interpretations of some details but little has been added to it. New types of drama were invented, as we shall see in Chapter V, for some of which new 'limbs' were devised. Many of these new types were more musical in character than the old types and were apparently of a more popular or ephemeral nature, using new kinds of dance and pantomime. It appears that some of these new types were described first by Kohala, an ancient critic who composed a supplement to the *Nāṭyaśāstra*, which seems to have been lost (his conjectural date would be in the +2 or earlier, and may be earlier than our present recension of the *Nāṭyaśāstra* itself, which some interpret as containing a reference to him and his work : XXXVI.65 Kāśī; the *Kāmasūtra* also refers to some of these new types, confirming that they existed before the +3). We shall review these types of drama in Chapter V. Some modern writers have conjectured that Kohala originated some of the interpretations of dramatic structure known to later writers, but there seems to be hardly any evidence to attribute particular ideas to him. An example is on the subplot *patākā* as optional, cited by Śāradātanaya (p. 210).

165. On the other hand a special theory of the structures of five different classes of play *nāṭaka* is attributed to the ancient dramatist Subandhu (apparently −3) [653], with comments by an unknown Drauhiṇi, by Śāradātanaya (pp. 238ff.).

Abhinavagupta also seems to be aware of Subandhu's special techniques (III p. 172). One class, called 'full' *pūrṇa,* has the regular five conjunctions discussed above [e.g. 1361]. The 'complete' *samagra* class also apparently has these [347, 653]. The other classes, called 'calmed' *praśānta* [984], 'brilliant' *bhāsvara* (e.g. the *Rāmābhyudaya* of Yaśovarman) and 'playful' *lalita* [1403], likewise have five conjunctions, but they are differently named and defined, indicating different types of plot. At the same time they draw on the regular *Nāṭyaśāstra* series of 64 'limbs', but different selections from these are required for the different classes of play. The five classes are also distinguished according to the four 'modes' *vṛttis* of stage business, which will be discussed briefly at the end of this chapter [181]. Thus the 'full' play is 'violent', as we find from its example [1354]. The 'calmed' is stated to be 'expressive' (by Drauhiṇi). The 'brilliant' is said to be 'eloquent'. The 'playful' is 'tender'. The 'complete' play has all four modes. This may be a very ancient system of dramaturgy, earlier than the present *Nāṭyaśāstra,* although Śāradātanaya gives some relatively late examples of these classes of play. Some further discussion on them will be found below when we come to discuss the examples. [2424, 3711]

166. The first of the later writers concerning whom we have firm evidence on theories of structure is Mātṛgupta (probably +400). His work, either a commentary on the *Nāṭyaśāstra* or a compendium of its doctrine, seems to have been lost, but substantial quotations are available, especially in Sāgaranandin. He expounded a coordination theory of the conjunctions, stages and elements of the matter (we have argued above that the *Nāṭyaśāstra* seems on the contrary to allow them to be independent). In this he does not go as far as some later writers, but according to Sāgaranandin (460ff., cf. also 103ff.) prescribes a 'triad' *traya* in each conjunction as follows. In the opening, a 'wish' or impatience for an object, with the commencement (stage) or thinking of the cause (probably the means), and the seed or connection with what is to be accomplished *sādhya.* In the re-opening, a gain or acquisition of means *sādhana,* with the continuity or relation to the means, and engaging in or extension of the action (this last may be the undertaking stage). In the embryo, enjoyment *saṃbhoga* and capability, germination *udbheda* and seeing success *siddhi*, the sub-plot *patākā* consisting of the success of a friend. In the obstacle (but this text reads 'pause'), destruction or loss of the means, something better but with an obstacle, again the acquisition of the seed. In the conclusion, acquisition of the desired object, success in accomplishing what was to be accomplished, concluding of what was commenced.

167. This incidentally introduces a group of five new terms in the analysis of the action, namely the 'accomplisher' (*sādhaka*, hero who succeeds in his object), the 'means' *sādhana*, that which is to be accomplished', 'success' *siddhi* and 'enjoyment'. In Mātṛgupta's 'triads' we find the elements seed and continuity particularly connected with the opening and re-opening (though the seed is mentioned again later) and the sub-plot with the embryo. There is no mention here of the intervention or the objective. It is not clear that all the stages are meant to correlate with the conjunctions, only the commencement being actually mentioned. The other stages could be read into the remaining triads (e.g. certainty of attainment of the fruit into 'again the acquisition of the seed' in the obstacle), but there seems to be no evidence that Mātṛgupta intended this [1309, 1317-21].

168. Abhinavagupta, as noted above, discussed the difficulties of the coordination theory (III. 26ff.), which had been proposed by predecessors whom he does not name, whilst Dhanañjaya, his contemporary, definitely accepts it (I.22f.). It is worth noting that Abhinavagupta also discussed the subject in his *Locana* on Ānandavardhana's *Dhvanyāloka* (336ff.), objecting to a rigid coordination as contrary to the *Nāṭyaśāstra*. In a model play mentioned by Ānandavardhana, he says, 'the five conjunctions are shown accompanied by *sahita* the five stages, filled with 'suitable' *samucita* limbs of the conjunctions, possessing elements of the matter' (not the 'five' elements)—but this is one example and not a rigid rule.

169. Dhanañjaya simply defines the conjunctions as produced one by one by the five elements of the matter when 'endowed with' the five stages; he can be translated as saying that the elements severally 'become' *jan* the conjunctions when so endowed. Thus the seed endowed with the commencement becomes the opening, and so on. The sub-plot endowed with the possibility of attainment becomes the embryo; yet there may be no sub-plot and the seed is again mentioned in connection with the embryo (I.36). It is implied here, though not actually stated, that the intervention endowed with the certainty of attainment of the fruit becomes the obstacle. Perhaps Dhanañjaya had some doubts about this.

170. Abhinavagupta points out the difficulty of connecting the obstacle, or even 'pause' (implying doubt), with the certainty of attainment. How can the stage of certainty 'pervade' (i.e. be concomitant with) the conjunction of the pause ? In this conjunction it would seem that the two parties in the dramatic conflict should be of equal strength and the outcome uncertain.

171. Śāradātanaya (+12 ?) accepts the coordination theory but holds that at least the limbs of the conjunctions are largely variable in order (pp. 207, 214 on the order in the opening). He further says that in the absence of any subplot the continuity or the seed may enter into the embryo (p. 210). Śiṅgabhūpāla (+14) accepts the theory (III.26 ff.) but likewise keeps it fairly flexible: the sub-plot may be omitted in some plays, in which case the continuity will extend through (the embryo) instead. Otherwise the embryo should conform to the possibility (or 'hope') of attainment and the sub-plot (III.50). The obstacle with its limbs should be in agreement with the intervention and the certainty of attainment (III.58). Presumably amongst the limbs of this conjunction, probably at the end of it (Śiṅgabhūpāla puts the 'resumption' limb last, cf. Mātṛgupta's 'again the acquisition of the seed' here), the certainty of attainment can be fitted in (when the obstacle is overcome). Vidyānātha (+1300) accepts the coordination theory rigidly (pp. 74f., quoting Dhanañjaya). Rāmacandra and Guṇacandra reject it (pp. 37 and 48 ff.). Viśvanatha knows the theory of coordination of stages and conjunctions, but explains the latter as conjunctions in the matter of the story, not between the stages and the elements (VI.74f.).

172. It is not known which earlier writers propounded the various theories of variable arrangement of conjunctions and stages referred to by Abhinavagupta, though he names Udbhaṭa (late +8) immediately afterwards and quotes him on the meaning of 'obstacle'. It was argued that one could please oneself about this and have any of the middle three stages in the embryo, or two of them in it. A similar flexibility applied to the re-opening and the obstacle. Śaṅkuka also is quoted in the vicinity of this discussion, partly reported by Abhinavagupta (III.17), on the relative importance of the different elements in particular plays (Sāgaranandin also mentions this).

173. As for the numerous limbs, various later writers rearrange some of them and substitute new ones for some of those we find in the *Nāṭyaśāstra*. Those who held the theory of coordination of the conjunctions with the stages seem to have been most inclined to rearrange the limbs to make this easier and to substitute new ones, also to regard many as optional. For our present purpose the details of all this are not important.

174. A new device of more interest, apparently not known to the *Nāṭyaśāstra*, is the play within a play (*garbhāṅka* or *antarnāṭaka* [104]). Despite what Abhinavagupta says (III.172 ff.) on the *nāṭyāyita*, a form of acting mentioned in the *Nāṭyaśāstra*, this does not in fact seem to have referred to this device. Abhinavagupta's example, however, lost to us, purports to have been extremely ancient (−3). It also seems incorrect to identify the device with one of the kinds of introductory scene described in the *Nāṭyaśāstra*, interpreting that as a play within a play (Bhoja, *Śṛṅgāraprakāśa* vol. II p. 477, thus interprets the *aṅkāvatāra*, but the latter as we have seen was not an introduction of an act, or a miniature play, but a scene at the end of an act 'introducing' the next act of the play itself, by hinting at the events leading up to it). The play within a play was used by several classical dramatists, for example Bhavabhūti, but the earliest references now available to us in theoretical works are those of Abhinavagupta and Bhoja, just mentioned, and of Kuntaka (early +11; p. 235 of the 3rd ed. of the *Vakroktijīvita*). Kuntaka explains the 'embryo act' as making something an embryo inside another act, and classifies it as a variety of what he calls 'contextual figurativeness' *prakaraṇavakratā*, meaning non-straightforward expression at the level of an extended context in a *kāvya* [281] (the theories of figurative speech will be discussed in the next chapter). Bhoja somewhat similarly describes the *garbhāṅka*, 'embryo act', as a *prabandhālaṅkāra*, 'figure of speech of the composition (as a whole)'. Kuntaka, incidentally, reserves the term 'figurativeness of the composition (as a whole)' for changes involving the whole *kāvya* as contrasted with its source, as when in adapting a story from Tradition, or from the *Rāmāyaṇa*, the aesthetic experience *rasa* is changed (p. 238). Abhinavagupta's so-called *nāṭyāyita* is also a play within a play, or even a play within a play within a play (but involving the prologue, which after all is a play introducing another play) [654]. The usual function of the play within a play is to produce, intentionally or unintentionally, a powerful effect on a character watching it, by reflecting on his own behaviour or by incidentally revealing important facts to him. A

175. As in the case of the *rasa* theory, the theory of dramatic structure was applied to other forms of *kāvya*. We do not know how early this extension was made, but Bhāmaha already (late +5) states that an epic poem has the five conjunctions (I.20) [1517]. Bhoja (Vol. II p. 485) says that the five conjunctions should be made in any full length composition, namely, besides the *nāṭaka* and *prakaraṇa* types of drama and the epic, the novel, biography, *campū* and *ākhyānaka* ('history').

176. No scenery and few props are used in the classical Indian theatre. A curtain is held at the front of the stage (near the central lamp), covering the two doorways to the green-room, and is lowered as the actors enter (*Nāṭyaśāstra* XIII.3), heralded by their themes played by the musicians (seated between the two doorways at the back of the stage) [306, 1614]. The stage is divided into moveable zones (XIV. 1ff.) and there are conventions, well understood by the audience, of the significance of an actor moving on from one to another. Space as well as time is flexible on the stage and characters may be imagined to move considerable distances without leaving it, entering and leaving houses, passing through streets or across the countryside and so on. More than one group of characters can be on the stage at the same time, but be unseen and unheard by each other because they are in different zones understood to represent distance or intervening trees, walls, etc. The absence of scenery further allows the actors to travel indefinite distances [1000], for example driving in a chariot (itself imagined and the driving mimed), even a celestial chariot borne through the air. The scene, stationary or moving, is described as elaborately as is felt necessary by the characters in the course of their speeches, especially in lyric verses or songs. Props likewise are often presented only in imagination by description or by handling them in mime, for which a rich vocabulary of gestures is available. However, the *Nāṭyaśāstra* (XXIII) also describes the construction of models of such things as mountains, vehicles, weapons, ornaments, diadems and so on from various materials, including mechanical devices. Models other than portable equipment were probably never much used, being restricted to special effects. Only in the case of the street play [324] do we hear of any painted scene, which serves in a special kind of performance as a basis for a narration by one of the actors [1075]. On the other hand the theatre is directed to be brilliantly decorated with sculpture and paintings, not in connection with any particular play but to create a suitable atmosphere. A

177. A gradually shifting scene as the characters go about their business or pleasure is characteristic of the Indian drama. Costume and make up are elaborate. The use of a variety of dialects places the characters as 'educated' (speaking Sanskrit) or as belonging to various strata of the lower orders. Sanskrit, however, is considered unsuitable for women, except for learned Buddhist nuns. The standard Prakrit used by upper class women and most inferior characters of the 'better sort' is Śaurasenī.

178. Śaurasenī was the dialect of the city of Mathurā, which suggests that the main classical tradition of drama as we know it came into being in that city. Mathurā rose from being the capital of a small kingdom, breaking away from the Magadhan Empire in *c*. —130, to become the Eastern capital of the Kuṣāṇa Empire towards the end of the +1. It flourished as metropolis throughout the +2. There is inscriptional evidence (*Ep. Ind.* I 43) of a company of actors of the Śailālaka school founded by Śailālin (known to Pāṇini, IV.3.110, in the – 4) in Mathurā during the +1 and +2. They were wealthy enough to endow the Buddhist community in the city. Unhappily we have no plays from their repertory. In the middle of the +2 Rudradāman I, the Śaka governor of Ujjayinī now effectively independent of the Kuṣāṇas, himself vaunting his classical scholarship, adopted Sanskrit as the language of his administration and, we may presume, patronised the theatre in Ujjayinī. At first this was evidently a branch of the Śaurasenī theatre of the imperial Kuṣāṇa capital, but soon it became the leading theatre in India. It was at a somewhat later stage—apparently during the +3—that the Māhārāṣṭrī dialect of the Deccan, already famous for its lyrics, was introduced in dramas as the dialect for verses uttered by characters who normally spoke Śaurasenī. We may conjecture that the *Nāṭyaśāstra* as we have it represents the final outcome of the Mathurā school, whilst the earliest plays we have stem from this Mathurā-Ujjayinī theatrical tradition.

179. A theory of types of hero and heroine was worked out [99, 1469]. The minor characters include stock types already mentioned in other connections, especially the 'fool' or companion (*vidūṣaka* —often a court jester) and the *viṭa* ('parasite').

180. In looking for the underlying principles of the drama the early theorists attempted to define drama as a representation of various situations in which characters find themselves [35, 42, 54]. The way in which it does this is through 'acting' *abhinaya*, and it is this visible representation which differentiates drama from other kinds of *kāvya* which are merely 'audible' (this is understood always to include silent reading). There was some disagreement later over dancing and ballet, in some types of which it was hard to draw the line between a performance involving enough actual acting (representation) to be classed as drama and one which was on the whole pure or abstract dancing (non-representational), 'rhythm and tempo' *tālalaya*. We shall touch on these discussions in Chapter V, when we take up the various types of play for study. See *Śāradātanaya*. p. 180.

181. The acting used in drama is said to be of four kinds : speech, expression (direct facial expression), gesture and props. Four corresponding 'modes' *vṛtti* of stage business are used (*Nāṭyaśāstra* XXII Kāśi): the 'eloquent' *bhāratī*, 'expressive' *sāttvatī*, 'violent' *ārabhaṭī* and 'tender' *kaiśikī*. There is a myth that these were originated by Viṣṇu when engaged in a struggle with some demons: Brahmā was watching and made a note of them for use later in the drama (the 'tender' was when Viṣṇu brushed back his hair during a moment of respite in the fight). This myth was useful to connect Viṣṇu with the creation of drama, along with Brahmā and Śiva, but it is hardly consistent with the First Chapter of the *Nāṭyaśāstra*. Later on there was controversy about the 'modes' and new proposals were made, but the results do not appear to be of much significance (there was a trend to assimilate them to literary styles). The 'eloquent' mode is where speech predominates, not action. It is interesting to note that it is regarded as especially suitable for the compassionate *rasa* and tragic plays [950], though also for comedies and street plays [326, 1075, 1090, 1106, 1120-4]. The 'expressive' (the meaning of which is a little vague and seems to tend towards what is 'elevated') is said to be suitable for the heroic and the marvellous, but also for the furious [984, 1585, 1627]. The 'violent' is the most energetic kind of acting, depending on gestures, and is suitable for the horrific, the apprehensive and also the furious [1354-60]. The 'tender' depends more on costume and on other props, is elegant and beautiful and appropriate for the sensitive and the comic [1172, 1403]. It is especially characteristic of the two most fully developed types of play, the *nāṭaka* and *prakaraṇa* [1212] (*Nāṭyaśāstra* XX.9), and even lacking in the others. On the other hand we have noted above [165] a probably very ancient distinction of five classes of *nāṭaka* according to the use of the four separate modes or all of them in combination. Each mode has four 'limbs' or 'parts' *bhedas*, which appear somewhat restricted as usually described. They are mostly illustrated in Vol. IV below [2276, 1779, 1836, 1826; 2287, 2365, 2285, 2199; 1850, 2103, 2233, 2234; 1761, 2204, 2238]. On the manner of performance see Vol. V [2793-9, 3420-40, 3544, 3604, 3742, 3867, 3869, 3872, etc.]. On the tender mode see [6639].

CHAPTER IV

INDIAN POETICS

182. We noted at the beginning of Chapter II that there has been a tendency in India to separate the study of figurative language, stylistics and the nature of poetic beauty from that of the techniques and theory of dramaturgy. The two studies overlap, however, and the separation represents a tendency on the part of critics and theorists to specialise in different aspects of the aesthetic and critical field relating to literature. The *Nāṭyaśāstra* regards dramaturgy as a comprehensive study, of which what we here call 'poetics' is simply one apparently rather minor part. Its chapters on the language of the drama (i.e. on speech as one of the media of dramatic representation) consider the characteristics *lakṣaṇas* of that language, the figures of speech *alaṅkāras* and the qualities *guṇas* of style as well as metres, dialects, intonation and the types and construction of plays. On the other hand even matters which might seem to have been specific to the drama, and may very likely have been so in origin, such as the *rasa* theory and the theory of the conjunctions *sandhis* in the presentation of a story, were widely recognised, at least in later times, as being in principle applicable to any form of literature. Some of the later writers, treating literature from a comprehensive point of view, incorporate the dramatic forms in their overall scheme alongside the forms which are merely 'audible' (epic, novel, etc.) and not also 'visible'. However, they omitted music (with dancing) and gesture as outside the scope of the literary art, if related to it.

183. The *Nāṭyaśāstra* happens to be the earliest available work which deals systematically with the 'composition of *kāvyas*' (*kāvyakriyā*—the term is used at XXII.23, Kāśī, and probably at XXII.8; *kriyākalpa,* procedure for composition', seems to have been synonymous, implying *kāvyakriyākalpa*, it is used in the *Kāmasūtra* in its list of sixty four arts and is noted by Ratnaśrījñāna, p. 6, as equivalent to *kāvyālaṅkāra*, the usual term later for poetics, which literally means 'figures of speech in *kāvya*'). Otherwise we have only a few incidental notes, especially those of Yāska (*Nighaṇṭu* III.13 and *Nirukta* III.13-18) on the simile *upamā*, of Kauṭalya in his *Arthaśāstra* (*c.* --300) on qualities and faults of style (but from the point of view of composing administrative edicts—II.10 on *śāsana*) and of the Pali literature on kinds of poet and composition (e.g. *Aṅguttara Nikāya* II 230). Yāska gives several kinds of simile, one of which (the *luptopamā*) is equivalent to the metaphor (later known as *rūpaka* and regarded as a separate figure). The simile or comparison has always been looked upon as the primary figure of speech. Many others are classifiable as derivatives of it in the sense that they involve a comparison of some kind. Clearly it is a natural and primaeval figure, much more ancient than *kāvya* and also very popular in *kāvya*, particularly in the earlier period of *kāvya* composition. A rather different means of securing decorative (*citra*, a term familiar in this sense already in Pali) composition is alliteration, also ancient and popular, and classed as a figure of speech from the *Nāṭyaśāstra* onwards.

184. In the period after the *Nāṭyaśāstra* the figures (*alaṅkāras*, 'ornaments') came to be regarded as the essence of *kāvya* composition, hence the later name *kāvyālaṅkāra* or *alaṅkāraśāstra* applied to the whole subject of poetics or composition of literature. In the *Nāṭyaśāstra*, however, we find instead an attempt to describe the specific language of *kāvya* in terms of what are called its 'characteristics' *lakṣaṇas*. These characteristics embrace the figures, but include also features of rhetoric sometimes resembling the 'limbs' of the conjunctions of dramatic construction. In fact two terms occur both as limbs and as characteristics (and a third in a variant version of the characteristics), though their technical meaning appears to be somewhat different as explained in the two different contexts. The characteristics are essentially dramatic.

185. Many of the 'characteristics' involve ambiguity of speech. No general definition of what is meant by a 'characteristic' here is offered; in fact we have, as usual in the *Nāṭyaśāstra*, an empirical collection of features intended together to define *kāvya* composition. The problem of interpreting them is further complicated by a wide discrepancy between the lists and definitions in the two versions of the text of the *Nāṭya-*

śāstra. Both have thirty-six items, but fewer than half seem to be identical. The two lists seem equally ancient among the manuscripts available to us and it is a difficult task, which has not yet been seriously attempted, to distinguish what the original form of the set of characteristics may have been. With the further development of the theory of figures of speech after the *Nāṭyaśāstra*, that of the characteristics perhaps became obsolete and few later writers attempted to develop it. Sāgaranandin (1464-1852), however, elaborates them into a set of 36 characteristics plus a set of 33 'ornaments of a play'. Studying the 'characteristics' in the context of dramaturgy, one comes to see them as in principle characteristics of dramatic expression, incidents in the dialogue which, like the 'limbs' of the conjunctions, help to give body to a play's action and to create interest in the characters.

186. Among the characteristics common to the two recensions, the first is 'ornamentation' *bhūṣaṇa* and is said to mean the use of the figures of speech *alaṅkāras* and the qualities *guṇas*, which are treated in detail afterwards in the same chapter (XVII Kāśī, XVI Baroda) of the *Nāṭyaśāstra* [1327]. The next two are both varieties of ambiguity, one, *akṣarasaṃghāta* [1607], apparently ambiguity in general and the other, *śobhā*, literally 'splendour', the special case where what has not been accomplished (yet) is combined with something which has been accomplished. 'Extolling' or 'illustrating' (*udāharaṇa*, in a different sense from that of the 'limb') is said to show much with little to those able to understand its significance. The 'example' *dṛṣṭānta* is similar to this, but perhaps distinguished as having logical form [1124]. 'Attainment' *prāpti* is again a kind of inference, but specifically from part to whole. The 'cause' *hetu* is also a seemingly logical statement. Opposed to all these proofs we have 'doubt' *saṃśaya* [1407]. The others are : etymology *nirukta*, success *siddhi*, in some matter, exaggeration *atiśaya*, accumulation of words (*padoccaya*, e.g. elaborate description), conciliation *anunaya*, (rhetorical) question *pṛcchā* [600, 763, 1610], similarity (*sārūpya*: apparently distinguished from simile as a similarity discussed by the characters) [1364], wish *manoratha* [826, 1602], praise *guṇakīrtana* and affectionate speech *priyokti*. A

187. When the theory of figures of speech was elaborated later, practically all these were incorporated in it under the various figures, making the doctrine of characteristics obsolete and offering in its place a more penetrating analysis. Those characteristics not in common between the two lists include more that are apparently simple expressions of emotion or other dramatic situations, for example in one list (Kāśī) distinction *viśeṣaṇa*, illustration *nidarśana* [1113], description *diṣṭa* [1607], admonition *upadiṣṭa* [1007], amiability *dākṣiṇya*, denunciation *garhaṇa*, implication *arthāpatti* [1606], excuse *leśa*, agitation *kṣobha* [1592]; in the other encouragement *protsāhana* [1407], obstinacy *mithyādhyavasāya*, cry *ākranda*, narration *ākhyāna* [1606], importunity *yācñā*, prohibition *pratiṣedha* [1456, 1481], benediction *āśis* [767], deceit *kapaṭa* [1363], forbearance *kṣamā*, remorse *paścāttapana* [1364]. A

188. In contrast with its long list of characteristics, the *Nāṭyaśāstra* gives only four figures of speech *alaṅkāras*: simile, metaphor, 'lamp' *dīpaka* and alliteration or 'rhyme' *yamaka*. Five kinds of simile are named and examples of them given, but without definitions. They do not appear to be mutually exclusive. The comparison may reflect praise or blame, it may involve something which is sheer imagination (there may be no real resemblance), there may be likeness or only partial likeness. For metaphor the *Nāṭyaśāstra* prefers a rather restricted sense, in which the object being described is compared with a series of other objects, the qualities of which it appears to have combined in itself; the example given is similar to what is elsewhere known as a 'complete *samasta* metaphor' [754], but here the several parts of two objects are named and identified, in this case a group of women and a pool: their mouths are the red lotuses, their teeth the white lotuses, their pretty eyes the blue lotuses, their mutual cries are like those of the wild geese. Since a word for 'like' is used, this would be a simile according to the usual later rule. After about +200 this kind of enumerating simile and metaphor went out of fashion in the literature. The 'lamp' is when a number of nouns, or pairs of nouns, radiate outwards from a single verb in one sentence, all having the same grammatical relations to it : 'They fill the lakes with wild geese, the trees with flowers, the lotuses with intoxicated bees and the woods of the park with parties *goṣṭhīs*' [757]. 'Rhyme' is dealt with at greater length and appears to include under one broad head all effects which depend on the repetition of sounds, including alliteration [887].

189. There are ten 'qualities' *guṇas* in *kāvyas* according to the *Nāṭyaśāstra*, and this number and the names remained standard for most later writers despite developments of meaning. These are 'union' (*śleṣa*, closeness of the words producing the desired meanings [1234, 1473, 1571]), 'clarity' *prasāda* of words and meanings [1347], 'evenness' *samatā* [1347, 1474], 'concentration' (*samādhi*: a degree of ambiguity seems intended here, by overlapping of meanings as in metaphor) [1332, 1347], 'sweetness' (*mādhurya* [1414, 1480], but there seems to be no English equivalent for this word: the *Nāṭyaśāstra* defines it negatively as that quality through which a sentence does not become troublesome even when repeated many times), 'strength' *ojas* [928, 1347], 'delicacy' *saukumārya* or softness of the words combined with delicate meanings [1347], lucidity or (immediate) 'manifestation of an object *arthavyakti* [1523], 'exaltation' *udāratā* [1523] and 'grace' (*kānti*, or 'graciousness' or 'charm', which favours or delights the mind) [1347, 1527]. As so often in the *Nāṭyaśāstra* the 'definitions' are too brief to be adequate for us, and it is not much use trying to read into them the conflicting interpretations of later and more systematic writers. There are also wide divergencies of reading in the text itself, as in the case of the characteristics. Thus 'exaltation' is on the one hand explained as variety and beauty of meaning and on the other as related to emotional exaltation in connection with the sensitive and marvellous aesthetic experiences. There seems to be much overlapping between the qualities, as of strength with exaltation, lucidity with clarity. Most of them relate to both sound and meaning, or to the proper combination of these. They are, as a group, contrasted with a set of ten faults *doṣas* in *kāvya*, such as irrelevance, meaninglessness, redundancy, confusion, illogicality and ungrammatical construction.

190. Whilst the study of poetics is thus at least as old as that of dramaturgy, the only hint we seem to have of any tradition of a conscious origin of literary criticism independent of either drama or linguistics (Yāska), except for our scraps of information about the development of the idea of *kāvya* in Magadha (in Pali sources and in other early *kāvya*, also Rājaśekhara's note on the tastes of the Emperor Śiśunāga of Magadha in the late – 5—*Kāvyamīmāṃsā* p. 50), is that given by Rājaśekhara (p. 10). In the form of a myth he says that *Kāvya* (personified as the son of the Goddess of Literature, Sarasvatī) married *Sāhityavidyā*, Theory of Composition, in effect Literary Criticism (also personified), in the delightful city of Vatsagulma in Vidarbha (Northern Mahārāṣṭra). If this is more than local patriotism on Rājaśekhara's part, it might mean that according to the ideas current in his day (+900) serious literary criticism first developed in Vatsagulma. This city flourished chiefly under the Vākāṭaka Empire (mid +3 to the beginning of the +6) and was an early centre of the widely praised *vaidarbha* style, which will be discussed below. It may at the same time have been the centre of the critics who first formulated the standards of *kāvya* for the early medieval period, but at present we have no evidence as to whether Bhāmaha, or his neglected predecessors such as Medhāvin, lived there.

191. Apart from the *Nāṭyaśāstra*, the earliest work on poetics now available is the Buddhist critic Bhāmaha's (late +5) *Kāvyālaṅkāra*. The title, 'Figures of Speech in *Kāvya*', implies restriction to the language of *kāvya*, or what we are here calling 'poetics'. Bhāmaha leaves aside everything connected with dramatic representation, and even the *rasa* theory (which he fully accepts and extends to all *kāvya* [405]), as dealt with by others, deals briefly with the forms of *kāvya* and concentrates on the study of figurative language, which according to him is the essential characteristic of *kāvya*. His work therefore belongs to the field of the 'procedure for composition (of *kāvyas*)', later known, apparently from his own title (but others might already have used this title, just as it is copied by some later writers), as 'figures of speech in *kāvya*'. If Bhāmaha was the first to propound the doctrine that it is figurative speech which is essential, then he may be regarded as the founder of the 'figures of speech' school of thought. He mentions several predecessors, however, such as Medhāvin, so that we cannot know how far his ideas were original or when the trend making the figures the central topic of poetics originated.

192. The general position of Bhāmaha is not unrelated to that of the *Nāṭyaśāstra*. The functions of *kāvya* (Bhāmaha

I.2) are to produce expertise in virtue, wealth, pleasure, liberation (this last in new, the 'fourth end', cf. the discussion on a 'calmed' aesthetic experience) and of the arts, to produce delight *prīti* and fame (*kīrti*—this last for the author). Of these it is clear that 'delight' is the essential, and the medium through which the others are produced. The author *kavi* must have genius *pratibhā* to produce a (real) *kāvya*—mere cleverness of speech will not do: one who is dull of intellect can learn a science (*śāstra*, any subject as a branch of learning) from a teacher, but one cannot learn to create *kāvya* in that way, it is produced only by genius (I.4-5). This again is new.

193. Bhāmaha then (I.8) announces that what must be studied (by those desiring fame as authors) is the 'characteristics' *lakṣaṇas* of *kāvya*. Clearly he uses the term characteristics here in a general sense for the essential features of *kāvya*, since in his work the figures have entirely superseded the 'characteristics' of the *Nāṭyaśāstra* (the *Nāṭyaśāstra* seems to consider its 'characteristics' of *kāvya*, including the figures of speech and 'qualities', essential, but of course not the only essential). Bhāmaha's figures are of speech and meaning.

194. Bhāmaha (I.13ff.) refers to two views of 'others' bearing on the essentials of *kāvya*. On the one hand, he says, there are those who make much of 'ornament' *alaṅkāra* in the sense of metaphor, etc. (the figures). By way of analogy they say a woman's face does not look beautiful without ornaments. On the other hand there are those who say that this kind of ornament (figures) is external, desiring rather 'ornamentation' *alaṅkṛti* in the form of the grammatical inflexions of the language itself, which they call 'good speech' (*sauśabdya*, i.e. correct, perhaps 'beautiful' speech). This, however, Bhāmaha objects, is to overlook the meaning (the figures are an essential part of the meaning, not something 'external'). There are in fact two kinds of 'ornament', namely speech and what is expressed, therefore the definition of *kāvya* (I. 16) is 'speech and meaning combined' *śabdārthau sahitau.* From the context we see that this does not mean any speech and meaning: both must be 'ornament' *alaṅkāra* to produce *kāvya*, in other words they must be beautiful. Beautiful speech with beautiful meaning, an essential part of the latter being that it is figurative [1523].

195. Beauty *cārutā* of speech cannot be secured simply

by the use of 'poetic' words (such as certain synonyms for 'very', e. g. *nitānta*): the ornamentation of speech must be that it is the expression, in speech, of something expressed, where both (speech and meaning) are *vakra*, 'figurative' (more literally but not necessarily more correctly 'crooked', 'indirect', 'winding') (I.36). Hence we have the term 'figurative expression' *vakrokti* as the defining characteristic of 'ornament' *alaṅkāra* in *kāvya*.

196. Bhāmaha uses figurativeness as a test for proposed ornaments, i.e. for approximately what we call 'figures of speech', really of the meaning, when he subsequently proceeds to collect, define and illustrate these. Thus hyperbole or 'exaggeration' *atiśayokti*, with a suitable (poetic) pretext *nimitta*, is very acceptable, since it is all figurative expression and by it the meaning is manifested (Abhinavagupta reads into this the manifestation or experience of *rasa*, the aesthetic experience, specifically) (II.84f.) [1502]. An author must be careful about figurative expression, for what figure of speech is there without it ? (II.85). 'Cause' *hetu* [823], 'hint' *sūkṣma* [822] and 'excuse' *leśa* are not figures of speech because there is no figurative expression in them, the same applies to mere 'news' *vārttā* (86f.). These were all accepted by some later writers whose standpoint was different; cause and excuse were among the 'characteristics' in the *Nāṭyaśāstra*. Similarly in discussing the merits of 'styles' based on the 'qualities' Bhāmaha holds that one of these is no more than merely pleasant to the ears, for all its qualities, if there is no figurative expression in it (I.34).

197. Bhāmaha mentions that some say 'naturalistic description' *svabhāvokti* is a figure, but appears to leave the question open (II.93f.). Later writers developed this controversy : if this alleged figure is taken to be the opposite of figurative expression *vakrokti* it will not be a figure on Bhāmaha's theory, but if this is not so and there is beauty in the situation described it can be a figure (there can be 'figurativeness' of the subject matter , even without the addition of a specific 'figure' in the expression) [632, 1478].

198. It would seem clear from Bhāmaha's Fifth Chapter, which is on (Buddhist) epistemology and logic (following Vasubandhu and Diṅnāga) as applied to *kāvya*, that figurativeness is not confined to the figures of speech. Here Bhāmaha is concerned with realism, but in poetic terms. He in fact has a figure 'realism' *bhāvikatva* in one of the chapters on the figures of speech, which, however, is **a** 'figure' or a quality *guṇa* of a whole work, where past or future objects are seen as if present before the eyes, where also the story is well presented (or 'acted' *abhinīta*) so that it is beautiful *citra*, exalted *udātta* and marvellous *adbhuta*, where finally the speech is not confused (*anākula*, consistent, orderly) (III. 53-4) [1347]. Now the Fifth Chapter may be seen as an extension of this last and pervasive figure, but what is in question is the subject, the story or content of a *kāvya*. It is *kāvya* and is mixed with the sweet aesthetic experience *rasa* of *kāvya* even when applying science *śāstra*, in fact in this way pungent medicine can be made drinkable (V.3, Bhāmaha here was perhaps thinking of the Buddhist poet Aśvaghoṣa, who consciously used this technique, mixing the philosophy of renunciation with the delights of *kāvya* [711]). Bhāmaha on the other hand proposes to compose *kāvya* in the guise of logical propositions and arguments based on experience. There must be verisimilitude, probability and agreement with both reason and the ways of the world. Udbhaṭa made inference a figure [254].

199. The initial proposition, corresponding to the statement of a thesis to be proved in logic, is in *kāvya* a promise or a declaration of purpose (*pratijñā* means both and is an appropriately ambiguous or 'figurative' word). The middle term, which proves it by the method of agreement and difference (linking the subject of the initial proposition with the predicate, by being found in the subject and in at least some examples of the predicate and by being absent from all examples of what is not the predicate, having thus three 'characteristics'), occurs also in *kāvya*, though the middle terms used there will be objects naturally beautiful, if equally liable to prove fallacious, in which case they must be rejected as no middle terms or reasons (*hetu*, the 'cause' which produces a valid argument) (V. 47-55). Finally the example *dṛṣṭānta* is in logic the empirical evidence adduced to establish the concomitance of the middle term with the predicate, that the middle term is found only in the predicate and nowhere apart from it (the 'major premise'); in *kāvya* also it must establish this concomitance, illustrating the matter being expressed. Mere analogy (*upamāna*, comparison) is not an example because it does not indicate any middle term: when a face is said to be like a lotus what is the predicate, what is the middle term ? (V. 55ff.). This might seem to make clear a difference between a figure of speech, such as a simile, which proves nothing and is confined to expressiveness, and figurativeness in the matter itself, when one proceeds by inference and argument. [cf254]

200. The omission of these logical members of discourse (proposition, reason and example) is listed among the faults in *kāvya* given by Bhāmaha, which otherwise are generally similar to those described in the *Nāṭyaśāstra*. Bhāmaha elaborates on the topic of faults in his fourth chapter, incidentally giving a definition of the sentence (it must have a complete meaning, its words being grammatically dependent on one another and requiring no further words).

201. He has another chapter, the sixth, however, for his discussion on grammar in relation to *kāvya*. There he reviews the theories on the nature of language, maintaining that it is purely conventional *samaya*. He criticises the Vedic tradition that words, i.e. the Vedic and Sanskrit speech, are eternal and a means of knowledge additional to the two means he accepts, sensation (experience) and inference (logical), as outlined in his fifth Chapter. He also criticises the view of another Buddhist philosopher (Diṅnāga), that words are related to objects not directly but only to the extent that they exclude other objects (*anyāpoha*, 'exclusion of what is other'). Bhāmaha says that if the word 'cattle' merely excludes non-cattle, then we shall have to find (presumably, agree on as a convention of society) another word for the cognition 'cattle', which will effectively refer to 'cattle'.

202. Having stated that words do in fact refer to four kinds of things, namely substances, actions, classes and qualities (noting that some—Diṅnāga again—add a fifth, 'chance' words, such as personal names), he goes on to discuss the use of 'figurative' *vakra* speech in the context of grammar (VI. 23ff.). Here one must have in mind ease of understanding, elegance (*agrāmya*, absence of vulgarity) and beauty *cārutā*. Bhāmaha recommends following Pāṇini and Patañjali as a general rule, but makes some selective suggestions about avoiding certain grammatical formations he feels unsuitable for *kāvya* and cultivating others, more poetic (thus he favours denominatives, verbs coined out of nouns). 'Figurativeness' of language at the grammatical level thus involves a deliberate selection of forms appropriate for literary purposes because they sound more beautiful than others, are clear, elevated and suggest ideas in a beautiful way (there is an element of surprise, freshness and figurativeness in using a noun stem on occasion where a verb is expected, for example; this is perfectly regular according to Pāṇini, with the proper suffix, but unusual in everyday speech).

203. Turning now to the figures of speech *alaṅkāras* in the more restricted sense, we find that Bhāmaha recognises about three dozen of these (in his second and third chapters). He propounds them not systematically but discursively, in the order, apparently, in which he found them in various earlier works. First (II.4ff.) he gives a very ancient group of five figures, similar to the four which alone are listed as figures in the *Nāṭyaśāstra* : alliteration *anuprāsa* [1543-4], rhyme *yamaka* [887], metaphor *rūpaka, dīpaka* ('lamp') [188, 757] and simile *upamā*. In the *Nāṭyaśāstra* alliteration is included in rhyme, being similar in principle (repetition of sounds). Bhāmaha gives various subdivisions of all these, but objects to too much technicality of construction, especially when it results in a commentary being needed to explain what an author is trying to do.

204. Metaphor is here described as actual identification of two objects, either complete *samasta* or partial *ekadeśa*, through their qualities. Simile is comparison expressed by various words meaning 'like'.

205. Some of Bhāmaha's sub-varieties are given as separate figures by some later writers (e.g. Udbhaṭa [254], who elaborated Bhāmaha's study of figures in the +8), which of course is a matter of the definitions chosen.

206. There follows (II.66ff.) a group of six figures given by 'others'. Among these is hyperbole or exaggeration, which we have already discussed [196] and which was originally a 'characteristic' [186].

207. The apparent prohibition, or insinuation *ākṣepa*, literally 'spurning', is when one seems to prohibit or suppress what one actually intended, but in such a way as to distinguish or emphasise it more; secondly it includes revoking what one has just said: 'It is wonderful that there is no pride in you, when you have conquered the world with your valour —but after all what cause would be adequate to effect a change in the Ocean ?' (the Ocean is the type of the steadfast hero, whose character is not affected by changing circumstances) [806, 1478].

208. Very characteristic of Indian literature is the 'corroboration' *arthāntaranyāsa*, literally 'adducing another matter', in which another proposition is adduced to corroborate what is said. Thus a particular case is adduced to illustrate a generalisation, or a generalisation is stated to enforce a particular remark. This figure gives scope for philosophical reflections [1537].

209. 'Contrast' *vyatireka* is a comparison designed to show the great superiority of the thing spoken of over that with which it is compared (there is a likeness—but...) [933].

210. The 'miracle' *vibhāvanā* is a causing of an effect although the proper cause is absent, by the extraordinary virtue of the thing which is being praised [892].

211. 'Condensed expression' *samāsokti* is the implication of an advantageous comparison by the use of epithets common to what is described and something else not actually named [cf. 1526].

212. A third group of two figures follows (II.88 ff.). The 'enumeration' *yathāsaṅkhya* is a list of dissimilar but excellent things, which are then found all to be related to the object described [888].

213. In some ways the most important figure of all, 'fancy' *utprekṣā* is the poet's imaginary activities of natural phenomena: fire (a forest fire), as if pretending to be (disguised as) red *kiṃśuka* flowers, climbs to the tops of the trees to see how much of the forest is burned and how much unburned. There is usually personification in this figure, but personification enters into other figures as well and pervades Indian nature poetry so thoroughly that it is rather one of the bases of figurative language than a particular figure [633, 1190, 1425, 1504, 1537, 1570-1].

214. The remaining figures accepted by Bhāmaha are given in one group (Chapter III) as from 'others'. The first

(III.5) is the 'affectionate' *preyas*, similar to the characteristic 'affectionate speech' and later magnified by some writers (e.g. Rudraṭa) into a *rasa* [549]. Bhāmaha's illustration is the expression of hoping to see a friend again. It is followed by two other figures also associated by later writers (Udbhaṭa, etc.) with *rasa*, one of which is a specific '*rasa*' figure in Bhāmaha himself.

215. This is the 'having *rasa*' *rasavant* (III.6) and its nature is that it shows the *rasas*, sensitive, etc., clearly [1426]. Bhāmaha's example of it presupposes Śiva watching as Devī (Umā or Pārvatī) approaches naked as ascetic *maskariṇi*, which would constitute an occasion for the sensitive *rasa*. We may presume that Bhāmaha intended to introduce the whole paraphernalia of the *rasa* theory of the *Nāṭyaśāstra* here, so that descriptions of the causes and effects of emotion, productive of *rasa*, would all constitute occurrences of this figure. There is no rule against the overlapping and mixing of various figures—on the contrary it is recommended—so that a *kāvya* might very well be regarded as containing many examples of the 'having *rasa*' figure scattered through it. Kuntaka (+11), though in general a follower of Bhāmaha, rejected 'having *rasa*' as a figure, holding that *rasa* is part of the subject matter of *kāvya* and could not therefore be a kind of figure of speech (in itself it could of course be figurative, but in the sense of a certain arrangement of the matter, not of its expression). But Bhāmaha's figures include the matter.

216. The other figure later associated with *rasa* is the 'exalted' or 'disdain' *ūrjasvin* (III.7), showing for example the pride and disdain of a noble hero such as Karṇa [1337].

217. There is another figure in this list so closely related to *ūrjasvin* that 'exalted' seems to be the nearest equivalent for it too, namely *udātta* (III.11ff.). We saw in our second chapter that Bhoja combined these in his 'exalted' *rasa*. In Bhāmaha, *ūrjasvin* has more to do with pride and might best be translated 'disdain', whereas *udātta* is rather magnanimity and forbearance, as in the character of Rāma [1642]. Already, however, Bhāmaha notes a variant interpretation of *udātta*, making it instead the opulence of wealth described through its rare luxuries. [99]

218. Some other figures introduce the idea later developed (by Ānandavardhana especially) of implied or indirectly revealed meanings, where what is intended is not the obvious surface meaning of the words but something hidden in them. Thus 'circumlocution' *paryāyokta* (III.8f.) is a paraphrase concealing a blunt statement: in Bhāmaha's example Kṛṣṇa says he does not eat food unless learned brahmans have first partaken of it; on the surface this suggests his piety and humility, eating only the leavings of priests who have been served first, but Bhāmaha points out that really it is a precaution against being poisoned. This figure is generally understood as a euphemism disguising the statement of disagreeable facts [1333].

219. 'Praise of what is not the subject' *aprastutapraśaṃsā* (III.29f.) is the apparent description of the excellences of something other than the intended subject of praise, which is not itself mentioned but which on reflection is realised to be the real subject because it is the cause of what is described (e.g. a happy state is described and seen to be due to freedom or naturalness) [1302, 1633].

220. 'Sham praise' *vyājastuti* (III.31f.) describes the wonderful achievements of great heroes, only to reflect on the absence of such accomplishments on the part of the person being spoken to, who is in fact being blamed [1606].

221. The 'simile-metaphor' *upamārūpaka* (III. 35f.) is a metaphor, asserting the identity of two things, but intended only as a comparison (simile): Viṣṇu's foot is the measuring rod of the revolution of the heavens. (it would not be very flattering to the Wielder of the Discus if this meant his foot was only a measuring rod).

222. The 'comparison as compared' *upameyopamā* (III. 37f.) is a simile applied both ways: your face is like a lotus and a lotus is like your face [cf. 931, which, however, is a hybrid between this and 'equal consequence'] [7818]

223. Comparison is also the basis of 'equal consequence' *tulyayogitā* (III.27f.), though on the other hand it resembles the 'lamp' *dīpaka* in respect of the parallelism involved: two or more objects, including that under description, are said to have identical qualities, effects, etc. [931, cf. 554].

224. 'Accompaniment' *sahokti* (III.39f.) is when a similar action of two things is stated with one word, thus: the nights *increase* (lengthen, in winter), along with the delights of lovers, fouling the regions with frost, causing close embraces [1533].

225. Failing anything else fit to be compared with the object of one's appreciation there is 'want of agreement' *ananvaya* (III. 45f.), as in: 'Your face is only like yours', —it can be compared only with itself [819, 886, cf. 554].

226. The pun *śliṣṭa* (III.14ff.), in which one word has two meanings, suggests their identification (cf. metaphor) though there is no actual resemblance in the objects meant (as there is in metaphor) [828, 1571].

227. 'Coincidence' *samāhita* (III.10) is illustrated by a description of a fortunate chance meeting [1407].

228. 'Revolution' *parivṛtti* (III. 41f.) is an advantageous exchange, gaining something excellent (e.g. reputation) by sacrificing something else (e.g. wealth) [821, 1470 : A8]. According to Bhāmaha it should be combined with a 'corroboration.'

229. 'Concealment' *apahnuti* (III. 21f.) or suppression, is when the reality is suppressed in favour of something imagined: this is not a noisy swarm of bees, humming continuously because of the honey, it is the sound of Love's (Pleasure's) bow being drawn. There is a partly hidden simile in this figure [1306].

230. 'Distinction' *viśeṣokti* (III.23f.) is a contrast or even paradox [1015], when, for example, despite the loss of one (important or seemingly necessary) quality another, which remains, proclaims the distinction of the subject. Thus : Love (Pleasure), alone, conquers the Three Worlds; though Śiva took away his body he has not taken away his strength (the reference is to the myth of the destruction of Love's body, making him incorporeal, invisible, purely mental) [892, 1234, cf. 1473]. The 'distinction' *viśeṣaṇa* which appears in one list of characteristics in the *Nāṭyaśāstra* was probably much broader than this.

231. 'Contradiction' *virodha* (III.25f.) also expresses the distinction of the subject, by expressing a quality or action of the subject, contradictory to another of its actions. Thus : your vanguard, though cool, makes the enemy hot (tormented). [888, 1260].

232. 'Illustration' *nidarśana* (III.33 f.), or 'evidence', indicates a special meaning through some action, a special significance of that action (there is a characteristic of this name in one list, which appears similar), thus: the Sun is about to set, his lustre diminished; this teaches fortunate men that rising is for the purpose of falling [1542].

233. 'Having doubt' *sasandeha* (III.43f.) is a form of praising through finding a difference between the object and something compared with it (the characteristic 'doubt' is similar, though the *Nāṭyaśāstra* does not say it is for praising). For example: 'Is this the Moon ? But that does not shine by day (as this person does). Is it Love (Pleasure) ? But this bow is not made of flowers (as Love s is). Reflecting thus, with astonishment, my thoughts, when you are seen, come to no conclusion as to the object (before me).' [1534].

234. Bhāmaha notes (III.49ff.) mixture *saṃsṛṣṭi* as a figure of special excellence, i.e. a combination of several figures. In other words he recommends using the figures in conjunction where possible, rather than keeping them separate. A particular combination which he mentions separately (III.47f.) is the 'partial fancy' *utprekṣāvayava*, mixing together some 'fancy', 'pun' and 'metaphor' [762, 1428].

235. Finally after this group, and after 'realism' which we have already discussed, Bhāmaha adds (III.55ff.) that some consider 'benediction' *āśis* a figure, without stating a decision either way. It is found in one of the lists of characteristics.

236. This set of three dozen figures became the basis of subsequent discussions by a series of critics. It is evident that they originated through the empirical investigation of the productions of poets and Bhāmaha presents them as a collection as it were of data of this kind. He does indeed propose 'figurativeness' as a criterion defining them and he excludes a few, as lacking this, from the lists he found in his sources. Nevertheless he does not present any theoretical analysis of figurativeness, nor does he classify and rearrange the figures according to the types of figurativeness and the relationships between them. Perhaps a predecessor had discussed figurativeness in detail and defined it. Later writers attempted more systematic and theoretical work on the figures, redefining some of them, adding to or subtracting from their number, classifying them according to their underlying principles. Above all, Kuntaka [269] wrote a monograph on 'figurativeness' *vakrokti*, examining its nature and its manifestations at all levels of composition, following Bhāmaha's general conception but working out its consequences thoroughly and freely revising such details as the status of individual figures.

237. Bhāmaha attaches little importance to the qualities *guṇas* or to the styles arising from their cultivation. He notes (II.1ff.) only three of the ten qualities given in the *Nāṭyaśāstra*. 'Sweetness' *mādhurya*, meaning that the matter is not too detailed, and 'clarity' *prasāda*, meaning that the matter is not too deunderstood (by those who are not scholars, and by women and children), are desirable, he says, and some recommend 'strength' *ojas*, meaning much compounding of words [1456, 1480]. Later writers are divided, the majority following Bhāmaha with only three qualities and stressing other elements in *kāvya*, an important minority developing the theory of the ten qualities as the most essential ornaments of literary expression. Elsewhere, as when dismissing the discussion of styles (I.31ff.), Bhāmaha makes further remarks bearing on the qualities, thus clarity, even(ness) *ṛju* and soft(ness) *komala* are merely pleasant, what is essential being developed meaning (*puṣṭārtha* or *arthya*) and figurativeness, together with 'fitness' (*nyāyya*, appropriateness) and the avoidance of crudeness *agrāmya* and confusion *anākula*. 'Realism' is a 'quality' *guṇa* of a work as a whole *prabandha*. Other 'qualities' are partly covered by figures (e.g. 'concentration' by 'condensed expression', 'exaltation' by 'exalted').

238. By Bhāmaha's time there were two schools of *kavis* named after the countries in which they presumably originated, Vidarbha (in Mahārāṣṭra) and Gauḍa (Magadha), cultivating opposed styles according to the use of the qualities. The *vaidarbha*, popular in the South, was also called after Vatsagulma, capital of Vidarbha and of the SW Vākāṭaka Empire of the Deccan in the +4 and +5. Its writers cultivated all the ten qualities. Bhāmaha (I.33) notes an *Aśmakavaṃśa* ('History of Aśmaka', another province of Mahārāṣṭra) as a leading *kāvya* (probably on epic; it seems to have been lost) in this style [938]. The *gauḍīya* writers preferred 'strength', with abundance of compounds, alliteration and display of recondite language, even at the expense of the other qualities such as clarity. No example is noted by Bhāmaha (unless

Rāmaśarman's *Acyutottara* was one, II.19), but Aśvaghoṣa (+1) sometimes tends that way [756]. Its greatest exponent, though in a very restrained and elegant manner perhaps not typical of the school, is Bhavabhuti (early +8).

239. Other schools of *kavis* followed. According to Bāṇa (+7, *Harṣacarita* verse 8) the Northern *udīcya* (corresponding to Gandhāra or North-West India) writers favoured double meanings, the Southern ones (i.e. the *vaidarbha* school) cultivated 'fancy', the Westerners (in Avanti, etc., perhaps Bhāravi [1491]) only meaning (developed) and the Gauḍas showiness of sounds. Later a *pāñcāla* ('of Pañcāla,' in the upper Ganges valley) style was generally recognised, a compromise between the *vaidarbha* and *gauḍīya*, of which Bāṇa himself was held to be the perfector. Still other styles are occasionally mentioned, but the *vaidarbha*, *gauḍīya* and *pāñcāla* are the only really important styles, unless we add that of double meaning (which is later rather a special genre of *kāvya* than a style).

240. The chief theorists of style are Daṇḍin (late +7), who calls it *mārga* ('road', 'way'), and Vāmana (+8), who calls it *rīti* ('flow', 'way'). Daṇḍin in his *Kāvyalakṣaṇa*, 'Characteristics of *Kāvya*', is the champion of the *vaidarbha* style, which he himself cultivated in prose in the novel [922, 937, 1347, 1380, 1484]. In this style the ten qualities are supposed to be exactly balanced, and he defines them as follows (I.41ff., in general agreement with the *Nāṭyaśāstra*). *Śleṣa* (or *śliṣṭa*) is 'union', well-knittedness, tightness or tautness of language (depending on a sufficiency of aspirated sounds). It should be noted that *śliṣṭa* (= *śleṣa*), literally 'combined', is used in two distinct meanings in poetics: (1) punning, (2) compactness and well-knittedness. *Prasāda* is clarity, lucid and unambiguous statements, not too far-fetched. *Samatā* is homogeneity or 'evenness' of sound within a line or verse (the *Nāṭyaśāstra's samatā* is different : evenness and balance of texture, and in one recension also easiness). *Mādhurya* is sweetness, as of honey, a kind of *rasa* (taste or aesthetic experience) produced by delightful words, it consists especially in the arranging of similar (not identical) sounds to echo each other at a small distance, giving thus an effect of balance; it further avoids any suggestion of coarseness or crudeness. *Sukumāratā* is delicacy or softness, avoidance of harsh sounds. *Arthavyakti* is lucidity and completeness of the objects in the words used, no additional words to be 'understood', not requiring further explanation or commentary. *Udāratva* is exaltation as elevated, 'enhanced' content. *Ojas* is strength through the use of compounds; this quality is used sparingly by the *vaidarbhas* except in prose, where it is essential. *Kānti* is grace or agreeableness as in polite and friendly conversation in everyday life and without the fantastic exaggeration of the *gauḍīya*. *Samādhi* is concentration or ambiguity as a kind of metaphor, as when speaking of flowers with words appropriate for eyes, words being used in a secondary and figurative sense—here it is also noted that some words which are coarse in their primary senses are not coarse but expressive in secondary senses, thus 'belch' is coarse but 'belched forth smoke' is expressive—'ambiguity' occurs also in words and phrases of double meaning.

241. Daṇḍin (himself a Southerner from Kāñcī [490]) is severely critical of the *gauḍīya* style and defines it as on the whole the reverse of the *vaidarbha*. At the same time he shows that in part the *gauḍīya* school take the qualities in a different sense. They cultivate strength *ojas* in verse as well as prose, and with it massive alliteration (they accept *śleṣa*, 'union', only in this sense). They love the display of command over language and showiness *ḍambara* in meaning and in figures of speech even at the expense of clarity and evenness. They prefer strong alliteration to 'sweetness', and brilliance *dīpta* to softness. On the whole they accept 'lucidity and completeness of meaning', 'exaltation', 'ambiguity' and 'grace', but in the last they like very exaggerated *atyukti* speech—which Daṇḍin says pleases nobody but scholars. The figures of speech take second place to the qualities in Daṇḍin's book (II and most of III), though he discusses them more elaborately than Bhāmaha.

242. Vāmana took up the study of style *rīti*, defined as a special arrangement of words (*Kāvyālaṅkārasūtra*, p. 4), and declared it to be the essence *ātman* of *kāvya* (Daṇḍin had placed it on a level with the figures of speech, though treating style first). He has the same names for the ten 'qualities' which constitute this special arrangement, but in each of them finds a double application: they are qualities of the sounds of *kāvya* and also of the meaning (p. 29). He describes (pp. 4ff.) the three main styles : *vaidarbhī* (feminine in Vāmana, as the word *rīti* is feminine) which has all the qualities and is therefore the best, *gauḍīyā* which has 'strength' and 'grace' and also can be excellent, and *pāñcālī* which has especially 'sweetness' and 'delicacy' (softness). The *gauḍīyā* and *pāñcālī* are thus diametrically opposed, and each avoids the two specific qualities of the other. 'Pure' *vaidarbhī* has no compound words.

243. Vāmana's descriptions of the qualities (pp. 30ff.), besides having two aspects of each, vary somewhat from Daṇḍin's. Thus 'strength' is firmness of structure (through suitable juxtaposition of sounds, not simply compounding of words) and expansion (boldness) of meaning. 'Grace' is distinction (brilliance, freshness, originality) of composition (arrangement of words) and has brilliant *rasas* [1527]. 'Sweetness' is separateness or distinctness of words and variety of expression. 'Delicacy' is avoidance of harshness of sound or meaning. 'Exaltation' means that the words seem to dance, whilst there is absence of vulgarity in the meaning. 'Clarity' is 'looseness' of sounds (therefore opposed to 'strength' and difficult to combine with this, but it is possible to achieve a varying balance of the two) and 'purity' (simplicity) of meanings (words used in direct, not transferred, senses), avoiding useless words. 'Union' is softness of sounds, so that many words seem like one, and (smooth, orderly) joining together of meanings [1473] (also said to be conspicuous in the works of Śūdraka [1234]). 'Evenness' is not changing the style of sounds and avoiding unevenness in the course of the meanings. 'Concentration' means climbing and descending of sounds (i.e. probably melodiousness, the quality of a well balanced melody —according to the commentators 'climbing' means having mostly long syllables and slow, 'descending' means having short syllables and unaspirated consonants) and 'seeing' (focussing) of meanings, whether spontaneous (original) or echoes of another *kāvya*. 'Lucidity of the object' refers to sounds which are the cause of the revelation and showing the nature of the objects (described) clearly.

244. There would seem to be a rather strong subjective element in Vāmana's qualities. The qualities are essential to *kāvya* and give it its beauty, says Vāmana (p. 30), whilst the figures of speech are unessential adornments which merely enhance the beauty. The proper combination of the qualities requires great delicacy and subtlety (especially in the case of 'clarity' and 'strength').

245. Perhaps it was the study of style which led Vāmana to a special interest in prose writing ('they say prose is the touchstone of *kavis*...' —p. 12), and he distinguishes briefly between three kinds of prose in *kāvya*: that 'which has the aroma of verse' *vṛttagandhi*, the terse (*cūrṇa*, 'pulverised'), which is without compounds and is 'playful', and the luxuriant *utkalikā*, which has compounds and is 'elevated.' [4541, 4581-2]

246. Most later critics find only the three qualities 'clarity', 'sweetness' and 'strength' of importance (as had Bhāmaha earlier), associating them particularly with the *vaidarbha*, *pāñcāla* and *gauḍīya* styles respectively.

247. It is in the *Dhvanyāloka*, 'Light on "Sound"', of Ānandavardhana (+9) that we find for the first time a clear organic synthesis of the theories of the aesthetic experience *rasa* and of figurative speech, of the ideas of dramaturgy and those of poetics. Seeking like his predecessors for a fundamental principle on which to build a theory of *kāvya*, Ānandavardhana appears to have been inspired by Bhāmaha's idea of 'figurative expression' *vakrokti* to analyse the nature of the most effective poetic expressions more deeply. His conclusion was that they owed their superiority to their allusiveness—the carrying of indirect meanings or overtones, We have two kinds of meaning, literal *vācya* and implied (*pratīyamāna* or *vyaṅgya*) (p. 43). In good *kāvyas* it is the implied meanings which predominate over the literal everywhere and even set it aside entirely.

248. This theory is not as recondite as it sounds. Splendid examples of the best kind of *kāvya* were culled by Ānandavardhana from the collection of Māhārāṣṭrī lyrics first compiled by the royal connoisseur 'Hāla' Sātavāhana (+2), which were drawn from nothing more sophisticated than folk song [830]. The subterfuges [812], insinuations [814], equivocations, mock defiances, hidden invitations [811], the idioms of everyday conversation and chatter which never carry literal meaning and can be understood only by the initiated : these regenerated literary criticism which sometimes tended to be overshadowed by minute grammatical analysis.

249. In language, sound carries meaning. If in linguistic analysis the grammarians studied how meanings were carried by 'sound' *dhvani*, and regarded sound as the basis of language (there were several theories about this, about the nature of the 'fundamental sound' which, for example, is repeated each time the same word is uttered, yet with slight variations)—then in good *kāvya* too there should be, as it were, 'sound' *dhvani* of such a kind that it can carry all the meanings, including the figurative and indirect, the aesthetic experience *rasa*, figures of speech, style and modes *vṛttis*, as well as the subject matter or story. Ānandavardhana uses the term 'sound' *dhvani* in a new sense, borrowing it from the grammarians (pp. 133ff.), to mean that which carries those excellences of good *kāvya* which he admired, so that it comes to mean the power which underlies suggestion or 'implication'. *Dhvani* in this special sense is that *kāvya* in which 'implication' predominates over literal meaning (p. 103).

250. *Dhvani* (*kāvya*) is of two main types (p. 136): that which does not intend the literal meaning at all *avivakṣitavācya*, but only the implied meaning [636, 1414]; and that which intends the literal meaning also, though the implied predominates *vivakṣitānyaparavācya*. Where the literal meaning predominates there is no *dhvani* in Ānandavardhana's sense, and there cannot be the best sort of *kāvya*. He recognises (pp. 458 ff.) a second class of *kāvya*, however, where the implied meaning is subordinate *guṇībhūtavyaṅgya* yet the literal meaning is beautiful *vācyacārutva* [813, 1302]. A third and lowest class is *citrakāvya*, 'decorative *kāvya*', in which the effects are purely verbal (pp. 494ff.). These decorative effects include for example rhyme, the construction of verses which read the same forwards or backwards or which can be laid out like a wheel, and a variety of other feats of mere dexterity of language.

251. Ānandavardhana investigates three main elements in *kāvya* from his new standpoint (p. 50); subject (*vastu*, reality matter, including the incident or situation in a single independent lyric verse), figurative speech *alaṅkāra* and aesthetic experience *rasa*. In good *kāvyas*, though there is always a literal sense *vācya artha*, the implied or revealed sense *pratīyamāna artha*, which has these three elements as its chief subdivisions, predominates. Such good *kāvyas* are called *dhvanikāvyas*.

252. Under 'subject' (pp. 52ff.), Ānandavardhana

analyses implied meanings such as those he found in the Māhārāṣṭrī lyrics collected by Sātavāhana [811, 812]. Under figurative speech (p. 77 and *uddyota* II) he discusses some examples of figures in these lyrics, or in Sanskrit epics such as those of Meṇṭha [1335, 1337] and Māgha, which carry primarily implied meanings. The aesthetic experience (pp. 78ff. and *uddyota* III), he contends (in harmony with Bharata's doctrine), can only be implied, not expressed literally. For this he gives examples, from the *Rāmāyaṇa* of Vālmīki (traditionally regarded as the 'first *kāvya*') and other epics, and from several dramas, of speeches or descriptions of action which produce aesthetic experiences, such as the compassionate or the sensitive, in the reader or audience. Ānandavardhana also discusses (pp. 309ff.) style (the 'qualities') in connection with aesthetic experience [1480], with particular reference to prose writing (biography and novels).

253. All *kāvya* should carry *rasa* in the same way as dramas and the best epics and lyrics (p. 526). The occasions producing emotion *vibhāva* and the expression of emotion by the characters *anubhāva* must be harmoniously created agreeably to the *rasa*, so that the effect of the work is not spoiled (p. 361). Likewise the style, modes *vṛttis*, and figures of speech, and incidental descriptive passages, must all harmonise with the *rasa*. In any *kāvya* (as in a drama) one *rasa* should be predominant (p. 378), though various other *rasas* should be drawn in in subordinate positions, just as there should be one main 'objective' *kārya*. All the techniques of drama, including the conjunctions (336ff.) and modes ([181] pp. 364, 401, 517, since 'expressive' actions, costume and violent or other gestures can all be described as well as acted), are appropriated for *kāvya* as a whole, and at the same time the techniques which have been evolved for *kāvya* are subordinated to *rasa* and the entire aesthetic system is presented as carried by *dhvani*, the non-literal power of language [1467].

254. Meanwhile the more specialised study of the figures of speech had continued. Udbhaṭa at the end of the +8 wrote a commentary on Bhāmaha's work, giving fuller discussions and more illustrations of the figures, and also compiled a short manual, *Kāvyālaṅkārasārasaṅgraha,* limited to an account of the figures, with improved definitions. He was, moreover, a poet himself, author of an epic, and, as we have seen, a commentator on the *Nāṭyaśāstra* [92, 133]. He added practically nothing to Bhāmaha's collection of figures and seems to have propounded no important new theories. He was probably a junior contemporary of Vāmana, and he and the school of poetics he founded upheld the traditional theory of the figures as the most important element in poetics (apart of course from *rasa*, treated separately) against the new school of stylistics founded by Vāmana. These two schools are well known among later critics. Udbhaṭa incorporated the logical 'reason' and 'example' [199-200] as simply two figures, 'literary middle term' *kāvyahetu* and 'literary example' *kāvyadṛṣṭānta* [2559] (VI.7 and 8). Thus he simplified Bhāmaha's exposition rather than adding to it. [823]

255. It was Rudraṭa in the +9, perhaps a contemporary of Ānandavardhana, who is the first writer known to us (which of course does not necessarily imply very much in view of the heavy losses of Sanskrit literature) to make serious modifications in the traditional enumeration of figures and to attempt a classification of those he accepted according to certain underlying principles. The lists given by Daṇḍin and Vāmana, as well as Udbhaṭa, are very similar to Bhāmaha's, in fact are the same basic list with a few additions or deletions. For example Daṇḍin adds 'cause', 'hint' and 'excuse' (which Bhāmaha had mentioned only in order to reject), asserting that they are excellent ornaments, whilst Vāmana rejects these and further rejects the sub-group 'affectionate', 'having *rasa*', 'disdain' *ūrjasvin* and 'exalted' *udātta*, which are concerned with the expression of emotion and the arising of aesthetic experience from this. It seems Vāmana regarded the qualities of style as the proper medium for producing *rasa*, not the figures: thus his 'grace' *kānti* 'has brilliant *rasas*'.

256. Rudraṭa has been regarded as a follower of Udbhaṭa in that he stressed the importance of the figures and attached little significance to style. He omitted the 'qualities' and defined a set of styles *rītis* simply on the basis of the degree of compounding (II.4-6) : the *vaidarbhī* is without compounds, the *pāñcālī* has compounds of two or three words, a style called the *lāṭīyā* has compounds of five or seven words and the *gauḍīyā* of any number (as many as the writer can manage). This seems to be the earliest reference now known, except for Bāṇa's [239], to 'Western' *pratīcya* writers, or to a *lāṭīyā* style, named after the Lāṭa country on the West coast of India (Southern Gujarat). We thus arrive at a scheme like Bāṇa's connecting four styles with the four points of the compass (*lāṭīyā* = West, *vaidarbhī* = South, *pāñcālī* = North, *gauḍīyā* = East), but defining them quite differently. Rudraṭa afterwards (his Chapters XIV and XV) noted that these 'styles' were 'appropriate' in connection with particular *rasas*, propounding (XV. 20) a principle of 'appropriateness' or 'harmony' *aucitya* between the form and content of a *kāvya*.

257. The bulk of Rudraṭa's work (called *Kāvyālaṅkāra* like Bhāmaha's) is concerned with detailed treatment of the figures. Those involving only the sounds of the language are dealt with first, under the headings 'equivocation', alliteration, rhyme, pun *śleṣa* and 'decoration' *citra* (II.13), this last being the kind of verse-game which had developed, and even got into serious literature in the form of cadenzas of verbal virtuosity, in which the sounds of a verse, laid out as a geometrical pattern, can be read in various amusing ways [1546]. Ānandavardhana's 'decorative *kāvya*' includes all the figures of sound. 'Equivocation' is here the meaning of *vakrokti* (not Bhāmaha's 'figurative expression') developed from its etymology *vakra* = 'crooked'. In this special sense a *vakrokti* verse is one deliberately calculated so that it can be misunderstood, with humorous effect [1472, 1478].

258. The figures of meaning are then discussed under four headings: 'objective' *vāstava*, 'comparative' *aupamya*, 'exaggerative' *atiśaya* and 'double meaning' *śleṣa* (VII.9). These are put forward as main divisions, though there is no theoretical limit to the invention of figures and the classes appear to overlap (a figure may belong to more than one, but then it must really be more than one figure). The underlying principle of each figure, then, is sought among these four.

259. The 'objective' figures are those whose point is found in the objects described rather than in the expression. According to Rudraṭa the 'lamp' belongs here, together with 'naturalistic description' (here called *jāti*, 'species', 'genre', but equivalent to *svabhāvokti* [1478]), 'contrast' *vyatireka*, 'circumlocution' *paryāya*, 'revolution' and 'enumeration'. 'Hint' and 'excuse' are also accepted here. 'Accompaniment' *sahokti* is classed under objective, but it appears again under 'comparative'. This means that there is another variety of 'accompaniment', which is based on comparison rather than on objective fact [1470]. In the same way many other figures appear under more than one class. 'Cause' thus appears here and under 'exaggerative'.

260. Rudraṭa adds a great many new figures not found in any of the writers mentioned above, in fact about as many as he takes up from the old standard list. It is not known whether he invented all or any of these himself. In the present state of our knowledge, therefore, he represents a major break with the tradition of the study of the figures in that he doubles their number and initiates a fashion of continually seeking new ones, quite apart from the innovation of the fourfold classification. Among the new figures we find 'intention' *bhāva* used in much the same sense as Ānandavardhana's 'implied' *vyaṅgya* meaning. Then we have 'inference' *anumāna*, 'exclusion' *parisaṃkhyā* (where the usual meaning is excluded by the context in favour of a secondary meaning [1569]), 'reciprocity' *anyonya* of action [808], 'essence' (*sāra* : a kind of climax in which one proceeds from the essence or most valuable part of an object to the most valuable part of that part and so on), 'opportunity' (*avasara*, or 'sally', a kind of circumlocution or euphemism [1478]), 'mingling' (*mīlita* : where through emotion an object changes its nature and merges with another in its character [1471: A18]), 'series' (*ekāvalī*: one object leads to another, much as in 'essence') and others under 'objective.' There are again new figures which appear under more than one class: 'conjunction' *samuccaya* of objects and 'reply' *uttara* may be objective or comparative; 'incongruity' *viṣama* may be objective or exaggerative [1411, 1477, 1541].

261. The 'comparative' figures include simile, metaphor, fancy (which appears also under exaggerative), concealment, 'doubt' (*saṃśaya*, equivalent to 'having doubt'), condensed expression, corroboration and 'spurning'. A most important new figure in this class is 'expression of something else' *anyokti*, where through the description of the nature or actions of 'something else'—usually some natural phenomenon such as a bird or animal—a comment is implied on the similar behaviour of something—generally good or bad men (cf. 'praise of what is not the subject', which this figure replaces). It is thus a kind of miniature fable. Collections of verses in this figure were popular from Rudraṭa's time on as vehicles for social criticism (e.g. Bhallaṭa, end of +9) [825-6]. Other new figures here include 'contrary' (*pratīpa*: reversed simile: Rudraṭa explains this as an apparently unfavourable comparison which is really favourable; later writers such as Jayadeva use the term differently), 'being in error' (*bhrāntimant*: through similarly of the objects taking one for the other [824, 1474]) and 'being reminded' *smaraṇa* by seeing something similar to the object. [2405, 2350]

262. The 'exaggerative' figures ('exaggeration' itself is not here given as a separate figure but is only the name of the whole class) include distinction, miracle and contradiction. New figures here include 'quality of that' (*tadguṇa*: not noticing the difference between objects because they have the same quality), 'surpassing' (*adhika*, this in effect replaces the traditional 'exaggeration' figure, but Rudraṭa restricts it somewhat to cases involving seeming contradiction), 'dissociation' (*asaṃgati*: cause and effect appear in different places), 'covered' (*pihita*: a quality or effect is attributed to a wrong but flattering cause) and 'opposition' (*vyāghāta*, between cause and effect, the cause not producing its usual effect despite the absence of obstacles). Rudraṭa defines the exaggerative figures generally as where the reality is altered or nature is exceeded. [3717]

263. The 'double meaning' figures depend on a plurality of meanings in the sentence (in more than one word by itself: the latter would be 'pun', a figure of sound). Nearly all the figures given here are new, though sometimes related to older ones. Thus we have 'apparent contradiction' *virodhābhāsa*, 'contradiction' *virodha*, 'surpassing' *adhika*, 'equivocation' (*vakra*: the meaning is not what it appears to be at first, because a series of words can apply to two different objects) and others. The double meaning must be in the meaning only, since these are figures of meaning, not in the concatenation of sounds, as in the figures of sound, though it would seem to require a considerable effort to keep these apart.

264. Though he has added so many new figures to the standard list, Rudraṭa omits a few old ones. He follows Vāmana in leaving out the sub-group connected with *rasa*. Here we should note that with Rudraṭa the 'affectionate' *preyas* has itself been classified as a *rasa* instead of as a figure [96]. He left it to Bhoja, as we saw in our second chapter, to combine the 'disdain' and 'exalted' (*ūrjasvin* and *udātta*) figures as another new *rasa* named after either of them and meaning 'exalted', and to set up a 'proud' *uddhata rasa* to incorporate the meaning left over from 'disdain'. Rudraṭa included some old figures under others which he accepted, thus he eliminated 'simile-metaphor', 'comparison as compared' and 'equal consequence' but distinguished a large number of sub-varieties of simile and metaphor which should include these variations. The same may be true of 'want of agreement', 'praise of what is not the subject' *aprastutapraśaṃsā* and 'sham praise'. 'Coincidence' and 'benediction' are omitted, probably as not being figures of speech at all. 'Illustration' *nidarśana* is replaced by the old characteristic 'example' *dṛṣṭānta*, as a 'comparative' figure (Udbhaṭa had both as figures).

265. In classifying the figures of speech in this way, Rudraṭa appears to have abandoned the old conception of 'figurative expression' *vakrokti* as their basis. The term *vakrokti* itself, in fact, had been appropriated by him to a particular figure only, in the very restricted sense of 'equivocation'. On the other hand Ānandavardhana had brought the figures and all other elements in *kāvya* under the conception of implied *vyaṅgya* meaning, very likely stimulated by Bhāmaha's idea of an underlying 'figurativeness' but looking for a possibly more comprehensive conception which would give adequate scope to subject matter and aesthetic experience as well as the figures within a single general theory. Other critics followed Vāmana's doctrine of stylistics or Nāyaka's aesthetic theory [85].

266. These are the leading views known to us as current by the end of the +9, if we regard the Udbhaṭa school as represented by Rudraṭa. The controversies among them perhaps tended mainly in the direction of the problem of the aesthetic experience, whilst there were also syncretistic trends (e.g. Rājaśekhara) aimed at collecting a variety of ideas within a traditionalist framework. A

267. At the same time there was some continuing discussion from the linguistic point of view concerning the nature of the kind of 'expression' *ukti* appropriate in *kāvya* (Bhāmaha—Vāmana—Ānandavardhana—Rājaśekhara). In stylistics Rājaśekhara proposed to define three styles on the basis of degrees of compounding, of alliteration and of the use of words in secondary senses (*upacāra*: transfer from the etymological meaning assumed to be primary, *yogavṛtti*). The *gauḍīyā* favours compounds and alliteration but uses words in their primary senses, in fact contains successions of words in their etymological senses. The *pāñcālī* is moderate in the use of both compounds and alliteration but favours the use of words in transferred senses. The *vaidarbhī* avoids compounds and limits alliteration to certain (appropriate) places, it also maintains words in their etymological senses (but without deliberately piling up successions of them) (pp. 8-9).

268. Here as in other parts of his work (e.g. on the figures) Rājaśekhara largely follows Rudraṭa, omitting the qualities and substituting rather some of their constituent elements as the basis of style, though he does not accept a fourth style (Raghavan has shown that it is likely that Rājaśekhara gave a critical review of the theories of 'qualities' in the at present lost Seventeenth *Adhikaraṇa* of his *Kāvyamīmāṃsā*—*Bhoja's Śṛṅgāraprakāśa*, pp. 336 ff.). He does, however, admit a further kind of stylistic differentiation through 'intonation' *kāku* [1528]. The bringing in of 'transfer' *upacāra* is a significant contribution to stylistic analysis. Several later writers, such as Bhoja and Śāradātanaya, further developed this type of stylistic analysis, adding other criteria and also inventing new styles, tending to the conclusion that there is no limit to the number of styles, each person having his own (Śāradātanaya).

269. Early in the +11 Kuntaka returned to the old conception of figurative expression *vakrokti* as used by Bhāmaha and set about deriving from it, as the one essential characteristic of *kāvya* expression, a comprehensive account of the nature of literature. Under the title *Vakroktijīvita* (perhaps 'Revival of *Vakrokti*', or better 'Figurative Expression as the Life [Essence—of literature]'), he discusses in detail the whole range of activity of the writer. The work is systematic throughout, basing all the topics of poetics on a single principle and showing how they are all related to it and to each other.

270. Literature *kāvya*, says Kuntaka, is the activity of the author *kavi*, aimed at beauty *vaicitrya*, which produces transcendent admiration (*camatkāra*, or 'delight') (pp. 2-3). This 'admiration' is in effect the aesthetic experience of the reader, seen from a broader standpoint than that of the special *rasa* theory and produced by all the elements of *kāvya*, not by its emotional content alone, though Kuntaka is far from diminishing the importance of *rasa*. We have touched on this idea in our second chapter [79, 95, 98]. Kuntaka uses 'admiration' (p. 5) for the 'experience' *anubhava* of the 'taste' (*rasa* in its original sense) of the ambrosia of *kāvya*, thus joining the two concepts and bringing *rasa* under *camatkāra*. He adds a further new idea of fundamental importance by saying that in reality *kāvya* is indivisible, it is not a combination of separable parts or ingredients, like a body with ornaments, because the author creates one beautiful whole and any analysis into figures, etc., is only theoretical abstraction (p. 7, top, no doubt inspired by Bhartṛhari's similar conception of language as indivisible utterances or sentences, grammatical analysis being only abstraction and not a discovery of real roots, suffixes, etc.; see e.g. *Vākyapadīya* II.58, *vākyavādins*).

271. Now the 'beauty' *vaicitrya* in literature, or its 'beautiful expression' *vicitrā abhidhā*, is precisely its 'figurative expression' *vakrokti* (p. 22). It is expression with skilful 'drawing' (*bhaṅgī* or *vicchitti*, terms taken from sculpture and painting and meaning originally the 'breaking' or 'cutting' of outlines; hence related in idea to the original meaning of *vakratā*, 'crookedness'). Consequently Kuntaka qualifies Bhāmaha's 'speech and meaning combined', as definition of *kāvya*, with 'in a composition distinguished by the figurative activity of the author *vakrakavivyāpāraśālini bandhe*. He adds further that the composition 'produces delight in the connoisseur' (*tadvidāhlādakāriṇi*, *āhlāda* being a synonym for *prīti*) (pp. 7-15).

272. The figurativeness in creative writing, as contrasted with the straightforward everyday expressions of ordinary treatises *śāstras*, etc., is of six kinds (p. 14 and pp. 29ff.), at six levels of expression: phonetic, lexical, grammatical, sentential, contextual and the composition as a whole (respectively of the phoneme *varṇa*; lexical unit *padapūrvārdha*; grammatical unit *pratyaya*; sentence *vākya*; context or section of a work *prakaraṇa*, i.e. the detailed arrangement of the story or matter; and composition *prabandha*). These six kinds of figurativeness are taken up in order and constitute the body of Kuntaka's book (unfortunately the end part is missing in the editions so far printed).

273. Phonetic figurativeness (first part of Chapter II) includes the use of alliteration and rhyme, but also the more subtle sound effects produced by the free and irregular repetition of similar or identical phonemes at varying intervals, which give texture and beauty to the expression. These effects are of great importance in the 'qualities', and the 'styles' based on them, of both of which Kuntaka gives a novel account in his first chapter. The qualities and styles also show the application of figurativeness at the other levels, however, and represent in effect the practice of writers, in groups and as individuals, choosing among the resources presented by the possibilities of figurativeness at the six levels. [1806, 2427, 3650]

274. Lexical figurativeness (pp. 87ff.) includes all effects based on the choice of vocabulary. Usage has conferred certain properties and associations on certain words [1606]. Synonyms in fact give different shades of meaning and different associations [1535]. Most important, however, is the effect of 'transfer' *upacāra*, when a word is used in a secondary sense, applied to an object with which it is not directly associated. This includes such devices as speaking of an abstract phenomenon as if it was something material which could be handled: 'gathering a *reputation* with his hands', for example, as if gathering flowers. Speaking of inanimate objects as if they were conscious (personification) is similar. Then there is euphemism *saṃvṛti* [1536] (105ff.). Such 'transfers' are often the basis of figures of speech (metaphor, etc.) at the sentence level and give life to them. [1676, 2407, 2443, 3642, 3703, 3725, 3741]

275. Grammatical figurativeness (pp. 122ff.) includes all possibilities of varying the grammatical construction of an expression. Here too personification can be effected by making an inanimate object appear as the agent (or 'subject'), thus: '*the multitude of tears* forcibly caused her wretched breasts to bathe.' [2121, 2125, 2407, 3643, 3648, 3656]

276. At the sentence level we have the discussion of the figures of speech *alaṅkāras* (Chapter III). Kuntaka follows the list given by Bhāmaha, but revising it and redefining the figures to attain greater precision and clarity in the analysis. The criterion of figurativeness is strictly applied in determining which of the proposed figures should be accepted. The definition of 'figure of speech' *alaṅkāra* which Kuntaka arrives at is given in a *kārikā* which the edition fails to restore (p. 174 *abhidhāyāḥ...*) but which fortunately is quoted by Subuddhimiśra in his (not yet printed—an edition is being prepared) *Sāhityasarvasva* Commentary on Vāmana (IV.3.14). This definition falls into three parts: it is called an *alaṅkāra* if it is a manner (*prakāra*, or 'figure') of expression (*abhidhā*, 'expressiveness' or 'speech'), a very great effort accomplishes it (i.e. the activity of the author) and it is a very great 'drawing' (*vicchitti*, implying a beautiful figurativeness or 'delineation') of a *kāvya* (or of literature). The second and third parts here appear to be equivalent to the requirements for literature in general [270], whilst the first indicates the particular kind of figurativeness, a 'figure of speech' at the sentence level. In the first place 'naturalistic description' *svabhāvokti*, about which Bhāmaha appears doubtful, is definitely not a figure of speech according to Kuntaka (pp. 23, 134ff.). It is not a figure or ornament but is itself that which is figured or ornamented *alaṅkārya*: it is part of the subject matter of a *kāvya*. It may be beautiful and productive of *rasa*, but this beauty is not at the level of the figures of speech, of figurative expression. This discussion leads naturally into one on the position of *rasa* and of some other figures in the traditional list, particularly the sub-group connected with *rasa*, which Vāmana and Rudraṭa had omitted already. It is the subject matter which is 'having *rasa*' *rasavant*, hence this too is not a figure of speech though it is certainly a figurativeness *vakratā* of the subject *vastu* as presented by the author's skill. This *rasa*-figurativeness must consequently be approached from the standpoint of the *kāvya* as a whole *prabandha*, the way the author treats his subject matter in order to secure the maximum *rasa*-effectiveness. This will include the simple selection of beautiful subjects, leaving aside what is uninteresting or unaesthetic (*virasa*, p. 239), as well as exaggeration and alteration of the story or of reality and the exercise of poetic fancy. At the level of the sentence the figures of speech will contribute in detail to this effectiveness, and in a sense all the figures should be 'having *rasa*' (pp. 174-5). But this is because the *rasa* gives life to them as part of their meaning and not because there is another kind of figure present, which could be called 'having *rasa*' Thus Kuntaka, unlike Bhāmaha, distinguishes figures from subject matter as strictly expression. [2427, 2447, 2473]

277. On the same grounds, that they are part of the subject being 'figured', not themselves figures, 'affectionate', 'disdain', 'exalted' and also 'coincidence' *samāhita* are rejected by Kuntaka. He discusses each in detail, reviewing the definitions proposed by his predecessors. On the ground of lack of beauty (*śobhā* or *vaicitrya*) he rejects 'condensed expression' *samāsokti* and 'enumeration', as well as 'distinction' *viśeṣokti*, which is no ornament but just well known qualities of the subject described, as in the actual example of it given by Bhāmaha [230] (which Kuntaka quotes). 'Cause', 'hint' and 'excuse', rejected already by Bhāmaha, contain no beauty and Kuntaka endorses the rejection. Such things may be part of the subject only and can be adorned by the use of those figures which are accepted. 'Benediction' similarly, about which Bhāmaha was undecided, is according to Kuntaka not a figure, but only subject matter capable of being figured. 'Simile-metaphor' has no application, i.e. its concept is illogical and does not apply to the facts of figuration, there is no such figure (alleged examples will be either similes or metaphors, if figures at all). Several other proposed figures are not separate figures but are particular cases of others, in which they should be included, as we shall note below.

278. Subject to revised, more precise, definitions in several cases, Kuntaka accepts eighteen figures only (as figures of meaning): 'lamp', 'metaphor', 'praise of what is not the subject', 'circumlocution', 'sham praise', 'fancy', 'exaggeration', 'simile', 'double meaning' *śleṣa*, 'contrast', 'contradiction', 'accompaniment', 'example' (*dṛṣṭānta*, taken from Udbhaṭa, not Bhāmaha), 'corroboration', 'spurning', 'miracle', 'having doubt' and 'concealment', These are defined in such ways as to distinguish carefully between them, for example between metaphor, fancy and simile. Along with the rejected and included figures they exhaust Bhāmaha's list. The arrangement (they are given in the order in which they are enumerated above, but 'sham praise' is possibly displaced in the manuscript) seems to be Kuntaka's own : there is grouping by kinds,

but with some overlapping and without apparent trace of Rudraṭa's classification; there are in fact no classes, but only certain associations and relations between the figures. The list is intended to be exhaustive of all possible figures, Kuntaka saying (p. 219) that any others proposed are either to be included in those he accepts or to be rejected as lacking beauty.

279. The definition of 'lamp' is restricted (generally following Udbhaṭa) to exclude purely formal arrangements lacking implied meaning. Metaphor is based on transfer *upacāra*, as noted earlier and now further developed. There is an element of transfer also in 'lamp' and in the figures immediately following, hence, presumably, Kuntaka's arrangement. Fancy leads on to exaggeration, since it partly resembles this, and to simile, since there is a superficial resemblance in their expression (*iva* in Sanskrit means both 'like' and 'as if') as well as an implied comparison in fancy. Under simile are included several figures which Kuntaka does not accept as separate; he follows Bhāmaha in including 'parallel-simile' *prativastūpamā* as just one kind of simile, whereas Udbhaṭa had separated it, but he also includes 'comparison as compared', 'want of agreement', 'equal consequence', 'illustration' *nidarśana* [1532] and 'revolution'. It should be noted in connection with 'illustration' that, in so far as it might not always, as defined by Bhāmaha, be included in simile, Kuntaka has a figure 'example' which would replace it. Wherever the expression of similarity is clear, Kuntaka declares that we have simply a case of simile. 'Double meaning' resembles simile, at least in appearance, but next we turn to 'contrast' as the opposite idea though it begins from a comparison. It may also have a double meaning, as may 'contradiction'. 'Accompaniment' requires careful distinction from simile (Kuntaka thinks Bhāmaha's example of it, quoted above [224], is in fact a simile) [1533]. 'Example' and 'corroboration' suggest comparison, or even logical identity (inclusion). 'Spurning' or apparent prohibition is related to simile, 'miracle' to exaggeration, 'having doubt' and 'concealment' both to fancy [1534].

280. Though this list is thus fixed and limited, the figures can be mixed, whilst Kuntaka states (p. 41) that the possibilities of figurativeness of the sentence are limitless because of the genius of writers. At the three higher levels, sentence, context and composition, Kuntaka introduces the story or subject matter *vastu* (for which the 'object' *padārtha* described is sometimes a synonym), because the complete meaning of utterances comes in only with entire sentences (following Bhartṛhari) and groups of sentences, where one can accordingly speak of figurativeness *vakratā* of this subject matter (p. 134). When the subject matter is naturally beautiful, for example young love, it is found that good authors do not generally embellish it much with figures of speech (pp. 135-8). The subject matter may be 'natural' *sahaja*, or 'imposed' *āhārya* by the author (pp. 139 and 41-2) [1404], alternatives which also interpenetrate with Kuntaka's distinction of styles varying from the natural or 'delicate' to the imposed or 'beautiful' (pp. 46 and 136) [288ff.]. [3071, 3725]

281. Some ten kinds of contextual figurativeness are described (first part of Chapter IV), the general purpose being to increase the *rasa* by a skilful arrangement of the parts of a *kāvya*. Details of the source story (e.g. the *Rāmāyaṇa* or the Great Epic) may be changed to make the characterisation more consistent. A hint of future developments may be attractive. The author may insert events he has invented into a story, in order to enhance the *rasa* [1391, making war on the God of Wealth] (this may be done to protect the character of the hero from what might seem an unworthy action [1419]). Besides invention of something new, what is in the source may be changed: authors are not restricted to the supposedly true, historical narrative [1531]. The parts of a *kāvya* are arranged and invented by the genius of the author so that they beautifully support the main plot and are supported by it [1368, Acts II and IV]. The successive acts of a play work to develop the *rasa*, and in either a play or an epic the main *rasa* can be 'tested', as with a touchstone, where the author has exercised the relevant kind of figurativeness, all the way through, in the sequence of acts, etc. [1530]. In a somewhat similar way the successive scenes or topics in a biography *ākhyāyikā*, i.e. the long descriptive passages, may develop *rasa*. The descriptive scenes in epics, such as bathing parties [1395], gathering flowers and so on, make them more beautiful. An episode may be introduced which has the effect of enhancing the main action by outlining sharply the characters of the protagonists [1626].

There is the device of a play within a play. Finally, the arrangement of the 'conjunctions' *sandhis* in relation to the *rasa* is noted, and with it the arrangement of the matter in the several 'contexts', here the acts in one example given, of a play [1369], or the equivalent scenes in epics [1422], [2372, 3662, 3897].

282. Unfortunately we depend on two incomplete manuscripts for this section of Kuntaka's work, which has not been adequately edited, and it is difficult to know how far we have the text intact. Our rough notes here may suffice to give the general drift of contextual figurativeness and clarify its level of application. [2130, 2140, 2331]

283. For figurativeness of a *kāvya* considered as a whole our position is even worse (pp. 238ff.), since the fragmentary manuscripts end without completing this section. The available text gives seven kinds of figurativeness of a whole work, besides the introductory remarks in the first chapter. These (pp. 42-3) say that the figurativeness of a work has the beauty of the combined complex of the (other) five kinds of figurativeness, describing a great hero and captivating the hearts of connoisseurs. It goes on that ultimately this reduces to (terminates in) instruction in virtue *dharma*, consisting of injunctions and prohibitions, such as, in the case of a *kāvya* on the Rāma story, 'act like Rāma, not like Rāvaṇa !' Also as in the (play) *Tāpasavatsarāja* (on the story of King Udayana, by Anaṅgaharṣa Mātrarāja, or Māyurāja, +7 ?), whose hero 'has a mind as delicate as a flower and is interested only in aesthetic diversions' : in reality this teaches that when one's own king is sinking in the ocean of disasters (as Udayana was) he may be enabled to cross over it by ministers having the sort of cleverness, in the application of policy by various means, which Udayana's ministers had. [2118]

284. In the main section on figurativeness of a whole work we find the following varieties of it described. The *rasa* of the original story may be changed in order to create delight. Thus the 'calmed' of the Epic and 'compassionate' of the *Rāmāyaṇa* are changed respectively in dramas to the heroic of Nārāyaṇa's *Veṇīsaṃhāra* and the sensitive of Bhavabhūti's *Uttararāmacarita* (p. 239, conflicting with other interpretations we have noted). Again one part only of the original story may be made the whole matter of a *kāvya*, leaving aside anything devoid of *rasa* and showing the rise of what is in effect a new character invented by the author, as in Bhāravi's epic *Kirātārjunīya* (based on a small part of the Great Epic [1529]). To illuminate the main *rasa* of his composition a writer may change the objective *kārya*, to eliminate a narrative without *rasa* leading to the original objective in his source (the interpretation of this piece of text is uncertain), as is done by Māgha in his epic *Śiśupālavadha* (from an episode in the Great Epic). [1834, 1901, 2327]

285. Again the hero may be made to attain a completely different result as his objective, unknown in the source story (the text is badly dislocated here: the example seems to be Harṣa's play *Nāgānanda*). Even the name of a *kāvya* may be figurative, indicating the way in which the author has contrived his version of the story, as in Viśākhadatta's 'Signet Rākṣasa' (*Mudrārākṣasa*: a historical play in which Rākṣasa is shown as defeated in political intrigue because his signet ring falls into the hands of his opponent Cāṇakya or Kauṭalya, who is able to seal a forged letter with it [1619]). Many works may be composed by as many writers on a single original story, yet the results may agree very little with one another, particularly in the case of plays. Thus the following six plays, and still others, are all based on the main story of the *Rāmāyaṇa*, yet the agreement between them is slight: *Rāmābhyudaya* (by Yaśovarman, who alone kept close to the original), *Udāttarāghava* (by Māyurāja), *Vīracarita* (by Bhavabhūti), *Bālarāmāyaṇa* (by Rājaśekhara), *Kṛtyārāvaṇa* (conjecturally by Meṇṭha [1349]) and *Māyāpuṣpaka* (author unknown). All are beautiful and delightful. Under this kind of figurativeness it is also noted that an extensive story may be abbreviated or a brief one expanded by the author. [2092, 3568, 3885]

286. The last variety of figurativeness in the available text states that the whole work of a great author may be figurative, giving instruction in the ways of policy creating new means of success. As examples the *Mudrārākṣasa* [1626] and *Tāpasavatsarāja* are noted. Here the available text ends and we do not know how much is missing. Comparing the detailed exposition with the summary introduction we might expect something further on 'instruction in virtue' as a culminating variety, after this last available variety which relates to wealth or political success *artha*, another of the ends of life. Pleasure and even liberation as ends might be added. From aesthetic considerations in relation to entire works Kuntaka may have worked round to ethical purposes. One might also expect something on entirely invented *kāvyas*, primarily novels and 'fiction' plays, after so much discussion on the originality of authors even when borrowing stories from old sources. Here of course the figurativeness in question would be as compared with real life as the original. Let us hope that this promising section of Kuntaka's book will be recovered intact from the still incompletely explored manuscript resources of India. [2263]

287. There is no evidence whether any further section beyond this one on the last kinds of figurativeness was written by Kuntaka. A possible further topic would be the literary genres. We have, however, to say something further about his views on quality and style, given at the end of his first chapter. Apparently following Vāmana, Kuntaka finds three styles, but he objects to the traditional geographical names for them and in any case reworks their definitions. He also objects to rating them in order of excellence: what is the use of describing inferior styles ? If they are inferior and do not delight connoisseurs they had better be omitted. But the three as defined by him are all good.

288. The 'delicate' *sukumāra* style is the old *vaidarbhī* redefined and named after an old quality (though one characteristic of *pāñcālī* according to Vāmana). It is natural, fresh and little ornamented. Emotion dominates and the cultivated skill derived from study is kept to the minimum: it is the natural beauty springing from genius which is found here. The poet Kālidāsa is typical of this style [1380, 1426], and Sarvasena in Prakrit [1269].

289. The 'beautiful' *vicitra* style is similar to the old *gauḍīyā*. Its beauty is increased by the intensive use of figures, and in this case the genius of the author is shown in the application of figurativeness to the expression and meaning. The work will be full of implied *pratīyamāna* meanings. This is a very difficult style to succeed in. Bāṇa has developed it, especially in his (biography) *Harṣacarita*, and Bhavabhūti and Rājaśekhara have used it in beautiful verses in their works (plays, i.e. amid the prose dialogue in simpler style). These and other known 'beautiful' writers quoted by Kuntaka are all +7 or later. [1650, 2379ff., 3337, 3691]

290. Thirdly there is the 'intermediate' *madhyama* style, comparable with some views of *pāñcālī*, which is a mixture of the other two, combining the excellent features of both: it has both natural and cultivated beauty. The masters in this style are Mātṛgupta [1304], Māyurāja and Mañjīra. [2123, 2134, 2470]

291. According to Kuntaka (p. 47) the individual styles of authors are in fact endless, corresponding to the nature and past experiences of each person, hence they could not be enumerated, but it is feasible to describe these three 'styles' as major trends and as accounting for some aspects of the appreciation of *kāvya*. His basic idea behind them is clearly that of natural versus cultivated writing as two poles in literature. The styles, Kuntaka says, belong to the particular characteristics of individual *kāvyas*, as distinguished from the general characteristics he thinks necessary in all good literature. In other words they represent individual variation among authors of similar excellence (not degrees of excellence).

292. There are both particular and general 'qualities'. The particular qualities are the same for all styles, but each varies according to the style. There are four such variable qualities : 'sweetness' and 'clarity' from Bhāmaha's set of three and two others not in the standard lists, 'sensuous beauty' *lāvaṇya* and 'nobility' *ābhijātya*.

293. 'Sweetness' in the delicate style means absence of compounds; in the 'beautiful' style it means avoiding softness *komalabhāva* but especially avoiding looseness of construction (a likely fault in writing which is studied rather than naturally flowing). The 'intermediate' style has a 'sweetness' intermediate between these (there is no discussion here: perhaps Kuntaka means it should have both aspects of the quality).

294. 'Clarity' in the delicate is being understood without difficulty; in the beautiful it is avoiding compounds yet maintaining 'strength' (*ojas*, actually Bhamaha's third quality). Compounds were characteristic of the old *gauḍīyā* and certainly occur in Kuntaka's examples of the 'beautiful'; what is meant here must be that compounding should be moderate and restricted within the limits that ensure clarity, and that avoiding them altogether on occasion can be a good point in the beautiful style. [3337]

295. 'Sensuous beauty' in the delicate is the beauty

of the arrangement of the sounds (phonemes) and words; in the beautiful it is the union of the words so that they seem 'like one' (again making a studied style appear natural) and some particular points relating to Sanskrit phonetics (maintaining *visarga* and having only short vowels before conjunct consonants). [2134, 2427]

296. 'Nobility' in the delicate means that it is pleasing to the ear and mind and is naturally 'fine' (*masṛṇa*, 'tender', 'soft', 'delicate'); in the beautiful it means that there is not too much of either softness or hardness.

297. As general qualities, developed in all good composition, Kuntaka first mentions 'charm' *saubhāgya*, which produces admiration, and then again 'sensuous beauty' *lāvaṇya*, the beauty of the combination of the sounds, etc. Later he explains that this 'charm' is what produces the success of a work with the connoisseurs, and adds another general quality, appropriateness or 'harmony' *aucitya*, which includes the proper figurativeness (and avoiding anything which would detract from the *rasa*) [1526]. Clearly it is as difficult to describe good *kāvyas* as good wines, though neither is impossible. It is a matter of developing a common terminology for experiences in which there is a high subjective component and people have private languages, if any languages at all, for communicating about them. Comment is hardly necessary on the difficulties of translating such terminology. [2141, 2427]

298. On later writers on poetics we can be brief for our present purpose. The most important of them, in terms of original contributions, is probably Mahiman (+11). We noted in Chapter II his theory of inference being the mechanism by which *kāvya* is enjoyed. In general he follows Ānandavardhana, and sometimes Kuntaka, but with the fundamental difference that in place of 'implied meaning' or 'figurativeness' as underlying principle he puts 'inference' *anumāna* (I.1). Implied meaning is accounted for within the limits of inference and requires no separate theory. In this way he brings literary appreciation into line with the theory of knowledge of the Buddhist (Dharmakīrti) school of logic. A further point is that all literature is educational, rather than aiming simply at delight (p. 20, TSS ed.; p. 101, Kashi ed.). It is concerned with injunctions and prohibitions (cf. Kuntaka on figurativeness of whole works). Following Nāyaka, he says that whereas scripture (the *Veda*) is predominantly a matter of words only (sacred utterances) and Tradition conveys its matter (meaning) without regard to the manner of expression, *kāvya* satisfies both requirements: matter expressed in an aesthetically (with *rasa*) acceptable manner, yet still aimed at education *vyutpatti* as a learned work *śāstra* (pp. 122 and 20, TSS ed.; pp. 483 and 101, Kashi ed.). In place of the figurativeness of whole works, of Kuntaka, Mahiman has a theory of enhancing *utkarṣa* or reducing *apakarṣa* the matter (p. 53, TSS ed.; pp. 264-5 Kashi ed.; Abhinavagupta II p. 298). A

299. The period that followed is characterised primarily by a growing scholasticism, typified perhaps by the ever popular (with the paṇḍits) manual of Mammaṭa (late +11), on which scores of commentaries have been written (partly because in a work which is syncretistic, though based on Ānandavardhana, numerous minor inconsistencies and problems of definition appear, partly because of the scholastic language borrowed from grammar and logic). There is an increasing component of linguistic and logical (or epistemological) analysis, interesting to the initiated but remote from the enjoyment of literature. There was also an encyclopaedic as opposed to analytical and critical trend, represented by Jayadeva's handbook of 'one hundred' (actually 108) figures of speech (+13), collected from miscellaneous sources. He at least criticised the traditional ten qualities and reduced them to eight. This simple work has long been a standard textbook for students in South India (it was written in Kaliṅga, modern Orissa). But Śobhākaramitra (+12) is the best analytic critic on the figures. Appayya (end of +16) added to the *Kuvalayānanda* 15 figures omitted or rejected by Jayadeva, and in that form the work has been in wide circulation since. These 123 figures are figures of meaning only: there was a similar proliferation of the figures of sound worked out by other theorists. A

300. What has been summarised in this chapter may perhaps suffice to indicate the main directions of Indian criticism, as well as something of the aims and techniques of the creative writers whose activity the critics sought to analyse. Good literature can be enjoyed without theoretical knowledge, but it can be enjoyed more when we have a vantage point and orientations provided by the ideas of the tradition which produced it, whether contemporary or, as must be the case with criticism, somewhat later but derivative from the literature itself. Understanding and enjoyment are easier when we have some first hand indication of the nature and aims of a literature, when we know what the authors sought to achieve and what current trends developed. Even when we look far back to the origins and early development of *kāvya*, the later perspective of critics reared in the *kāvya* tradition is helpful, since, for all the changes of fashion and taste, those critics were by-products of the long tradition itself and the ultimate sources of some of their guiding ideas must be sought at the beginnings of the *kāvya* movement.

301. The critics in turn influenced the creative writers. The dominating theory of the aesthetic experience *rasa*, which is very ancient but which has grown steadily in scope and pervasiveness throughout the history of *kāvya*, had a powerful effect on the work of the *kavis*. Thus the earlier *kāvyas* are remarkable for their variety of stories, whereas in later times we find the same stories, only with endless variations, selected again and again by writers who are in fact most anxious to be original. The reason for this lack of obvious novelty is to be found in the theory, particularly in the works of Ānandavardhana and Kuntaka : it is new ways of producing *rasa*, new expressions rich in implication, new incidents and situations in human intercourse, which authors wish to create—and an old and familiar story will serve very well as a vehicle for these. Indeed it may serve much better than a new one, for the familiarity of the characters and of the general outline of the story serve as common ground for writer and reader, which need not be laboriously described in order to bring the reader on the scene and acquaint him with the situation. The writer can get down immediately to the more intimate and congenial task of creating universal types of the infinitely varied incidents of life—let the 'hero' be 'Rāma' or 'Yudhiṣṭhira' or 'Udayana' or 'Sītā' or 'Vāsavadattā'—common humanity, common emotions link the reader, the author and the hero in a moment of struggle or repose, joy or sorrow or anger. The reader enters easily into relationship with the familiar hero, and so appreciates fully his surprise or delight at the unexpected incidents with which the author's originality upsets the course of the struggle. Not all late *kāvya* is like this, but such cases typify an important trend in literature which originated before the +5.

302. A secondary, but to the modern reader very important, effect of the critical work of the later theorists has been the recommendation of certain classics to connoisseurs and the neglect of others. In the disastrous period of the +2nd millennium, when the entire classical heritage was so nearly lost in the conflagrations of an alien fanaticism, the survival of books depended on the multiplication of copies and their dispersal all over India. Unfortunately the largest libraries, where alone many less favoured works were available, were destroyed when the Turks conquered Northern India (end of the +12). Subsequently many other libraries were destroyed, and. perhaps equally important in the long run, the patronage of governments and wealthy individuals, on which the production of copies and collection of libraries depended, was gradually abolished over the greater part of India. The extant literature comes from provincial collections which escaped and from the small libraries of private individuals and of the impoverished schools of the brahmans of Northern India. The most popular classics, and especially those preferred by the paṇḍits or traditional teachers, have come down to us in vast numbers of manuscripts, provided moreover with several dozen commentaries each, written by these paṇḍits, but by far the greater part of the *kāvya* written before +1200 has been lost.

303. The literature now available thus represents basically a selection made according to the tastes prevailing among the paṇḍits, which included a strong leaning towards grammatical and other complexity, worthy of a teacher's endeavours, and a distinct avoidance of novels unless their language was quite exceptionally difficult. The earlier *kāvya* has suffered severely through this rigorous selection, which was only partially compensated by some variation in the tastes of paṇḍits scattered all over India and by the continuance of the classical theatre and government patronage in the far South. Happily a fair number of neglected *kāvyas* have come to light in recent years in remote libraries, mostly in Kerala, and quite frequently classics long forgotten or known only by name are restored to us. Long may these discoveries continue ! The drama suffered the extreme persecution of the prohibition of the theatre on religious grounds in the greater part of India. A people for whom the drama was an essential and regular element in ordinary life, regardless of class or caste, and who possessed the world's richest dramatic heritage, were suddenly deprived of liberty and of the theatre, two precious possessions which have often been thought to be inseparable from one another. Here the total loss of the heritage except in the far South was prevented by the devotion of the paṇḍits to the drama, which as we have seen they regarded as the highest form of literature and of art, and by the widespread habit of reading plays.

304. The changed political circumstances and the tastes of the paṇḍits of course affected the writing of new *kāvyas* as well as the preservation of old ones. The work of *kavis* was scattered over the outlying regions, mainly in the South, which remained under Indian rule. Reinforcing the trend in literature noted above, in a period of heroic and desperate wars against a better armed (especially better mounted, at a time when cavalry was the decisive weapon) enemy, who aimed to destroy Indian civilisation completely, well known heroes of ancient legend and also of recent history formed the most popular subjects for *kāvya*. Fiction, whether in plays or novels, was not much cultivated. We have Devakavi (+13), Jinaharṣa and Ratnaśekhara (+14), Cāritrasundara and Arjunadāsa (+15), Narasiṃhasena, Sūranna and Jāyasī (+16), Ājñāsundara (+17) and Upendrabhaṃja, Rāmacandra, Timmakavi and Viśveśvara (+18). These are not many in comparison with the dramas and epics. Like the drama, the novel has been thought to have special connections with political liberty, in fact or at least (especially ?) in aspiration. Whatever truth there may be in this (and it requires a study of the precise types of novel in question), in India the novel flourished throughout the +1st millennium, having developed out of the imaginative prose stories of the —5 or earlier (of which we have rather special samples in the Pali Buddhist Canon). In the dark period, when much of India was gradually lost to the Turkish invaders, the novel seems to have found few *kavis* to cultivate it for five centuries, even in the independent regions. Heroic and romantic legend, not realism, inspired the Indian warriors of that period, and the novel revived only after the tide had finally turned against the Turks in the +18. The taste of the paṇḍits contributed strongly to the neglect of the novel, despite the interest in it evinced by the critics of the +11 (Bhoja, Soḍḍhala) and +12 (Hemacandra). Telling a story was evidently regarded by the learned as too unsophisticated a function for real literature, whilst the popular demand for stories was amply provided for by the literature of Tradition (the Great Epic and the *Purāṇas*) and by the making of numerous popular collections of short stories of simple style and rapid narrative. In *kāvya*, prose biographies *ākhyāyikās* continued to be written, but as they were usually of reigning monarchs, or enlightened princes and ministers, the undesirability of publishing anything which could be represented as a libel against a powerful or wealthy person ensured that the writers would cast their subjects as very generic heroes. At the same time most *kavis* who wished to cultivate prose did so in the new form called *campū*—prose with mingled verses—which has been immensely popular as a medium for reinterpreting the legends of Tradition since the +11.

CHAPTER V

THE LITERARY FORMS : THE DRAMA

305. If we except certain special applications such as panegyric (*praśasti* : the official bombast in *kāvya* style used especially in inscriptions [1292], and fashions such as the *campū* (a story usually from Tradition told in mixed prose and verse—ancient as a popular narrative form but admitted to the class of *kāvya* only late and reluctantly, then much cultivated from the +10 onwards as a medium for epic, historical or fictitious matter), then the main forms of *kāvya* are five in number (as laid down by Bhāmaha, 1. 18) :

A. Drama *nāṭya*,

B. Epic (*sargabandha*, 'canto composition', or simply *mahākāvya*, 'great *kāvya*'),

C. Lyric (*anibaddha*, 'independent verses', or *khaṇḍakāvya*, 'short *kāvya*'),

D. Biography (*ākhyāyikā*, 'history' —usually of a living or recently living person),

E. Novel (*kathā*, 'story', 'tale'—the 'short story' was sometimes admitted as a sub-variety).

306. A. The drama is in mixed prose and verse : prose dialogue interspersed with lyrics, some or all of which are intended to be sung. Music is in fact very important in the production : musicians perform an 'overture' before the play, including several movements with songs and dances, and certain themes *dhruvās* may be heard during the play at appropriate moments (entrance of a character, change of *rasa* or of place, etc.) to produce the right atmosphere or to enhance the effect of the plot [1096, 1614]. Characters singing lyrics would sometimes be accompanied, and sometimes leitmotivs would herald the entrance of a character or an important event. Bharata, who deals with music at great length within the framework of the *Nāṭyaśāstra*, recommends certain musical modes (*jātis*, the ancestors of the modern *rāgas*) as appropriate for the successive conjunctions *sandhis* in the development of the plot (Chapter XXIX, Kāśī ed.; also XXXII 23f, 335ff, 453ff.).

307. These musical arrangements were normally not the concern of the *kavi* but only of the producer *sūtradhāra* and the musical director on any particular occasion of performance. The extant texts of dramas contain only the words and stage directions (the latter are copious). Later critics pay little attention to the musical aspect of the drama, and the extant plays are purely literary in appearance, suggesting that at least from an early period the music was an ornamental adjunct rather than an integral part of the drama. We know also from some writers, including at least one dramatist (Rājaśekhara, early +10), that plays were written with readers in mind as well as audiences (*Bālarāmāyaṇa* 1.12). Nevertheless the surviving practice of the theatre upholds in principle the musical conventions of Bharata. In fact it is probable that performances have varied greatly in response to changes in fashion. The full length plays are very long, as we have seen in Chapter III, so that if the verses are sung an act must take up the greater part of a day or a night even if the songs are kept as simple as possible. In Indian theatrical custom such long sessions are quite normal, and on the other hand the practice developed or was even original, as we have seen [161], of performing only one act at a day's session, so that a complete play would take several days. In these productions the performance is extremely elaborate and unhurried. The *Naṭāṅkuśa* (+15?) resists the trend by saying that music should be confined to the *pūrvaraṅga* [309] except for the *dhruvās* [2794].

308. In origin as in its later history the drama appears to have been connected with festivals. It was associated with dancing and seems to have developed gradually out of displays of dancing on festive occasions, when myths and legends were represented. Acting probably grew out of dancing, and a rich gesture language remained common to both. The festival of the Vedic god Indra, especially, was the ancient occasion for a play, though later his position was usurped by the Goddess of Literature, Sarasvatī. The festival performance includes a great deal of preliminary ritual and dancing apparently quite unconnected with the play : we are perhaps present at an originally religious function. The *Veda* itself contains certain dialogue poems suggestive of dramatic representation (see Chapter IX below), and the Buddhist *Āgama* has similar dialogues and dramatic episodes (see Chapters XI and XII below).

These may be the relics of the earliest phase of the Indian drama. [510, 544, 562, 570-2, 587-607]

309. There are other indications, especially in the *Nāṭyaśāstra*, that the drama is much more ancient than *kāvya* generally. As soon as it matured sufficiently to become independent of its presumed religious origin and to be cultivated for its own sake, drama became the dominant form of *kāvya*. A conjectural date for this development would be not later than *c.* –400. We shall see, however, that besides this probable source in religious festivals at least two other streams of dramatic performances appear to have converged to constitute the drama as a form of *kāvya*. Before discussing these we may review briefly the opening proceedings *pūrvaraṅga*, or ritual, which ought in theory to precede any performance of a play, though in practice it was often abridged (*Nāṭyaśāstra* V, Viśvanātha VI.23 [3869]).

310. In outline the *pūrvaraṅga* consists of : music, a song with gestures, a dance, the setting up of Indra's 'standard' *jarjara*, the *nāndī* (opening benediction), a musical theme appropriate for the particular occasion of the performance, a transition from ritual to drama, dramatic songs and verses and finally the actual prologue, usually provided by the author, generally some humorous 'business' leading to the announcement of the play.

311. In more detail (V.17 ff.), the ritual begins (*pratyāhāra* and *avataraṇa*) with the musicians and singers taking their places behind the curtain (which is in the middle of the stage: it is used for the 'entrance' of an actor; the musicians are thus at the back of the stage). The singers and instrumentalists then exercise their voices *ārambha* and tune their instruments *āśrāvaṇā*, and proceed to practice various kinds of music together (these *bahirgītas*, 'outside songs', are described in detail in the musical section of the *Nāṭyaśāstra* XXIX. 115ff., Kāśī).. [2504]

312. The curtain is now removed and a song *gītaka* with gestures is performed : here the *tāṇḍava* dance (of Śiva) may be used [361]. After this comes the theme *dhruvā* called *utthāpanī*, 'setting up', which announces the entrance of the producer, who, with two assistants, offers flowers to Brahmā and sets up Indra's standard, which one of the assistants has carried on to the stage. With a second theme called *parivartinī* ('moving round') the producer moves about the stage and makes reverence to various gods, after which a third assistant brings him more flowers and he offers these to Indra's standard. He (or another actor in old dramas) then (or alternatively after another, very slow, theme with song : *geyāvakṛṣṭā*) recites the *nāndī*. This is followed by a theme without words (but with meaningless syllables sung to it: *śuṣkāpakṛṣṭā*) in honour of the standard. [2763]

313. Another verse in honour of Indra's standard (which seems at this point to be removed) indicates the 'entrance to the stage' *raṅgadvāra*, which from now on is the scene not of ritual but of drama. Dramatic songs follow, *cārī* [3915] and *mahācārī* each with its own theme. The first (called *aḍḍitā*, V. 119) is 'sensitive' (e.g. on Śiva and Pārvatī, according to Abhinavagupta, I. p. 219), thus introducing an element proper to drama, not ritual; the second is addressed to Śiva (e.g. celebrating his destruction of demons) and includes a 'furious' *rasa* verse (another dramatic element) and a song *gāna* of the class called *natkuṭaka* (V. 135, characterised by a group of semimusical metres used for the verses—XXXII. 304 ff.).

314. At last we have reached the *trigata* [cf. 326 below], in which the producer addresses the audience. The texts of plays generally begin here with a prologue *sthāpanā* [950, 1013]. Usually there is a humorous interlude or interruption at this point (comic business written by the dramatist to introduce his play), but either directly or indirectly the producer announces the play *prarocanā* and this ends the *pūrvaraṅga*. By various devices the producer here introduces the first character to appear in the play, as indicated above [139] in discussing the structure of the drama (prologue with rhetorical devices for leading in to the play XXII. 26 ff). [2763]

315. In practice these preliminaries were varied (V. 160 ff.), and might be abridged to almost any degree, provided only that the benediction was retained. Thus it appears that from perhaps about the +3 onwards severe abridgement was usual and long ritual preliminaries no longer tolerated: from this period the dramatist himself supplied the benediction and announcement, including mention of the occasion of performance, with business leading on through the prologue to the play. Some musical preliminaries, however, a kind of 'overture', would doubtless be retained to divert the audience and prepare their mood whilst accommodating latecomers.

316. We see then that dramas were often performed on the occasions of festivals originally religious in character, that they originally at least opened with the worship of various gods, especially Indra, Brahmā and Śiva, that they were performed at temples (especially of the goddess Sarasvatī—this does not mean in a temple proper, but in a theatre built within the temple grounds, as may be seen today in Kerala) as well as in other theatres, and that traces of a religious function appear in the inclusion of benedictions (opening and final) and in the auspicious ending.

317. Turning to the actual stories of the early drama we find that, of the ten main types of drama usually recognised, three are religious in content (the types called cooperation *samavakāra*, fight *ḍima* and rape *īhāmṛga*). They are religious in the sense that they are based on the mythology and legends of the Vedic tradition or of those of the worshippers of Śiva or Viṣṇu. It is remarkable that in spite of their theoretical prominence hardly any plays of these types are extant in the classical heritage. The few that are available are in fact quite late, moreover they seem somewhat artificial in composition, as if written to supply an occasional connoisseur's demand for plays of all the theoretical types, rather than as a natural form of expression for their writers or their period. Yet we are told in the *Nāṭyaśāstra* that a *samavakāra* and a *ḍima* were the first two plays ever performed when the drama was invented. Admittedly this tradition is mythical, since the inventor was Brahmā, the Creator, and the performances took place in Heaven before the gods, but there is no reason to suppose that the myth would be false in asserting the great antiquity of these types of play. We conclude then that religious plays were important in the earliest known period of drama but that they were obsolete from an early date in the history of *kāvya*. This agrees with the basically secular character of the heritage of *kāvya* as now known to us, which we have already noticed.

318. If the religious stream contributing to the early drama was of great importance at first, but dwindled to an irrelevant vestige when *kāvya* was consolidated as an essentially secular art, the second stream, flowing from Tradition, has remained powerful and predominates in the extant heritage. Tradition, that is the Great Epic and the constantly growing body of legends and history which clustered round it, occupies a position intermediate between scripture (canonical religious literature) and *kāvya*. Though not admitted to the status of scripture by the prevailing orthodox opinion, not being a supernatural revelation, it nevertheless claimed to be a fifth *Veda* and was recognised by some as authoritative on religious matters because uttered by ancient sages. Like the Buddhist, Śaiva, Vaiṣṇava and other Non-Vedic canonical literature it was accessible to everybody, whereas the other four *Vedas* were supposed to be restricted to the twice-born upper classes. Thus Tradition became a medium of religious instruction as well as of entertainment for the masses of the people, and came to be widely accepted as a source of religion, though the orthodox opinion remained that any religious statement in it, if true, was so only because it had been taken from the *Veda* (the Four *Vedas*), and that anything in it which conflicted with the *Veda* was false (in other words it had no independent authority and was not reliable——discussions in the Mīmāṁsā schools on the interpretation of Jaimini 1.3.3). This position turned out to be privileged and influential, since it reached the majority of the people, since political revolutions from time to time swept away the old aristocracy and created a new one of upstarts from the lower orders and since the Epic was always appreciated by the aristocratic and military class, whether of genuinely ancient twice-born families or only so by adoption or fictions. In fact Tradition gradually usurped the position of being a major and even dominant factor in the religion of the Indian people, and for *kāvya* provided, amongst other things, what may be regarded as the religious moment of orientation and assumptions in the comprehensive reproduction of life. Drama also is claimed in the *Nāṭyaśāstra* to be the fifth *Veda*, as we have seen [34]. It thus claimed to replace Tradition in this rôle. In fact public recitations of the Epic have never lost their popularity, but dramatised versions of episodes from it were produced in an early period and three of the main types of drama (the 'play' or history *nāṭaka*, heroic play *vyāyoga* and pathetic play *utsṛṣṭikāṅka*) have stories taken from Tradition (including more recent history) and a fourth type (the street play *vīthī*) may use such a story. The majority of dramas now extant have stories from Tradition, though the dramatists have interpreted them with the utmost freedom [285]. A

319. The third stream converging to provide the range of types of drama recognised in *kāvya* is also ancient, as is attested by theory, by examples from the earliest period from which dramas are extant, and perhaps by human probability. This is the stream of plays composed primarily for amusement, though they may have a spice of instruction and philosophy. From this most secular stream come the comedy *prahasana* and the satirical monologue *bhāṇa* among the ten main types of play, and probably also the street play (which however may also use a story from Tradition), whilst the sophisticated *prakaraṇa* ('fiction') is a larger scale comedy evolved from it.

320. The ten main types-of-play *rūpakas* generally recognised from the *Nāṭyaśāstra* onwards are as follows (*Nāṭyaśāstra* XX Kāśī, XVIII Baroda).

321. I Formally the simplest, and possibly the most primitive, is the satirical monologue *bhāṇa*, in one act [1101, 1444]. The single actor, however, invariably acts the part of a parasite *viṭa* [27,30]. Usually engaged in some errand for a *nāgaraka*, the parasite progresses without undue haste through the streets of some great metropolis where all the follies and vices of mankind are likely to flourish (the city is normally the capital of the country in which the play was written and so probably the place where it was first produced). On the way, the actor mimics his meetings with a variety of acquaintances, such as geisha girls, actresses and a selection of foolish or vicious men, including bogus ascetics, sterile tutors, vain poets and the pleasure-seeking sons of wealthy merchants, officers or ministers. The parasite describes the scene, and the characters imagined to be met, and in the supposed conversations repeats what they say: 'What do you say? "...." ?' (this is called *ākāśabhāṣita*, 'speech in space'). He is often detained on the way with requests to undertake fresh business, but is usually able to postpone this after consoling his client with flattering talk. His brilliant repartee is equal to most emergencies, but sometimes he has to take evasive action. Chiefly, however, he laughs at the characters he observes in their absurd vanity, or deplores the foolishness of those who deceive themselves—for example those who imagine they have inspired sincere affection in a geisha——

though always perfectly polite and reassuring to their faces. Eventually he succeeds in performing his errand, or finds that by that time it has become superfluous. Evidently the plays of this type now extant (and their theory) are as far as possible from a really primitive drama except in having only one actor, which we might presume to represent the first step in a conjectured development of drama out of a recited narrative.

322. II Similar in some respects is the one act *vīthī*, 'street (play)', of which, however, with one possible exception [1074-5], only very late examples seem to be available (other earlier examples are referred to and quoted from in theoretical works, but seem to have been lost [1151]). This type may have either one or two actors and is normally a dialogue (one critic finds three also : Sāgaranandin 2906; in fact there are three parts in the *Mālatikā* : the heroine, the king and the jester [1151]). There is no restriction on the kinds of character represented, nor on the type of story. The paucity of examples preserved in the classical heritage suggests that this type of play, perhaps more genuinely primitive than the satirical monologue, flourished only in a popular milieu --on the streets-- and was generally ignored by the classical dramatists and critics, who were interested in serious drama in a regular theatre or a palace, assembly hall or temple precinct.

323. It is of course clear that the classical heritage as preserved is primarily a collection (or rather collections) of serious and substantial literary works such as seem most rewarding to readers. We have hardly such a thing as a classical theatrical repertory, since over a period of centuries nearly all the theatres of India were closed by the Turks or the British. Only in the South and in Nepal has the living theatre survived to the present day, and it is noteworthy that it is precisely in the South, and nowhere else, that street plays are available in some numbers from recent centuries and are still flourishing in performance. Where acting was suppressed the minor works of classical dramatists were forgotten and the popular, as opposed to the literary, theatre vanished.

324. Most extant street plays have been written from the +16 onwards in Āndhra, Karṇāṭaka, Tamilnāḍu and Kerala. In Āndhra, where they are still performed in some villages, they are mostly in the Telugu language; they are there called either *vīthī* or *yakṣagāna*, the latter name being more usual. In the far South, in Tanjore (Tañjanagara), Madurā and Trivandrum (Anantaśayana), the type flourished in court circles in the same period, being often in Sanskrit and acted in the court assembly. The stories are often taken from Tradition, including especially the exploits of Kṛṣṇa, though a Tanjore prince composed a *yakṣagāna* celebrating the deeds of his father, whilst a geisha girl at his court wrote one with the prince himself as hero. Comedies of palace intrigue are also found, with *nāṭikā*-like plots (cf. below [339]). The *yakṣagānas* may have a single actress who speaks, sings and dances the story, but the classical-type *vīthīs* are dialogues with two actors, e. g. a king and his jester. Another feature in what may be the oldest extant *vīthī* (if in fact it is a *vīthī*), is the use of a painting depicting the traditional story described in the dialogue [1075, 1151]. *Yakṣagānas* may now have many actors.

325. In connection with the street play the *Nāṭyaśāstra* (XX. 117ff.) describes a set of thirteen rhetorical devices called its 'limbs' *aṅgas*. Practically all of these depend on equivocation (*vakrokti* in Rudraṭa's sense [257] : *Nāṭyadarpaṇa* 116 f.) and thus indicate that the type had its basis in witty repartee in the 'eloquent' mode. These limbs may be used in other types of play also, and it is remarkable that in the theory they should have been introduced under the street play and named after it. This seems to confirm that the type is extremely ancient and that these devices, evolved for its dialogue, were later taken over for the drama as a whole. The street play technique appears especially in the latter part of the opening proceedings *pūrvaraṅga* (*trigata*, etc.) or the prologue of plays of all types.

326. The limbs of the street play are as follows. The first two, the misunderstood word *udghātyaka* and parallelism *avalagita*, are the same as the two rhetorical devices so named for leading in from a prologue to the play proper [139], but used elsewhere in a play. Thus Bhoja (see Raghavan, *Bhoja's Śṛṅgāraprakāśa*, p.887) quotes the street play *Mālatikā* [1151] for an example of misunderstood word, where the heroine mentions 'transmigration' and the king brings in the stock analogy of the 'ocean' in order to turn the conversation towards his own 'ocean of unhappiness' (the same example is given by Bahurūpamiśra on *Daśarūpaka* III 13f). The *trigata*, which might be interpreted as 'open speech' or apparently letting out the truth (but it may be a misunderstanding and not true at all), has been mentioned already in a special application as part of the *pūrvaraṅga* [314] or prologue; the essential feature seems to be that a third party overhears what is being said [1611]—which in the *pūrvaraṅga* means the audience. The *Nāṭyadarpaṇa* (p. 126) illustrates *trigata* from the street play *Indulekhā* [1151], where a king speaks to his jester of anklets jingling like the sweet cry of a duck, a remark which presumably is overheard. Outwitting *adhibala* is also a limb of the embryo [148]: an example given in the present connection is from the *Kṛtyārāvaṇa* [1350], where Śūrpaṇakhā impersonating Sītā criticises Lakṣmaṇa for not going to help Rāma and thus succeeds in shaming him into going, opening the way for Rāvaṇa. Simple equivocation *chala*, for purposes of deception, is another limb, also the slip (of the tongue) *avasyandita* [1364], nonsensical speech *asatpralāpa* [1407], play on words *vākkelī* (for purposes of repartee) [1236] and a joke *vyāhāra*, the last for example where the jester on seeing a geisha's mother asks how they got her through the gateway of the house after it was built [1187]. Ironical flattery *prapañca* is usually for teasing [1188,1376]: Sāgaranandin (3025) says it may be known in the street play called *Rādhā*, but unfortunately does not quote from it. The riddle *nālikā* is illustrated by Cāṇakya 's secret agent speaking of the Moon (Candra, meaning Candragupta) to the pupil so that the master may recognise who he is [1637]. Bhoja gives an example of it from the street play *Mālatikā* (Raghavan, *Bhoja's Śṛṅgāraprakāśa*, 888f., omitted in Josyer's edition), which in the absence of any context is a riddle for modern readers. The *gaṇḍa* is a speech having a double meaning which suddenly becomes clear and as a rule portends something bad. Sāgaranandin (3004 ff.) finds an example in the Exaltation of the Rāghava [1584], where Sītā mentions 'separation' in speaking to Rāma. Distortion *mṛdava* is speech contrived so as to make a fault of a good quality or a good quality of a fault, as in debating. For example the general in the *Abhijñānaśākuntala* [1418] praises hunting (II.5) insincerely (as good exercise, etc.), because he thinks that is what the king expects of him, whilst hoping the jester's opposition to it will be successful.

327. III The comedy *prahasana*, as also all the remaining main types of play, may have any number of actors. It normally has one act, but more rarely two. The favourite victims of satire in this type of play are *yogins* and other saintly characters, whether bogus or even genuine in their pretensions[1085]. It was for satirising the sages in heaven in comedies that the actors were cursed by their victims to be of low (*śūdra*) class, according to the *Nāṭyaśāstra* (Kāśī XXXVI. 29ff). All the rascals, charlatans and fools met with in great cities and described in the satirical monologues appear in comedies, and also corrupt officers, crooked ministers and disastrous kings. The critics classify comedies according to the characters appearing in them [1598]. Śiṅgabhūpāla (*Rasārṇavasudhākara* pp. 290 ff) seems to be the only critic to describe ten 'limbs' of comedy, namely in special senses : parallelism, jumping in, transaction, deception, application, fear, untruth, confusion, faltering and chatter. We have discussed these below in connection with an actual comedy [1094-5].

328. IV From Tradition, from the Epic usually, we have (besides some street plays) the one act heroic play *vyāyoga* presenting a short episode [946]. [6600 ff]

329. V Likewise from Tradition arises the one act tragic, compassionate or pathetic play *utsṛṣṭikāṅka*, the neglect of which in the extant heritage emphasises the disappearance of the idea of tragedy in Indian literature after the (true) Epic had been largely displaced by *kāvya*. It was in any case a convention in *kāvya* that the ending must be auspicious, but this was not so much a theoretical restriction as a simple reflection of the prevailing outlook in Indian society from at least the –6, which we have discussed above [63-67]. Moral causation—that everyone reaps the just reward of his actions—and transmigration——allowing this to happen after death and robbing death of its significance—— annihilated tragedy. Only the Lokāyata philosophers denied moral causation and transmigration, but tragedy would hardly appeal to these advocates of the pursuit of happiness. Tragic episodes from the Epic, which is full of tragedy, thus became in *kāvya* transitory pathetic incidents (such as death and separation) ending not with tragic finality but with the attainment, or the prospect, of a happier state [950]. There was however the convention that death should not be represented on the stage : this was easily satisfied by converting death into transformation or into the direct translation of the dying hero to Heaven [954]. The type could be adapted to Jainism [3192, 7012 ff] A

330. VI Among the religious plays the *samavakāra*, 'cooperation', in three acts, represents a myth. At the same time it has sensitive and comic elements and uses the limbs of the street play. Although sophisticated in form (besides having three acts the detailed structure of the type is peculiarly complex as laid down in theory[154], this traditionally primaeval play (after the initial experiment, which almost ended in disaster through provoking a section of the audience [41], a cooperation was the first play performed before the gods and demons) is primitive in its story. The myths represented are cooperative ventures by the gods in the remotest antiquity, sometimes also by the gods *devas* united with their rivals the demons (*asuras*, also heavenly beings, but often disputing the possession of Heaven with the gods and ultimately being expelled and forced to live below the Earth instead of above). The *Nāṭyaśāstra* says the 'seed' is the gods and demons, as if these should always be present in a cooperation. It is laid down that there must be a large number of joint heroes in a cooperation, that they must be divine, not human, and that they must all gain their desires. The type thus seems to reflect the most ancient social reality, that of primitive communism, and, as we shall see in the action of the first cooperation, its ethos and perhaps its break up into a society of antagonistic groups or classes [37-40].

331. The first cooperation, according to the *Nāṭyaśāstra* (IV. 2ff.), represented the myth of the Churning of the Ambrosia (from the Ocean), in which the gods and demons together churned a variety of precious things out of the primaeval ocean (which resembled milk), including the ambrosia of immortality, the Moon, the goddess Lakṣmī (Fortune, who became Viṣṇu's wife) and Indra's elephant. Conflict, essential to drama, is produced by the avarice of the demons, who attempt to appropriate the highest fruits of the venture (especially the ambrosia) to themselves, denying the gods their share. The gods counter deception with deeper deception and the demons are foiled (the theory prescribes deception and disguise as prominent in a cooperation). [6521 ff]

332. Another myth dramatised in a cooperation is the

Origin of Kumāra (the God of War). Here the gods, overcome by the demons, seek a liberator. Only a son of the Great God Śiva, according to an oracle, can conquer the powerful enemy, but Śiva (the Great *Yogin*—probably originally of the non-Aryan, non-Vedic Indus Civilisation) is absorbed in meditation and inaccessible even to the gods. At last they attain their end through the intervention of the goddess Umā, whom Śiva marries for the sake of *dharma* (religion, duty). The hero Kumāra is born, defeats the demons at once in his mere infancy and frees the gods from oppression, (see Abhinavagupta II p. 440) [1147]. There are several myths on the theme of the wars of the gods and demons [513, 589], glorifying various divine hero-liberators and of diverse origin as various religions coalesced with Vedic Brahmanism to form the Purāṇic Tradition. Abhinavagupta's mention of Śakra (Indra) and Ahalyā (p. 440) perhaps refers to the story of the *Śakrānanda*, a cooperation named by Sāgaranandin (2812), though it could hardly have been more than one incident in an otherwise cooperative venture of the gods. Perhaps in harmony with its mythological character the cooperation is said to use 'crooked' (Vedic) metres (*Nāṭyaśāstra* XX. 80, v. 1.).

333. VII The *ḍima*, 'fight', is in four acts and represents a victory of a god or gods over the demons, or more rarely the victory of a human hero [658, 1148]. The 'expressive' and 'violent' modes are used. The action is violent throughout and no female characters appear. The sensitive and comic experiences are excluded. The initial experiment in Heaven, performed before the assembled gods and demons to celebrate the Festival of Indra's Standard, was apparently of this type, since it is said to have represented a victory of the gods over the demons[41]. After the performance of the cooperation 'Churning of the Ambrosia', composed by Brahmā, the next drama performed is definitely stated to have been a fight, the *Tripuradāha* representing a victory of Śiva over 3 demons (*Nāṭyaśāstra* IV. 10). This was played before Śiva in the Himālayas (his home). He was delighted and suggested that instead of a plain performance the play could be adorned with his dance, the *tāṇḍava*, in its *pūrvaraṅga* (see earlier in this Chapter [312] and No. XXIII below). Accordingly he arranged for the actors ('Bharata' and his company) to be instructed in its numerous gestures and movements. [6559 ff]

334. VIII The third type of religious play is the *īhāmṛga*, 'rape', which usually has four acts but may have only one (*Nāṭyadarpaṇa* p. 116; *Nāṭyaśāstra* silent on this point but interpreted by Abhinavagupta, II p. 442, as indicating only one, as in a heroic play; other works 'four'). A heroine, who must be divine (a goddess, or at least a 'nymph', *apsaras*), is carried off after the defeat of her relatives by a hero, who may be either divine or human. The stories are taken from the Vedic myths and legends or from those of the Kṛṣṇa tradition [658, 1149]. [6578 ff.]

335. After these eight relatively primitive types of play we come to the real territory of the classical drama and the greatest dramatists with the remaining two main types, the *nāṭaka* and the *prakaraṇa*, which provide the utmost scope for development and alone use the 'tender' mode of stage business (*Nāṭyaśāstra* XX. 7 ff.) [181]. It is worth noting here that the *Nāṭyaśāstra* divides drama into two classes according to the manner of performance or acting *prayoga*, the 'violent' *āviddha* and the 'delicate' *sukumāra* (XIV. 57 ff.). The former corresponds roughly to the expressive and violent modes. The three types of religious play are all classed as 'violent', along with the heroic play. The *nāṭaka* and *prakaraṇa*, which we are about to discuss, are classed with the satirical monologue, street play and the pathetic play as 'delicate'. The comedy is not mentioned here, it might perhaps belong to either kind of acting. It is evident that the 'delicate' drama, which is more human (XIV. 62), outstripped the 'violent' and divine (XIV. 61) in popularity, probably by about the +1. The classification, however, refers to the manner of playing rather than to the subject simply, though of course appropriate to it. Thus the *nāṭaka* usually has a story taken from Tradition, like the heroic play, yet it is 'delicate'. It is in fact treated by the dramatists in a very different way from the more primitive types of play: the emphasis, as befits the sophisticated theory of the aesthetic experience outlined in the *Nāṭyaśāstra*, is on the psychological aspect of drama instead of merely on the outward action.

336. IX The *nāṭaka*, 'play' (par excellence, or 'history'), which may have from five to ten acts, has a 'well-known' *prakhyāta* story *vastu*, that is one taken from Tradition or from more recent history. It is understood that the details may be to some extant invented (see Mātṛgupta, quoted by Śāradātanaya p.234). The theory of the arrangement in acts and introductory scenes has particular reference to the *nāṭaka*. There was a tendency among the most celebrated dramatists to prefer seven acts for this type of play[161], but five or six acts remained quite regular and eight, nine or ten are occasionally found [1044, 1309, 1026, 964, 1033, 1349, 1616, 1586, 156, 717, 1161]. This type gave scope for the full application of the theory, both of the structure and modes and of the psychological and aesthetic development. The general theory in fact applies primarily to the *nāṭaka*, which is taken as a standard from which other types diverge. Only certain kinds of violent action found in fights, cooperations, rapes and heroic plays are excluded from it. Though the majority of *nāṭakas* are dominated by either the sensitive or the heroic, and this is recognised as appropriate by the critics, a number of them centre on other kinds of aesthetic experience. Besides the dominant *rasa* and a related secondary kind, touching sporadically on the whole gamut of the others was approved in a major play. On the other hand in the types of play having four or fewer acts the full structure of conjunctions and so on is not deployed and the kinds of aesthetic experience produced are limited and specialised: e. g. heroic (heroic play), compassionate (tragic play), comic (comedy), furious (fight). It is noted (*Nātyaśāstra* XX. 40) that in the (more restrained) *nāṭaka* and *prakaraṇa* there should not be a great crowd of of characters on the stage but only four or five, whereas in the four violent types there will be ten or twelve. Subandhu's theory of five classes of *nāṭaka* has been noted above [165].

337. X The *prakaraṇa*, 'fiction', has a story 'invented' *utpādya* (or *autpattika*, *Nāṭyaśāstra* XX. 49) by the dramatist, but in other respects generally resembles the *nāṭaka*, as especially in having from five to ten acts (but with a preference for the maximum of ten) [998, 1367, 1011, 1373, 1182]. The fact of the invented story, however, as opposed to one from Tradition or history, results in the *prakaraṇas* dealing with bourgeois and other private and lower class life including the circles of the *nāgarakas* and the milieu of the satirical monologue, instead of being practically confined to the warrior princes of antiquity and other public figures as are the *nāṭakas*. Since a *prakaraṇa* seems also to have been allowed to borrow a story from an earlier *prakaraṇa*, or from a novel, the border line between it and the *nāṭaka* is not always clear, or may be arbitrary depending on the exact definition of 'well-known' versus 'invented'. The *Nāṭyadarpaṇa* (p. 104) sets out a scheme of seven degrees of inventedness, which in fact would cover some *nāṭakas*, as when a well-known hero attains an invented objective. In a sense also all plots of plays are invented, in that the dramatist is expected to produce a new interpretation and new incidents in any story : a dozen superficially similar dramas, which might seem to repel interest, will be found on reading to agree only on the barest outline and to be completely different in characterisation and the other essentials.

338. Generally the critics seem to have regarded as *nāṭakas* any plays dealing with Tradition or history (the translation 'history' would almost fit this type, but as it may be confusing it is convenient to keep the Sanskrit term), and as *prakaraṇas* any plays dealing with stories of fictitious origin even if they had been told before (the stories of Tradition are supposed to be actual history, as many of them doubtless really are based on historical events). Regrettably, far fewer *prakaraṇas* than *nāṭakas* have been preserved (though we know from the critics that many once existed : for example there was a division of them into 21 sub-varieties, or even 42 in theory, which presumably had some practical basis—*Nāṭyadarpaṇa* p.105 and Abhinavagupta II p. 433), owing to the preoccupation of late medieval India with the upholding of its traditions and ideals against alien aggressors. In the era of heroic wars against the Turks the Indian kingdoms were inspired by the glory of ancient heroes and just rulers; neither a type of drama often critical of social conventions (which a staunch Brahmanical traditionalist might prefer to idealise), nor the novel, were much appreciated. Like the *nāṭaka*, the *prakaraṇa* provides scope for the deployment of the full practice of drama and generally the same kinds of aesthetic experience, with probably a greater infusion of the comic. It tended indeed to rather greater length and complexity, and there is a preference for the *prakaraṇa* to have ten acts.

339. XI Besides the ten main types-of-play, the *Nāṭyaśāstra* (XX. 60 ff.) describes one secondary type, called the *nāṭī* or *nāṭikā*, 'little play'. It has only four acts but in other essentials resembles the *nāṭaka*, whilst in character it is usually a pure comedy (and mostly fictitious though the hero is a historical king, sometimes a contemporary one). On the conjunctions in a light play see below [997]. The theory notes song and dance as appropriate for this type. Examples have been preserved from all periods [990]. [6637 ff.]

340. The *Nāṭyaśāstra* does not mention any other types of play, though it deals so thoroughly with all aspects of the theatre. Later writers describe a large number of other types of play or theatrical performance, including plays or musical plays as well as dances or ballets, adding altogether about thirty new items to the ten main types of play of the *Nāṭyaśāstra*. Some of these are evidently derived from the system of dances given in the *Nāṭyaśāstra*, especially the *lāsya* ('dancing') actually described at the end of its chapter on the types of play in one version (Kāśī XX. 136ff.) but in the chapter on the construction of plays in the other (Baroda XIX. 117 ff.). This *lāsya* is danced by one person, for which reason it is compared with the satirical monologue, but is to be used 'in a play' *nāṭake*, hence presumably not independently as a performance on its own. Before we consider this *lāsya* (as No. XXIV below [362]) and how it gave rise to independent dances, let us review those other types of performance mentioned by later writers which are more like actual plays. These types-of-play (and dance production or ballet) not recognised by the *Nāṭyaśāstra* are probably of later development, rather than simply of minor importance. They are poorly represented in the extant heritage of Indian theatre, which as we have noted earlier reflects primarily the literary tastes of scholars in the later middle ages and more recent times, not the real situation when the classical theatre was flourishing. Some minor productions of a more 'popular' character would obviously be ephemeral, corresponding to changing tastes and transient novelties of form.

341. The later writers agree that it was Kohala who first described some of these minor types of performance, and a Kohala and his *Uttaratantra*, *i.e.* 'Supplement', are actually mentioned in the available *Nāṭyaśāstra* text (at the end : XXXVI. 65 Kāśī). This supplement is not now available : it is presumably to be dated at the end of the successive periods of elaboration of the *Nāṭyaśāstra* text which we discussed in Chapter II, perhaps in the +2, possibly a little earlier. It is not clear how many minor types Kohala mentioned; from Abhinavagupta we can see that he seems to have dealt with at least the *toṭaka*, *saṭṭaka*, *rāsaka* and (*rāga*) *kāvya* (I pp. 171, 182; III p. 72; manuscript text quoted by Raghavan, *Bhoja's Śṛṅgāraprakāśa*, p. 536). Abhinavagupta says that Bharata himself had them in mind in mentioning *saindhava* ('of the Sindhu country') as a 'limb' (kind) of *lāsya* [363], because this implies a Prakrit dialect and many of the minor types were in Prakrit, such as a *rāsaka* he refers to as in the Saindhava language itself (III. 72). But this is reading far too much into the solo *lāsya*.

342. The *Kāmasūtra* (p. 154: II. 10. 25) mentions *hallīsaka* (which is in fact a group dance; Bhāsa includes one in his *nāṭaka Bālacarita* [1049], probably+2; variant spelling *hallīśa*) and *nāṭyarāsaka*; *prekṣaṇaka* there (p. 45, etc.) may mean drama generally rather than the specific minor type of that name known later. Bodhāyana in the prologue to his *Bhagavadajjukīya* mentions *sallāpa* and *vāra* with the main types (making twelve main types) [1085]. An apocryphal section in the old Poona edition of the *Harivaṃśa*, a supplement to the Great Epic, of perhaps the+4, mentions *chālikya* (a dance) [367], and Bhāmaha (I.24) mentions *dvipadī* (No. XXVIII below) [370], *śamyā*, *skandhaka*, 'etc.,' along with *rāsaka*, as branches of drama (dramatic *kāvya*, to be acted). A group of dances prominent later, beginning with the *ḍombī* (No. XXX below [377]), usually called *nṛtyas* ('dances,' 'ballets'), may have developed out of the *rāgakāvya* (see No. XXXVIII below [389]) or directly from the *lāsya*.

343. XII The *toṭaka* (or *troṭaka*) is usually described as a variety of *nāṭaka* (Sāgaranandin 2766 ff., Śāradātanaya p. 238). Several of the theorists omit it altogether, presumably considering it not distinct from the *nāṭaka*. Its main characteristic is said to be that the story (which must be well known, as in a *nāṭaka*) shows the meeting of gods and men, and in practice the examples seem mostly to be myths and legends concerning the nymphs *apsarases*, who are divine beings, in their affairs with men [1402, 1581]. There might seem to be some resemblance to the 'rape', but the atmosphere is different, romantic and 'delicate', not 'violent', and the *toṭaka* has five or more acts like any other *nāṭaka*. A feature which does not appear to be mentioned in the available theoretical works, but which is prominent in at least part of the only *toṭaka* which seems to have been printed (Kālidāsa's *Vikramo-*

rvaśīya, act IV), is the insertion of songs and dances showing the emotion of the hero[1407]. One might speak here of a'musical play', and on this account regard the *toṭaka* as a secondary kind of drama akin to the dances or ballets *nṛtyas*. The *Nāṭyaśāstra* in fact is said in a commentary on the play to describe the kinds of songs and dances found in the *Vikramorvaśīya*, though it is difficult to identify them in the available texts, so that perhaps they could occur in other types of play in the early period (Raṅganātha's commentary, pp. 85ff.: 'Bharata'). It may be noted here that an ancient theorist named Subandhu distinguished five sub-varieties of *nāṭaka*, not including the *toṭaka* [165]. He is quoted for this later (Śāradātanaya pp. 238 ff.), but his distinctions are obscure and probably became obsolete quite early, since they do not appear to be further developed by the later writers beyond Śāradātanaya's, or his source's, assigning some plays as examples of them.

344. XIII **A play in four scenes which is entirely in Prakrit** (or more specifically in the 'best' Prakrit, i. e. Māhārāṣṭrī), but which in subject matter resembles a *nāṭikā*, is called a *saṭṭaka* (Sāgaranandin 3198 ff., Śāradātanaya p. 244). It has certain other peculiarities, particularly the total absence of introductory scenes. The popularity of Māhārāṣṭrī has ensured the writing of plays of this type over a long period, and the survival of a number of them, though the earliest now available is Rājaśekhara's *Karpūramañjarī* (+900). [3592-8]

345. Some writers distinguish a *prakaraṇī* (or – *ikā*) as a four act play like a minor *prakaraṇa* (fiction), taking the *nāṭikā* to be like a minor *nāṭaka* (Abhinavagupta mentions this view, II. 436). Its hero would be such a character as a merchant, whereas a *nāṭikā* usually has a king as hero. No examples seem to be available, though this proves nothing since few *prakaraṇas*, even, have survived.

346. XIV The *sallāpa* ('dispute', 'contention') is a play of violent and heroic character, based on either a well known or an invented story (Sāgaranandin 3028, Śāradātanaya p. 256). It has three acts (the later and not very reliable *Sāhityadarpaṇa* says it may have three or four : this may be a confusion with the four conjunctions stated for this type by Śāradātanaya), with 'panic' *vidrava* in the first act, abundance of rhythms (i. e. dancing) in the second and deceit in the third. It has the furious and heroic *rasas* and is in the expressive and violent modes. The omitted conjunction is the re-opening, not the obstacle (cf. Chapter III, this contrasts with the 'cooperation' and with the general rule). The hero is of unorthodox *pāṣaṇḍa* beliefs and angry, engaged in a battle of deceit as a result of fate or an enemy's action. No example of this interesting type seems to have survived [cf. 957] : the theorists mention a *Māyākāpālika* ('Illusion Kāpālika-Ascetic'—— a Kāpālika is a Śaiva of an extreme mystic school) as representative.

347. XV The *vāra* ('turn' or 'series') mentioned by Bodhāyana is more obscure. Śāradātanaya (p. 241) has a term *nṛttavāra*, alternative reading *nṛttacāra*, as a kind of *nāṭaka* of one of Subandhu's types (the *samagra*, 'complete', type). To make the matter still more obscure, rather than to elucidate it, Abhinavagupta (III p. 172) refers to a *nāṭyadhārā* (which can easily be a mere scribal error for *-vāra* since the characters *dh* and *v* closely resemble one another in Indian scripts) on Vāsavadattā by a dramatist Subandhu, placing him in the reign of the emperor Bindusāra (-293 to-268), which is not available to us[653]. If this date is correct we have to do with a very ancient and presumably obsolete type. Abhinavagupta refers to this play for the emboxing of one play within another, and apparently further of the emboxing of these within a third, which conceivably is what was meant by the term 'series' *vāra*. The type does not appear in any known list of minor types or ballets and Bodhāyana places it and the *sallāpa* among the main types.

348. XVI The *śilpaka* (the *ṣidgaka*, Abhinavagupta I p. 181; or *śiṃgaka*, Hemacandra, *Kāvyānuśāsana* VIII. 4; appears to be different—see No. XXXVI below) has four acts (Sāgaranandin 3029 ff., Śāradātanaya p. 257). It has all the *rasas* and is in any mode according to Sāgaranandin, but Śāradātanaya excludes the comic. The hero is a brahman and there is an inferior subsidiary hero and daughters of ministers or brahmans as heroines, unmarried, married or remarried. The theory prescribes a set of twenty seven 'limbs' for this type, mostly emotions to be portrayed in it, but which are used also in plays of other types. These are : eagerness, dissimulation, undertaking, knotting (mutual understanding or decision), wishing, reasoning, doubt, remorse, affliction innocence, lassitude [1136], perplexity, lamenting, perversity, following, astonishment, means, breathing (reviving), admiration, emptiness (forgetting), enticement [1196], confidence, altercation [1194], reassuring, knowing (comprehending), delight, panegyric. [Respectively according to Sāgaranandin: *utkaṇṭhā*, *avahittha*, *prayatna*, *grathana* (Śāradātanaya : ? *yukti*, but near the end of the list), *āśaṃsā*, *tarka*, *saṃśaya*, *tāpa*, *udvega*, *maugdhya* (*mauḍhya*), *ālasya*, *apratipatti* (*kampa*), *vilāpa* (?*ātaṅka*, but later), *vāmya* (? *pramada*, near end), *anugamana*, *vismaya*, *sādhana*, *ucchvāsa*, *camatkāra* (? *pramāda*, near end), *śūnyatā*, *pralobha*, *vaiśāradya* (?*nāṭya*), *saṃpheṭa*, *āśvāsana*, *bodhana* (? *prarocanā*, penultimate), *praharṣa* and *praśasti* (Śāradātanaya's terms in brackets, with notes on their displacement; rest similar to Sāgaranandin's and in same order).] Some of these we have met before as elements in structure, one is a basic emotion and a few are transients. They apparently replace the usual 'conjunctions' and limbs. We here follow the list of Sāgaranandin : that of Śāradātanaya has some minor variations, which may be synonyms or in some cases corruptions in the manuscript tradition of the text. Sāgaranandin gives illustrations of all these 'limbs' (mostly from *nāṭakas* and 'fictions'), which serve as a check on our readings of their names and interpretation of their meanings. Śāradātanaya (pp. 278 ff.) gives briefer definitions and illustrations which seem to enable us to identify all his variant terms with synonyms in the other list. No *śilpaka* is known to have been preserved; Sāgaranandin names a *Kanakavatīmādhava* as example, its title is evidently formed from the names of the heroine and hero. A

349. XVII The *durmallikā* (Sāgaranandin 3187ff., Śāradātanaya p. 267;—the *Nāṭyadarpaṇa*, p. 191, and Bhoja, Raghavan p. 547, write *durmilitā*) is a humorous play in four acts. The lengths of these acts are laid down (as in the case of the 'cooperation' above, Chapter III) as successively three, five, seven (Śāradātanaya;— Sāgaranandin says ten) and ten *nāḍikās*. These figures are apparently equivalent to an hour and twelve minutes for the first act, two hours for the second, two hours and forty eight minutes for the third and four hours for the fourth, altogether ten hours. The increasing length of the acts is contrary to the usual diminishing length we noted in Chapter III [154]. There are four conjunctions,

in this case the 'embryo' being omitted (again contrary to the usual omission of the obstacle in a play with four conjunctions). It is further stated that the first act consists of the play of the parasite, the second of that of the jester, the third of that of the tutor and the fourth of that of the *nāgaraka* (or of all three of those 'ministers' of his, according to Śāradātanaya). The *nāgaraka* is the hero in this type of play, and the plot is of 'stolen' love, with a deceitful female messenger who continually raises the price of her work as go-between, using low stories (Raghavan suggests this means blackmail—*Bhoja's Śṛṅgāraprakāśa*, p. 547) to effect this end. It is deeply to be regretted that no examples of such plays seem to have been preserved, in which the life of the *nāgaraka* with his 'ministers' was so fully displayed. Probably they did not appeal at all to the scholars of the later middle ages. Sāgaranandin mentions a *Bindumatī* (presumably the name of the heroine) as example, and perhaps the theme of the deceitful messenger is noted from this actual play rather than being a necessary feature of all examples of the type.

350. XVIII The *goṣṭhī* is a one act play with three conjunctions (Sāgaranandin 3026 f., Śāradātanaya p. 256, *Nāṭyadarpaṇa* p. 191, *Śṛṅgāraprakāśa* Vol. II p. 468). The sources are rather brief on this type. Śāradātanaya says first that it has an invented story, the sensitive *rasa*, five or six heroines and nine or ten heroes. This might suggest the 'circle' *goṣṭhī* of the *nāgarakas* as the scene. He ends however, perhaps following another predecessor (and he seems usually to be compiling from earlier theorists in his work), with a brief reference to the deeds of the young Kṛṣṇa (as 'lord of the milkmaids', not actually naming him), the 'boy of the *goṣṭha*', killing various demons. This would not be 'invented' in the accepted sense of that term and contradicts the first explanation. A *goṣṭha* may mean, and presumably means here, a cattle pen or station. The other sources seem to support the second explanation : the *Nāṭyadarpaṇa* and *Śṛṅgāraprakāśa* have the same verse, similar to this and saying that it is the deeds of the Enemy of Kaiṭabha (i. e. Viṣṇu or Kṛṣṇa, Kaiṭabha being a demon killed by him) at the cattle station; Sāgaranandin naming as an example a *Satyabhāmā* (who became one of Kṛṣṇa's wives; however she was not a milkmaid but a more aristocratic lady who was one of the prizes he acquired by invading the Underworld and defeating Jāmbavant). Finally, the later and less reliable *Sāhityadarpaṇa* follows (only) the explanation of the first part of Śāradātanaya's text, adding as an example a *Raivatamadanikā* (p. 346), a title perhaps meaning Madanikā (the heroine) of Raivata (a hill near Dvāraka—this suggests the Kṛṣṇa legend again [368]). It is possible that there were two kinds of *goṣṭhī* play. The *Harivaṃśa*, however, combines the two themes in its Kṛṣṇa *goṣṭhi* (II. 88). At least two examples are preserved in Orissa (Jayadeva III and Anādimiśra).

351. XIX The *prekṣaṇaka*, 'spectacle', is a one act play which may be performed in the street as well as in the theatre (Sāgaranandin 3192ff., *Śṛṅgāraprakāśa* Vol. II p. 468, Śāradātanaya p.263, *Nāṭyadarpaṇa* p. 191). The story seems usually (perhaps always) to be taken from Tradition. It is said that the producer does not appear, though there is the usual opening benediction and the announcement *prarocanā*, both from off-stage. However, some rare examples of plays called *prekṣaṇakas* in their manuscripts, which have survived, seem to conflict with this theoretical statement. These examples are relatively late (+14 and later, by Bhāskara and Virūpākṣa) and may show a new development. They are brief and portray anxiety in time of disaster. Four older examples are named by the critics, all violent episodes : the killing of Vālin, Nṛsiṃha's victory, crushing of Tripura and burning of Kāma.

352. XX The *preraṇa* is a one act farce featuring deformed and fantastic characters and riddles *prahelikās*, as well as agreeable music (Abhinavagupta I pp. 172, 181 [385], *Kāvyānuśāsana* p. 446, manuscript of *Nāṭyasarvasvadīpikā* quoted by Mankad, p. 128). No example is named or known. [2656, 4938] A

353. Śāradātanaya (pp. 267 f.) describes after the *durmallikā* what he calls a *mallikā*, in two (or more?) acts dominated respectively by the jester and the parasite. This looks like a variation on the *durmallikā*. However, he goes on with a description of the *maṇikulyā* or mystery story, a subdivision of the novel which we shall discuss in Chapter VII [455], saying finally that the *mallikā* is the same as the *maṇikulyā*. No other writer seems to know of a *mallikā* and this appears to be an extraordinary confusion on the part of the compiler, who has blunderingly mixed together two categories of literature in selecting information from his sources. Whether there ever was a *mallikā* drama we can hardly establish from Śāradātanaya, who seems to have been trying to 'restore' a missing description from materials which may not have contained it at all : his first statements may be mere conjecture spun out of the description of the similarly named *durmallikā*. A verse he gives on the *maṇikulyā*, identifying it with the *mallikā*, is found in Bhoja (*Śṛṅgāraprakāśa* Vol. II p. 469) but with the name of an example of the *maṇikulyā* replacing the word *mallikā*. Perhaps Śāradātanaya was simply compiling from a manuscript of Bhoja's book which was damaged or corrupt at that point.

354. Śāradātanaya also seems to be alone in describing a *kalpavallī*, as a comic and sensitive play with an 'exalted' but playful hero, supported by the tutor, a heroine either waiting to welcome him or going herself to meet him and much song and dance (p. 268). He names a *Māṇikyavallikā* as example. A possible source for this 'type' would be the *nāṭyarāsaka* (see below No. XXII).

355. The same writer mentions finally a *pārijātalatā* (or *pārijātaka*), as a one act play, heroic or sensitive, with a king or warrior as hero, a heroine separated from him on account of a quarrel, or alternatively a geisha whose company he enjoys, the jester and a group of dancers. A *Gaṅgātaraṅgikā* is given as example—evidently the name of the heroine. Since the *daṇḍarāsaka* dance is mentioned (see below under *śamyā*—No. XXVII) it is possible that Śāradātanaya has again become confused, although such dances may of course be inserted in longer plays (p. 268).

356. XXI With the *rāsaka* or *rāsakāṅka*, which is among the earliest of these types of play, we approach the borderline of ballet. Alaka in his commentary on Ratnākara's *Haravijaya* (XVII. 108) quotes Kohala on the *rāsakāṅka* ('*rāsaka*-act') as a kind of play *nāṭya*. Śāradātanaya (p.263), the *Nāṭyadarpaṇa* (p.191) and Bhoja (*Śṛṅgāraprakāśa* Vol. II p. 468; see also p. 491) have the same verse on *rāsaka* but with slightly different readings. There are sixteen or 32 or eight female singers (so Alaka; the others read simply heroines) who perform group dances *piṇḍībandhas* in this kind of performance. The *Nāṭyaśāstra* mentions these *piṇḍībandhas* (IV. 252 ff., and 287 ff.) and we have Abhinavagupta's comments on them (I pp. 167 f., and 190ff.).

The dancers, in fact a corps de ballet, form various decorative patterns, often representing various objects. There is a tradition (*Śṛṅgāraprakāśa* II p. 469, Śāradātanaya p. 265) that these dance forms were invented by the gods, when they danced to celebrate after drinking the ambrosia churned from the primaeval ocean.

357. That a *rāsakāṅka* was as much a play as a ballet seems to be attested by Abhinavagupta's references to and quotations from Bhejjala's *Rādhāvipralambha* as an example of the type (III. pp. 63, 72; I. p. 214 if from the same play). This was largely in the Saindhava language, a form of Apabhraṃśa; from its title it presumably dealt with the story of Rādhā's (temporary) separation from Kṛṣṇa (it could also mean the 'deceiving' of Rādhā). Bhoja (p. 491) notes also the presence of the jester along with Rādhā. Sāgaranandin (3205 ff., cf. Śāradātanaya p. 269 and the Appendix, p. 408—different readings from other manuscripts) in his brief prose account of the *rāsaka* states that it has one act, five characters, an 'exalted' hero, an innocent (if we read *mugdha*) heroine, tender and exalted emotions, a predominance of dialogue (the significance of this is not clear), the 'limbs' of the street play (see above) and no producer (appearing on the stage). It can be in any language. It is also said to be instructive in the arts (presumably those listed in the *Kāmasūtra* as branches of pleasure). An example is the *Madanikākāmuka* ('Madanikā's Lover'—presumably Kṛṣṇa). The *Sāhityadarpaṇa* (p. 348) has a similar description (with variants of unknown value) and adds a *Menakāhita* as example (Menakā is one of the nymphs, who first married Nahuṣa [1581], then seduced Viśvāmitra and thus became the mother of Śakuntalā). No example seems to have survived (but cf. below [421 as well as 360]). [2494, 2503]

358. XXII Our sources appear to distinguish a *nāṭyarāsaka* from this *rāsaka* type, though through the similarity of names there is a good deal of confusion between them (we are accustomed to Śāradātanaya being confused; Bhoja also seems confused here, since he inserts the description of the *nāṭyarāsaka* into the middle of that of the *rāsaka*, but this may be the result of manuscript corruption). Despite the name, which would seem to suggest that the *nāṭyarāsaka* is more like a play, the description indicates that it is more of a dance than the *rāsaka*, and it should perhaps be grouped with the *lāsya* and other dances which we are going to discuss next. According to Sāgaranandin (3210 ff., cf. Śāradātanaya p. 264, lines 7 and following, and *Śṛṅgāraprakāśa* II p. 468, lines 13 to 20) the *nāṭyarāsaka* has much dancing ('rhythm and tempo', i. e. the elements of pure dancing, not representative or expressive of emotion), but is adorned with the comic and sensitive. It has one act and the ten 'limbs' of the *lāsya* (cf. under *lāsya* below [363]). The hero is exalted, the tutor is the secondary hero and the heroine is waiting ready for her lover (she is a *vāsakasajjā*, 'one who has her home ready', one of the eight types of heroine given in the *Nāṭyasāstra*). A *Vilāsavatī* (evidently the name of the heroine) is given as example. The *Sāhityadarpaṇa* (pp. 346f.) notes differences of opinion concerning the number of conjuctions in this type and adds a second example, a *Narmavatī*.

359. Bhoja and Śāradātanaya have a variant description, noting that the *nāṭyarāsaka* is also called the *carcarī*, which originally was the name of a *tāla* (rhythm). In this case dancers, representing girls in love *kāminīs* in the springtime, enter in pairs, dancing the actions of their lovers, or of a king, passing left and right and then remaining stationary with their right knees advanced (*ālīḍha*—see *Nāṭyaśāstra* XI. 65-6 Kāśī). Other dances follow; finally they exit in pairs. There are *carcarī* dances in some longer plays (of the *nāṭikā*, *toṭaka* [1407] and *saṭṭaka* types) and Uddyotana (+8) introduces one in his novel *Kuvalayamālā* (pp. 4 f.). The latter begins with a theme which becomes a refrain repeated after each of four following verses in a different metre. The piece is in Māhārāṣṭrī, like the novel in which it is found. These descriptions are not immediately reconcilable. It would seem that the *carcarī* might form part of a *nāṭyarāsaka* as described by Sāgaranandin, not the whole of it, and be followed by other scenes. [1781, 2710, 3603, 3620-3]

360. A further obscure point in connection with the *rāsaka* and *nāṭyarāsaka* is the relationship between these and the *rāsa* of late medieval and modern India. This may be nothing more than etymological resemblance, whilst the term *rāsa* itself is used for at least two very distinct things : heroic poems equivalent to epics, especially in Hindī; sets of lyric stanzas, especially in Apabhraṃśa and Gujarāti, which might belong to the tradition of the *nāṭyarāsaka*. A *rāsa* dance has survived, especially in

Gujarāt. Etymologically the word *rāsa* seems originally to have meant a sound, cry or speech. Secondarily it was felt to mean 'connected with *rasa*', which would help to explain the popularity of the term. It is also possible that historically the word was related to *lāsya*, since there is a merely dialectal variation between *r* and *l* in some of the Indian languages. In that case the original meaning would be simply 'dancing'. Finally the apocryphal *Harivaṃśa*, II. 89. 67 and 93. 24, describes women dancing a *rāsa*, with gestures, etc., and the language of the country *deśa*, describing the life of Kṛṣṇa. [6724-40,6744 ff.]

361. XXIII The first dance mentioned in the *Nāṭyaśāstra* is the *tāṇḍava*, Śiva's dance (IV. 13ff.), which he presents to Brahmā for use in the opening proceedings *pūrvaraṅga* of the drama, along with its stock of movements and gestures [312]. Despite the descriptive possibilities of some of the gestures, this is a pure dance, used for direct but abstract expression of emotion and not for description or narrative. It is *nṛtta* (dancing, simply) and has no 'meaning' *artha* in the sense of a 'programme' (IV.260 ff.). It is introduced in the theatre because it is beautiful and as a diversion which the audience enjoy. When it is combined with singing it becomes what is called *nṛtya* (IV. 264 ff.), which is descriptive and narrative dance, perhaps translatable approximately as 'ballet'. From this Abhinavagupta would derive eventually some of the minor forms of stage production, such as the *ḍombikā*, which we shall discuss below (see No. XXX). Whereas the original *tāṇḍava* is a solo dance, groups of women could form group dances *piṇḍībandhas* (cf. above under *rāsakāṅka*) from it (IV. 276 ff.; Śāradātanaya p. 297 *aṅgas* of *tāṇḍava*).

362. XXIV The *Nāṭyaśāstra* says (IV. 246 f. Kāśī) that Pārvatī, Śiva's consort, watched him dancing and then danced herself, introducing more delicate movements and gestures. Although the *Nāṭyaśāstra* does not appear to make the identification, Abhinavagupta and other later writers state that the dance thus created by Pārvatī was the *lāsya*. According to the *Nāṭyaśāstra* (XXXI, 476 ff.), in its chapter on rhythm *tāla*, the *lāsya* is a sensitive solo dance. It has ten (or twelve in the Kāśī text of Chapter XX) 'limbs', however, each of which is a separate dance item which again may contain several individual dances. A full *lāsya* performance, if it contained all these, would be a very substantial programme. These limbs can be used separately and in other types of drama; for example the satirical monologue, being a solo performance, gives scope for their application, particularly when the parasite has to imitate the actions and emotions of the people he meets. Elsewhere a soliloquy would offer an opportunity for this kind of development. Some later writers illustrate the limbs of the *lāsya* from various kinds of drama (e.g. Sāgaranandin 2850 ff.). [6496 ff.]

363. In brief outline the limbs are as follows.

(1) The *geyapada* has three main sections; first a singer sits and sings a 'dry' (i. e. without words, meaningless syllables [312]) *āsārita* song, with instrumental accompaniment, including a flute; then there is an *āsārita* song with words, in *mārgāsārita* rhythm, consisting of three musical phrases and ending with an *upohana* (a kind of cadenza of meaningless syllables, or else purely instrumental, sometimes an instrumental prelude to a song or dance; literally a 'piling up', cf. *Saṅgītaratnākara* V. 41 and Commentary); finally there is a *paridhānaka* in 3-time with a conclusion describing the gaining of the object. (2) The *sthitavādya* or *sthitapāṭhya* is a dance with gestures *nṛtya* by a woman describing the qualities of her lover; it begins in mixed rhythm (i. e. a complex rhythm resulting from the combination of the basic 4-time and 3-time, here the *pañcapāṇi*), switches to 4-time (as in *gaṇacchandas* or 'bar metre' verse) and returns to the mixed rhythm at the end [1189]. (3) The *āsīnavādya* after a prelude *upohana* in 3-time, continues with a song expressing anxiety and grief; there are changes of rhythm and drum accompaniment. (4) In *puṣpagandhikā* a woman dancer acts the part of a man reciting for the diversion of his friends, using the Sanskrit language and gestures. (5) The *pracchedaka* is a romantic song, in a series of sections in different metres and rhythms, of women oppressed by the moonbeams, fancying the reflections of their lovers in water or in a mirror as they wait for them to come[1375]. (6) The *trimūḍha* is soft and in the *gāndhārī* musical mode *jāti*, it has various metres or rhythms and enacts the emotions of men. (7) The *saindhava* is a compassionate song when a rendezvous *saṅketa* has been forgotten (i. e. the lover has not come); it has gestures but not very distinct ones, uses the Saindhava language and music, with much drumm-

ing but not syncopated and with mostly long syllables (producing the effect of a slow measure). (8) The *dvimūḍha* consists of a prelude followed by a dance, with singing and acting; it uses both 3-time and 4-time, and has clear emotion, producing *rasa*. (9) In *uttamottamaka* there are many *rasas* and beautiful stanza structures, with a dramatic song *natkuṭaka* [313] and mixed rhythm [1407]. (10) The *vicitrapada* (missing in the shorter list and rejected by Abhinavagupta) is a love song, diverting the mind after seeing a likeness (painting, etc.) of the beloved. (11) In *uktapratyukta* there are many gestures and much expression of emotions, especially of anger and the propitiation of it (presumably propitiating an offended mistress), with accusations and pacifying excuses; it is a 'dispute', but evidently a lover's quarrel; it begins in mixed time and ends in 3-time [1479]. (12) In *bhāvita* (missing in most lists and probably a later addition; Abhinavagupta rejects it) various emotions are expressed when tormented by love after seeing the beloved in a dream (*Nāṭyaśāstra* XX. 152; the above are from XX. 136 ff. and XXXI. 476 ff.). A

364. We should note that the *Nāṭyaśāstra* takes it for granted that performances of this sort produce *rasa*, the full aesthetic experience, whilst some later writers try to establish a rather artificial distinction of only drama proper *nāṭya* producing *rasa*, ballet (*nṛtya*, representational dance) producing only emotion *bhāva* and dance *nṛtta* being just diverting rhythms (e. g. *Daśarūpaka* pp. 2—3), Abhinavagupta on the other hand thinks there is no real division between these three kinds of performance, since all should be included in a full scale dramatic production (I p. 170). The *Nāṭyaśāstra* notes (XX. 137) that the 'objective' in a *lāsya* performance is invented, as in a 'fiction' [1189].

365. In later times the *lāsya* as an independent production seems to have been superseded by a variety of ballets *nṛtyas* which probably grew out of it. The *nāṭyarāsaka* was very likely one of these. Daṇḍin (I.39) mentions as 'shows' *prekṣyas* the *lāsya*, *chalika*, *śamyā*, 'etc.', where Ratnaśrījñāna in his commentary says 'etc.' means '*skandhaka*, etc. (he also reads *chalina* for *chalika*). Earlier, Bhāmaha, as we have already noted, without giving any general name but saying they are varieties of drama, gives in a group (after *nāṭaka*) *dvipadī*, *śamyā*, *rāsaka*, *skandhaka*, etc. (I.24). Bhoja (*Śṛṅgāraprakāśa* Vol. II pp. 381 f.) much later gives a list of six *prekṣyas*: *lāsya*, *tāṇḍava*, *chalika*, *śamyā*, *hallīsaka* and *rāsaka* (which afterwards appears as *rāsa*). Later he says (p. 468) that *nartanaka* ('dancing') includes *śamyā*, *lāsya*, *chalika*, *dvipadī*, etc. Jīvānanda, a late commentator on Daṇḍin, follows a similar tradition in completing the 'etc.' of Daṇḍin as *tāṇḍava*, *hallīśaka* and *rāsa* : he also calls these *prekṣyas* '*nṛtyas*' (ballets).

366. We have already discussed *lāsya*, *tāṇḍava* and *rāsaka* (*and nāṭyarāsaka*). We have noted the confusion over *rāsaka* and *nāṭyarāsaka*; the former, simple, term is also used for a lyric poem, of several strophes in different metres in Prakrit or Apabhraṃśa (e. g. by Virahāṅka, IV. 37-8), which is of the same general structure as the *carcarī* and suitable for the kind of performance with song and dance we are here studying. Thus it seems we should identify this *prekṣya* with the *nāṭyarāsaka* discussed above . Let us now see what is known of the other ballets grouped with these and which seem to be closely related to them.

367. XXV The text of a *chalika* contains four strophes, called *vastus* ('subjects'). Kālidāsa (+5) brings in a performance of part of one, its fourth *vastu*, in his *nāṭaka Mālavikāgnimitra* [1384] (see end of Act I, after verse 19, for the name *chalika* of this composition and the beginning of Act II for the performance—the *Nāṭyadarpaṇa*, however, loosely refers to this as a *lāsya* performance, p.117), with a Prakrit song (strophe), and its appreciation by an audience. There seems to be an introductory song too, which perhaps would be a refrain repeated as in the *carcarī* (see under *nāṭyarāsaka* above, No. XXII [359]). The solo dancer successfully shows the emotions in the song by her acting, according to the *rasa* (the sensitive) to be produced. Perhaps a little earlier, but not very clear, is the mention of a *chālikya* play in the *Harivaṃśa* (II, *Viṣṇuparvan*, 89. 67 ff and 93.23). The nymph Rambhā dances to a *chālikya geya* song, accompanied by a group of musical instruments. According to the anonymous *Hṛdayaṃgamā* commentary on *Daṇḍin* (I.39) the *chalika* is in fact a musical instrument itself, presumably used to accompany this kind of dance. Bhoja (*Śṛṅgāraprakāśa* II. 382) says that the *chalika* is based on both *lāsya* and *tāṇḍava* and thus may be sensitive , furious or heroic. He illustrates it with a verse depicting a hunting scene, in **Apabhraṃśa.** A

368. XXVI The *hallīsaka* (*or hallīśa* (*ka*)) is a group dance resembling the *rāsaka* (according to Bhoja (II. 382) the difference of rhythm is the chief distinction). The *Harivaṃśa* in the scene noted above mentions a *hallīsaka* (89.68) as one of the instruments used to accompany the *chālikya*. Bhoja says that a group of women, representing e. g. milkmaids, dance in a circle with one 'hero', e. g. Hari (Kṛṣṇa), and in fact this dance seems usually to be about Kṛṣṇa. We have already mentioned Bhāsa's introduction of a *hallīśa* in a *nāṭaka* about Kṛṣṇa, where the hero in fact dances with the milkmaids (Act III) [1049]. It consists of song, instrumental music and dancing, but no words are given for it. The *hallīśaka* is the only one of these ballets described separately by Sāgaranandin (3154 ff.), Śāradātanaya (pp. 266 f.), Abhinavagupta (I p. 181) and the *Nāṭyadarpaṇa* (p. 191). It has seven, eight or nine female dancers and much rhythm and tempo (i. e. abstract rather than expressive dancing), with one male dancer. Example : *Keliraivataka* ('Pleasure-Raivataka', the latter being a hill near Dvārakā where Kṛṣṇa enjoyed himself when living there and where in fact the *Harivaṃśa's chālikya* was danced [cf. 350]. Ex. Gopālabhaṭṭa, *Govardhanayātrā*—Vema.

369. XXVII The term *śamyā*, 'time-beat', is used in the *Nāṭyaśāstra* simply for visibly beating time, apparently only with the right hand or fingers. According to the *Hṛdayaṃgamā* (on Daṇḍin I. 39), however, it is a coloured stick used in the dance named after it. This would identify the dance with a *daṇḍarāsaka*, 'stick dance', mentioned elsewhere. A transition from beating time with the hand when dancing to using a stick for that purpose would be natural enough. This seems to be a group dance, or it may later have developed into one. The *daṇḍarāsaka* as a kind of *carcarī* (cf. No. XXII above) is described in Rājaśekhara's *saṭṭaka Karpūramañjarī* (Act IV. 11) as performed by thirty two women dancers; they appear to form two lines of sixteen facing one another (beating their coloured sticks together, we may add from the *Śuddhānandaprakāśa* quoted by Raghavan, *Bhoja's Śṛṅgāraprakāśa*, p. 565, then forming other patterns). Bhoja says (II. 382) the *śamyā* is about gods and fairies (or centaurs). Virahāṅka (p. 42) gives a *śamyā* metre as necessarily in Sanskrit (Bhoja's verse is not), but this may have no special connection with the dance. [3620] A

370. XXVIII The *dvipadī*, 'two-metre', which stands first in Bhāmaha's list of these ballets, is a metrical structure (not a particular metre) very prominent in Virahāṅka's work. As this structure is of the same type as the *carcarī* and *chalika*, it would appear likely that the dance was a representation of a text (poem) of the type Virahāṅka describes. The name *dvipadī* evidently means that the poem is in a mixture of two metres. These are used alternately : there are four strophes, called *vastukas* (cf. the *vastus* of the *chalika*), in any one of a series of metres collected in Virahāṅka's third chapter as suitable for this use; each *vastuka* is followed by a *gītikā* (in *gīti*, or other *gaṇacchandas*, 'bar' or musical metre). From this basic pattern various *rāsakas* are derived by substituting other metres for the *vastuka* metres (Virahāṅka II and IV. 37 f.). The other metres named here are described in the fourth chapter. cf. Svayambhū: *Chandolakṣaṇa* [3264, 3266].

371. A variant form which perhaps is to be regarded as a sub-variety of *dvipadī* is the *dvipadīkhaṇḍa*. Here the *khaṇḍa* is another metre used in conjuction with the *gītikā*. However, the resulting structure is much shorter than an ordinary *dvipadī* : merely two *khaṇḍas* followed by a single *gītikā*. Svayaṃbhū in his work on metres (+9) gives the *khaṇḍa* (III. 3.1) and then the *dvipadīkhaṇḍa* (IV. 1. 1), with an example from Harṣa's *nāṭikā Ratnāvalī* (+7), where in the play the stage direction is for two actresses to act and sing a *dvipadīkhaṇḍa* (I. 13-15 and preceding direction). It is of some relevance that the jester afterwards displays his ignorance by calling the *dvipadīkhaṇḍa* a *carcarī* and trying to dance it, for which he is suitably teased and buffeted by the dancers. Of course this tells us only that the two forms are different and that everyone knew the difference, but there must be at least some vague resemblance between them for the jester's mistake to seem natural, even in a fool. The *dvipadīkhaṇḍa* poem here describes the effects of Kāma on young women in the first month of spring. Other examples are found in one recension of Kālidāsa's *toṭaka Vikramorvaśīya* [1407]. [2673, 2717, 3126, 4162]

372. XXIX It is difficult to glean much information about the *skandhaka* beyond the fact that it is the Prakrit name for the metre *āryāgīti*, a form of *gaṇacchandas* (musical 'bar' metre). This metre is in fact used for epic poetry in Prakrit (but not in Sanskrit), for example in Sarvasena's (+4) *Harivijaya* [1267] and Pravarasena's (+5) *Rāvaṇavaha* [1433]. Presumably it was used for dance and song performances as well, not mixed with other metres but probably diversified with the many variations it itself possesses [413, 415].

373. Though little remains of these dances in the extant literature, their significance as a popular element in the classical theatre should not be underestimated. They appear fairly often as episodes in the more substantial plays preserved, where they offer a little musical relief by way of interlude in the main drama. It is natural that this should happen more often in the *nāṭikā* and other kinds of play outside the *Nāṭyaśāstra's* ten main types, i. e. in plays for which there is other evidence of musical tendencies (*toṭaka*, *saṭṭaka*). Outside such interludes their ephemeral nature is obvious. They were regularly in the vernacular languages and dialects (Prakrit, later Apabhraṃśa), they were short, and we can see in the theoretical works which touch on them (particularly those on metres) how each style and fashion in such popular song making and metrical arrangement (and dance steps corresponding to the latter) was superseded by another. Many similar dance and song performances can be found in late medieval and modern India. Sometimes they are similarly named. Though the similarities are generic rather than specific we can say that after many changes in fashion and in influences of all kinds these modern performances in part represent the ephemeral extension of the classical theatre of India. The more substantial classical dramas themselves drew new ideas and expressions from this popular background, as did Sanskrit lyric and epic poetry.

374. What we have sketched above indicates something of the state of these ephemeral performances during the period from the final codification of the *Nāṭyaśāstra* down to about the + 8, after which the changes of fashion appear to have been so great that the critics had some difficulty in relating the terms they found in the earlier writings on minor forms of drama (Kohala, etc.) to current practice. The majority of our later sources in fact omit most of these minor *prekṣyas*. Bhoja (*Śṛṅgāraprakāśa* II 438) and the *Nāṭyadarpaṇa* (p. 191) mention but do not adequately define the *śamyā*, *lāsya* (though its limbs are treated elsewhere following the old *Nāṭyaśāstra* account), *chalika*, *dvipadī* and the useful 'etc.', *ādi*, lumping them together under a new heading as one type of secondary drama, the *nartanaka*, 'dancing', which could accommodate whatever new fashions might be current within the framework of traditional theory. As long as they contain acting *abhinaya* they count as forms of drama and are not pure dance.

375. By the +8, and possibly much earlier, we find a new group of *nṛtyas* mentioned by the critics from Abhinavagupta and Dhanika onwards. These seem to be of the same general character as the *lāsya*, *chalika*, etc., i. e. acting-dancing, usually solo, with songs. They clearly existed a considerable time before the writers who are first known to us to discuss them, since these quote earlier sources on their characteristics, which may well include Kohala for some of them. Dhanika enumerates a set of seven types of *nṛtya*, which he says (as the *Nāṭyaśāstra* says of the old *lāsya*) are 'like the *bhāṇa* (satirical monologue)' —presumably in that they feature a solo performer (even if some may have a corps de ballet accompaniment). He and Dhanañjaya also describe *nṛtyas* as a basis for emotion *bhāva* only, not for *rasa*. This however is an extreme view not shared by Abhinavagupta and others, who value the *nṛtyas* more highly. There is on the other hand general agreement that the *nṛtyas* contain acting of the meanings of words, whereas drama proper (*nāṭya*, the main types) is the acting of the meanings of sentences. The distinction here is that in *nṛtya* the dancer uses gestures representing words and proceeds word by word in acting out a song, whereas in *nāṭya* the actor uses gestures corresponding to complete ideas or sentences. A

376. Dhanika's (pp. 2—3) seven types of *nṛtya* are : *ḍombī*, *śrīgadita* , *bhāṇa* (sic, different from the homonymous satirical monologue), *bhāṇī*, *prasthāna*, *rāsaka* and *kāvya* (sic, in a special sense, probably the same as the *rāgakāvya* and known already to Kohala). The *kāvya* here stands a little apart and may be left till afterwards (see No. XXXVIII below). Abhinavagupta's corresponding group (I p. 166 ff., especially 181) is: *ḍombikā*, *bhāṇaka*, *prasthāna*, *ṣidgaka*, *bhāṇikā*, *preraṇa*, *rāmākrīḍa*, *hallīsaka* and *rāsaka*, with a sprinkling of 'etcs.' suggesting there may be others. He keeps the *rāgakāvya* separate. He regards them as derived from the *tāṇḍava* [361], as all dances are (p. 180). Among these the ever popular *hallīsaka* is the one dance among the ancient set of *prekṣyas* we have just discussed to retain its independent position, after the others were forgotten or lumped together as *nartanaka*. We noted the *preraṇa* or farce earlier, as it seems to depend more on dialogue and to be a minor *nāṭya* rather than a *nṛtya*. Probably it was a borderline case. We have also discussed the difficulties of distinguishing various kinds of *rāsaka*. In the present context we may have even a third kind of *rāsaka*, since there is a brief description given by Abhinavagupta (I.p. 181), Śāradātanaya (p. 266, lines 13-4) and Hemacandra (p. 446) to the effect that it has up to sixty four female dancers in pairs and varied rhythms and tempi. This is too brief to show whether it should be identified with the types noted above as *rāsaka* or *nāṭyarāsaka*, at some stage in their history. Vāgbhaṭa (+12) in his *Kāvyānuśāsana* (p. 18) has a list of eleven types, plus 'etc.', which he calls *geya rūpakas*, explaining that this means, according to the 'ancients' or 'old' *cirantanas*, acting the meanings of words (not sentences [375]). These are the *ḍombikā*, *bhāṇa*, *prasthāna*, *bhāṇikā*, *preraṇa*, *śiṅgaka*, *rāmākrīḍa*, *hallīsaka*, *śrīgadita*, *rāsaka*, *goṣṭhī*, etc. This includes all the above except the *rāgakāvya*, but adds the *goṣṭhī* [350, second explanation]. The 'old' source, whose descriptions of these types are quoted here, appears to be the same as that quoted by Abhinavagupta (I p. 181), but including the *śrīgadita* and *goṣṭhī* as well as the explanation with *geya* [588]. A

377. XXX The *ḍombikā* (or *ḍombī*) appears as the type of this group of dances. Abhinavagupta (I p. 175) explains *ḍombī* as 'disguising' (*viḍambi*, which may cover imitating, deception and mockery). Then (I p. 176) he says it shows the nature of the world in the guise of Rāma, etc., through an actor. The actor, or rather actress, does not conceal her own person (to show the hero by dress) by appearing in his form, but shows him only by acting in her dance. It seems that it is in the song that the 'disguise' or 'deception' takes place, for this has 'another meaning' (I p. 166), i. e. alludes covertly to matters of interest to the audience, or some of them. It is concerned only with pleasure (love) as an end of life, and in it we find the utmost secrecy of a hidden passion (I p. 172). Similarly in the *bhāṇa* (*ka*), *preraṇa*, *bhāṇikā*, etc., Abhinavagupta says that we see instruction given in the purposes of men through fables of lions, boars, bears, buffaloes, etc., with 'praise of what is not the subject', 'corroboration','example' and other figures of speech. The purpose of a *ḍombikā* is to please kings and princes with the adventures of secret lovers (I p. 175), the actress (called a *ḍombī*) making them think she is praising them. In brief, then, in the verse from an 'old' writer quoted by Abhinavagupta (I p. 181), the *ḍombikā* is about a hidden passion, thus attracting a king's mind. As examples Abhinavagupta notes a *Guṇamālā* (I p. 175) and a *Cūḍāmaṇi* (I p. 171, IV p. 271), the latter perhaps by Rāṇaka (I p.188). It seems that the Saindhava language, Apabhraṃśa originally of Sindhu, was usual in *ḍombikās*, *prasthānas*, etc. (IV p. 280), as in *rāsakas* and even in minor types of drama generally (see above [341, 357]). Hemacandra (445 ff.) has the same 'old' verse and repeats much of Abhinavagupta's discussion. Śāradātanaya has the 'old' verse (p. 265) on *ḍombikā*, but under a heading *ḍombī* he gives what other writers offer as a description of the *bhāṇikā* (257 f.; see below on *bhāṇikā*, No. XXXIII). [2857ff.]

378. No *ḍombikās* seem to have survived. The historian Kalhaṇa (+12) in his *Rājataraṅgiṇī* (V. 354 ff.) gives an interesting account of a visit of a *ḍomba* company to the court of Kaśmīra in the + 10. Its leader was a *ḍomba*-singer named Raṅga, and he had two beautiful daughters who seem to be *ḍombī* dancers (though the actual word is not applied to them). The king (Cakravarman, represented as extremely foolish by the historian) is seduced by the singing and gestures of the two girls, and through the mediation of a parasite of whom he is fond he takes them into his palace and makes one of them his chief queen, in the blindness of his passion. After this the court and the government are run by the *ḍomba* company, until the deluded king, victim of flatterers, is murdered by some of his barons.

379. Though this group of dances is regarded as being of the one act form, Abhinavagupta says (I p.188) that Rāṇaka and others in their *ḍombikās*, etc., arrange four exits *apasārakas* when the dancers leave the stage. This structure may correspond to that in four *vastus* of a *chalika* (see above [367]) and other dances. We may understand it as four scenes played on one day.

380. XXXI The *śrīgadita* is described by Sāgaranandin

(3157ff.) as having one act , in which a woman, seated, recites something pathetic *karuṇa* from a well known story. The eloquent *bhāratī* mode of stage business predominates and the type is therefore very different from those, like the *ḍombikā*, which are primarily dancing with songs. This may be why Abhinavagupta omits it from his group. Bhoja (II p. 466) describes it as having a woman singing to her friend about her absent husband, describing his heroic qualities, sometimes complaining of his unfaithfulness. 'Śrī' in the name of the type refers to the Goddess Lakṣmī, Fortune, consort of Viṣṇu-Kṛṣṇa, well known for his infidelities. Sāgaranandin's example is a *Krīḍārasātala*, which presumably was about Kṛṣṇa's expedition to conquer the Underworld (Rasātala), in the course of which he incidentally won Jāmbavatī and Satyabhāmā, a sufficient cause of distress to his consort. The *Nāṭyadarpaṇa* (p. 191) has the same words as Bhoja. Śāradātanaya combines the descriptions in Sāgaranandin and Bhoja but gives a different example, a *Rāmānanda*. If this was a complaint by Sītā about Rāma's absence we are left to conjecture in what way the paragon of fidelity was supposed to have been enjoying himself whilst away: perhaps the episode was from the apocryphal Seventh Book of the *Rāmāyaṇa*, Sītā's renewed exile when Rāma was finally reigning as king (the rival 'woman' would then be the Earth). On the other hand *rāmā* (fem.) means simply a beloved woman, so that this need not be a Rāma play but a "Joy of the Beloved." One play has been published which calls itself a *śrīgadita* in its prologue (Mādhava's *Subhadrāharaṇa*, early +17? : 'because it is coloured with the word *śrī*'—p, 3). However, it contains no scene which could be described as coming under the above type and as a whole can hardly be accepted as a *śrīgadita* of the classical kind. It seems the author based his play on the brief sketch in the *Sāhityadarpaṇa* (p. 349), making a one act sensitive drama with many characters, like a one act 'rape' but with a human heroine (Subhadrā, Kṛṣṇa's sister). [cf. 385]

381. XXXII The *bhāṇaka* (or *bhāṇa*) is described by Abhinavagupta (I p. 166) as predominantly instrumental music with 'broken' (syncopated?) rhythms. This distinction is relative to other types of dance in this group. There is little speech in it (IV p. 281). As a dance it is bold or vigorous, in contrast to the gentle or delicate manner of most of the dances

(I p. 181) (this would relate it to *tāṇḍava* rather than *lāsya*), and it describes the acts of Nṛsiṃha (the Man-Lion incarnation of Viṣṇu), the Boar (Sūkara incarnation), etc. It is curious that here the incarnations of Viṣṇu are spoken of, whereas earlier (I p. 172), as we noted above, the *bhāṇa* and other types of dance are explained as fables with (ordinary) lions, boars (and other animals). There seems to be some confusion, as it is unlikely that both interpretations can be correct. Bhoja (II p. 467) gives three kinds of *bhāṇa* dance, pure, mixed and varied *citra*, according to the manners and speech employed. He supports the view that it is the acts of Viṣṇu which form the subject matter of the *bhāṇaka*. There are verses preceding this and following those on the *rāgakāvya*, which according to Śāradātanaya's version (pp. 258 f.) belong to *bhāṇa* (this is not clear in Bhoja's text). They say that, besides Viṣṇu, other gods may form the subject (Śiva, the Sun, etc.), but female subjects are avoided (though the dance is performed by a woman dancer). Details on the changes of rhythm follow. A long further description follows (pp. 260 f.), in which amongst other things it is said that Brahmā and Indra may be the subject of this dance, perhaps an archaic feature. The *Nāṭyadarpaṇa* (p. 192) has some of Bhoja's verses, confirming a reading in one of them that the *bhāṇaka* is difficult to act, which is likely enough on account of the complexity of rhythms.

382. XXXIII A dance similar to this but delicate and usually having Viṣṇu as subject (presumably as Kṛṣṇa) is according to Bhoja (II p. 467) a *bhāṇikā*. The representation of females is not here avoided. There are nine or ten scenes *vastus* in a *bhāṇikā*. Abhinavagupta has an 'old' verse (I p. 181) on *bhāṇikā* referring to the play of a child (Kṛṣṇa?) and also boars and lions and play with a standard (or staff). All this is for us ambiguous since it may relate to gods or to beast fables and children's play. Sāgaranandin (3160 ff.) gives the *bhāṇikā* an exalted heroine, fine costume, one act, the tender and eloquent modes, a gentle (?—*manda*) hero and seven 'limbs'. The latter are : resignation [1371, the despair of Nandayantī], proposal [1371, complaint of Nandayantī], check, continuance, fright [1421, these three limbs all in Act VI, Duṣyanta's remorse], reproach [1760] and consummation (*vinyāsa*, *upanyāsa*, *virodha*, *anuvṛtti*, *sādhvasa*, *samarpaṇa* and *saṃhāra*). These are illustrated from a *prakaraṇa* and two *nāṭakas* (thus presumably they can be used in any play), but an example of the type is named as the *Kāmadattā*. Śāradātanaya gives some of this information and the 'limbs' under *ḍombī* (p. 257), but under *bhāṇikā* (p. 262) he gives Bhoja's account and what might be a garbled version of a fragment of Sāgaranandin's. The *Sāhityadarpaṇa* (p. 351) follows Sāgaranandin's account, the *Nāṭyadarpaṇa* just the first point of Bhoja and Hemacandra (p. 446) the 'old' verse of Abhinavagupta with a variant reading which does not help. Finally Śāradātanaya defines the 'limbs' separately (pp. 280 f.) and the manuscript reading there appears to be *bhāṇī-aṅgas*, in which case the confusion with *ḍombī* may be merely the modern editor's. A

383. XXXIV Sāgaranandin distinguishes from his *bhāṇikā* a *bhāṇī* (3184 ff.). It has one act, the sensitive *rasa* and is adorned with the ten limbs of the *lāsya* as well as with the parasite, jester and tutor. Example : *Viṇāvatī* (name of the heroine). The presence of the parasite, jester and tutor may seem surprising, but perhaps they are merely described or impersonated by the dancer, if this is a solo performance as the use of the *lāsya* limbs might imply. Śāradātanaya tacks on some lines corresponding to this at the end of his description of the *bhāṇikā* (p. 262). The other writers do not seem to have anything resembling this.

384. XXXV The *prasthāna* according to Abhinavagupta (I p. 166) is characterised by descriptive gestures. It is very delicate and represents going abroad *pravasana*, with imitation of the gait of elephants, etc. (I p. 181). The word *prasthāna* means 'departure' and presumably the scene is of someone setting out on a journey. Whether the traveller is riding an elephant, etc., or whether the gaits referred to are just dance conventions does not seem to have been clarified. Bhoja (II p. 466) says that the description may be of anything suggesting the longing of lovers, such as spring or the rainy season. As travel did not take place during the rains, this seems to imply that after the first scene of departure there will be a later one depicting love in separation, the emotions intensified by the season. At the end the heroic *rasa* is included. There are four 'exits' *apasāras*, presumably four scenes. According to Sāgaranandin (3148 ff.) the heroine is a maidservant carrying a pitcher for water or the like. The mode is very tender.

The hero is a slave or the like. A parasite is secondary hero. There is drinking of spirits. There is plenty of rhythm and tempo. Example : *Śṛṅgāratilaka*. The *Nāṭyadarpaṇa* gives the same account as Bhoja (p. 191). The *Sāhityadarpaṇa* is similar to Sāgaranandin (p. 347) but says the heroine is a slave, adds the eloquent mode as well as the tender, states that the drinking is because of union (or preparation?—*samāyoga*) at the consummation of the object intended (reunion at the end?) and that there are two acts. Śāradātanaya's account (p. 262) is similar to Sāgaranandin's, but adding like the *Sāhityadarpaṇa* that there are two acts. Possibly the four scenes of Bhoja could be divided between two acts, although the impression from elsewhere is that the 'scene' arrangement is an alternative to the act organisation. Later (p. 265) Śāradātanaya repeats the description in Bhoja and then (p. 266) the verse from Abhinavagupta (I p. 181). He has obviously compiled from older sources and not succeeded in organising the result properly. Hemacandra (p. 446) as usual has the same (old) verse as Abhinavagupta. Exx. *Dhūrtānanda, Vaiśikānanda*—Vema, *Sāhityacintāmaṇi*.

385. XXXVI The *ṣidgaka* is dominated by singing according to Abhinavagupta (I p. 166). His 'old' source says it is telling a woman friend of the bold conduct of a husband , delicate and sometimes about the acts of a rascal (it is not absolutely clear that this is the husband and not a lover)(I p. 181). Bahurūpamiśra on *Daśarūpaka* II. 8 connects the obscure term *ṣidga* with the 'tutor'. It is possible that this type is really the same as the *śrīgadita* of Sāgaranandin, Bhoja and others, with merely its name corrupted. Hemacandra follows Abhinavagupta or his source (p. 446), with variant spellings (*śiṃgaka*, etc.). In a rather obscure passage (I p. 181) Abhinavagupta (followed by Hemacandra) compares some of these types : the *bhāṇaka* is bold, but it is proper to admit the bold style of dancing into the delicate; when there is a little bold dancing in a delicate type we have the *prasthāna*, when there is much we have the *ṣidgaka*; when on the other hand the delicate enters into the bold we have the *bhāṇikā*. Finally the *preraṇa*, *rāmākrīḍaka*, *rāsaka*, *hallīsaka*, etc., can be included in this classification according to their degrees of variation. Śāradātanaya (p. 266) has the verse on *ṣidgaka* (but reads *śilpaka* !) as well as a section on *śrīgadita*, which however does not establish a distinction. Hemacandra also has both types separate, with a verse similar to Bhoja's on the *śrīgadita*. Though he keeps them separate and lists both in his preliminary enumeration, his two verses are close enough in content to have diverged from some common ultimate origin.

386. XXXVII The *rāmākrīḍa* is very briefly characterised in Abhinavagupta's 'old' source as a description of the seasons (I p.181). Śāradātanaya (p. 266) has the same line and it occurs also in Hemacandra (p. 446). The *Nāṭyasarvasvadīpikā* manuscript referred to by Mankad (p. 128) adds that it is sensitive. No one appears to know anything further about it.

387. Reviewing this group of dances we can see, despite some obscurities and the lack of examples preserved, that they all have some resemblance to the *lāsya* and other dances associated with it. Some apparently use the *vastu* structure; at least one uses the limbs of the *lāsya*. Many of the musical details, which we have omitted here, such as particular rhythms and dances, draw on the same repertoire as the *lāsya*. Abhinavagupta says they can be classified according to the proportions of in effect *lāsya* (delicate) and *tāṇḍava* (bold) dancing in them. The actual subject matter can be very varied and is also in part a basis of classification, especially as suggesting different styles as appropriate for the performance. Abhinavagupta further suggests a classification according to the proportions of pure dance, descriptive gesture (especially *prasthāna*), instrumental music (*bhāṇaka*) and song (*ṣidgaka*) (I p. 166).

388. It would appear that any story could be presented through the medium of these dances and any character depicted, but generally by a solo dancer miming the various persons supposed to appear (probably the same was done by the actor in a satirical monologue as he repeated the words they are supposed to utter), not by separate dancers taking various parts. Our sources are not always clear, when they mention a set of characters, whether these are separate parts or merely persons occurring in the story. There is one other source available to us which describes some of these dances, along with other types of drama : Amṛtānanda's *Alaṃkārasaṃgraha*. It is very close to Sāgaranandin and to the *Sāhityadarpaṇa*, and its date seems not far removed from that of the latter. The edition is not satisfactory and where its readings differ from Sāgaranandin's it has not seemed satisfactory to rely on them.

However, one point may be worth noting : for Sāgaranandin's *bhāṇī* it gives the name *lāsikā* (p. 158). This may be merely coining a new word from *lāsya* (the limbs of which are used), but it might be original. The *Sāhityadarpaṇa* seems to follow it in coining *vilāsikā* (p. 350).

389. XXXVIII Abhinavagupta distinguishes from these dances, i. e. the '*ḍombikā*, etc.', the *rāgakāvya* or simply *kāvya* often appearing in association with them. He quotes (I p. 182) a verse definition of the *kāvya* from Kohala, to the effect that it has a well sustained (or well finished) story *kathā*, with various *rasas* and marked by *rāgas* with acting in different tempi. The word *rāga* means originally 'passion' and that may be all it meant in Kohala's time. Later, however, and certainly before Abhinavagupta (for example in the work on music of Mataṅga), it was adopted as the term for a musical 'mode', replacing the old term *jāti* of the *Nāṭyaśāstra*. The connection of ideas presumably was that a mode was supposed to arouse a particular emotion, or express a particular passion. In time the word 'passion' came to be substituted, at least for the many new modes created in the medieval period, for the colourless word 'class' *jāti* : so many modes, so many passions. From the point of view of drama, *rāga* is a stronger and more specific term than *bhāva* to indicate emotional content, since *bhāva* in fact may mean any activity in thought, not emotion only. Thus Kohala may have been stressing the acting of the effects of passion in this type of performance. Abhinavagupta on the other hand seems to think that the reference is to the use of the *rāgas* as musical modes as a feature of this *kāvya*. He speaks particularly of such modes in his discussion which follows. In the name *rāgakāvya*, applied to this form by Abhinavagupta, we may understand the meaning 'passion-*kāvya*' (poem expressing passions, or poem with acting of passions) or 'mode-*kāvya*' (poem set to certain musical modes).

390. In his discussion Abhinavagupta names two examples, the *Rāghavavijaya* (Rāma's Victory) and *Mārīcavadha* (Death of *Mārīca*), and says that the former is sustained by the *ṭhakka rāga* and the latter by the *kakubha grāmarāga*; thus they are *rāgakāvyas* because they are essentially songs or song cycles. Earlier (I. p. 172) Abhinavagupta notes that such *rāgakāvyas* deal with all four ends of life, whereas the *ḍombikā*, etc., deal only with pleasure. Both are drama *nāṭya* because they involve acting *abhinaya*. The *ḍombikā* group is called *nṛttakāvya*, 'dance - *kāvya*' (I p. 175), though the *rāgakāvya* also contains dancing (I p. 180), hence its association with them. There is *tāṇḍava* in the *Rāghavavijaya*, etc., when the scene is appropriate for it (I. p. 198). Hemacandra (pp 445, 447 and 449) follows Abhinavagupta. [3924]

391. Sāgaranandin (3151 ff.) begins his account of the *kāvya* by saying it is adorned with *khaṇḍamāna*, *mātrā*, *dvipadī*, *bhagnatālaka*, etc. These may be metrical structures or dance forms (the *Nāṭyadarpaṇa* and Śāradātanaya have some of these and add others in their descriptions of the *kāvya*). All four modes of stage business are used and the *rasa* is predominantly the sensitive or the comic. There are three conjunctions (the embryo and obstacle being absent). It is in one act. Example: *Utkaṇṭhitamādhava* (presumably on Kṛṣṇa). The *Nāṭyadarpaṇa* (p. 192) has merely something like the first bit of this description. Śāradātanaya has a similar verse (p. 265) with some different readings and a further description (pp. 262 f.). This is very close to Sāgaranandin's wording but adds that sometimes the *lāsya* is used in it, and there may be the parasite and maid-servant, whilst the heroine is of good family or a geisha and the hero exalted but playful. Example : *Gauḍavijaya*. Or, he continues, there may be a brahman, minister, merchant, a brilliant hero and heroine, joyful speech and actions of young women, or the parasite, servant, etc. Example : *Sugrīvakelana*. None of this is very clear, except that all kinds of stories likely to produce the sensitive and the comic are used. Bhoja (II p. 466) has the same opening verse as Śāradātanaya, who probably borrowed it from him, but continues that there is a *kāvya* with various *rāgas*, which is called *citra* ('varied', 'decorated'). This apparently is the *rāgakāvya* : from the text of Bhoja it does not seem that he necessarily means this as a sub-variety of the *kāvya*, whilst the name implied is *citrakāvya* (this is used also in another sense, 'decorative *kāvya*', see the preceding chapter [250]). [3256, 3269]

392. Raghavan (*Bhoja's Śṛṅgāraprakāśa*, p. 549) suggests, however, that there is a simple *rāgakāvya* with only one *rāga* and a *citrarāgakāvya* with several *rāgas*. He further suggests (p. 551), rather convincingly, that the *Gītagovinda* (+12) is a *citrarāgakāvya* since its text indicates various *rāgas* to be used in singing its songs and it was intended for acting [cf. 420]. He mentions later examples of a similar type. We might add here the somewhat similar *Kṛṣṇagīti* (date, +1652) of Mānaveda, still performed daily in Kerala as a drama (Guruvāyur), as an example of the later continuation of the type. These are substantial dramatic poems containing many songs linked by narrative. The *campū* form and performance, at least in later practice, should be noted here as a related phenomenon (see Chapter VII [434]). The *kathakali* of Kerala may also be regarded as a variety of *rāgakāvya*. Like those described by Abhinavagupta, it may have any kind of story. It has many actors but they use gesture, not words, and are accompanied by separate singers who provide the dialogue songs, usually in Malayālam, and some connecting narrative verses, usually in Sanskrit.

393. XXXIX One minor type of drama remains, the *ullāpyaka*. The *Nāṭyaśāstra* (XXXI. 273 ff. Kāśī, 194 ff, Baroda) knows a song form called *ullopyaka* (variant reading *ullāpyaka*), and describes how with other songs it is to be set to the rhythm or metre. It is in three sections or 'limbs' *aṅga*, but one or two of these can be dropped, leaving an *ullopyaka* in two limbs or with one only. The *lāsya* is mentioned in the same context and, as we have seen, later in the same chapter of the *Nāṭyaśāstra* the details of the setting of its limbs to rhythms are given. The *ullopyaka* can also be built up to twenty limbs (XXXI. 301/221). In his comments Abhinavagupta does not appear to connect the *ullopyaka* with the *nṛtyas* or the *rāgakāvya* as a type of drama. Sāgaranandin, however, describes an *ullāpyaka* as a form of drama at the end of his account of the other types (3213 ff.). He says it consists of songs and has three limbs (reading uncertain: possibly three acts; he does not detail these to indicate whether they are the three limbs mentioned in the *Nāṭyaśāstra* and we do not know whether the three 'acts' version is a mere misreading or a real development in the type). It has an exalted hero, brilliant costumes, many props and represents the acts of the gods. It is adorned with the (twenty-seven) limbs of the *śilpaka* (see above [348]) and may have the comic, compassionate and sensitive *rasa*. Example : *Devīmahādeva* (evidently on Pārvatī and Śiva).

394. Now if the *ullāpyaka* has the twenty seven limbs of the *śilpaka* it may seem unlikely that it has its own three as well; hence perhaps we should accept the reading three acts : the *śilpaka* has four acts and three or four acts would seem to be needed for so many limbs. Śāradātanaya (p.266) has a generally similar description (the reading is *ullopyaka*) but states that the type has one act and three limbs. He adds also that there is no obstacle (i. e. there are four conjunctions: this also would indicate a long play needing at least three acts). He notes further that the type is explained in the *Gāndharvanirṇaya* (apparently a treatise on music). He adds a second example, an *Udāttakuñjara*. The *Sāhityadarpaṇa* (p. 347) has a description similar to Sāgaranandin's but states that the type may have one act but 'some say' it has three acts. He adds that it has four heroines, tearful songs and a war (reading doubtful). Amṛtānanda has one act and a happy conclusion, otherwise reads as Sāgaranandin. We thus do not get a very clear idea of the *ullāpyaka*. It was well known in ancient and early medieval times as a song form and seems to have undergone development into a dramatic form fairly late. Probably it remained essentially a series of song movements, like an opera or a *rāgakāvya*, but was extended to a considerable length in some cases, to accommodate four conjunctions and the limbs of the *śilpaka*.

395. We may seem to have given too much scope here to a number of obscure forms which we shall hardly meet in our historical study of *kāvya* literature. This may be justified, however, by the reflection that these minor dramatic types were probably of some importance and influence in the days when they flourished, that some of them are found as episodes in extant plays, whilst from the rarity of extant specimens we shall hardly touch on them again. Instead we find a great variety of still living modern descendants in different parts of India continuing the same popular traditions of dramatic dance and song. The major and more serious literary forms will claim plenty of space in our later chapters and do not require much discussion here : the minor and ephemeral forms deserve detailed attention somewhere in a study of *kāvya* literature and the present chapter has seemed the best place to collect what information we can find about them.

396. Very few dramas of any of the secondary types have

been preserved, though they were probably popular and numerous before the prohibition of the theatre over most of India. Their literary value being presumably accounted small by the learned taste of the scattered and impoverished scholars of the classics , on whom the preservation of the *kāvya* heritage devolved, they have been almost completely ignored in recent centuries and hence mostly lost. Some popular performances resembling some of these types, however, have survived in the folk traditions of favoured regions of India.

397. It is important not to overlook the secondary dramas and *nṛtyas*, which formed an essential part of the literary scene when *kāvya* flourished freely, merely because that part of the heritage has for the most part accidentally perished. If it was a relatively minor part, it complemented the serious and sophisticated drama and enriched the scene with some kinds of satire and farce of social interest little represented in the major classical plays extant, particularly the *durmallikā* and *preraṇa*, perhaps the *bhāṇī*, *ḍombikā* and *ṣidgaka*. Examples of satire are found among the other forms of *kāvya* but there too they have suffered badly from neglect.

398. The existence of a flourishing tradition of satire in ancient and medieval *kāvya* must be reckoned with in assessing the literature as a whole, and some knowledge of it is indispensable to the appreciation of the more elevated literature, which was at all times strongly influenced by the coexistence of satire, threatening to overwhelm the pompous or affected in a flood of ridicule. Hence the majority of the great *kāvyas* have a strong vein of humour, of laughing at themselves—their conventions, their milieu, the society they describe, religious rituals, *kavis* and vanity or humbug of whatever kind. The efforts of many satirists whose work has perished were not in vain, for it is perhaps the gentle irony, into which their criticisms were distilled in more fortunate works, that has done more than anything else to humanise and universalise the classics of *kāvya*, to make it resist the threat of being reduced to a literature merely of and for a feudal aristocracy.

399. Instead, *kāvya* flourished as a literature of the whole of society, with different genres appealing to different classes, with a variety of languages, with dramas regularly performed at popular festivals in the towns and villages. This society was not static, as the revolts and revolutions of the more detailed histories make clear to us, but on the other hand no better form of government than some form of feudalism could be established as the ancient monarchies, empires and republics gradually disintegrated between the —2 and the +4, and for many centuries afterwards only military groups were able to establish and hold power, that is to form an aristocratic ruling class. The questions remained, who should form such groups and such a class and how they should rule. The former question depended partly on the latter, since a tyrannical regime which alienated its subjects could be overthrown by a vassal who revolted and gained popular support, or by a revolution which, if it replaced one ruling feudal group by another, served as a check on oppression and a support for the traditional conception of a just rule as it was supposed to have been exercised by the greatest and most envied heroes of old. The new ruling group claimed to re-establish justice and to serve all humanity, and probably believed in this claim.

400. Social criticism in literature was thus not impotent, and at the same time literature was not exclusively at the service of the ruling class as such and without reserve, although the rulers provided much patronage for authors and found a sufficiency of servile flatterers to please them. Finally, feudal India had very many kings, many separate states. The *kavi* who sought an enlightened patron could often find one if he wandered far enough, for the tradition of the just and wise ruler was not entirely vain : Indian princes customarily received a broad education, including the *kāvya* classics and training in *kāvya* composition, and the royal contribution to *kāvya* has not been negligible. The *kavi* need not serve a tyrant, and his criticism of a bad government would be well received by one which sought the reputation of being better.

401. It is desirable to look more closely into the milieu of *kāvya* and the life and outlook of the *kavis* than we have done so far either in this brief historical digression or earlier in connection with the *nāgaraka* circles and the theory of pleasure, but first we must complete our review of the forms of *kāvya*.

Chapter VI

THE LITERARY FORMS : EPIC AND LYRIC POETRY

402 B. The epic is a large scale work entirely in verse, divided into cantos *sargas*, the average number of which is in the region of twenty. The average number of verses (invariably quatrains) in a canto is probably about seventy, but any number between forty and a hundred and twenty is quite common. The essential feature, from the point of view of the definition, is the length, and the term 'epic' may not be quite appropriate, though Bhāmaha says it is called a 'great' *kāvya* because it is 'of great things' (I. 19). In any case we are concerned with an artificial epic as opposed to the true Epic of more ancient times. As the aim here is comprehensiveness, the *kavi* displays his skill in lyric descriptions as well as in epic narrative. Nevertheless the original inspiration for such works seems to have been the true Epic narratives of Tradition, and in outline an epic is always a narrative, a story. A

403. The manner of telling the story, however, is so different from the naive narration of events, found in true Epic and ordinary story telling, that the reader who plunges in unprepared will be disappointed or at least baffled and frustrated. The *kavi* shows no urgent interest in unfolding the events of his story. What he seeks is the situation at a point in the story, the content of a single moment. With infinite patience he concentrates on drawing out the possibilities of the moment, describing it with all the imaginative detail his inspiration can evoke. His epic is a series of chosen moments, and the transitions between them, the passage of time , are handled as lightly as possible. The moment of action, for example a battle, is no exception : it is invariably the moment, not the movement, which is evoked. There is a good analogy in a gallery of paintings depicting a story, and such picture galleries were in fact common in the palaces of ancient and medieval India and probably influenced poetry.

404. In these epics the ancient narrative metre (the *vaktra*) of the true Epic, and the few longer metres it occasionally uses to heighten the conclusion of a canto, are overshadowed by dozens of more sophisticated metres of the type peculiar to *kāvya*. Whereas in true Epic the effective unit is the line, and moreover the lines are not independent but continuous, in that the sense and the grammatical construction often run over from line to line; in the *kāvya* epic the unit is the quatrain, and it is an absolute unit, detached from its neighbours in grammar and sense and usually having its own figure of speech (figurative speech being the essence of *kāvya* according to Bhāmaha, as we have seen). The combination of two or more quatrains in a complex description is rare. When it occurs, each quatrain will be a separate clause in the resulting period. The quatrain or strophe consists of four quarter verses in the given metre (including variations in 'uneven' metres); the narrative 'line' of true Epic on the other hand consists of two quarter verses, it being a feature of the *vaktra* that its alternate quarter verses are of contrasting rhythm and form a natural unit : when the *vaktra* is used in *kāvya* two lines are taken as an absolute quatrain. A

405. The story is presented in accordance with a theory not unlike that of the structure of drama and applying the same five conjunctions (see Bhāmaha I. 19 ff.) [744, 1517]. The varied episodes and incidents which abound in true Epic are here carefully subordinated to the main action, which itself is simple. The rise of a single hero is narrated, who dominates the whole poem. The aim, however, is to range over the whole field of human experience , expressing the four ends of life but especially 'wealth', and Bhāmaha holds that the eight classes of aesthetic experience *rasa* should all be produced by a good epic. Among the topics covered, Bhāmaha notes particularly the elements of politics: political debate or counsel *mantra* [728, 1334, 1520], embassy [728, 1267], expedition [714, 1399] and war [622, 714, 728, 1267, 1338, 1399, 1439, 1510-4]. The story itself must be well known, taken from Tradition (including legends from the Buddhist and Jaina canons) or more recent history (sometimes contemporary history, we find : Bhāmaha leaves the question open). What is imporant here for Bhāmaha is that an epic should be based on what is good (should therefore have moral as well as aesthetic purpose) and should be 'meaningful' *arthya*, whilst the expression must be elegant (avoiding vulgarity *agrāmya*). Finally it should be realistic : congruent with the nature of the world.

406. If the manner of developing the story is not straightforward, the story itself is far from being a naive tale of adventure. The epic takes on a philosophical character: the action is not simply a particular enterprise by the hero, it is a seeking and attaining of the recognised ends of human existence : wealth (*artha*, including power), pleasure *kāma* and virtue *dharma*; sometimes 'release' (*mokṣa*, release from transmigration) is added (as by Bhāmaha) as a fourth end. Thus the story tends to lose its individual character and to become a general expression of the pursuit of these ideals, a generalised symbol of human endeavour [1516].

407. Daṇḍin (I. 14ff.) modifies Bhāmaha's description slightly, introducing some new points. There should be a sufficient development of the story and of the aesthetic experience (i. e. sufficient length), but at the same time the cantos should not be too long (the proper length he leaves to the poet's judgment). They should be well fitted together (to make the whole poem a unity). The metres should be carefully chosen. Suggesting that an epic should be rich in content, as well as significant in action and sophisticated in language, he gives a list of descriptive topics, both naturalistic and human, with which it may be ornamented. Here he adds to Bhāmaha's political list cities [729, 1267], the ocean[1399, 1435, 1442], mountains[729, 741, 1267, 1424, 1438, 1442, 1500 -1], the seasons[1505; e. g. spring 729, 1399, 1426, summer 1399, rains 637, autumn 1399, 1434, 1442, 1499, winter 624, 633], moonrise[1424, 1438,1442, 1504], sunrise, sport or play in a garden or park or in water [1335, 1399, 1503], drinking [1267, 1504, 1520], lovemaking [728, 740, 1399, 1438, 1504, 1520], frustration [1392, 1434], weddings [1392, 1422] and the rise (presumably the youth) of a prince [728,1391]. Daṇḍin also suggests three ways of beginning an epic, with a benediction *āśis* (this is comparatively rare, examples are Śivasvāmin's *Kapphiṇābhyudaya*, +9, and Lakṣmīdhara's *Cakrapāṇivijaya*, +11), a salutation or invocation *namaskriyā* [1434] or by plunging straight into the story *vastunirdeśa* [1332, 1495], the last being by far the most usual. [3104; 3074, 4822]

408. Rudraṭa extended this list further (XVI. 7ff.), suggesting still more the old (true) Epic abundance of incidents (cf. Hegel's 'totality of objects') and contrasting with the concentration on action of the drama. The proper government of a realm should be shown and a king engaged in his cabinet, deliberating what action to take against an enemy (this is an expansion of 'counsel'). There may be descriptions of the agitation of the ladies of a city (when the hero passes) [731], countries and islands of the world, rivers [1399, 1502], forests [629, 630, 1503], the desert, encampment of an army, sunset [1427, 1438], twilight (evening [1438] and dawn [1439]), night [646, 1336, 1428, 1438, 1504], festival *samāja* [28] and musical entertainments. At the end the hero, with difficulty [1440-1], will be successful. The various topics should be brought in in necessary connection *prasaṅgāt* (15) with the story. **[4359, 2439, 1908]**

409. Bhoja, (*Śṛṅgāraprakāśa* II 470 ff.) sets out a system of 'qualities' and 'ornaments' of entire compositions *prabandhas*, to be used in epics, 'etc.' Several of these are derived from Daṇḍin's description of an epic, i. e. sufficient development, the cantos being not too long in order to keep it attractive, the cantos being fitted together so that the composition becomes a single whole, and so on . He adds and develops Bhāmaha's moral purpose : an epic should show the rise of the good and the fall of the bad, thus teaching injunctions and prohibitions *vidhiniṣedhavyutpāda* (this may be derived from Kuntaka, along with some other points applying to whole compositions, there called figurativeness of a *kāvya* as a whole [283-6]). The metres used should be suited to the aesthetic experiences (Bhoja gives details of this). Some of his 'ornaments' concern the details rather than the work as a whole, such as the ways in which poets change the natural order of things [1521]. Bhoja adds one or two topics to Rudraṭa's list, including hermitages [728, 737-9, 1520] and hunting [1393, 1399], and gives many details of the others, subdividing them and citing examples for all of them from fifteen or more epics, sometimes also from dramas, novels and biographies. **For the qualities see [1551] .**

410. The extant epics vary considerably in content, especially in accordance with the dominant *rasa* (from the truly epic heroic [1519] to the compassionate[623], the sensitive [1429] or the calmed[714]–which latter is often supposed to be that of the Great Epic itself as it has come down to us, since it ends with the renunciation of the world by its hero; the comic [715] appears only as a secondary *rasa*, usually to the sensitive but also to the calmed). Epics vary also in style[756, 1347, 1443, 1525], as the form passed through various fashions in its evolution, tending in some times or places to greater sophistication and difficulty, or reacting towards relative simplicity and sweetness (e. g. especially Abhinanda, +9, in his *Rāmacarita*). As is appropriate for such a major form, and the aim of universality, the epics often discourse on philosophy [728], though without abandoning the essential characteristics of *kāvya*, or less directly offer profundity of meaning and implication [1518].

411. A. quite separate category of literature, in effect, is the *citrakāvya*, primarily concerned with merely verbal decorativeness as we noted above [250]. It may however run to the length and outward form of an epic. These verbal **firework** displays are of very minor literary interest, and Ānandavardhana relegated them to the lowest rank of *kāvya*, but we may note that there are long poems having as main characteristic rhyme (in all its forms, including for example internal rhyme and play on homonyms—e. g. Vāsudeva's *Yudhiṣṭhiravijaya*, *c.* +900) or double meaning *śleṣa*; in the latter variety we have entire double epics in which two stories are narrated simultaneously, each verse having two possible interpretations, one appropriate for each story (e.g. Mādhavabhaṭṭa, +12). Eventually triple epics were produced and there is even one telling seven stories simultaneously (Cidambara's *Rāghavayādavapāṇḍavīya* tells three epics simultaneously, *c.* +1600; Meghavijaya's *Saptasandhāna*, +17, tells seven). A variety which can be very amusing, and also instructive, is the grammatical epic, in which the writer contrives to deploy as fully as possible each topic of Sanskrit grammar in rotation, marshalling in turn the hosts of forms of as many verbs as he can for each tense, especially rare or irregular verbs, and so on through the grammar book, in blocks of verses bristling with, for example, concentrated perfects or imperatives, yet still telling the story (Bhaṭṭi's *Rāvaṇavadha*, + 7?, is the most popular example). Otherwise the more difficult points of Sanskrit grammar may be less systematically mingled in an epic of higher literary value for the edification of the reader [755]. Even the greatest *kavis* sometimes felt that the universality of epic demanded the inclusion of a canto of *citrakāvya*, an appropriate place being the description of a battle, where the manoeuvres or rout of troops, or certain kinds of oratory, could be reflected in verses of extraordinary construction [1543-6].

412. Inadmissible as epics, or perhaps even as *kāvyas*, are the long narrative poems in simple language which continued to be written in answer to popular demand. They are usually easy abridgements of famous stories, from the Great Epic or other branches of Tradition to the most celebrated novels [667].

413. When an epic is written in Māhārāṣṭrī or Apabhraṃśa certain formal characteristics are changed along with the language. These concern the metres and the organisation of cantos. The Māhārāṣṭrī language is associated—it would seem necessarily associated — with a certain form of verse construction popular in folk song in ancient times, which may justly be called 'musical metre' on the ground of its actual musical organisation of long and short syllables in bars (whence its name *gaṇacchandas*, *gaṇa*='group', in this case a bar or half bar of music) [567]. Most of the other metres known to *kāvya* in Sanskrit are found in Prakrit literature also, especially in the earliest period, and the musical form on the other hand is frequently used in Sanskrit; but the musically constructed metres, which appear to have originated in Prakrit poetry and been subsequently borrowed into Sanskrit, having been the vehicle of the celebrated collection of lyrics or songs with which Māhārāṣṭrī *kāvya* made its début [781], remained standard for all Māhārāṣṭrī *kāvya* afterwards. This holds good even for the epic, in total contrast to the Sanskrit epic where these musical metres are avoided by almost all writers (they are common in Sanskrit only in the drama). Some slight variation is possible within the musically constructed metres themselves, so that the cantos need not all be in a single metre [1443]. One famous Māhārāṣṭrī epic, however, Vākpatirāja's *Gauḍavaha*, +8, is not divided into cantos at all, though conforming in length to the scale of an epic, so that along with the avoidance of the great variety of metrical forms of a Sanskrit epic there seems to have developed a dissatisfaction with the canto organisation interwoven with it. The cantos, if any, in a Māhārāṣṭrī epic are usually called *āśvāsas* (not *sargas*), and the form is also called *skandhakabandha* after its main metre [1266].

414. It is clear in fact that, in the vernacular languages of India, poetry was taking a definite direction based on the musical organisation first attested in the—5 or—4, to the exclusion of the older organisation of metres, based on counting syllables, and further of the hybrid organisation where the number of syllables in a line is fixed but so also is their quantity (which quantity is significant rhythmically in the strictly musical sense : a long syllable is exactly twice as long as a short one). The musical metres underwent gradual evolution from those of Pali to those of the modern languages of India, but retained their essential characteristics : the total length of a line or verse is fixed in quantity (in terms of bars) but the number of syllables in it is variable (two shorts may substitute for one long and vice versa). The overall organisation of an epic meanwhile tended towards shorter blocks of verses than the old canto, more homogeneous in subject matter and constituting paragraphs clustering round a certain topic. The standard canto epic in Sanskrit consists of verses which, though often forming groups describing some object, are nearly all completely isolated from each other and self contained. This organisation existed for a time in Māhārāṣṭrī, but was partly abandoned under the pressure of a more flowing organisation : instead of isolated verses there are clusters linked in subject and sometimes linked grammatically as well. This may reflect in part a song consisting not of a single verse but of several verses. Despite this trend the most famous Māhārāṣṭrī epics observe in general the rules and conventions of epics outlined above [1431].

415. In Apabhraṃśa this trend has proceeded much further. The simple canto organisation is replaced by one recognising smaller paragraphs or blocks as a regular textual unit. Daṇḍin (I. 37), after saying that in Sanskrit we have *sargabandhas*, etc. and in Prakrit (i. e. Māhārāṣṭrī) *skandhakas*, etc., states that in Apabhraṃśa we have *osaras*, etc. This seems to refer to the earliest phase of Apabhraṃśa composition from which no literature seems now to be available. The *osara* probably corresponds (as Apabhraṃśa equivalent) to the *apasāraka* which we interpreted as an 'exit', i. e. complete dance, in the *ḍombikā* [379], also to the *vastu*, 'subject', 'scene', of four strophes as in the *chalika* [367] and to the *nāṭyarāsaka carcarī* [359] of four verses each followed by a refrain. In other words the *osara* may be a group of four strophes followed by a refrain, used as a regular unit in epic composition in Apabhraṃśa, as the *skandhaka* or single musical strophe was used in Māhārāṣṭrī and the quatrain in Sanskrit. The minor dramatic types mentioned here seem usually to have been in Apabhraṃśa, so that the four verse plus refrain unit may have been characteristic of all early Apabhraṃśa literature. Ratnaśrījñāna in explaining Daṇḍin here names a *Valayakarambaka* (apparently unknown) as example of an *osara* and adds that 'etc.' means *rāsakas* [359], etc.

416. The available Apabhraṃśa epics, which are later than Daṇḍin (+7), show a further stage in development. The smaller unit of four verses or eight lines is called a *kaḍavaka*, whilst a larger unit called the *sandhi*, comparable with the canto, is established, consisting of about fifteen *kaḍavakas*. As opposed to Māhārāṣṭrī the metres, though all of the musical type, are extremely varied in construction, new lengths of line and new rhythms being introduced. The standard small unit *kaḍavaka* consists of four, sometimes more, verses of one metre followed by a single refrain verse in another. Rarely an introductory verse in some other metre is prefixed (at the beginning of a larger unit—the *sandhi*—there must be an introductory verse). The metres used in these three places are distinct, and there are quite a number of each class. Generally each *kaḍavaka* is a unit also as regards meaning, having a single topic; in origin it appears to be a song and might be so translated. The Apabhraṃśa epics are of considerable length, being of the order of a hundred *sandhis* in some cases. The same organisation and the same metres have continued without serious modification down into the epics of the modern languages of India. Poetry in Apabhraṃśa seems invariably to be rhymed, another feature which distinguishes these epics from those in Sanskrit and Māhārāṣṭrī. The pioneering epic of this type organised in *sandhis* was apparently Caturmukha's *Abdhimathana*, +7? (Bhoja : *Śṛṅgāraprakāśa* II p. 470), and the greatest Apabhraṃśa epic poets perhaps Svayambhū, +9, and Puṣpadanta, +10 [491]. [3255, 3261 ff., 3978 ff.]

417 C. The lyric also is in verse. In the strict sense of *anibaddha* or *muktaka*, 'independent' verse, it may consist of detached single verses (*gāthā*, *śloka*) [575], almost always quatrains, some of which are single-verse songs (the performance of such a song includes generally a good deal of repetition of lines, parts of lines, and sometimes the whole quatrain). On the other hand as *khaṇḍakāvya* or 'short *kāvya*' we have more highly organised lyric poems of various lengths [1238]. Clusters of two or more verses are recognised as distinct units (linked in meaning and generally in grammatical construction), and we find again the standard song of **four** verses (i. e. the *kaḍavaka*), of which cycles are built.

418. A convention developed of publishing independent verses in collections of a hundred *śataka* [1455] or of several hundreds [777]. Sometimes these are uniform in content as sensitive *śṛṅgāra*, relating to policy or worldly wisdom *nīti* (the most famous is by Bhartṛhari, +7?), dispassionate and philosophical (*vairāgya* : 'renunciation') or religious, the hymn *stotra* addressed to the gods (notably those of Mayūra and Bāṇa, both+7), to the Buddha [890] or the Jinas. Thus we find again the four ends of life as basic themes. Other themes, however, are also found. Further, such a 'hundred' might be formed round some episode or incident with a story unifying the whole, being thus a 'short *kāvya*'. A favourite device is to introduce the theme of separated lovers, with a fanciful sending of a message provoked by some poetic incident such as seeing a bird or a cloud. Here the poet takes the opportunity to describe some of his favourite scenes, in the guise of giving directions to the supposed messenger for his journey [1410]. The *anyāpadeśa*, 'citation of something else', is another type of lyric found in 'hundreds', in which human life and society, and especially the causes of bitterness such as unfairness and fickleness and the preferment of the worthless, are criticised in the veiled character of natural phenomena (the type of which is Bhallaṭa's, +9, famous verse on the dust blown to the highest places by the fickle wind). Lyrics, like epics, may cross the borderline of *citrakāvya* [1079]. **[3330 ff.]**

419. Anthologies of lyrics were made of favourite verses from many poets. The best Sanskrit anthology known, and apparently the earliest available, is Vidyākara's *Subhāṣitaratnakośa*, *c* +1100. These are extremely valuable for preserving examples of the work of poets not otherwise known at present, and for indicating the taste of their period in relation to the heritage of poetry then extant. Though lyric in content they are far from being restricted to poems of the lyric form as sources, since especially dramas and to some extent epics abounded in detachable verses of a descriptive character. The contents of the anthologies are arranged by topics, such as the seasons, the times of day, mountains, the wind, poverty, the gods, the enjoyment of love, the pain of separation, the Moon authors, good and bad men, corroborations *arthāntaranyāsas*, *jāti* ('class', here untranslatable : 'nature' or 'genre', meaning the characteristics of animals and birds, the types of village and country life, the idiosyncrasies of authors and scholars), and the popular *anyāpadeśa*.

420. The most highly organised lyric poems, where in fact we find ourselves on or beyond the borderline of drama, are those based on the *kaḍavaka* or four-verse song, which appears to have originated in Apabhraṃśa when it was the vernacular of most of northern India. This, with its great variety of metres, formed the unit of construction of epic as well as lyric poems in Apabhraṃśa (and following it in the modern languages). In Sanskrit it was occasionally adopted for lyrics; never, it seems, for epics. Like the musical metres of Prakrit earlier, it easily gained popularity in Sanskrit as a vehicle for songs, reflecting the folk songs of the day, but was found contrary to the epic spirit. Because of its vitality in the vernaculars, on the other hand, the song cycle persistently grew to epic proportions and embraced epic subjects in the popular (Apabhraṃśa and modern) literature. An example of a very elaborate Sanskrit lyric composition of this construction is the *Gītagovinda* (+12), describing the loves of Kṛṣṇa in twelve cantos (really *sandhis*) each containing one to four songs of four verses: The songs are sung by Kṛṣṇa or Rādhā or by Rādhā's friend (confidante), and (unlike the Apabhraṃśa epics but suggesting instead drama) are connected by brief narrative or descriptive passages. The appropriate musical mode *rāga* and rhythm *tāla* for each song are noted in the text. The metres of the songs are those of Apabhraṃśa. As noted above [392], it has been suggested that this poem is really a kind of drama, of the *rāgakāvya* type, since it is usually acted.

421. A few examples of Apabhraṃśa lyrics built up of *kaḍavakas* are extant from about the period of the *Gītagovinda*.

For example a number have been preserved in Apabhraṃśa such as Vajrasena's *Bharateśvarabāhubalighora* and Śālibhadra's *Bharateśvarabāhubalirāsa*, which might be described as 'ballads' rather than lyrics. Vijayasena's *Revantagirirāsa*, describing the Girinagara Mountain, is more strictly a lyric, as is Pālhaṇa's *Āburāsa*. Still more lyrical are Śālibhadra's *Buddhirāsa* (a kind of *nīti* collection) and the sensitive *Bārahamāsās* by Pālhaṇa and Vinayacandra. They are usually called *rāsas*, and were generally intended to accompany a dance, hence, presumably, may properly be identified as minor dramas, i. e. as *rāsakas* [356, 360]. There are early examples consisting of four or more *kaḍavakas* in different metres, but there are other slightly later, examples uniform in metre and not arranged in *kaḍavakas*. These song cycles sometimes grew into the vernacular epics also called *rāsas*. Some connection with the dramatic *nṛtya* type called *rāsaka* seems probable. Unfortunately no certain example of the latter is available : we have no more than a couple of quotations by Abhinavagupta from one called the *Rādhāvipralambha* [357], by the otherwise unknown Bhejjala. Here evidently we have the Kṛṣṇa and Rādhā theme again. The language is stated to be the Saindhava (of Sindhu) and is a form of Apabhraṃśa. (At least three other *rāsakas* are known by title only, and indicate a variety of themes besides the popular Kṛṣṇa story.) From the period +800 to +1200 we have numerous Buddhist lyrics in Apabhraṃśa, called *dohās* and *caryāpadas*, of varied form by Saraha, Kambala, Kṛṣṇācārya and others. [2494, 2503-7; 2512-9, 2913-21]

422. In connection with lyrics we may note that Sanskrit, the Prakrits and Apabhraṃśa possess an enormous repertoire of metres. They are used, with some restrictions, in the drama and epic also, as briefly indicated above, but as they are nearly all of lyric origin, and are all freely used in lyric poetry, this is the most appropriate place for a note and recapitulation on them. Hundreds of metres are attested in use, of which some scores (about sixty to eighty) are of common occurrence, each distinct in rhythm and associations. They may be grouped as the old primarily narrative metres (syllabic, and nearest in feeling to European metres), the musical metres (strictly, musically, quantitative, i.e. more strict than for example those of Greek or Latin, and organised in musical bars) and the 'fixed' quatrain metres (simultaneously syllabic and strictly musical : each has its characteristic pattern of long and short syllables, its special rhythm, extending over a whole line—quarter verse—instead of a mere foot or bar, or even over two or all four lines of the quatrain). The last class is the most numerous, though the proliferation of musical metres in Apabhraṃśa and modern Indo-Aryan brought these to the dominant position in the literature of those languages. [538, 567, 581-2, 615-6, 659-60, 752, 781, 1268, 1412, 1443, 1448, 1485, 1547, 1919, 2532, 2673, 3030, 3117, 3126, 3262-9, 3313, 3609, 4383, 4786, 5503]

Chapter VII

THE LITERARY FORMS : BIOGRAPHY AND THE NOVEL (INCLUDING THE *CAMPŪ* AND SHORT STORY)

423 D. The biography or 'little history' *ākhyāyikā* is in prose, though it may have a few introductory verses, sometimes two verses at the beginning of each of its chapters and rarely a verse elsewhere. The division into chapters, called *ucchvāsa* or by some synonym, corresponds to the division into cantos of an epic, whilst some critics seem to regard the biography practically as an epic in prose sharing the usual epic characteristics other than metre. Unfortunately few biographies are extant and those extant are mostly unprinted, so that it is difficult to get a practical idea of the form and of the scope of its content. It appears to have originated as a branch of Tradition or history *itihāsa* and later to have been assimilated into the *kāvya* movement. Thus Kauṭilya (–4?) in the *Arthaśāstra*, I. 5, lists 'biography' among the branches of Tradition. Vararuci (Kātyāyana, –3?) in his *Vārttika*, on Pāṇini IV. 2.60 and IV. 3.87, mentions biographies and Patañjali (–2?) explaining this gives the titles of some of them [652]. It is not clear whether these grammarians regarded biography as already a *kāvya* form, but Bhāmaha (I. 18) and other later critics are quite categorical that it was one for them.

424. Tradition consists largely of 'histories' *ākhyānas*, as for example the main story of the Great Epic and also its episodical stories. In Tradition the extant *ākhyānas* are mostly in narrative verse *vaktra*, though there are exceptions in prose or in mixed prose and verse. In the more ancient literature of the Veda, however, there are a number of *ākhyānas* mostly in prose, preserved in ritual texts (*Brāhmaṇas*) [512]. It appears then that the prose history was an extremely ancient form, used for the narration of stories believed to be true, concerning celebrated persons. Whilst the bulk of the historical traditions of ancient times were incorporated in the *itihāsa*, the ancient practice of composing accounts of famous men and women, in narrative prose, evidently continued independently and then became a branch of *kāvya* composition [610]. As *itihāsa* tended to become indistinguishable from *purāṇa*, 'antiquity', which originally (e.g. *Arthaśāstra* I. 5.14) was simply one branch of it, biographies of contemporary or recently living persons, such as an *ākhyāyikā* seems generally to have been, might appear inappropriate as part of it. Biographies then found a suitable home among the branches of *kāvya*, whose stylistic characteristics and figurative language they acquired and developed.

425. The characteristic feature of the biography, as a form of prose *kāvya*, is that it is an account of what actually happened *vṛtta* (Bhāmaha I. 26), of matters perceived *upalabdha* (Amarasiṃha : *Nāmaliṅgānuśāsana*, I.5.5), as contrasted with fiction or works of imagination *kalpanā*. Amarasiṃha clearly contrasts the novel *kathā* (I. 5. 6.), as imaginary, with the biography, as factual, and his commentator Kṣīrasvāmin (+12) explains 'perceived' as 'happened' *vṛtta* and 'imagination' as 'invented' *utpādya*. Bhāmaha begins his description of the biography (I.25-7) by saying that the narrative follows the order *anākula* of what was done *prakṛta*, 'performed'. At the same time its speech and meaning are 'audible' *śravya* (recited?). The matter should also be connected with what is exalted *udātta* and divided into chapters. The hero (or heroine) in it narrates his own actions as they happened. Verses in certain metres (*vaktra* and *aparavaktra*) are used occasionally to indicate future matters (for example, we may add, at the beginning of a chapter). The narrative may be marked *aṅkita* by some special words (read *aṅkana* with Ratnaśrījñāna, p. 21, i. e. 'markings') indicating the intentions of the author *kavi*. It also contains the abduction of a girl, a battle, frustration (in love) and (then) success *udaya*. Since Bhāmaha says afterwards that a novel may be either in Sanskrit or not, it is inferred (e. g. by Ratnaśrījñāna) that the theory accepted by Bhāmaha requires that a biography be in Sanskrit. If so, this is the only branch of *kāvya* so restricted, which possibly was a relic of its origin from Tradition. In connection with the content we may note that the traditional story of Vāsavadattā, the heroine of an ancient biography [652], includes her abduction by Udayana. For biographies in Pali see [610, 4099-114].

426. Raghavan has pointed out (*Bhoja's Śṛṅgāraprakāśa*,

p. 615) that Sarvānanda, commenting on the passage noted above in the *Nāmaliṅgānuśāsana*, quotes a verse from Kohala on the biography and novel. This confirms the distinction between the novel as imaginary and the biography as deriving from a 'succession' *paramparā* (i.e. a tradition of persons reporting the events, ultimately the original hero). If this quotation from Kohala suggests that that author wrote on *kāvya* in general as well as on drama, we may turn next to an interesting passage in the *Kāmasūtra* (p. 29), where biographies are spoken of as if they were actually a kind of dramatic performance. Among the branches of pleasure we read 'showing plays and biographies' *nāṭakākhyāyikādarśana*. This may be understood, in the light of the performance of *campūs* (e. g. as *kūttus*) in Kerala (see below [434]), as a kind of public recitation, or rather dramatic monologue, by an actor narrating the story, with appropriate intonation, expressions and gestures.

427. Daṇḍin (I. 23ff.) denies that there is any validity in the distinction between biography and the novel : there is just one class here, namely prose *kāvya*. In fact he has only three classes of *kāvya* : verse, prose and mixed, lyric poetry being just part of epic; drama is mixed, as is *campū*, but he does not make it quite clear whether he regards it as a fourth distinct class. He also points out that some of the description given by Bhāmaha had been infringed in practice : that there were biographies in which someone other than the hero narrates his actions; that metres other than those mentioned by Bhāmaha had been used; novels had been known to be divided into chapters; that the topics, abduction, etc., were found in epics; that marking by special words could be used elsewhere (Ratnaśrījñāna gives the *Kirātārjunīya* [1495] as an example for this in epic). Ratnaśrījñāna (p. 21) adds that there were biographies in languages other than Sanskrit. These seem relatively minor points; the criticisms do not touch the major distinction between history and fiction, which originally differentiated the two types, as it differentiated *nāṭaka* from *prakaraṇa* in drama. For the rest, Bhāmaha's description may have been accurate in his own day, whilst later *kavis* by Daṇḍin's time had introduced novelties (as we may see for example in a biography by Bāṇa, +7, which we must examine in a moment).

428. Rudraṭa (XVI. 24ff.) adds some further points, reflecting these same developments in the conventions of a biography. It may begin with a salutation to gods or teachers and praise of *kavis* (this latter convention led to the idea of a kind of historical review of the great authors inserted in a *kāvya,* of which we have several very useful examples later). Then the writer may give an account of how he came to compose his work, with his autobiography included. The chapters are like the cantos of an epic; each may begin with two *āryā* verses (a musical 'bar' metre) introducing the matter. When doubt is expressed about an unseen matter, whether present or past, or about something which might be seen but lies in the future, it may be resolved by a recitation of verses in various metres, using the figures 'expression of something else' *anyokti* [261], 'condensed expression' [211] or 'double meaning' [263], in the presence of the doubter when he provides an opportunity. Rudraṭa indicates that in general the biography should resemble an epic in construction, ending with success : if there is a disaster for the hero he will eventually retrieve his fortunes.

429. Ānandavardhana says (323ff.) that a biography should have compounds, moderate or long, but not where the aesthetic experience is the sensitive in frustration or the compassionate. Bhoja (*Śṛṅgāraprakāśa* II p. 469) follows Bhāmaha, but adds that a biography may be narrated either by the hero himself or by a follower of his. It should definitely be in Sanskrit prose. In discussing the features of epics, etc., as entire compositions, he includes some illustrations from a biography (the *Harṣacarita* by Bāṇa) for the salutation type of beginning (p. 472) and other features, such as the youth of a prince (p. 475). Mammaṭa says (end of VIII) that a biography should not be delicate *masṛṇa* in style (language) even when the experience is the sensitive, which Ruyyaka in his *Saṃketa* explains as because the biography is predominantly 'bold' *vikaṭa* in composition.

430. The earliest biography other than in Pali, Bāṇa's *Harṣacarita* (+7, slightly earlier than Daṇḍin and much later than Bhāmaha), exemplifies the later phase of these discussions. It begins with a salutation and verses praising great authors The first two chapters are autobiographical [484], including an account of how the author met the subject of his biography.

The actual biography then begins in the third chapter and occupies six chapters; it is narrated by Bāṇa himself, no doubt in the capacity of a 'follower' of his royal subject. In most other respects the work agrees with Rudraṭa's description, including the doubt resolving verses heard by the characters, the *āryā* verses opening chapters and the disaster and recovery. There are massive descriptive passages and plenty of compounds, the former rather more detailed and realistic than those in epics—an advantage deriving from the prose form.

431. It is perhaps in the nature of biography that relatively few should survive, their subjects being eclipsed in interest on the one hand by the ancient heroes of Tradition, of classical antiquity, and on the other hand by more recent celebrities. The *Harṣacarita* has been treasured for the sake of Bāṇa's brilliant Sanskrit writing and wealth of ideas, for the appealing personality of the author and not for his subject. To the historian who can understand this kind of composition, however, often allusive (figurative and full of implications rather than direct statements, as befits a great *kāvya*) and generally difficult in style, Bāṇa offers an illuminating interpretation of contemporary events and attitudes. The work is primarily heroic, with much of the compassionate and marvellous also [1644].

432. About half a dozen generally similar biographies of contemporary characters are known, written from the +12 to the +18, and no doubt there are others yet to come to light. At the same time it should be noted that biographical epics from the same period are more numerous, representing a kind of fusion of the two forms which had become popular by +1000. On the other hand we have a smaller number of biographies of heroes of antiquity (of the Jaina prince Jīvandhara, of Kṛṣṇa and of Rāma). Krishnamacharya lists (pp. 432 f. and 488 f.) quite a number of other Sanskrit prose works which may be biographies but have not yet been printed or examined to determine their contents. As far as is known, all the ancient biographies have been lost (apart from the Vedic and Pali prose narratives we have noted). It is noteworthy that, unlike the available medieval biographies, they were all of women [652, 1264].

433. The *campū*, or *kāvya* in mixed prose and verse, is a form which became extremely popular after the +10, though apparently rare earlier, and to some extent replaced the biography. This continuity seems to be confirmed by the practice of 'showing' or performing both biographies and *campūs*. On the other hand the contents of the *campūs* are extremely varied: in fact no limitation is found either in theory or practice. Some are biographical in the limited sense (e. g. Somanātha's *Vyāsayogicarita*, +16), most retell stories from Tradition (e. g. Vidarbharāja's *campū* on Rāma), but a *campū* may be a history (e.g. Vāsudevaratha's, +18), a novel (e. g. Soḍḍhala's) or a satire (e. g. Veṅkaṭādhvarin's, +17), a description of a festival (e. g. Ahobala's, +14) or a sacred place (e. g. Rāmavarman's *Syānandūrapuravarṇana*, +19), in fact anything whatever in content as far as can be seen from the practice. The critics have very little to say about them. Bhāmaha says nothing. Daṇḍin (I. 31) merely mentions the *campū* as a mixture of prose and verse in form, like the drama. Ratnaśrījñāna explaining this says that occasional verses in novels, etc., are disregarded in this connection as inessential, in other words in a *campū* the verse and prose are both important. In practice the proportions of verse and prose vary considerably, but both occur at fairly regular intervals throughout a *campū*. As examples Ratnaśrījñāna mentions the *Jātakamālā* [915] and a *Damayantī* which seems to have been lost. Bhoja (*Śṛṅgāraprakāśa* II p. 470) says that, like a biography (a significant comparison), a *campū* is divided into chapters, is 'marked' (with special words peculiar to the author and suggesting his aims) and is in *divya* verse and prose, which, if the correct reading, apparently means it is in Sanskrit. He too gives the *Damayantī* as a model, and a *Vāsavadattā*, also apparently lost. Raghavan has shown (*Bhoja's Śṛṅgāraprakāśa*, p. 815) that this *Damayantī*, from which Bhoja quotes, is quite different from Trivikrama's *Nala* (+10) on the same story from Tradition. The *campū* thus seems usually to be a narrative retold from Tradition, but it is allowed complete freedom of content. Any *kāvya* in mixed prose and verse is a *campū*, unless it is a drama (in regular form introduced by the producer, etc., with its speeches assigned to the characters).

434. In Kerala, where the Indian tradition survives in its purest form, *campūs* are performed in theatres by actors. Dr. Kunjunni Raja (*The Contribution of Kerala to Sanskrit Literature*, p. 238; 'Kūṭiyāṭṭam', *Samskrita Ranga Annual* II, 17ff.—

see pp. 20, etc.) has given some account of this, but it should be noted by those unfamiliar with Kerala or South India that when he says 'temple' he means not a building but the whole enclosed area, a sort of park or campus; for the theatres of Kerala, though usually attached to temples, are large detached buildings, designed according to the recommendations of the *Nāṭyaśāstra* (II) as theatres. A *campū* is generally presented as a *kūttu*, 'acting', or properly *prabandham kūttu*, 'acting of a composition'. The solo actor appears in the rôle of the jester or fool on a small stage: in the Kerala tradition he is free to add translations and explanations in the vernacular (Malayālam) and to insert comic business of his own.

435. It should be added that a *campū* may be of any length. The chapters (and probably those of the biography before them) probably represent the equivalent of an act of a play, a part to be performed in one continuous session, but they too are very variable in length. A rather regular and average number of chapters for a *campū* is eight, but some of those written for the Kerala actors have only one short chapter, probably reflecting the elaborate performance intended, whilst long *campūs* continued to be written alongside them. The *Jātakamālā* is in thirty four chapters, each of which is a separate story. On account of the extreme flexibility of the *campū* form it is perhaps not surprising that *campūs* are often referred to simply as 'compositions' *prabandhas*. The name *campū* itself is obscure : it might be translated 'movement'. The form of mixed prose and verse is very ancient and examples of it can be found in the Veda [512, 515]) and in the *Tripiṭaka* (for example in the *Jātaka* [611]). It should be noted finally, as characteristic for *campū*, that the prose and the verse perform the same functions in the narrative, not different functions [930]. [2696, 3927] A

436 E. The novel or 'story' *kathā* (the term is used in both the general sense and the specific sense of 'novel', though for the latter we sometimes find as synonym *mahākathā*, 'great story') is a fiction invented by the author. We have already noted, in contrasting it with the biography, Amarasiṃha's qualification of the novel as imaginary, with Kṣīrasvāmin's explanation 'invented'. It is normally in prose, though there are examples in verse, the latter especially when the language is not Sanskrit (or Paiśācī [666]) but Māhārāṣṭrī [772] or Apabhraṃśa (an example of the last is Dhanapāla II's *Bhaviṣyadatta*, c. +1000). There is also the overlap with *campūs*, which occasionally are novels in content (e. g. Soḍḍhala's *Udayasundarī*, +11, in Sanskrit; Uddyotana's *Kuvalayamālā*, +8, in Māhārāṣṭrī). Bhāmaha (I.28f) notes that the novel does not have the verses in *vaktra* and *apara-vaktra*, characteristic of a biography, which indicate future matters, nor is it divided into chapters. This implies a different organisation and perhaps that it is simply for private reading, not for any kind of 'performance'. Bhāmaha also notes that a novel may be in Sanskrit or not in Sanskrit, for example in Apabhraṃśa and finally that the hero's story is told by another person, not by himself (explaining that a noble person would not reveal his own qualities, which would appear to reflect on the characters of the heroes of biographies). Daṇḍin as we have seen, though a major novelist himself, has nothing to say except that there is such a thing as prose *kāvya*. By implication he denies any significance in an attempt to separate fiction from history. [1696-732, 4180-202, 4587-629]

437. Rudraṭa (XVI. 20 ff) gives a fuller account of what he calls the *mahākathā* (literally 'great story'), i.e. full length novel, which in principle is equivalent in scope to an epic. It starts with some verses of salutation to gods or teachers and further verses briefly mentioning the family of the author. Then the main story begins in prose. Alliteration is favoured for the prose, together with a preponderance of short syllables (this will give an impression of lightness and rapidity). Instead of beginning with the main story [1560], the author may start with a subsidiary narrative and later introduce the main story into it as necessarily connected. The commentator Namisādhu names Bāṇa's *Kādambarī*, +7, as a standard example of this construction. In fact we find, in such novels as those of Bāṇa and Dhanapāla I, that several pieces of narrative may be emboxed one within another; it is this which provides a structure for the whole, in place of chapter divisions, the reader being led deeper into the story, learning more about the characters by going back into their pasts, until at the end the last piece of narrative falls into place and everything is understood. The form of a novel may thus be extremely complex, contrasting with the straightforward passage through time of a biography or epic. Instead of following the course of history, we follow the experiences of certain characters, who learn of past events from one another in an apparently chance sequence. [4211-89]

438. Rudraṭa continues that the conclusion of a novel may be 'obtaining a girl', thus the aesthetic experience will (frequently) be the sensitive. If it is not in Sanskrit a novel need not be in prose (as we have noted). [2567-616]

439. Afterwards Rudraṭa (XVI. 33f.) discusses the 'short story' *khaṇḍakathā* as a form of minor *kṣudra kāvya* (see below), mostly disastrous for the hero, instead of ending with his success, and producing the compassionate experience. Alternatively it may be sensitive, with frustration, e. g. through the hero going abroad, but with success at the end.

440. Namisādhu in his further comments notes that the introductory verses in a novel may include praise of good men [1577] and blame of scoundrels [1576]. If the conclusion is not union with a girl it may be winning a kingdom and so on.

441. Finally, after commenting on short stories, Namisādhu notes the *parikathā*, presumably as a form of minor *kāvya* (see below[449]), which is mostly in verse and is a condensation of a narrative (i. e. apparently an abridgement or summary from which the story can be extemporised). Ānandavardhana and Bhoja, followed by Hemacandra, have these and other subdivisions of *kathā*, which we may examine below.

442. Being a form of *kāvya*, the standard novel shares the common characteristics of 'fine literature', such as the free use of figures of speech, the occurrence of long descriptions [1566] and organisation with reference to the theory of *rasa* and the purposes of *kāvya*. The prose form allowed a fuller development of the 'styles' (*mārga* or *rīti*) and 'qualities' *guṇa* than verse, and the theorists of style took a special interest in prose. Daṇḍin was himself a novelist, though both in theory and in practice he rejected some of the usual definitions, particularly the distinction between the novel and biography, preferring to confound history and fiction. Vāmana seems to have regarded prose as the highest form of expression in *kāvya* (p. 12). He disregards the characterisations or definitions of different forms of *kāvya*, novel, biography, epic, etc., as not very interesting (p. 14). Whilst Daṇḍin was an exponent of the *vaidarbha* style in his novel *Avantisundarī*, the novelist Subandhu in his *Vāsavadattā* carried the *gauḍīya* to an extreme

[1559]. According to Mammaṭa (end of VIII) a novel should not be completely 'bold' *uddhata* in style even when the experience is the furious, which Ruyyaka in his *Saṃketa* explains as because the novel is mostly delicate *sukumāra* in composition. It thus contrasts with the biography [429].

443. The essential characteristic of the novel is that it is a fiction (this holds good for the *Avantisundarī*, despite Daṇḍin's theory and his attempt to graft his story onto actual history—an attempt by no means unusual in Indian novels). In the pre-*kāvya* period the *ākhyāna* was a narrative definitely held to be factual, adduced as historical corroboration of some ancient ritualistic custom or to supply the biography of some celebrated person regarded as historical. At first, *kathā*, as simply 'story' in general, had a wide meaning embracing in ordinary speech *ākhyānas* as well as fictions and narratives of any sort. At the time of the origin of *kāvya* India was extremely rich in narrative literature, in the form of short stories told in prose and more sophisticated stories in verse tending to greater length [570, 579, 608-9]. Of the latter, we have numerous examples, developed at all lengths from a few verses requiring elaboration in prose (cf. the *parikathā*) up to the full blown epic. A high proportion are evident fictions, though generally given some kind of circumstantial presentation suggesting the opposite. A few seem of genuine historical origin; quite often we find a doubtless historical character built up into a legend no longer containing more than a few distorted scraps of real history. Excluding the *ākhyānas* and the epic tradition (which latter employed different methods of holding interest), the story-teller thus developed his art for its own sake and for conveying truths in his own way without being bound to historical fact. The realism which the ancient storytellers developed is that of characterisation and social criticism of their own times, not of historical research [579, 608-9]. Historical characters are merely occasional props adding atmosphere, but the circumstantial presentation implying actual history is designed to make the story seem as realistic as possible (this does not prevent the story being ostensibly set in a remote past). Otherwise, in defiance of sober reality, the storyteller may give his tale a pattern of an artistic, poetic, kind in order to enhance its effect [611]. This is especially the case in the numerous stories having a moral which have been preserved, for example by the Buddhists [579, 608-9]. Popular short stories have been written in very large numbers throughout the history of *kāvya*, but being generally simple in style they have been neglected by the critics. The serious novel of their theory must have the stylistic sophistication of *kāvya*, it must also be of some length, a 'great story'. [1964-2062]

444. The effective beginning of the novel in this sense, as far as we now know, was the *Bṛhatkathā* ('Great Story') of Guṇāḍhya, who is revered as a great *kavi*, one of the early pioneers, by many later *kāvya* writers [665, 704]. Unfortunately the original is not now available, being written in the obsolete Paiśācī language and regrettably replaced by Sanskrit and other later versions. Its date has not been exactly determined, the traditional association of Guṇāḍhya with a Sātavāhana emperor in the +2 being in defiance of the archaic language. If Guṇāḍhya lived at that time he was hardly the real author, since the language appears to have been one current in perhaps the—2 or even earlier. If we suppose he revised or in some way edited an older book we have to look for an older author and an older form of the novel. Whatever its date, and despite the fact that other early novels may have shared and may have anticipated its characteristics (but of these, such as the supposed *Cārumatī* of Vararuci,—3 ?, we know practically nothing [650]), the *Bṛhatkathā* was long looked upon as the type of the novel. It was pure fiction, though grafted onto history at a conveniently romantic point (the hero is the imaginary scion of an uprooted dynasty). It was in prose and of considerable length : difficult to estimate now but apparently quite as long as any later *kāvya* novel, or even much longer.

445. Despite the prominent featuring of supernatural elements—the *vidyādharas* or 'wizards' with their magic sciences such as the power of flight and their imagined empire beyond the Himālaya—there was a great deal of realism in the *Bṛhatkathā*, strongly apparent in the earliest Sanskrit version and very likely still stronger in the original (in the version it is constrained by abridgement and by being put into verse). This is seen in the characterisation and in scenes of deceit and intrigue, also in a concern with technology. In fact it was taken as a model of all that a novel should be, ranging from scenes of real life to the fabulous conquest of the empire of the wizards, from sordid robbery to the attainment of the maximum prosperity and happiness conceivable, including marriage with princesses of the wizards. Bāṇa (*Harsacarita*, introductory verse 17) seems to suggest that the *rasa* of the *Bṛhatkathā* was the marvellous *adbhuta*, though the sensitive and the heroic were prominent and as in the majority of later novels it may be nearer the truth to suppose that the sensitive was in fact the dominant *rasa*. The attainment of this kind of success gave a pattern often adopted by later novelists. A peculiarity of the *Bṛhatkathā* is the working in of numerous episodes, usually leading to new amorous adventures by the hero. Unlike the standard later novel, the book is divided, largely on the basis of these episodes, into chapters. In short we have in the *Bṛhatkathā* a fiction of epic proportions, possibly rivalling those of the Great Epic itself. Unlike the Great Epic it is a fiction, moreover it is entirely free from any concern with religion or *dharma* (virtue as conformity to duties laid down by religious authority): it is absolutely secular in outlook. It is a true *kāvya*. Seemingly it was new and unorthodox, and it is reported to have met with very adverse criticism when first published [670].

446. The later **critics** divide the *kathā* into a number of sub-varieties, sometimes as many as a dozen. Novels were also classified according to their characters (human, divine or mixed) and according to the ends of pleasure, wealth, virtue or a mixture of these pursued by the hero (see e. g. Haribhadra : *Samarāditya*, p. 2; Uddyotana p. 4). Some add liberation as a separate end [1449]. As to virtue *dharma*, an early example of a *dharmakathā* was the Prakrit *Taraṅgavatī*, extant in a Prakrit abridgement and in an Old Gujarātī translation, by the Jaina author Pādalipta (probably + 2), in which the *dharma* eventually realised is naturally that of Jainism [839—40]. Of the dozen formal varieties sometimes mentioned, two are the *ākhyāna* and *upākhyāna*, the epic and episodical narrative of Tradition, presumably, and certainly dealing with 'well-known' heroes, not fictitious characters. It seems misleading to mention them in discussions on branches of *kāvya*. Bhoja (*Śṛṅgāraprakāśa* II, p. 461) seems to have had no better motive for doing so than to help bring the total number of types of 'audible' *kāvya* up to twenty four, the same as his types of 'visible' *kāvya* and a favourite number of his.

The *upakathā* is apparently a supplement or sequel to a well known older work [1579] (Bhoja, p. 469). There was, not surprisingly, some fluidity in the terminology, and a word indicating an 'episode' of Tradition may perhaps have been used for what in fact was a *campū* or other work by a *kavi* based on that episode. We are left with eight or nine effective varieties of fictitious story or novel.

447. I. The first is the *Bṛhatkathā* itself, when distinguished from other *kathās* and raised to the dignity of a separate branch of literature—unless indeed there were imitations unknown to us (Bhoja, p. 470; Hemacandra, p. 465). Bhoja makes the *paiśācī* language part of the description and Ratnaśrījñāna (p. 26) knows another novel in that language, a *Ratnaprabhā* (presumably the name of the heroine). Its irregular, or at least idiosyncratic, construction and form, with divisions into chapters, might have made some critics hesitate to group it with the standard novels [665]. [2591?]

448. II. The standard *kathā*, or 'novel' (Bhoja, p. 469; Hemacandra, p. 463; Ānandavardhana, pp. 323, 326ff.), is the novel in the limited sense, a long prose fiction without chapter divisions, contrasted with the meaning of *kathā* as a term for 'fiction' or even 'story' in general. This is the central type of prose fiction as we have already described it above, which Rudraṭa more appropriately calls the *mahākathā,* 'great story' [839, 1559]. It can be in any language. Bhoja names the *Kādambarī* and the *Līlāvatī* [772] as examples. [2567-616]

449. III. The *parikathā* according to Ānandavardhana (p. 325) is confined to the story *itivṛtta* only, therefore presumably without any descriptive elaboration. It illustrates one end of life, or perhaps one topic *artha*, only, and is not very productive of *rasa*. In other words it would seem to be primarily instructive. As we saw from Namisādhu it appears to be a summary or synopsis from which the narrative can be extemporised [570]. This would agree on the whole with the use of the term *parikathā* by Buddhist writers (see Chapter XVII below [877, 880, 896, 899, 904-5]) for short moral tracts, though these latter are as a rule not particular narratives or stories but general ethical expositions, almost sermons; sometimes, however, these Buddhist tracts have in view particular stories handed down in Buddhist tradition, which could be extemporised as illustrations. No non-Buddhist work extant seems now to be entitled *parikathā* [1297]; the type was perhaps assimilated to the 'illustration' *nidarśanā* or the short story *khaṇḍakathā* discussed below. The paraphrases and abridgements of novels are presumably not in question here. [1934?] A

450. IV. The *sakalakathā* ('entire story') follows its hero through a series of lives (Ānandavardhana, p. 325; Hemacandra p. 465). The available examples (e. g. the *Samarāditya* by Haribhadra, +8, the *Upamitibhavaprapañcā* by Siddha, +10) are not unexpectedly of very great length. The theme of the narrative is the complete working out of actions and their results through several lives. Saṃghadāsa's *Vasudevahiṇḍi* [1452] shows the trend towards these novels. [2639-75, 4123-79]

451. V. The *khaṇḍakathā* ('short story') or *kathānaka* ('little story') narrates a brief episode (Ānandavardhana, p. 325; Bhoja, p. 469; Hemacandra, p. 465). Many collections of these were made in all periods and they are continuous with those of the ancient storytelling mentioned above : sometimes the same story has a long history of retelling. Usually there is a rather tenuous frame story round such a collection. An example of such a collection would be the anonymous *Vetālapañcaviṃśati* (+10?). The form was not much noticed by the critics, the simple unpolished language not appealing to connoisseurs of *kāvya*. When highly organised it tended to become a *nidarśanā* or satire [452]. As Rudraṭa noted (XVI. 33f.), in short stories the hero often meets with disaster, in contrast to the happy ending of the standard novel [1251, 1255—6]. Both the *sakalakathā* and the *khaṇḍakathā* are often in Prakrit, moreover their prose narrative may be interrupted from time to time by groups of verses (Ānandavardhana). The strict novel *kathā*, on the other hand, at least when in Sanskrit, contains hardly a single verse except by way of prologue. When in Prakrit or Apabhraṃśa, however, it may be entirely in verse, in the 'musical' metres widely used for narrative in those languages. [579, 672, 4394-500, 4630-68, 5010-165] A

452. VI. The *nidarśanā*, 'illustration', 'example' or 'lesson', in effect 'satire', is didactic in purpose (Bhoja, p.469; Hemacandra, p. 463). To this type belong a number of brilliant satires, as well as the exceptionally popular *Pañcatantra*, which teaches mostly through the medium of the beast fable [1250—1].

These *nidarśanās* are eminently readable simply as literature, without regard to the purpose of instruction. The satires are directed against social vices and human weaknesses. The *Pañcatantra* illustrates policy *nīti*, public and private; the *Mugdhakathā* [1254] folly; Haribhadra's *Dhūrtākhyāna* illustrates religion; Dāmodaragupta's *Kuṭṭanīmata*, +8, harlotry; Kṣemendra, +11, wrote several satires against bureaucracy, arrogance, etc. In all cases the stories are invented, but highly realistic. A *nidarśanā* may consist of a single long story or of several shorter ones enclosed in a frame story. It may be in unmixed prose or verse, or a mixture of the two. The satirical *campūs* may be regarded as continuing the *nidarśanā* tradition.

453. Of the three remaining types of fictitious narrative few examples have been identified. Like some of the minor types of drama which have been annihilated, they may once have been popular, however, if not sophisticated enough to attract much attention from the critics. Whereas the drama was wiped from the face of most of India by hostile governments, and preserved there only as an antiquarian pursuit of scholars, minor branches of popular story or novel were superseded by new fashions, especially in the modern languages.

454. VII. The *matallikā* (which appears to be identical with the *manthulli(kā)*), is said to be a minor *kṣudra* story in Māhārāṣṭrī, especally a satire against priests, ascetics and ministers. It would seem that it might very well have been included under *nidarśanā*. Apparently it must be in prose (*Śṛṅgāraprakāśa* I p. 122, according to Raghavan's reading, p. 822 of his book on this work), like the biography and (standard) novel, i. e. unmixed with verse. The persons satirised undertake something but do not succeed in finishing it (*Śṛṅgāraprakāśa* II p. 469; Hemacandra, p. 464). The examples named by Bhoja are *Gorocanā* and *Anaṅgavatī* (perhaps the names of their heroines). The name might be translated 'excellent' and thus the *varā kathā* mentioned by Uddyotana (p. 4) may be the same [2708]. Other remnants of the form might be found in the Jaina Māhārāṣṭrī prose literature. [2732]

455. VIII. The *maṇikulyā* is described (*Śṛṅgāraprakāśa* II p. 469; Hemacandra, p. 464) as a mystery, the secret of which is revealed at the end. Example : *Matsyahasita* (Fish Laugh). As Raghavan has suggested (p. 816), this type of story was probably organised round some extraordinary occurrence, the mystery of which is solved at the end. The two 'fish laugh' stories he refers to in other works may have been borrowed from the original *Matsyahasita* : both are concerned with a secret affair of a queen, exposed by a clever person who penetrates the meaning of the laughter of a dead fish, provoked by the absurdity of human behaviour (see e.g. *Kathāsaritsāgara* I, *taraṅga* 5, 14 ff.). [4407, 4421, 4554-60]

456. IX. The *pravahlikā* was a kind of enigma or riddle (Amarasiṃha I.5.6, next to the novel), presented as a dialogue in a mixture of Sanskrit and Prakrit and in mixed prose and verse with the prose predominating (*Śṛṅgāraprakāśa* I p. 122, reading *Ceṭaka*, an example of the type, and II p. 469; Hemacandra, p. 464). From an allusion to the type in Harṣa's (+12) *Naiṣadhacarita*, XVI. 102, we glean something of its form: a girl hides her intentions and a boy with her tries to decipher them—this is like a *pravahlikā* and an attempt to write a commentary on it. The word *pravahlikā* was anciently used for a riddle. *Kāvyamīmāṃsā* p. 6 [4440-6, 4480] A

457. The novel has suffered particularly badly from the ravages of the +2nd millennium. Of some forty or more standard novels known to us by name from the critics as presumably famous examples written by the +11, only about 13 have as yet been retrieved, one of these in extensive fragments only (the *Avantisundarī*) and three others in abridged paraphrases (the *Bṛhatkathā*, *Taraṅgavatī* and *Malayasundarī*). These forty were of course only the most successful products of a long flourishing tradition, the critics—at least those critics whose writings have been preserved—paying little attention to the form. In addition we have a few *nidarśanas*, *sakalakathās* (by Jaina writers), *campū* novels, collections of short stories and some Buddhist *parikathās* (which contain practically no narratives). The scholars of the +2nd millennium neglected all fictitious writing and concentrated on a few favourite historical plays and epics dealing with heroic antiquity. Only two novels were at all widely read among them: those of Subandhu and Bāṇa, which were appreciated not for their content but for their form, since it offered difficulties of interpretation worthy of their learning. As noted above relatively few novels were written between the +12 and +18.

Half a dozen survive from the +11 [4611]; from the +12 (two extant?— Mahendra, Nemicandra) the number seems to fall off. [304]

458. If the lost *maṇikulyās* were mysteries, the standard novels also usually hold back key links in their stories until the end, thus maintaining the reader in suspense. This is the real formal construction of the novel, which outwardly is a single uninterrupted piece. There is a great deal of individual variation, but some of the novels are extremely complex in structure. Splendid examples of this are Bāṇa's *Kādambarī* and Dhanapāla I's *Tilakamañjarī* (+10). The narrative is introduced piecemeal in apparently chance order from a seemingly remote and external starting point. The sequence seems random, not being chronological but beginning somewhere about the middle. The mystified reader receives the pieces of a puzzle in haphazard order, but essential connecting pieces are kept back till the end. The characters in the story, however, who are generally the narrators, know even less than the reader about the significance of certain events or about certain of their mutual relationships. As they are progressively enlightened the reader moves with them, or just ahead of them, and is thus made to feel he is participating in their experiences. Eventually, emboxing and seemingly irrelevant matter, including the opening scene, resolves into continuations of the main narrative. In this way the novel works up to a dénouement much as a drama does. The reader experienced in this kind of literature may foresee vaguely what might happen, but the skilful novelist involves his narrative in unexpected turns which heap up fresh interest. [1696-732, 1810-23, 4211-89]

459. The belief in transmigration, and consequently in faint recollection of previous lives, gives a further dimension to the narrative : it may for example account for the mystery of love at first sight (in fact with the beloved of a previous life). Certain events, or objects previously familiar, may strengthen a faint recollection of the remote past to full recognition.

460. It turns out, then, that the novel has an extremely complex organisation, merely camouflaged as casual and in fact as unified in plot as the drama. This is appropriate to the content and not an irrelevant mystification or mere virtuosity in the storyteller's art. It enhances the feeling of uncertainty which truly reflects the experience of real life, and follows from the fictitious nature of the story –as opposed to the 'well-known' stories of the epic, the *nāṭaka* or the biography. The reader or spectator perhaps more easily accepts a well known hero, and in that case a different kind of art is required of the *kavi*. With an unknown, fictitious hero the novelist uses the technique of mystery and suspense to draw in his reader and develop his sympathy. The organisation of a novel is thus psychological as well as aesthetic, and appropriate as a setting for its generally realistic narrative and characterisation, particularly the psychology of young people in love as in the two great novels just mentioned.

461. The prose style of the novels is very variable, as already noted, and the form might be used as by Subandhu [1559] not at all as a realistic narrative but as a study in pure style. The true novelists, however, evolved a prose technique within the domain of *kāvya* which was suited to their purposes. Free from the restrictions of verse, they found rhythms and cadences for prose which were no less finished for being indefinitely variable. Mature or ripe *pāka* (Vāmana, p. 11) prose has the same feeling of inevitable rightness as polished verse. Free from metrical embarrassments, the prose writer has the wealth of the Sanskrit vocabulary more fully at his command. He can elaborate his descriptions with less encumbrance of cadence and figure. He can call to his aid a rapidity of language impossible in even the simplest and flattest verse, since he follows the natural word order and construction of sentences. Though he may lengthen his sentences in descriptive passages, he can make them such as the reader may take in his stride, without an objectionable delay in the essential narrative. He may occasionally do the reverse of this, stopping the reader to work out double meanings or other recondite constructions, but unless he goes towards the extreme represented by Subandhu these excursions will not slow his narrative to the deliberate pace of an epic. As in the case of the descriptions, the action of a novel also is regularly cast in long rhythmical sentences, phrase balancing phrase and pressing on eagerly with a minimum of stops or periods. Alternatively, in dialogue passages, a succession of short sentences is sometimes used for a different effect. In length there is no theoretical limit to the Sanskrit sentence; in practice it is just a question of maintaining a particular set of simple grammatical relationships throughout and stepping from clause to clause without loss of balance. The Sanskrit language responds readily to the skill of the accomplished writer, who is supported by its peculiar strength and plasticity.

462. If the characteristic of prose is speed, it is nevertheless fair to prepare the impatient modern reader for the great Sanskrit novels by warning him that this is a relative speed, and that all *kāvya* is an art for real leisure, for long periods of recreation and not short breaks. The *kavi* could afford to pile up his words, his imagined scene, as richly as his art allowed and expect his reader to follow gladly into his fictitious world. [1697-9, 4212-6, 4589-91]

CHAPTER VIII

THE AUDIENCE AND THE READERS OF *KĀVYA* AND ITS SOCIAL FUNCTIONS; THE AUTHORS

463. *Kāvya* probably met its widest audience in the form of drama at popular festivals. We have noted already the social function of the drama in Indian civilisation, an essential part of the lives of the people, and the public festivals *samājas* at which dramas were the most important events 28-29, 34-5, 40, 43]. At these festivals the drama was to some extent in competition with other forms of entertainment, primarily the ever popular recitations from Tradition, which rivalled the drama for the position of the Veda of the people. Other forms of *kāvya*, however, are found alongside the drama at public festivals, especially in later times the *campū* recited by an actor and in earlier times the *ākhyāyikā* (biography) similarly presented [426, 434]. Nevertheless the drama with its innumerable forms could satisfy any need, down to modern times has continued to throw off new varieties as demand and fashion changed, and so has always been the major public form of *kāvya*. As to the rivalry with Tradition, the so-called 'First Kāvya', the epic *Rāmāyaṇa*, has proved at least as popular as the Great Epic and other works of Tradition for recital at festivals. [2196]

464. As *kāvya* found a wide audience among the Indian people, so it drew a considerable part of its content and inspiration from the people in the broadest sense. Folk song was a perennial source of *kāvya* forms (metres, lyrics of various constructions [538]) and of an important part of the content of *kāvya* (village life [770, 782, 784 -97], but also inspiration for the aesthetic theory of the implied meaning [248]). The great heritage of popular stories contributed alongside Tradition to the content of *kāvya*, and to the art of narrative, including realism [443]. Since its origin, *kāvra* has absorbed many new languages, expanding its resources of expression.

465. A more direct reflex of its popular basis is the literature of social criticism [563, 926, 933, 1016], satirical stories or novels [1251, 1254] and dramas [1101, 1084–1125, 1187, 1194-8, 1367, 1373, 1445, 1631], also lyrics reflecting poverty and misery [793—8,1307], occasionally cantos of an epic contrasting the rule of bad kings with the ideal [1398]. Here the people found expression for their needs, a means of protest against oppression and corruption, ideals to appeal to and to demand [575, 1011, 1200, 1202]. *Kāvya* has always kept before the eyes of Indian rulers the highest ideals of Indian civilisation [1642], and satirised social evils [1223—4, 1398, 452]. [2742]

466. To some extent performances of plays by small groups of actors, or by a single actor, and public recitations of *kāvyas* (especially of the *Rāmāyaṇa*) might be supported by contributions or gifts by the ordinary people, in the same way as many religious teachers and reciters of Tradition have found support among the villages of India [551]. *Kāvya* on the scale we in fact find, however, depended on the more substantial patronage which could be offered by the ruling classes. This patronage has been complex in its operation. In the first place there was the support of writers and the theatre by kings, aristocrats, ministers and wealthy merchants [653, 1304, 470, 491]. Then the hereditary scholars, *brāhmaṇas*, many of them extremely poor, though well educated, some very wealthy and living as gentry on their own estates, were traditionally expected to take up creative writing as well as learning. The obligation, social if not legal, of the *nāgarakas* to provide public entertainment at festivals and assemblies, as well as their traditional interest in *kāvya* and the other arts and private cultivation of literature and criticism, perhaps provided the most widespread and regular basic support for *kāvya* [28—9]. Sometimes wealthy geishas are recorded to have provided patronage for the drama, particularly for performances in their houses, and acting and even composition were normal accomplishments of these purveyors of pleasure [1187, 1225]. Persons having the necessary leisure, including queens and princesses (e. g. Gaṅgā [1554]) as well as wealthy scholars, and also kings, aristocrats and ministers in intervals of recreation, sometimes wrote *kāvyas* as a diversion [1159, 1299, 1431, 1604, 471]. In addition to the hereditary class of *brāhmaṇas*, India has had throughout the history of *kāvya* non-hereditary schools of scholars, mainly the Buddhist and Jaina monks, many of whom wrote *kāvyas*, usually with a didactic or educational aim [580, 709, 1275, 835]. Some lyrics purport to be actual folk songs created by the peasants [776, 782, 830]. [2715, 3062]

467. As with most literatures, therefore, we see two aspects of *kāvya*. It is to a substantial extent the literature of the people as a whole, embodying their experiences and traditions; on the other hand it generally has a strong bias towards the ruling classes, who adopted it as their own, supported it, and to a great extent wrote it. This last point depends on how far the hereditary *brāhmaṇas* are regarded as a ruling class, even when poor: traditionally they regarded themselves as the highest class, so that even when very poor they would not share the outlook of labourers, artisans or peasants. In rare cases they did work as peasants, cultivating their own land for subsistence, but this represented extreme and abnormal adversity and still did not cancel out the literary education they almost invariably received, however poor. The position of *kāvya* thus reflected the state of society, the relationship between the rulers and society as a whole: when this was relatively harmonious, and the rulers governing as much in the general interest as could be expected, the outlook of literature might be broader, if too optimistic; when the government was oppressive, or merely inefficient, and the rulers tended to isolate themselves, the literature produced by or for them would be restricted in outlook and wildly unrealistic if it affected to describe contemporary events. The latter tendency would be quite compatible with an opposite tendency elsewhere, including in another stratum of the same society, and we shall see that sometimes the emergence of new ruling groups was accompanied by new movements in *kāvya* with a broader and more social-critical outlook (see Chapters XIV—XVI, XXVIII—XXIX, the +8). [2386-93, 5040]

468. Dramas were frequently performed at the courts of kings, it being usual for a royal palace to contain a permanent theatre. The regular festivals were observed with performances in the theatre, in addition to which special occasions were marked by similar festivities. [2328, 3637, 3869, 1772]

469. It was held to be the duty of a king to maintain a regular assembly *samāja* of scholars and *kavis* (Rājaśekhara: *Kāvyamīmāṃsā* pp. 54 f.). This would meet, in a hall *sabhā* built for the purpose, under the chairmanship of the monarch. It was the custom for *kavis* to submit their work to the criticism of the *samāja* by reading or reciting it before the assembled scholars and authors, and also members of the court who might attend. On these occasions the king made suitable awards to successful *kavis*. Sometimes they were given titles of poetic rank. In addition to these practical exercises in criticism, theoretical discussions concerning *kāvya* were prominent at the meeting of the *samāja*. There were also lighter literary games such as completing verses. [1699, 2551, 4504, 4586-7]

470. The practice of kings was imitated by princes and by ministers who were connoisseurs of literature. For example the poet Maṅkhaka, (+12) tells us how he presented his epic *Śrīkaṇṭhacarita* in the hall *sabhā* of his brother, who was foreign minister in Kaśmīra at the time (canto XXV of the epic). Those present included scholars, authors, poets, philosophers, ritualists, theologians, grammarians, historians (the great Kalyāṇa = Kalhaṇa, and also the foreign minister of neighbouring Rājapurī, who wrote the history of his king), physicians and diplomats— notably the ambassadors from kingdoms in North and South India (Āryāvarta and Koṅkaṇa = the Deccan, their capitals at Kānyakubja and Śūrpāraka, both of which were flourishing centres of *kāvya* at the time). The poet probably regarded as the culminating point of the proceedings the delivery of an appreciation by his teacher the critic Ruyyaka (author of several theoretical works on *kāvya*), who expressed satisfaction that his pupil was now a fully matured *kavi* and a successful worshipper of Sarasvatī.

471. Patronage of *kāvya* by the merchant class seems generally to have been less direct. At all times some merchants have been generous supporters of the Buddhist and Jaina schools, so that there has often been a certain community of outlook between them and the Buddhist and Jaina authors, the latter in particular have written a good many *kāvyas* with a bourgeois audience or readership in mind, stories of their own class and of travel and adventures in distant countries [702, 849, 1451]. Wealthy merchants and especially their sons indulged in the pursuit of pleasure in the great cities, and thus lent some support to those authors and actors who provided dramatic entertainments. They emulated with more or less success the *nāgarakas*, and probably joined their ranks if they had enough leisure from business and some pretensions to culture. More rarely we hear of direct patronage by powerful *vaiśyas* (members of the mercantile class) able to maintain a *samāja* and support authors. The best known examples of this are in Gujarāt in the +13, when, as the feudal monarchy approached its nadir, this country which lived by commerce had the good fortune to have two *vaiśya* brothers, Vastupāla and Tejaḥpāla, of ancient and respected family, appointed as ministers to save the kingdom from the Turks. They proved as skilful in military as in commercial operations. They patronised both the Jaina (their own) and the Brahmanical religions. They were themselves authors, not without distinction, they collected libraries, and above all they maintained an assembly of *kavis*. [1945, 4180, 5397]

472. The majority of the *kavis* known to us are probably *brāhmaṇas* (brahmans), this vocation along with many other intellectual professions being above all open to this class of scholars. Their education commanded respect, even when they were poor, and the young *brāhmaṇa* able to display at court the wit expected of a *kavi* could hope to gain a royal or ministerial patron and carry through his cherished aim of writing a great *kāvya*, bringing him present success and perhaps immortality. *Brāhmaṇas* who had no need to seek patronage might still have the ambition to achieve fame and preeminence as *kavis*, or wish to leave behind them a monument which would endure. [1646, 1656]

473. The life of the *nāgarakas* as amateurs and patrons of *kāvya* has been discussed already [27], with their literary circles ***goṣṭhis*** **and their regular public entertainments *samājas* paralleling** those of the courts. Their milieu, the social life of great cities where various human passions luxuriated in private and in public, is reflected in some of the branches of *kāvya* which we have just reviewed. In the remnant of these now available the satirical monologues take first place, ridiculing the vanities of private life in this environment, of scholars and merchants' sons as well as of the young women (mostly geishas), the rascals *dhūrtas*, tutors, false ascetics and monks, old actors, arrogant young *brāhmaṇas*, vile courtiers and of course the poets, who seek amusement or else try to eke out a livelihood in the inexhaustible depths of a metropolis [1105—9, 1117—24, 1220—5, 1446]. Here the *nāgaraka* is king, commanding his parasite 'ministers' and sending them as ambassadors to the girl with whom he desires a probably temporary alliance. The girl is usually a geisha, and the 'minister' as much hers as the *nāgaraka*'s—for the latter has to share his empire with her. She is well educated, protected and maintained by the state, often wealthy. She is not merely decorative and charming, providing dalliance for privileged citizens and courtiers, for it is her function also to provide entertainment as musician, dancer, actress, poetess, painter, as well as through the minor decorative arts such as flower arrangement. Thus *kāvya* finds a place in her house. [2119, 2752, 4510, 4949 ff., 6496]

474. Besides the satirical monologues, comedies, sometimes *prakaraṇas*, *durmallikās* [349], *bhāṇis* [383], other minor types of drama, some novels, often the *nidarśanā* [452], perhaps the *matallikā* [454], and an occasional satirical *campū* reflect this same environment in many cities through the history of *kāvya* [1191, 1600, 1020, 1368—74, 692]. Next to the satirical monologues it is the *nidarśanās* which give the best descriptions of this world among the *kāvyas* extant. A *brāhmaṇa* could become a *nāgaraka*, so presumably could an aristocrat or a merchant. Though the proper and original place of the *nāgaraka* is the city, the type appears in smaller towns all over India, and as feudalism developed, and more and more petty barons and country gentry set up on estates, some of these emulated the *nāgarakas* as well as princes in literary pursuits, and held meetings of their 'circles' at scenic spots in the country (waterfalls, for example—Tod : *Annals and Antiquities of Rajast'han*, Vol. II, p. 573) instead of in city gardens and parks [28]. [4506]

475. Kings often aspired to the title of *kavi*. From an early period literary prowess was widely accepted as a distinction of the highest order, as appropriate for a king as military success. Thus the royal president of a *samāja* could seek to justify his position as a genuine eminence in the republic of letters, rather than as an accidental facet of autocracy. In fact, unless we have frequently been deceived, by patrons passing off as their own *kāvyas* which they have merely paid others to write for them, several Indian kings have found deserved immortality as *kavis* (usually as dramatists). Probably these royal plays are genuine, though their authors doubtless benefited from the guidance of their assembled scholars, authors and critics. Critics have found in some of them perfect models of dramatic construction (e. g. the plays of Harṣa and Yaśovarman). The fashion was thus set for the cultivation of literature by individuals with wealth and leisure. Nothing could bring greater honour than the status of *kavi*. It was equally honourable for the wives of princes or of wealthy *brāhmaṇas* to be creative in literature, and they have left us some interesting dramas and epics (the princess Śīlā, probably late +7, was acclaimed for mastery of the *pāñcāla* style, alongside Bāṇa, and perhaps like him was a novelist ; unhappily none of her works seem now to be extant). [770, 1159, 1299, 1431]

476. The majority of *kavis* being *brāhmaṇas* would have received the education customary for their class. Part of this consisted of the study of the *Veda*, varying in the amount covered and also as between the different Vedic schools and specialities. A minimum of Vedic scriptures was learned by all. Originally in close connection with Vedic studies, and as a basis for them and for all other literary education, a boy started from the age of about six on grammar (i. e. Sanskrit grammar) and phonetics and in due course took up a lexicon and the study of metre. He was supposed also to study two other ancillaries to the *Veda*, namely 'ritual' (*kalpa*, which included religious law and customs) and astronomy (the original application of which was to the calendar), including mathematics. [2729-31, 3581]

477. Partly derivative from these subsidiary Vedic studies, and to some extent superseding them, are certain other subjects, the writings on which (and on grammar and the other ancillaries just mentioned) belong to the category of *śāstra*. These are *smṛti* (or *dharmaśāstra*, primarily law and ethics, including civil and criminal law and the duties of the various social classes and stations), *mīmāṃsā* (Vedic interpretation and systematic study of ritual, metaphysics and theology) and philosophy (*ānvikṣikī*, primarily logic and epistemology, secondarily metaphysics). In addition to *dharmaśāstra* i.e. the study of virtue, the sciences of wealth *arthaśāstra* and pleasure *kāmaśāstra* (with the arts [23]) might be taken up.

478. *Itihāsa* (Tradition) was essential, especially for one who might become a *kavi* (being the inexhaustible store of myth, legend and history—see Chapter X below). It consists primarily of the Great Epic and the *Purāṇas* [519]. The latter are books similar in language and style to the Great Epic, which contained originally narratives concerning the evolution and dissolution of the universe and the sequence of its aeons and ages, leading to the generations of kings and sages. Many myths and legends were incorporated in them, and eventually miscellaneous subjects making them almost encyclopaedias: some of them have sections on poetics, for example, and on other arts such as architecture, sculpture and painting. [74, 76]

479. The literary critics have given various accounts of the educational qualifications for becoming a *kavi*. Rājaśekhara's *Kāvyamīmāṃsā* (see its first two chapters), in particular, sets out a comprehensive educational scheme and also deals with numerous details of study and practice. These authors stress proficiency in grammar, metrics, lexicon, Tradition, logic (with reference to training the judgment : *yukti*—some critics, for example Bhāmaha, require an advanced study of formal logic and theory of knowledge), and of course poetics, knowledge of the arts *kalās* and of the world, and reading of *kāvyas*. This brings in the study of poetics *alaṃkāraśāstra* as an addition to the ancient curriculum. This study in time took its place prominently in the general educational system, a place which it holds even today in the traditional schools as an optional subject following after the basic grammar, logic and *mīmāṃsā*. As to the 'arts', these are the traditional sixty-four arts, crafts and amusements generally regarded as branches of the science of pleasure, which we have noted above [23]. They include *kāvya*, though the literary critics gave it a more dignified and independent position and held that in fact *kāvya* was the supreme art and all the others subordinate to it. [358 1]

480. If the 'arts' were anciently branches of 'pleasure', 'wealth' *arthaśāstra*, which included politics and military science, also had its branches, namely politics, economics, agriculture, cattle breeding, trade, mining and mineralogy, and military science including weapons, horses, elephants and chariots. Of course a *brāhmaṇa* becoming a minister would need to be familiar with at least some of these, but the *kavi*, whose knowledge, it appears, ought to be universal, should have a smattering of all these matters in order to be able to deal adequately with politics and war, particularly in an epic. Archery was regarded as a kind of subordinate *Veda*, along with music and medicine. These would be studied professionally only by warriors and by specialists, but again the *kavi* should include something of them in his general knowledge. [2296-8]

481. Education for other classes of Āryan society (aristocrats or warriors : *kṣatriya*; the productive class, of peasants, originally, from which the bourgeoisie derived: *vaiśya*) was similar in essentials but was carried on for shorter periods and with different specialities appropriate for their stations. The education of the aristocrat, at least, did not fall too far short of the brāhmaṇical standard and was very broad. [1705, 3938]

482. The schemes of the Buddhists and Jainas were generally parallel to that of the *brāhmaṇas*, substituting their own philosophical and religious doctrines for study of the *Veda*, and their own versions of some of the other branches of study. In place of Tradition they had their own account of the evolution of the universe, their own histories, and above all their own revered legends, which provided them with 'well-known' stories for *kāvyas*. [609f. 854ff.]

483. Some *kavis* have left us autobiographical fragments in their works, or discussions on the life of the creative writer. There was a convention in some kinds of *kāvya* of including passages of this sort, explaining the origin of or otherwise apologising for the work, occasionally claiming divine inspiration or in other ways briefly introducing the author. Here and there we can glean something of the manner of life of a poet or writer.

484. Thus the wealthy brahman Bāṇa (+7: first three chapters of his *Harṣacarita*) had no material need to court royal patronage, but did so when invited and left a biography of the emperor Harṣa. Bāṇa lived in his ancestral home in a village in Magadha or Vatsa, where his family, a branch of the Vātsyāyana clan, maintained the complex ceremonial life inherited from antiquity by their class. With his cousins he studied Tradition, listening during a presumably typical day to a professional reciter chanting from the *Vāyu Purāṇa* in the morning and after dinner. A bard rouses the household just before sunrise by singing appropriate verses, and sings also at other regular times of the day and occasionally by request. The *kavi* washes, performs the sunrise ritual and takes betel nut to clean his mouth. The main work of the day takes place in the morning—in the present case, however, Bāṇa is telling his kinsmen the story of the emperor he has just visited (or we may suppose writing his biography—but as we noted in Chapter VII 'showing a biography' was a kind of performance). Dinner is in the afternoon, and the time between it and sunset is spent in recitations and discussion. At sunset the cows are milked and there is ritual and sacrifices, for which fires are lit. Then in the evening boys and students repeat the texts they have learned, ascetics take up their postures for meditation, the women, their work ended, wander restlessly about, and Bāṇa sits in the house for a time with his kinsmen before retiring to sleep.

485. This secluded and traditional life of a wealthy brahman family may not be typical of many. Here the writing of *kāvyas* seems incidental only, to entertain relatives. On the other hand we learn that occasional travel was not unusual, and we see in his works that Bāṇa made good use of it (cf. Rājaśekhara, *Kāvyamīmāṃsā*, p. 78). For other writers there was the serious business of earning a livelihood.

486. Rājaśekhara (early +10), *kavi* and critic, was also a wealthy brahman, the son of a minister and 'preceptor' to the emperor Mahendrapāla. He concerns himself with the life of a *kavi* in a theoretical manner and we do not know how far he was able to realise his ideal in practice (see *Kāvyamīmāṃsā*, Chapter X). His character is quite different from Bāṇa's. He proposes a very strenuous timetable for the *kavi* (p. 52). After the sunrise ritual he studies for three hours and then spends three hours on the composition of his *kāvya*. At noon he baths and has dinner. The next three hours are spent in a *kāvya goṣṭhī* (literary circle) in discussion and poetical exercises with his friends. Afterwards he examines the morning's work alone or (better) with a select group—since (he says) a *kāvya* with *rasa* cannot be written with an isolated view. He then revises it, cutting out superfluous matter and making up deficiencies. After the sunset ritual he makes a fair copy of the revised work, then he may wish for feminine company. At night he takes six hours' sleep (from 9 p. m. to 3 a. m.). In the early morning when his mind is calm he reflects on various matters. [6522]

487. Rājaśekhara's *kavi* (having inherited or acquired some affluence) should have a spacious house and garden, offering accommodation suited to each of the six seasons of the Indian year. The garden should be shaded by many trees and have a miniature mountain, a lake, a lotus pool, streams, and a whirlpool where they meet, and a canal or river. There should be birds such as parrots, peacocks, pigeons, ospreys and ornamental geese, an arbour of creepers, fountains, swings and hammocks. The writer should employ menservants speaking Apabhraṃśa and maids speaking Māgadhī. The ladies of his house should speak Prakrit and Sanskrit. He should have friends speaking all languages and should employ a fast scribe and calligraphist skilled in all languages and scripts. The *kavi's* clothes should be expensive but not extravagant, he should wear flowers on his head and anoint his body (pp. 49f.).

488. Rājaśekhara notes (p. 50) that the *kavi* should have always ready for use a bag containing a writing tablet and chalk, a casket (presumably to store completed work), palm leaves or birch bark (the standard writing materials) with writing ink and a metal stylus, and tablets prepared for writing on (?—this seems to be meaning of the words, Vākpatirāja 1185, Ratnākara XX.21, Kuntaka 145, a stone block, also a *bhittiphalaka* for writing or painting on: the word *bhitti*, which ordinarily means 'wall', may also refer to a kind of slab or board for scribbling on). Numerous other pieces of advice are scattered about in this theoretical book, such as knowing one's own powers and the current fashion, studying the linguistic peculiarities of different parts of the country, and having plenty of copies made of one's *kāvya* as an insurance against loss (hence we find that every writer who was able to employed a scribe to multiply copies of his work). It should be noted in connection with the physical condition of literature in India that printing has been practised only recently. Although it was adopted in neighbouring Tibet perhaps before Rājaśekhara's time, the Indians seem to have considered it impracticable, doubtless because it meant using paper, which in the Indian climate is a highly unsatisfactory and ephemeral material. Palm leaf books when properly stored and kept clean last many centuries.

489. Glancing a moment longer at the careers of some of these writers, we find Bāṇa tells us he lost his parents when he was young (first his mother, then his father when he was 14). After mourning his father he for a time led a wild and dissipated life. He gives us a list of the friends he had at this time : *kavis*, teachers, musicians, gamblers, an actor, an actress, a scribe, a goldsmith, a painter, a sculptor, a potter, a widow, a maid, a doctor, a Jaina monk and other ascetics, and many others from all classes of society. He travelled and enjoyed himself, using his large inheritance. At first he got into disgrace through his wild behaviour, but gradually through frequenting courts and assemblies and meeting scholars he 'regained' his hereditary wisdom. Eventually he returned home and lived in tranquility, settling down to write, as we have seen.

490. Daṇḍin also lost both his parents when young (*Avantisundarī* p. 12; *Sāra* I. 33). His mother died when he was 7 and he fancies the Goddess Sarasvatī then looked after him. His ancestors had gradually migrated south from Gujarāt, and one of them, a poet, had settled at Kāñcī several generations earlier, attracted by the patronage of the Pallava emperor. Daṇḍin's father died soon after the boy's brahmanical initiation *upanayana* (presumably when he was eight years old). Just at that time (*c.*+670)the Pallava army was routed by the Cālukyas and the country temporarily occupied. As a result there was chaos, ruin and famine, and Daṇḍin wandered abroad for many years (he later worked the theme of enemy conquest and exile into his great novel). He was able to study in famous schools, and in fact we find his learning was immense. After peace was concluded and the country restored, the Pallava king invited Daṇḍin to return, and he went home and lived among his friends. At a gathering at Daṇḍin's house the architect Lalitālaya (skilled in building all kinds of palaces and in constructing various kinds of 'engines' *yantra*, i. e. fountains, robots, war engines for throwing missiles, and the like) asked the company to go with him to Mahāmallapura, on the coast about 50 miles from Kāñcī. There, at the temple on the shore, he had restored a statue of Viṣṇu, of which an arm had been broken, and he wanted them to tell him whether the restoration was worthy of the original. Daṇḍin makes this excursion the occasion for beginning his novel *Avanti-sundarī*. The friends are unable to make out which arm was broken, so the architect is very gratified. As the waves of the Indian Ocean break wildly against the base of the magnificent temple, the friends, filled with awe, fancy that a red lotus is thrown up against the foot of the statue, and turns into a wizard *vidyādhara*, who salutes Viṣṇu and vanishes. Daṇḍin says it must have been the liberation of a wizard from the effects of a curse. Afterwards he writes his novel, the hero of which eventually becomes emperor of men and *vidyādharas*, the story being revealed to him by divine inspiration. [1977]

491. The Apabhraṃśa poet Puṣpadanta (Apabhraṃśa : **Pupphayaṃtu,** +10) was extremely poor, though a brahman. His parents had originally been of the Śaiva religion, but were converted to Jainism, which Puṣpadanta followed. Puṣpa-danta had no property, 'only a noble mind.' At the first court he attended he was humiliated and withdrew in disgust, becoming a homeless wanderer living like an ascetic. His wanderings bring him eventually to the outskirts of a city (Mānyakheṭa), where he stays in a park, sleeping under the trees. Two passers-by invite him to visit the city, but he objects that he would rather eat grass on the mountains than see the faces of wicked and contemptible kings. However, they manage to persuade him to visit a minister who is a great patron of literature, especially Prakrit literature (which includes Apabhraṃśa). He still goes reluctantly owing to his bitter previous experience. This time his reception is good : he is given food, clothes and a place to live and the minister commissions him to write an epic. He spends six years writing his epic (which is one of the greatest masterpieces of Apabhraṃśa literature), whilst enjoying the minister's generosity (full maintenance, also secretarial assistance). Even after the minister's invitation the poet hesitated, saying it seemed futile to write poetry in a wicked world, and anyway he felt unequal to the great subject proposed (the legends of the sixty three 'great men', which may be regarded as the Jaina version of Tradition). His patron says he should ignore wicked men as the Moon ignores the barking of dogs. Thus given his opportunity Puṣpadanta settles permanently, the patronage continuing after he has finished his first commission and in due course being kept up by the minister's son after his father's death (see *Mahāpurāṇu*, *sandhi* I, *kaḍavakas* 3 to 9; with supplementary information from the editor's introductions, especially Vol III pp. xivff.). [3978, 4007, 4022]

492. Enough has been said to indicate that a variety of opportunities might be open to the *kavi*. There was a tradition that the young *kavi* or scholar should set out to wander the length and breadth of India in search of congenial patronage, and in all periods we hear of such wanderings. Older writers also quite often migrate, sometimes invited to a distant place on account of their fame. At most times India contained numerous independent or semi-independent kingdoms, whose capitals were normally centres of culture, so that the fate of the aspirant could not be settled by the caprice of a single emperor or the fears of some 'establishment' of mediocre *kavis*. Even in the darkest days of Turkish and British domination there were always Indian courts in various places where *kāvya* was patronised. [5280]

493. This decentralisation must be stressed as characteristic for India, and for understanding Indian history and Indian culture. It is of one piece with, perhaps the basis of, the tolerance of Indian religion : no imposed orthodoxy, rarely the possibility of imposing an orthodoxy—so that even aggressive Islam, that antithesis of everything that India stands for, and the most ruthlessly intolerant and presumptious of all orthodoxies, failed to impose itself. The spirit of India has been, in the earliest literature which survives to tell us of it and ever since, the spirit of freedom, of endless variety. It is a dangerous and tragic spirit, disunited and anarchic in the face of the invaders who aimed to obliterate it. It survived not so much by uniting against tyranny (as at Vijayanagara, which preserved for us the main part of the extant heritage) as by infinite division, so that the tyrants, for all their insatiable appetite, failed to destroy it all (so when Vijayanagara was eventually sacked its heritage, diffused over Southern India, did not all perish with the city). Every centre of freedom was capable of generating others without end and replenishing the land. Much was obliterated, but more was created, so that the heritage is with us still. Freedom has proved greater than tyranny, infinitely greater, as infinity is greater than one. Thus variety is the great principle of civilisation and of art, not unity.

494. Such was the environment of the *kavi*. The critic need not be separately discussed—he was usually a *kavi* himself (as were Daṇḍin and Rājaśekhara) and what has been said above applies to him as well. His field of action was generally the *goṣṭhī* or the larger public assembly *samāja* [28, 469] rather than the private study, his weapons quotation and analysis, leading to general theories such as we have reviewed in earlier chapters. He naturally presupposes, or rather observes in others and doubtless in himself, the 'connoisseur' *sahṛdaya*, or one capable of aesthetic appreciation *rasika*. This is the member of the audience at the theatre, the listener, the reader envisaged by the critic as reacting to a *kāvya*, being delighted, especially enjoying the *rasa* but also appreciating the implied meanings or delighting in figurative language or in clarity and balance of style. The *Nāṭyaśāstra* (XXVII) enumerates the ideal qualifications of an audience : impartial, well informed, of good judgment, sympathetic, etc., though not all these can be found in any one spectator. The term *bhāvaka*, 'appreciator', as a general one for the readers, etc., who will circulate a *kāvya*, seems to have been introduced by Rājaśekhara (*Kāvyamīmāṃsā* IV). His idea is of a counterpart in the reader to the genius *pratibhā* (which is creative) in the author, making the latter fruitful (pp. 12ff.). [2551, 4589]

495. Realism and social criticism in *kāvya* have to some extent been indicated above. To complement these we find (apart from the element of feudal court flattery which sometimes obtrudes, though as court panegyric it was for the most part a separate department of ephemeral composition) the poetic fancy which seeks to improve on nature either by the invention of surprising conceits or by the construction of an ideal system wherein poetic elements are grouped in unnatural profusion and unpoetic elements passed over. Whilst admitting that the author arranges his subject matter, we must claim that that is inevitable in any form of art. Kuntaka in introducing his work (p.1) rejects two extreme views of art, naturalism or simple factual description of the world, which would have no aesthetic effect, and pure fancy having no reality in it. Art evidently lies in the successful combination of these two aspects. Mere reporting of exact reality would not be art, but—more important—as no report can be complete, reporting too is in fact selective and tends to become an art itself when some degree of clarity of presentation and balanced coverage of events is aimed at. The poet may achieve realism in a highly imaginative or impressionistic manner instead of by direct imitation. As it is essential to realism to bring the subject vividly before the eyes of the reader, imaginative reproduction may be more effective than imitation (cf. Abhinavagupta's objection to mere imitation [83]). In *kāvya* both methods are used, and often mingled in an alternation of bold but fanciful images and keen observations. [1922, 2524-6, 3330ff., 3971-2]

496. Among pure poetic fancies which became commonplaces of *kāvya* we have inventions such as the *aśoka* tree which bursts into flower when kicked by a woman and the partridge *cakora* which drinks moonbeams. The system of the seasons is revised and regulated, so that a critic can complain that it appears cuckoos sing only in the spring and peacocks are heard, and seen to dance, only in the rainy season, whilst the jasmine is not supposed to flower in the spring (though in fact it does). Reality is exaggerated, though not without a genuine basis, when any mountain falling in the way of a poet is found to be full of gold, precious stones and other mineral wealth (on such conventions *samayas* see Rājaśekhara, *Kāvyamimāṃsā*, Chapters XIV and XV). [631, 3601, 3752, 4082]

497. Then we have the interplay of the conscious or sentient and the insentient aspects of the universe. There is a basis for this, as in the influence of the seasons on sentient beings, but the poet, ever seeking out what is typical, symbolic and general, again exaggerates the facts in the interests of poetic organisation. The sky, 'the elements', inspire, then actually reflect, the yearnings of conscious beings. Thus we arrive at the personification of inanimate nature. This is aided by mythology, which had already endowed the whole universe with life, making living gods of the Sun, fire, the ocean, and goddesses of the Earth and rivers. So a *kavi* describes the Himālaya alternately as the inanimate mountain with its snows, clouds, rocks and minerals (and its partly supernatural population of living beings) and as the god with his (human) concern for his daughter (Umā, who marries Śiva) [1424]. To its infinite advantage as art, all *kāvya* is pervaded by the sense of life of the *kavi's* universe. The presentation of everything described is charged with the vigour, the aura, the tension and coherence of life. The description and the subject are given organic wholeness. Yet this personification is not contrary to reality, for it brings nature closer to the reader, makes him see it vividly and in relation to the living inhabitants whose adventures he is following. The artist sees not the mass of insignificant, though true, detail, but picks out a few lines which are significant in relation to his purpose, and it is at the level of this purpose that the aesthetic truth of his work offers itself for judgment : if true at this level, his work will be congruent with the logical, literal facts of his subject matter, but also related (here is the 'significance') to many other subjects; in short, his images are generic rather than specific and the enjoyment of his work is *rasa* (aesthetic experience), not *bhāva* (emotional experience). [213, 646]

498. In the first part of this chapter it has been suggested that *kāvya* literature, like almost all other literature (perhaps all literatures so far, in fact), has been the literature of a society divided into classes, and that, though it reflects the outlook of the whole of that society to a considerable extent, it inevitably reflects more fully and directly the outlook of the ruling or privileged class of society. It is only in the present epoch of human history that the ideal of a society not divided into classes, with equality of opportunity for everyone, has perhaps become a realisable political programme. Up to now, to devote one's life to writing is a privilege given to very few, and in most places it is extremely hard, indeed usually impossible, for an individual from the unprivileged class, whatever his abilities, to force his way into a position in which he can devote his main energy to creative writing. So in India we find that *kavis* are usually brahmans, otherwise aristocrats, rarely merchants, sometimes however persons from unprivileged classes who have found entry to literature through becoming Buddhist or Jaina monks. What ideals should we expect these writers to express? Sometimes, especially among the Buddhists, we do in fact find an ideal of perfect justice, freedom and equality which can only be called utopian. It is absurd, however, to criticise the *kavis* (this must be mentioned, because it has been done by people who on other matters command respect for their opinions) for not putting forward a political programme which would have been totally inapplicable under the conditions of their times. More realistic than some modern critics, they in fact supported ideals and programmes which did apply in their day. They gave expression to the ideals of Indian civilisation, which have been touched on already, and to programmes of good government under the inevitably feudalistic system of the period in which most of them lived. [563-4, 575, 912, 1885-6, 1925, 2465, 3833]

499. The ideals of Indian civilisation are not simply very fine : they are in great part still desirable, indeed necessary, for humanity. This is perhaps the main reason why *kāvya* is still worth reading, and it is because it is worth reading in this sense that we can reject the suggestion that *kāvya* is merely the literature of a class, and not of India or of humanity. The programme of social harmony of the Indian *dharmaśāstra*, or its more thoroughgoing and egalitarian but seemingly less practicable Buddhist or Jaina variants, was progressive in its day, advanced by contemporary standards elsewhere, and anything more revolutionary was pure utopia until at least the +13—and then India was for centuries locked in desperate struggle with barbarous invaders, during which it consequently entered a period of economic and social regression. In the earlier period , and in the later period of heroic struggle, *kāvya* was a national literature, or more correctly the literature of a civilisation, not the literature of a class. In the darkest days it kept the Indian tradition alive. It handed on the best ideals and inspired the struggle to expel tyrannical invaders and realise these ideals. In this context it sounds pedestrian to say that *kāvya* is important for its educational function—the 'aesthetic education'—but we may usefully recall that the drama is the *Veda* of the people, the whole people, according to Bharata himself, and the best vehicle, along with the *rāsas* and other forms of *kāvya* in the vernacular languages (from Apabhraṃśa onwards), for reaching the whole people with the ideals of Indian civilisation and its defence. Ideals apart, *kāvya* is a permanent record of a mighty stream of human experience, and in part a comedy, a critique, of that experience. Having carried our survey some way we may reaffirm the thesis suggested at the outset, that *kāvya* is the heritage of Indian civilisation and that in the present fusion of world civilisations it is necessary, if we value happiness and our very existence, that this inheritance should be appropriated by the whole human race. [567, 589, 742, 892, 1116, 1396-8, 1445, 1506-7, 1618, 1639]

BIBLIOGRAPHY FOR VOLUMES ONE TO THREE

The works referred to have been arranged in the order of the English alphabet, under the names of the authors where known. Translations of *kāvyas* have been included along with their texts, even when they are of poor quality, which is usually the case. They may give some idea of the original to a reader able to ignore their language and style and sceptical enough not to be misled by their substitution of non-Indian ideas. Unfortunately there is no way of suspecting what is entirely omitted in a translation, beyond the mere feeling that the work is so incredibly dull that something must be wrong. Few of those able to write tolerable English have had the time and patience to acquire a sufficient command of the vast vocabulary of Sanskrit, along with a sensitivity to shades of meaning, to the life and nature reproduced in *kāvya* and to the vision of its writers, to be able to produce accurate translations. Mostly they have taken the easier way of substituting their own vision, or the atmosphere of a favourite English classic, hoping thus to hit on something equivalent to the original. We must be grateful to these translators, however, despite these criticisms, for the task is of extraordinary difficulty, whilst even the roughest pioneering work enables later students to find their way much more quickly. The majority of English translations of *kāvyas*, on the other hand, have been written by people who were not native speakers of English and whose acquaintance with that language was extremely limited. These are students' cribs prepared by Indian professors. Their style may be explained by observing that for their authors English is a dead language : it died in the +19 and must be studied through the classical writers of that period. Handbooks are available in which are collected the quaint 'idioms', metaphors and clichés which English is supposed always to prefer to simplicity or to original expression. Indian professors find it characteristic of English always to use as many words as possible to express even the simplest ideas, whilst its vocabulary is totally inadequate to convey any subtleties of thought or to offer equivalents for even a thousandth part of the riches of the Sanskrit lexicon.

Abhijñānaśākuntalacarcā (anon.), ed. K. Raghavan Pillai, University of Kerala Sanskrit Series (Trivandrum Sanskrit Series), Trivandrum, 1961.

Abhinanda: *Rāmacarita*, ed. K. S. Rāmasvāmin, Gaekwad's Oriental Series, Oriental Institute, Baroda, 1930.

Abhinavagupta : *Abhinavabhāratī* or Commentary on the *Nāṭyaśāstra*, ed. M. R. Kavi, K. S. Rāmasvāmin and J. S. Pade, Gaekwad's Oriental Series, Baroda, 1926-64, in 4 volumes, of which the second edition of Vol. I (1956) should be used (references to this are usually given simply by volume and page, e. g. 'Abhinavagupta I p. 272').

: *Locana* or Commentary on the *Dhvanyāloka* of Ānandavardhana, ed. Paṭṭābhirāma, Kashi Sanskrit Series, Benares, 1940.

: *Tantrāloka*, ed. M. Kaul, Kashmir Series of Texts and Studies, Research Department, Kashmir State, Srinagar, 1918-38, in 12 volumes.

Āgama, Buddhist, see *Tripiṭaka*.

Agastya : *Kṛṣṇacarita*, MS in Tanjore, Burnell's *Catalogue* No. 10203. ed. T. Veṅkaṭācārya, Tanjore Sarasvatī Mahal, 1975

Bālbhārata I-III, ed. Subrahmanya Śrirangam, Vani Vilas Press, 1939

Nalakīrti Kaumudī, II and IV ed. T. Veṅkaṭācārya; Delhi; D.K. Publishing House, 1975

Agni Purāṇa, ed. H. N. Apte, Ānandāśrama, Poona, 1900; translated by M. N. Dutt, Calcutta, 1903.

Ahobala : *Virūpākṣavasantotsava*, ed. R. S. Panchamukhi, Kannada Research Institute, Dharwar, 1953.

Aitareya Brāhmaṇa, see *Ṛgveda*.

Alaka: commentary on Ratnākara's *Haravijaya*, ed. Durgāprasāda and Parab, Kāvyamālā, Bombay, 1890 .

Amarasiṃha: *Nāmaliṅgānuśāsana*, ed. with the commentary *Amarakośodghāṭana* of Kṣīrasvāmin by H. D. Sharma and N.G. Sardesai, Poona Oriental Series, Oriental Book Agency, Poona, 1941; ed. with the commentary *Ṭīkāsarvasva* of Sarvānanda (and also Kṣīrasvāmin's commentary) by Gaṇapati, Trivandrum Sanskrit Series, Trivandrum, 1914-7.

Amaruka: *Śataka*, ed. with Arjunavarman's *Rasikasaṃjīvinī* by Nārāyaṇa Rāma Ācārya, Nirṇaya Sāgara Press, Mumbaī (Bombay), 3rd. edn. 1954; ed. with Vemabhūpāla's

Śṛṅgāradīpikā and a translation by C. R. Devadhar (unfortunately the editor has merely reprinted and translated the Nirṇaya Sāgara text, above, instead of Vemabhūpāla's), Poona Oriental Series, Poona, 1959; MS of Acyutarāya's *Śāradāgama* commentary in Poona Ānandāśrama No. 7052; MS of Rudramadeva's commentary in London, British Museum No. Or. 3566 (from Nepal); critical. edn. of the *Śataka* by R. Simon, with notes from several commentators, Haeseler, Kiel, 1893. See also the article by Friš.

Amṛtānanda : *Alaṃkārasaṃgraha*, ed. V. Krishnamacharya and K. Ramachandra, Adyar Library Series, Madras, 1949.

Ānandavardhana: *Dhvanyāloka*, ed. with the commentary *Locana* of Abhinavagupta (*q. v.*); there is an edition with an English 'Exposition' by Bishnupada Bhattacharya, Mukhopadhyay, Calcutta, 1956 in progress; translation by K. Kṛishnamoorthy, Poona Oriental Series, Poona, 1955.

Anaṅgaharṣa, see Māyurāja.

Anantaśarman : *Mudrārākṣasapūrvasaṃkathānaka*, ed. D. Sharma, Anup Sanskrit Library, Gaṅgā Oriental Series, Bīkāner, 1945.

Aṅguttara Nikāya, ed. Morris and Hardy, Pali Text Society, London, 1885—1900; Buddhaghosa's commentary *Manorathapūraṇī* ed. Walleser and Kopp, Pali Text Society, London, 1924—56.

Anuyogadvāra Sūtra or *Aṇuogaddārāiṁ*, critical edn. in the Jaina Āgama Series, No. 1, by Puṇyavijaya, Mālvaṇiā and Bhojak, Shri Mahāvīra Jaina Vidyālaya, Bombay, 1968; ed. with the commentary of Maladhārin Hemacandra in the Āgamodaya Samiti Series, Bombay, 1924.

Appayya Dīkṣita : *Kuvalayānanda*, ed. Nārāyaṇa Rāma Ācārya, Nirṇaya Sāgara Press, Bombay, 10th. edn. 1955, with Jayadeva's *Candrāloka* and Vaidyanātha's *Candrikā*; ed. Vāsudevaśarman, Nirṇaya Sāgara Press, Bombay, 3rd. edn. 1927, with Āśādhara's *Dīpikā*.

Arnold E.V. : *Vedic Metre*, Cambridge University Press, 1905.

Arthaśāstra, see Kauṭalya.

Ārya Śūra, see Śūra.

Asaṅga: *Madhyāntavibhāga*, ed. with the *Bhāṣya* of Vasubandhu by G. M. Nagao, Suzuki Research Foundation, Tokyo, 1964; first part translated by Stcherbatsky, Biblotheca Buddhica, Moscow/Leningrad, 1936.

Aśoka : Inscriptions, ed. and translated by J. Bloch, *Les inscriptions d'Aśoka*, Institut de Civilisation Indienne, Collection Emile Senart, Paris, 1950; see Warder, *Indian Buddhism*, Chapter 8, for an English translation of a selection, with discussion. Vol. II below, Appendix pp. 395 ff.

Aśvaghoṣa : *Buddhacarita*, ed. and translated by E.H. Johnston, Panjab University Oriental Publications, Calcutta, 1935-6 and *Acta Orientalia*, 1937; see also Weller, *Zwei Zentralasiatische Fragmente des Buddhacarita*, *Abhandlungen der Sachsischen Akademie der Wissenschaften*, Leipzig, 1953.

: *Rāṣṭrapāla Nāṭaka*, referred to by Dharmakīrti, *Vādanyāya*, p. 67.

: *Śāriputra*, fragments ed. Lüders, *Sitzungsberichte der königlich preussischen Akademie der Wissenschaften*, Berlin, 1911, pp. 388ff.; see also Lüders, *Bruchstücke buddhistischer Dramen*, Königlich preussische Turfan-Expeditionen, Kleinere Sanskrit-Texte I, Reimer, Berlin, 1911.

: *Saundarananda*, ed. and translated by Johnston, Panjab University Oriental Publications, Oxford University Press, London, 1928 and 1932.

: *Somadatta*, fragments ed. Lüders in *Bruchstücke* (see *Śāriputra* above).

: fragments of an allegorical play also in Lüders, *Bruchstücke*.

Atharvaveda: Śaunaka recension, *Saṃhitā* ed. Roth and Whitney, Dümmler, Berlin, 1856, 2nd. edn. by Lindenau, 1924, ed. with Sāyaṇa's commentary by Vishva Bandhu, Vishveshvaranand Vedic Research Institute, Hoshiarpur, 1960ff. in 5 vols, translated by Griffith, Lazarus, Benares, 1895-6, also by Whitney, reprinted Motilal Banarsidass, Delhi, 1962; Paippalāda recension, *Saṃhitā* ed. Durgamohan Bhattacharya and Dipak Bhattacharya, 1964, 1970 in progress; the *Gopatha Brāhmaṇa* appears to belong to the Śaunaka recension (ed. R. Mitra and H. Vidyābhūṣaṇa, Bibliotheca Indica, Calcutta, 1872), the *Paippalāda Brāhmaṇa* seems to be lost; the *Muṇḍaka Upaniṣad* probably belongs to the Paippalāda (ed. Hertel, Leipzig, 1924).

Ātmabodhendrasarasvatī, see under Sadāśivabrahmendra.

Avadānas: apocryphal Buddhist texts sometimes added to the *Khuddaka Nikāya* or *Kṣudraka Āgama* of the schools, in which legends were collected; in Sanskrit the best known collections are the *Avadānaśataka* (ed. Speyer, Bibliotheca Buddhica, St. Petersburg, 1902-9, translated by Feer, *Annales du Musée Guimet*, Paris, 1891), the *Divyāvadāna* (ed. Cowell and Neil, Cambridge, 1886 and Vaidya, Buddhist Sanskrit Texts, Darbhanga, 1959) and the *Bodhisattvāvadānakalpalatā* (see Kṣemendra), see separately the *Maṇicūḍāvadāna*; an *Aśokāvadāna* is known only in two Chinese versions (Przyluski, *La légende de l'empereur Açoka*, Annales du Musée Guimet, Paris, 1923) and sections of the *Divyāvadāna* probably based on it.

Āvaśyakaniryukti, see Bhadrabāhu.

Bahurūpamiśra: *Daśarūpakadīpikā* commentary on Dhanañjaya's *Daśarūpaka*, MSS in Trivandrum (complete, save for some small lacunae) and Madras (incomplete, Government Oriental MSS Library No. R. 3670 and 4188), transcripts kindly loaned by Professor T. Venkatacharya.

Bāṇa: *Harṣacarita*, ed. Śūranāḍ Kuñjan Pilla, with Raṅganātha's commentary *Marmāvabodhinī*, Trivandrum Sanskrit Series, 1958; translated by Cowell and Thomas (one of the best translations of any Sanskrit text), Royal Asiatic Society, London, 1897.

: *Caṇḍīśataka* (*stotra*), ed. and translated by Quackenbos in *The Sanskrit Poems of Mayūra*, Columbia University Indo-Iranian Series, New York, 1917 .

: *Kādambarī*, ed. Peterson (very accurate), Bombay Sanskrit Series, 1883, reprinted with a few misprints by Vaidya, Poona Oriental Series, 1951; ed. with the commentary of Bhānucandra and Siddhacandra by K. P. Parab, Nirṇaya Sāgara Press, Bombay, 9th. edn. 1948; translated by C. M. Ridding, Royal Asiatic Society, London, 1896.

Bhadrabāhu : *Āvaśyakaniryukti* or *Āvassayanijjutti*, ed. with Haribhadra's *Ṭīkā*, Āgamodaya Samiti, Bombay, 1916-7; see Leumann, 'Āvaśyaka-Erzählungen', *Abhandlungen für die Kunde des Morgenlandes*, Leipzig, 1897, and 'Übersicht über die Āvaśyaka-Literatur', posthumously ed. Schubring, Hamburg, 1934.

Bhāgavata Purāṇa, ed. and translated by Burnouf and others, Imprimerie Royale Nationale, Paris, 1840-98 in 5 volumes; ed. Paṇśikar, Veṅkaṭeśvara Press, Bombay, 1920 in 12 volumes; translated by M. N. Dutt, Calcutta, 1895.

Bhallaṭa: *Śataka*, ed. Durgāprasāda and Parab, Kāvyamālā Gucchaka IV, Bombay, 3rd. edn. 1937.

Bhāmaha : *Kāvyālaṅkāra*, ed. Baṭukanāthaśarman and Baladevopādhyāya, Kashi Sanskrit Series, Vārāṇasī, 1928; there is an inferior edition with a practically useless translation (because the translator did not understand the subject matter, in this case) published in Tanjore by the Wallace Printing House in 1928; Gnoli has edited some fragments of a manuscript of the text with a commentary, which he believes to be Udbhaṭa's, Serie Orientale Roma, Rome, 1962.

Bhānudatta: *Rasataraṅgiṇī*, ed. Regnaud in *La Rhêtorique Sanskrite*, Leroux, Paris, 1884; also Venkatesvara Press, Bombay, 1914.

Bharata, see *Nāṭyaśāstra*.

Bhāravi: *Kirātārjunīya*, ed. with Mallināthaʼs commentary by Nārāyaṇa Rāma Ācārya, Nirṇaya Sāgara Mudraṇālaya, Bombay, 14th. edn. 1954; translated into German by Cappeller, Harvard Oriental Series, Cambridge, Massachusetts, 1912; cantos I—III ed. with Citrabhānu's *Śabdārthadīpikā* by Gaṇapati, Trivandrum Sanskrit Series, 1918.

Bhartṛhari : *Vākyapadīya*, *Kāṇḍa* I ed. K. A. Subramania Iyer, with the *Vṛtti* and *Paddhati*, Deccan College Monograph Series, Poona, 1966, translated, with the *Vṛtti*, by K. A. Subramania Iyer, Deccan College Building Centenary Series, 1965, *Kāṇḍa* II ed. Gangādhara, Benares Sanskrit Series, with Puṇyarāja's commentary, 1887ff., *Kāṇḍa* III, 1-7 ed. K. A. Subramania Iyer, with the commentary of Helārāja, Deccan College Monograph Series, Poona, 1963, 8-14 ed. Sāmbaśiva and Ravi Varman, with Helārāja's commentary, Trivandrum Sanskrit Series, 1935 and 1942; for a useful study (but based on the early editions and requiring revision) see Gaurinath Sastri, *The Philosophy of Word and Meaning*, Calcutta Sanskrit College Research Series, 1959.

: commentary on *Mahābhāṣya*, see Patañjali.

Bhartṛhari (II, presumably): *Triśatī* (lyrics), critical edn. by D. D. Kosambi, Singhi Jain series, Bombay, 1948; translated by B. S. Miller, Columbia University Press, New York, 1967.

Bhāsa: *Bhāsanāṭakacakra*, ed. Devadhar, Oriental Book Agency, Poona, 2nd. edn. 1951 (reprinted from the original editions of the plays by Gaṇapati in the Trivandrum Sanskrit Series), containing the *Svapnavāsavadatta*, *Pratijñāyaugandharāyaṇa*, *Avimāraka*, *Daridracārudatta*, *Pratimā*, *Abhiṣeka*, *Pañcarātra*, *Madhyama*, *Dūtavākya*, *Dūtaghaṭotkaca*, *Karṇabhāra*, *Ūrubhaṅga* and *Bālacarita*; the same plays translated by Woolner and Sarup as *Thirteen Trivandrum Plays attributed to Bhāsa*, Panjab University Oriental Publications, Oxford University Press, London, 1930-1 in two volumes; the *Dāmaka*, *Traivikrama*, *Yajñaphala* and *Ghaṭakarpara* have been entered separately under their titles as probably by other, at present unknown, authors.

Bhaṭṭanṛsiṃha, see under Dhanañjaya.

Bhaṭṭi : *Rāvaṇavadha*, with the commentary of Jayamaṅgala, Nirṇaya Sāgara Press, Bombay, 1887; with Mallinātha's commentary ed. Trivedin, Bombay Sanskrit Series, 1898 (despite his grammatical virtuosity, Mallinātha is remoter from the ideas of Bhaṭṭi than Jayamaṅgala, following later critics for the figures of speech, etc.).

Bhavabhūti : *Vīracarita* or *Mahāvīracarita*, ed. with the commentary of Vīrarāghava, by T. R. Ratnam Aiyar and S. Rangachariar, revised by W. L. Paṇśīkar, Nirṇaya Sāgara Press, Bombay, 4th. edn. 1926; critical edn. by Todar Mall, Panjab University Oriental Publications, Oxford University Press, London, 1928; translated by J. Pickford, London, Trübner, 1871.

: *Mālatīmādhava* (fiction), ed. with the commentary of Pūrṇasarasvatī by Mahādeva, Rāmasvāmin and several others, Trivandrum Sanskrit Series, 1953; ed. with the commentaries of Tripurāri and Jagaddhara by M. R. Telang, Nirṇaya Sāgara Press, Bombay, 6th. edn. 1936; translated into French by G. Strehly, Leroux, Paris, 1885; there are editions with English cribs by Kale, Bombay, 1928, and R. D. Karmakar, Poona, 1935; translated by H. H. Wilson, Asiatic Press, Calcutta, 1826.

: *Uttararāmacarita*, ed. Nārayaṇa Rāma Ācārya, Nirṇaya Sāgara Press, Bombay, 10th. edn. 1949, with Vīrarāghava's commentary; ed. and translated by Stchoupak, Institut de Civilisation Indienne, Collection Emile Senart, Paris, 1935 (recommended); translated by S.K. Belvaikar, Harvard Oriental Series, Cambridge, Massachusetts, 1915.

Bhaviṣyant Purāṇa, Veṅkaṭeśvara Press, Bombay, 1897.

Bhoja : *Sarasvatīkaṇṭhābharaṇa*, ed. with the commentary of Ratneśvara (I—III) and Jagaddhara (IV) by Kedāranāthaśarman and Vāsudevaśarman, Kāvyamālā, Bombay, 2nd. edn. 1934.

: *Śṛṅgāraprakāśa*, ed. Josyer, Coronation Press, Mysore, 1955 in progress (Vol. II in 1963 carried the text to the end of Chapter XIV); Chapters XXII-XXIV ed. Yadugiriyati, published by the editor, Madras, 1926; see Raghavan's book on this work.

: *Samarāṅgaṇasūtradhāra*, ed. Gaṇapati and revised and made more complete by V. S. Agrawala, Gaekwad's Oriental Series, Baroda, 1966.

Bloch, see under Aśoka.

Bodhāyana : *Bhagavadajjukīya*, ed. P. Anujan Achan, with Nārāyaṇa's *Diṅmātradarśinī*, Mangalodayam Press, Trichur, 1925; ed. Veṭūri Prabhākara, Vāvilla Press, Madras, 1925; translated into Italian as *L'asceta trasmutato in etèra*, by F. Belloni-Filippi, Carabba, Lanciano, 1931, reprinted in M. Vallauri, *Teatro Indiana*, Nuova Accademia Editrice, Milan, 1959.

Brahma Purāṇa, Ānandāśrama, Poona, 1895.

Brahmāṇḍa Purāṇa, Veṅkaṭeśvara Press, Bombay, 1913.

Brahmavaivarta Purāṇa, ed. Jīvānanda Vidyāsāgara, Calcutta, 1888; translated by R. N. Sen, Sacred Books of the Hindus, Allahabad, 1920-2.

Bṛhatkathā, see Guṇāḍhya.

Buddhist *Āgama*, see *Tripiṭaka*.

Buddhist Historical Tradition, for a sketch see Warder, *An Introduction to Indian Historiography*, Chapter V.

G. Bühler : *Die indischen Inschriften und das Alter der indischen Kunstpoesie, Sitzungsberichte der kais. Akademie der Wissenschaften*, Philosophisch-Historische Classe, Vienna, 1890.

Bu-ston : *Chos-ḥbyung* (= 'Dharmodbhava' or 'Production of the Doctrine', the origin and history of the texts of Buddhism), translated by Obermiller in *Materialien zur Kunde des Buddhismus*, Heidelberg, Vols. 18 and 19, 1931-2.

Cālukya inscriptions, see e. g. *Epigraphia Indica* Vol. VI.

Candragomin : *Lokānanda*, Tibetan text ed. R. Handurukande, Pali Text Society, London, 1967.

: *Śiṣyalekhadharmakāvya*, ed. J. Minayeff, *Zapiski* of the Imperial Russian Archaeological Society, Oriental Section, Vol. IV, 1889, pp. 29 ff.

: *Deśanāstava* and *Udānakathā* in the Tibetan *Tripiṭaka*.

: *Cāndravyākaraṇa*, ed. Liebich, *Abhandlungen für die Kunde des Morgenlandes*, Leipzig, 1902.

: *Cāndravṛtti*, ed Liebich, *Abhandlungen für die Kunde des Morgenlandes*, Leipzig, 1918.

Cappeller : *Die Gaṇachandas*, Leipzig, 1872.

Hari Chand : *Kālidāsa et l'art poétique de l' Inde*, Champion, Paris, 1917.

Chāndogya Upaniṣad, see *Sāmaveda*.

Chavannes: *Cinq cents Contes et Apologues extraits du Tripiṭaka chinois*, Leroux, Paris, 1910-34 in 4 volumes.

Cidambara : *Rāghavayādavapāṇḍavīya*, MS in Government Oriental Manuscripts Library, Madras (*Descriptive Catalogue*, XX. 7829).

Comprehensive History of India, see Nilakanta.

Dāmaka, ed. and translated by Venkatarama, Panjab Sanskrit Series, Moti Lal Banarsi Dass, Lahore, 1926.

Dāmodaragupta: *Kuṭṭanīmata*, ed. M. Kaul , Bibliotheca Indica, Calcutta, 1944.

Daṇḍin: *Kāvyalakṣaṇa*, ed. with Ratnaśrījñāna's commentary *Ratnaśrī* by A. Thakur and Upendra Jha, Prācīnācāryagranthāvalī of the Mithilā Institute, Darbhanga, 1957 (the *Ratnaśrī*, +10, is by far the oldest and best commentary now available); ed. and translated under the corrupt modern title *Kāvyādarśa*, with Jīvānanda's commentary, by V. Narayana Iyer, Ramaswamy Sastrulu, Madras, 1952; the anonymous *Hṛdayaṃgamā* commentary has been ed. by M. Rangacharya, along with Taruṇavācaspati's commentary, Madras, 1910; ed. with Vādijaṅghāla's commentary by V. Krishnamachariar, Srinivasa Press, Tiruvadi, Madras, 1936.

: *Avantisundarī*, ed Śūranāḍ Kuñjan Pilla, Trivandrum Sanskrit Series, 1954, covering the first part of the text from fragmentary manuscripts; a further part, from the middle of the text, has been edited several times under the episodic and inaccurate title '*Daśakumāracarita*' ('*Aṣṭakumāra*' would be accurate for the available fragment, '*Ekādaśakumāra*' would be accurate for the number of *kumāras* associated in the intact novel), by Godabole and Parab, Nirṇaya Sāgara Press, 5th, edn. 1906 (pp. 56 to 278, the rest is spurious), by Wilson, Society for the Publication of Oriental Texts, London, 1846 (pp. 49 to 202), the spurious parts being apparently attempts to restore the novel from an inaccurate Telugu translation or conjecturally (there are variant versions of the conclusion, but those printed are meagre and do not carry out what is indicated in the opening nor tie up some of the loose ends of the first part); the connection between the two available original parts is covered by a free versified paraphrase, the *Avantisundarīkathāsāra* (anon.), ed. Harihara, Kuppuswami Sastri Research Institute, Madras, 1957 (this also is incomplete, starting from the beginning but breaking off in the middle of the second part).

Devacandra : *Śāntināthacarita*, MS in Jessalmere (Dalal's *Catalogue*, p. 52).

Devavijaya (gaṇi) : *Rāmacarita* (Krishnamachariar p. 480).

Dhammanandin : *Sīhalavatthu* (*ppakaraṇa*), ed. Buddhadatta, Anulayantālaya, Colombo, 1959.

Dhammapada, ed. Fausböll, London, 2nd. edn. 1900; translated by C. A. F. Rhys Davids, with a text, Pali Text Society, London, 1931.

Dhammapada Commentary (*Aṭṭhakathā*), ed. H. C. Norman, Pali Text Society, London, 1906-14; translated by Burlingame, Harvard Oriental Series, Cambridge, Massachusetts, 1921 in 3 volumes.

Dhanañjaya : *Daśarūpaka*, ed. with Dhanika's *Avaloka* by Parab, Nirṇaya Sāgara Press, Bombay, 5th. edn. 1941 (references in the text are generally to this edition, as the best available when it was being written, but there is now a better edition, with the *Avaloka* and also Nṛsiṃha's *Laghuṭīkā*, by T. Venkatacharya, Adyar Library Series, Madras, 1969); unsatisfactory edn. and translation by Haas, reprinted Motilal Banarsidass, Delhi, 1962; *Dīpikā*, see Bahurūpamiśra.

Dhanapāla (I) : *Tilakamañjarī*, ed. Bhavadatta and Parab, Kāvyamālā, Bombay, 2nd. edn. 1938.

Dhanapāla (II) : *Bhaviṣyadatta* or *Bhavisayattu*, ed. Dalal and Gune, Gaekwad's Oriental Series, Baroda (1923), reprinted 1967.

Dhanika, see under Dhanañjaya.

Dharmakīrti : *Pramāṇavārttika*, I and *Vṛtti* of Dharmakīrti ed. Mālavaṇiyā, Hindu Vishvavidyalaya Nepal Rajya Sanskrit Series, Vārāṇasī, 1959, also by Gnoli, Serie Orientale Roma, Rome, 1960; II-IV ed. with Prajñākaragupta's *Bhāṣya* by Sāṅkṛtyāyana, Tibetan Sanskrit Works Series, Patna, 1953 (Index 1959); I-IV with Manorathanandin's *Vṛtti* (easier) ed. Sāṅkṛtyāyana, Appendices to Vols. XXIV, XXV and XXVI of the *Journal of the Bihar and Orissa Research Society*, Patna, 1938-40, reprinted in the Bauddha Bharati Series, Varanasi, 1968; first part of I (to *Kārikā* 51), with Dharmakīrti's *Vṛtti*, translated by S. Mookerjee and H. Nagasaki, Nava Nālandā Mahāvihāra Publication, Patna, 1964.

: *Vādanyāya* ed. Sāṅkṛtyāyana, Appendices to Vols. XXI and XXII of the *Journal of the Bihar and Orissa Research Society*, Patna, 1935-6.

Dharmaśāstras, the most important and probably the earliest extant of these is the *Mānava Dharmaśāstra*, ed. Deslongchamps, Levrault, Paris, 1830, translated by G. Bühler as *The Laws of Manu*, Sacred Books of the East, Oxford University Press, London, 1886; eventually as many as 36 such books of legal institutes were recognised, all in principle equally authoritative and teaching an identical law if rightly interpreted, thus to be taken collectively as the law, supposedly drawn from the *Veda*; this universally applicable law of the *Dharmaśāstras* superseded, for society as a whole, the more ancient *Dharmasūtras* of the Vedic schools of brahmans, which belonged to the *Kalpa Vedāṅga*; for a good introduction to the subject see R. Lingat, *Les sources du droit dans le système traditionnel de l'Inde*, Mouton, Paris/La Haye, 1967; of the medieval *Dharmaśāstras*, that of Yājñavalkya is the most important, ed. Paṇśīkar, Nirnaya Sāgara Press, Bombay, new edn. 1949, translated by J. R. Gharpure, Hindu Law Texts, Bombay, 1936-44,

Dharmasena, supplement to *Vasudevahiṇḍi* in press, Ahmedabad.

Dhīranāga: *Kundamālā*, ed. K.K. Dhavana, Bhāratīya Saṃskṛta Bhavana, Jālandhara, 1955; translated by Woolner as *The Jasmine Garland*, Panjab University Oriental Publications, Oxford University Press, London, 1935.

Dīgha Nikāya or *Dīrgha Āgama*, Pali recension ed. T. W. Rhys Davids and J. E. Carpenter, Pali Text Society, London, 1890-1911 in 3 volumes; translated by Rhys Davids as *Dialogues of the Buddha*, Pali Text Society, London, 1899-1921in 3 volumes, since reprinted; Chinese translation of another recension ed. Takakusu and Watanabe in Vol. I of the *Taishō Tripiṭaka*, Tokyo, 1924; of the Sanskrit recension, the *Mahāparinirvāṇa Sūtra* has been ed. by Waldschmidt, *Abhandlungen der Deutsche Akademie der Wissenschaften*, Berlin, 1950-1.

Dīgha .Commentary, *Sumaṅgalavilāsinī*, of Buddhaghosa, ed. T.W. Rhys Davids, Carpenter and Stede, Pali Text Society, London, 1886-1932 in 3 volumes.

Diṅnāga: *Miśrakastotra*, Tibetan version ed. D. R. S. Bailey as Appendix II of his edn. of the *Śatapañcāśatka*, see under Mātṛceṭa.

: *Pramāṇasamuccaya* and *Vṛtti*, Tibetan translations in the Peking edn. of the Tibetan *Tripiṭaka*, reprinted Otani University, Kyoto, 1957, Nos. 5700, 5701 and 5702, also in the Sde-dge edn., Nos. 4203 and 4204; only fragments, as quotations, of the original Sanskrit are now available, see the footnotes to Kitagawa's Japanese translation of parts of Chapters II, III, IV and VI in his *A Study of Indian Classical Logic—Dignāga's System* (*Indo Koten-Ronrigaku no Kenkyū*), Suzuki Research Foundation, Tokyo, 1965; Hattori similarly has collected fragments of Chapter I in his English translation in *Dignāga on Perception*, Harvard Oriental Series, Cambridge Massachusetts, ,1968, and is doing the same for his forthcoming translation of the remaining Chapter V, on *anyāpoha*; for a study, but based mainly on the later work of Dharmakīrti, see Stcherbatsky, *Buddhist Logic*, Vol. I, Bibliotheca Buddhica, Leningrad, 1932, reprinted Indo-Iranian Reprints, Mouton, 'S-Gravenhage,- 1958.

Durvinīta Gāṅgeya, see e. g. *Mysore Archaeological Reports*, Bangalore, 1916, 36.

Epigraphia Indica, Supplement to the Reports of the Archaeological Survey of India, Calcutta, 1892-1929.

Faddegon, B. : The *Vaiśeṣika System*, Verhandelingen der Koninklijke Akademie van Wetenschappen, Amsterdam, 1918.

Fris, Ô : 'The Recensions of the Amaruśataka', *Archiv Orientalni* Oriental Institute, Prague, Vol. 19, 1951, pp. 125ff.

Gaṇḍavyūha Sūtra, ed. Suzuki and Idzumi, Sanskrit Buddhist Texts Publishing Society, Kyoto, 1934-6, ed. Vaidya, Buddhist Sanskrit Texts, Mithila Institute, Darbhanga, 1960.

Gaṅgā: *Madhurāvijaya*, ed. and translated by Thiruvenkatachari, Annāmalai University, Annāmalainagar, 1957.

Gaṅgādhara, see under Sātavāhana.

Garuḍa Purāṇa, Veṅkaṭeśvara Press, Bombay, 1905; translated by M. N. Dutt, Calcutta, 1908.

Gershevitch, I : *The Avestan Hymn to Mithra*, Cambridge University Press, 1959.

Ghanaśyāma : *Ānandasundarī* (*saṭṭaka*), ed. Upadhye, Motilal Banarsidass, Banaras, 1955.

Ghaṭakarpara, ed. and translated as *The Broken Pot* by Peiris and van Geyzel, Colombo Apothecaries, Colombo, 1961; ed. and translated by J. B. Chaudhuri, published by the editor, Calcutta, 1953; ed. with Abhinavagupta's *Vivṛti*, Kashmir Series of Texts and Studies, Research Department, Kashmir State, Srinagar, 1945.

Gītagovinda, see Jayadeva.

Gnoli, R. : *The Aesthetic Experience according to Abhinavagupta*, Serie Orientale Roma, Rome, 1956.

Godakumbura, C.E. : *Sinhalese Literature*, The Colombo Apothecaries, Colombo, 1955.

Govindarāja, see under Vālmīki.

Guṇacandra, see Rāmacandra.

Guṇāḍhya: *Bṛhatkathā*; the main versions available are 1) Budhasvāmin, *Bṛhatkathāślokasaṃgraha*, ed. and translated into French by Lacôte, Leroux, Paris, 1908-29 (see also his *Essai sur Guṇāḍhya et la Bṛhatkathā*, Leroux, Paris, 1908); 2) Kṣemendra, *Bṛhatkathāmañjarī*, ed. Śivadatta and Parab, Kāvyamālā, Bombay, 2nd, edn. 1931; 3) Kongu-Vēḷir, *Perunkatai*, ed. V. Swaminatha Iyer, Madras, 1935 (Tamil, a new study of this version is reported to be in preparation); 4) Saṃghadāsa, *Vasudevahiṇḍi*, ed. Caturavijaya and Puṇyavijaya, Ātmānanda Jaina Grantharatnamālā, Bhāvanagara, 1930-1 (on this see Chapter XXV); 5) Somadeva (II), (*Bṛhat-*) *Kathāsaritsāgara*, ed. Durgāprasāda and Parab, Nirṇaya Sāgara Press, Bombay, 2nd. edn. 1903, translated by Tawney, Bibliotheca Indica, Calcutta, 1880-4, new edn. with (mostly irrelevant) notes by Penzer as *The Ocean of Story*, privately printed by Sawyer, London, 1924-8 in 10 volumes; 6) there is another *Bṛhatkathāmañjarī*, by Bāṇa or Vāmana, perhaps the author of the *Vīranārāyaṇacarita* (+15), of which, however, only a small part is known to be available, manuscript in the Adyar Library, see Krishnamachariar, p. 216. Dharmasena's *Majjhimakhaṇḍa*, LD, 1988

Haribhadra : *Samarāditya* or *Samarāicca*, ed. Jacobi, Bibliotheca Indica, Calcutta, 1908-26; the sixth 'existence' has been ed. and translated by M. C. Modi, Prakrit Granth Mālā, Ahmedabad, 1936.

: *Dhūrtākhyāna*, ed. Jinavijaya, with a study by Upadhye, Singhi Jain Series, Bombay, 1944.

Haripāla : *Saṅgītasudhākara*, MSS in Madras and Tanjore.

Hariṣeṇa : inscription (*praśasti*), ed. Bühler, see above.

Harivaṃśa, ed Kinjawaḍekar, Citraśālā Press, Poona, 1936 (this edition, the 'vulgate' with Nīlakaṇṭha's commentary, is the one generally referred to, but two thirds of its text is apocryphal); ed. and translated into French by Langlois, Oriental Translation Fund, Paris/London, 1834-5 (2 vols. in 3 parts); critical edn. by Vaidya, Bhandarkar Oriental Research Institute, Poona, 1969 (text, second volume with the apocryphal additions to follow).

Harṣa (I) : *Nāgānanda*, ed. and translated by Karandikar, New and Second Hand Book Stall, Bombay, 1953.

: *Ratnāvalī*, ed. and translated into French by M. Lehot, Institut de Civilisation Indienne, Collection Emile Senart, 1933.

Harṣa (II) : *Naiṣadhacarita*, ed. Nārāyaṇa Rāma Ācārya, Nirṇaya Sāgara Press, Bombay, 9th edn. 1952, with Nārāyaṇa's commentary; translated by K. K. Handiqui, Deccan College Monograph Series, 2nd edn. 1956.

Hazra, R.C. : ***Studies in the Upapurāṇas*, Sanskrit College, Calcutta,** 1958, 1963, in progress.

Hemacandra : *Kāvyānuśāsana*, ed. R. C. Parikh, Sri Mahavira Jaina Vidyalaya, Bombay, 1938 in 2 volumes.

Hiuen Tsang : *Si Yu Ki*, translated by S. Beal, reprinted Oriental Books Reprint Corporation, Delhi, 1969.

Hōbōgirin (Dictionnaire encyclopédique du bouddhisme d'après les sources chinoises et japonaises), ed. Demiéville, Maison Franco-Japonaise, Paris/Tokyo, 1929ff.

Hṛdayaṃgamā, see under Daṇḍin.

Indurāja, see under Udbhaṭa.

Indus Civilisation, see Mortimer Wheeler, *The Indus Civilization*, Cambridge University Press, 1953; John Marshall, *Mohenjo-Daro*, Probsthain, London, 1931 in 3 volumes; E. J. H. Mackay, *Further Excavations at Mohenjo-Daro*, Government of India, Delhi, 1937—8 in 2 volumes; M. S. Vats, *Excavations at Harappā*, Government of India, Delhi, 1940 in 2 volumes; B. and R. Allchin, *The Birth of Indian Civilization*, Penguin Books, Harmondsworth, 1968.

Iśvaradatta, *Dhūrtaviṭasaṃvāda*, ed. M. R. Kavi and S. K. Ramanatha in *Caturbhāṇī*, Dakshinabharati Series, Bombay, 1922.

Iśvarakṛṣṇa : *Sāṃkhyakārikā*, ed. and translated by Colebrooke, Collingwood, London, 1837; ed. with the commentary *Yuktidīpikā* by R. C. Pandeya, Motilal Banarsidass, Delhi, 1967.

Itihāsa, see *Mahābhārata*, *Harivaṃśa*, *Purāṇas*, *Upapurāṇas*, *Sthalapurāṇas*, Pargiter, etc.

Jaimini : *Mīmāṃsā Sūtra*, ed. with Śabarasvāmin's commentary by Subbā, Ānandāśrama Sanskrit Series, Poona, 1929-34; translated by Ganganatha Jha, with the commentary, Gaekwad's Oriental Series, Baroda, 1933-4 in 3 volumes.

Jaina tradition and historical sources, see Warder, *Introduction to Indian Historiography*, Chapter VI, and e.g. *Vyākhyāprajñapti*, *Kalpasūtra* (especially the *Jinacarita* section), *Sthānāṅga*, *Samavāyāṅga*, *Jambudvīpaprajñapti*, *Jñātādharmakathā*, Vimala, Jinasena (I), Jinasena (II) and Guṇabhadra, Prabhācandra and *Purātanaprabandhasaṃgraha*.

Jalhaṇa: *Sūktimuktāvalī*, ed. E. Krishnamachariar, Gaekwad's Oriental Series, Baroda, 1938.

Jambudvīpaprajñapti, Devcand Lālbhāī Jaina Pustakoddhāra, Bombay, 1920.

Jātaka, ed. Fausböll, Trübner, London, 1877-96 in 6 volumes with its commentary (*Aṭṭhakathā*), recently reprinted by the Pali Text Society; translated, with the commentary narratives, by Cowell, Chalmers, Rouse, Francis and Neil, Cambridge University Press, 1895-1907, also reprinted by the Pali Text Society, London, 1957.

Jayadeva I: *Gītagovinda*, ed. and translated by Laksminarasimha, V. Ramaswamy Sastrulu, Madras, 1956.

Jayadeva II: *Prasannarāghava*, ed. Paṇśīkar, Nirṇaya Sāgara Press, Bombay, 3rd. edn. 1922.

: *Candrāloka*, see under Appayya.

Jayānaka: *Pṛthvīrājavijaya*, ed. G. S. H. Ojha with Jonarāja's commentary, Ajmer, 1941.

Jayaratha, see under Ruyyaka.

Jāyasī : *Padmāvatī*, ed. Ram Candra Shukla, Nāgarī Pracāriṇī Sabhā, Banāras, 1924; partly ed. with a translation by Grierson and Dvivedi, Bibliotheca Indica, Calcutta, 1896-1911, and continued by Lakshmi Dhar, Luzac, London, 1949; complete translation by A. G. Shirreff, Bibliotheca Indica, Calcutta, 1944.

Jayasiṃha : *Hammīramadamardana*, ed. C.D. Dalal, Gaekwad's Oriental Series, Baroda, 1920.

K. P. Jayaswal : *Hindu Polity*, (1924) 3rd edn. Bangalore Printing and Publishing Company, 1955.

Jinabhadra : *Viśeṣāvaśyakabhāṣya*, ed. Malvania, Lalbhai Dalpatbhai Series, Ahmedabad, 1966 in progress.

: *Viśeṣaṇavatī*, Jainabandhu Press, Ratlam, 1927.

Jinaprabha : *Vividhatīrthakalpa*, ed. Jinavijaya, Siṃghī Jaina Granthamālā, Śāntiniketana, 1934.

Jinaṣena I : *Harivaṃśapurāṇa*, ed. Darabārīlāla, Māṇikyacandra Digambara Jaina Granthamālā, Bombay, 1930.

Jinasena II and Guṇabhadra : *Ādipurāṇa* and *Uttarapurāṇa*, ed. Pannālāla, Bhāratīya Jñānapīṭha, Vārāṇasī, 2nd. edn. in 3 volumes 1963, 1965 and 1968.

Jīvānanda, see under Daṇḍin.

Jīvandhara, biography of, see Vādībhasiṃha.

Jñātādharmakathā, Āgamodaya Samiti, Bombay, 1919.

Johnston, E.H. : *Early Sāṁkhya*, Royal Asiatic Society, London 1937

Kalhaṇa : *Rājataraṅgiṇī*, ed. Stein (1892), reprinted Munshi Ram Manohar Lal, Delhi, 1960; translated by Stein (Westminster, 1900), reprinted Motilal Banarsidass, Delhi, 1961 in 2 volumes.

Kālidāsa : *Mālavikāgnimitra*, ed. Nārāyaṇa Rāma Ācārya, Nirṇaya Sāgara Press, Bombay, 9th. edn. 1950 with Kāṭayavema's commentary; translated by Tawney, Thacker, Spink and Co., Calcutta, 2nd. edn. 1891.

: *Raghuvaṃśa*, ed. and translated by G. R. Nandargikar, Radhabhai Atmaram Sagoon, Bombay, 3rd. edn. 1897, with Mallinātha's commentary.

: *Vikramorvaśīya*, ed. Parab, Nirṇaya Sāgara Press, Bombay, 2nd. edn. 1897 with Raṅganātha's commentary; ed. Velankar, Sahitya Akademi, Delhi, 1961 (claims to be 'critical' but shows no knowledge of textual criticism and retains the apocryphal verses); translated by Wilson in his *Select Specimens of the Theatre of the Hindus*, London, 3rd. edn. 1871.

: *Meghasandeśa*, ed. Hultzsch with Vallabhadeva's commentary, Royal Asiatic Society, London, 1911; ed. R. V. Krishnamachariar with Pūrṇasarasvatī's commentary, Sri Vani Vilas Press, Srirangam, 1909; ed. Gaṇapati with Dakṣiṇāvarta's commentary, Trivandrum Sanskrit Series, 1919; ed. and translated by M. R. Kale with Mallinātha's commentary, Booksellers' Publishing Co., Bombay, 5th. edn. no date; the Sahitya Akademi edn. again is uncritical, being based on previous editions and neglecting the Southern recensions, no MSS from Kerala were used except indirectly through the Trivandrum edn. above (Pūrṇasarasvatī also probably represents the Kerala recension) and the editor shows a distinct prejudice against Southern recensions (Delhi, 1957, ed. S. K. De).

: *Abhijñānaśākuntala*, ed. Nārāyaṇa Rāma Ācārya with Rāghavabhaṭṭa's commentary, Nirṇaya Sāgara Press, Bombay, 11th. edn. 1947; translated by Monier Williams, Oxford, 2nd. edn. 1867, reprinted in a Mentor Book *The Genius of the Oriental Theater*, New York, 1966; see separately the *Abhijñānaśākuntalacarcā*.

: *Kumārasambhava*, ed. with Mallinātha's commentary by Govinda, Khemarāja Śrīkṛṣṇadāsa, Mumbaī (Bombay), 1924; ed. with the commentaries of Aruṇagirinātha and Nārāyaṇa by Gaṇapati, Trivandrum Sanskrit Series, 1913-4; ed. and translated, with Mallinātha's commentary, by Karandikar, Booksellers' Publishing Co., Bombay, 1950 (first five cantos only); the Sahitya Akademi edn. (1962) is incredibly bad, showing no knowledge of how to collate MSS and totally ignoring even printed editions from the South, let alone MSS, whilst accepting the apocryphal conclusion as genuine; for a reliable introduction to Kālidāsa textual criticism see H. Chand's book above.

Kalpasūtra, ed. Jacobi, *Abhandlungen für die Kunde des Morgenlandes*, Leipzig, 1879; translated by Jacobi, Sacred Books of the East, Oxford University Press, London, 1884.

Kāmasūtra, by Mallanāga Vātsyāyana, ed. Dāmodara, Kashi Sanskrit Series, Benares, 1929 with Yaśodhara's commentary; English translation by Burton and Arbuthnot, guided by pandits, reprinted R. K. Champion, London, 1963; German translation, including the commentary, by R. Schmidt, Barsdorf, Berlin, 6th. edn. 1920.

Kambala, see e. g. the collection (by various Buddhist lyric poets) *Caryāgītikoṣa*, ed. Bagchi and Śānti Bhikṣu, Visva-Bharati, Santiniketan, 1956, pp. 26ff.

Kane, P.V. : *History of Sanskrit Poetics*, published by the author, Bombay, 1951.

Kathāsaritsāgara, see under Guṇāḍhya.

Kauṭalya : *Arthaśāstra*, ed. Gaṇapati, Trivandrum Sanskrit Series, 1924-5 in 3 volumes; ed. and translated by Kangle, University of Bombay, 1960 and 1963; a fragment, with a fragment of an old commentary, ed. Kosambi, Singhi Jain Series, Bombay, 1959.

Kavikarṇapūra: *Alaṅkārakaustubha*, ed. Sivaprasad Bhattacharya, Varendra Research Society, Savita Memorial Series, Rajshahi, 1926 and 1934, with Lokanātha's commentary.

Khuddaka Nikāya or *Kṣudraka*, the Pali recension consists of about 15 texts, including the *Jātaka*, *Suttanipāta*, *Dhammapada*, *Theragāthā*, *Therīgāthā*, *Udāna* and *Niddesa* which have been entered separately; see also *Avadāna*.

Konow, S. : *Das indische Drama,* Grundriss der indo-arischen Philologie und Altertumskunde, de Gruyter, Berlin/Leipzig, 1920.

Kramadīpikā MSS in Trivandrum, etc., for various acts.

M. Krishnamachariar : *History of Classical Sanskrit Literature*, Oriental Book Agency, Poona, 1937.

Kṛṣṇacarita, *ākhyāyikā*, see Agastya.

Kṛṣṇācārya or Kāṇhapāda: *Dohākoṣa*, ed. Haraprasād in *Bauddha Gāna o Dohā*, Vaṅgīya Sāhitya Pariṣad, Calcutta, 1916;

some of his *gītis* are in the *Caryāgītikoṣa* given above under Kambala.

Kṛṣṇaśarman : *Mandāramaranda*, ed. Kedāranāthaśarman and Vāsudevaśarman, Kāvyamālā, Bombay, 2nd. edn. 1924.

Kṣemendra, satires, the *Kalāvilāsa*, *Darpadalana*, *Deśopadeśa*, *Narmamālā* and *Samayamātṛkā* have been reprinted in *Minor Works of Kṣemendra*, ed. Rāghavācārya and Padhye, Osmania University, Hyderabad, 1961; the same volume contains also his critical writings *Aucityavicāracarcā*, *Kavikaṇṭhābharaṇa* and *Suvṛttatilaka*; these last three have been translated by Sūryakānta, Poona Oriental Series, 1954 (the satires have apparently been thought too highly spiced for the chaste English tongue, though the *Samayamātṛkā* has been translated into German, under the peculiar title *Das Zauberbuch der Hetären*, by J. J. Meyer, Altindische Schelmenbücher I, Lotus-Verlag, Leipzig, 1903); for the *Bṛhatkathāmañjarī* see under Guṇāḍhya; the *Bodhisattvāvadānakalpalatā* is ed. by Vaidya, Buddhist Sanskrit Texts, Mithila Institute, Darbhaṅga, 1959 in 2 volumes.

Kṣīrasvāmin, see under Amarasiṃha.

Kulaśekhara : *Tapatīsaṃvaraṇa*, ed. Gaṇapati, Trivandrum Sanskrit Series, 1911.

Kumāradāsa : *Jānakīharaṇa*, ed. Paranavitana and Godakumbura, Ceylon Academy of Letters, Colombo, 1967 (the only authentic and complete text); Cantos I-V ed. (reconstructed and inferior text) and translated by Nigudkar and Joglekar, The Oriental Publishing Co., Bombay, 1908.

Kumāralāta: *Kalpanāmaṇḍitikā*, ed. Lüders, Kleinere Sanskrit-Texte II, Leipzig, 1926.

Kumārasvāmin, commentary on the *Pratāparudrīya*, ed. with the text by Sankararama, see under Agastya.

Kunhan Raja: *Survey of Sanskrit Literature*, Bhāratīya Vidyā Bhavan, Bombay, 1962.

Kunjunni Rāja: *The Contribution of Kerala to Sanskrit Literature*, Madras University Sanskrit Series, 1958.

: 'Kūṭiyāṭṭam : the Staging of Sanskrit Plays in the Traditional Kerala Theatre', *Samskrita Ranga Annual*, II, Madras, 1961, pp. 17ff.

Kuntaka: *Vakroktijīvita*, ed S. K. De, Mukhopadhyay, Calcutta, 3rd. edn. 1961, ed. K. Krishnamurthy, Dharwar, 1977

Kūrma Purāṇa, ed. N. Mukhopadhyaya, Bibliotheca Indica, Calcutta, 1890.

Kūṭiyāṭṭakrama, MS in the Pāliyam Manuscripts Library, Chennamangalam, Jayantamangalam (now in Trivandrum).

Kutūhala : *Līlāvaī*, ed. Upadhye, Singhi Jaina Series, Bombay, 1949.

Lakṣmīdhara: *Cakrapāṇivijaya*, ed. Kāśīrāma, Rājasthāna Purātana Granthamālā, Jayapura, 1956.

Laṅkāvatāra Sūtra, ed. Nanjio, Kyoto,1923, reprinted by Vaidya, Buddhist Sanskrit Texts, Mithila Institute, Darbhanga, 1963; translated by Suzuki, Routledge, London, 1932.

Līlāvatī or *Līlāvaī*, see Kutūhala.

Lin li-kouang : *L'aide mémoire de la vraie loi*, Annales du Musée Guimet, Adrien—Maisonneuve, Paris, 1949.

Liṅga Purāṇa : Veṅkaṭeśvara Press, Bombay, 1906.

E. J. H. Mackay : *Further Excavations at Mohenjo-Daro*, see under Indus Civilisation above.

Mādhava, see Vidyāraṇya.

Mādhava : *Subhadrāharaṇa*, Kāvyamālā Gucchaka IX, Bombay, 1899.

Mādhavabhaṭṭa Kavirāja : *Rāghavapāṇḍavīya*, ed. and published by Bhavadeva Caṭṭopādhyāya with Premacandra Tarkavāgīśa's commentary, Calcutta, 2nd. edn. revised by Kṛpāmaya, 1925.

Māgha : *Śiśupālavadha*, ed. with the commentaries of Vallabhadeva and Mallinātha, by Anantarāma, Kashi Sanskrit Series, Benares, 1929; excerpts translated into German by Cappeller, Kohlhammer, Stuttgart, 1915 as *Bālamāgha*.

Mahābhārata, critical ed. by Sukthankar and others, Bhandarkar Oriental Research Institute, Poona, 1933-66; translated (from the inferior 'vulgate' text) by P. C. Roy, Bhārata Press, Calcutta, 1884-96; ed. with the commentary of Vādirāja by P. P. S. Shastri, Ramaswami Sastrulu, Madras, 1931ff.

Mahādeva : *Adbhutadarpaṇa*, ed. Bhavadatta and Parab, Kāvyamālā, Bombay, 2nd. edn. 1938.

Mahāparinirvāṇa Sūtra, see under *Dīgha Nikāya*.

Mahendravarman : *Mattavilāsa*, ed. Gaṇapati, Trivandrum Sanskrit Series, 1917; translated by L. D. Barnett, *Bulletin of the School of Oriental Studies*, Vol. V, London, 1930, pp. 697ff.

Mahendrasūri : *Narmadāsundarī*, ed. P. Trivedī, Singhi Jain Series, Bombay, 1960.

Mahiman : *Vyaktiviveka*, with Ruyyaka's commentary, ed. Gaṇapati, Trivandrum Sanskrit Series, 1909; ed. Dwivedi, Kashi Sanskrit Series, Varanasi, 1964.

Majjhima Nikāya, ed. Trenckner and Chalmers, Pali Text Society, London, 1888-99 in 3 volumes, reprinted 1948-51; translated by I. B. Horner as *Middle Length Sayings*, Pali Text Society, London, 1954-9 in 3 volumes.

Majjhima Commentary, *Papañcasūdanī*, of Buddhaghosa, ed. Woods, Kosambi and Horner, Pali Text Society, London, 1922-38 in 5 volumes.

R. C. Majumdar (editor) : *The History and Culture of the Indian People*, Bhāratīya Vidyā Bhavan, Bombay, 1951-1969 (the most complete general history of India so far published; the chapters on literature are to some extent useful for bibliographical purposes).

Maladhārin Hemacandra, see under *Anuyogadvāra Sūtra*.

Malayasundarī, original (in Prakrit ?) attributed to 'Keśin' and apparently lost, there are several abridgements in various languages, including Dharmacandra's *Malayasundarīkathoddhāra* in Sanskrit prose (+14), based on a Prakrit source (the original?), apparently unprinted but translated into German from a manuscript by J. Hertel in *Indische Märchen*, in the second series of 'Die Märchen der Weltliteratur', Diederichs, Jena, 1919, pp. 185-268, Māṇikyasundara's *Malayasundarīkathā* also in Sanskrit prose (+15, based on Dharmacandra?), ed. Amṛtalāla, Nirṇaya Sāgara Press, Bombay, 1918, Jayatilaka's *Malayasundarīcaritra* in Sanskrit verse and a Gujarātī paraphrase of the +18.

Mallanāga Vātsyāyana, see *Kāmasūtra*.

Mammaṭa: *Kāvyaprakāśa*, ed. Sivaprasad Bhattacharya with Śrīdhara's commentary, Calcutta Sanskrit College Research Series, 1959, 1961 in 2 volumes; ed. H. Harihara with Vidyācakravartin's commentary, Trivandrum Sanskrit Series, 1926, 1930 in 2 volumes; ed. and translated, with edn. of Vidyācakravartin's commentary and of Ruyyaka's commentary by R. C. Dwivedi, Motilal Banarsidass, Delhi, 1966, 1970 in 2 volumes; ed. Vāsudeva with Māṇikyacandra's commentary, Ānandāśrama Saṃskṛta Granthāvali,

Poona, 1921; ed. Abhyaṃkara Vāsudeva with Govinda's *Kāvyapradīpa* and Nāgojī's *Uddyota*, Ānandāśrama Saṃskṛta Granthāvali, Poona, 1911; ed. Durgāprasād and Parab with Govinda's *Kāvyapradīpa* and Vaidyanātha's *Prabhā*, Kāvyamālā, Bombay, 1891; ed. R. C. Parikh with Someśvara's commentary, Rajasthan Pracya Vidya Pratisthan Jodhpur, 1959 in 2 volumes; *Kāvyaprakāśakhaṇḍana* by Siddhicandra ed. R. C. Parikh, Bhāratīya Vidyā Bhavan, Bombay, 1953 (a critique); the *Candrikā* commentary to which De refers in his footnotes to Kuntaka (e. g. p. 31) is presumably the *Udāharaṇacandrikā* by Vaidyanātha (+17), which appears not to have been printed yet, MS in India Office Library, London.

Mānava Dharmaśāstra, see under *Dharmaśāstras*.

Mānaveda: *Kṛṣṇagīti*, ed. P. S. Ananthanarayana, Mangalodayam, Trichur, 1914.

Mandāramaranda, see Kṛṣṇaśarman.

Maṇicūḍāvadāna, ed. and translated by R. Handurukande, Pali Text Society, London, 1967.

Māṇikyacandra, see under Mammaṭa.

Mañjuśrīmūlakalpa, ed Gaṇapati, Trivandrum Sanskrit Series, 1920-5 in 3 volumes; reprinted by Vaidya, Buddhist Sanskrit Texts, Mithila Institute, Darbhanga, 1964 (under the uninformative title *Mahāyānasūtrasaṁgraha* Part .II); the *Rājavyākaraṇa Parivarta* translated by K. P. Jayaswal in his *An Imperial History of India*, Motilal Banarsi Dass, Lahore, 1934.

Mankad, D.R. : *The Types of Sanskrit Drama*, Urmi Prakashan Mandir, Karachi, 1936.

Maṅkhaka : *Śrīkaṇṭhacarita*, ed. Durgāprasāda and Parab, Kāvyamālā, Bombay, 2nd. edn, 1900.

Manorathapūraṇī, see under *Aṅguttara Nikāya*.

Mārkaṇḍeya Purāṇa, ed. K. M. Banerjea, Bibliotheca Indica, Calcutta, 1855-62; ed. Kṣemarāja Śrīkṛṣṇadāsa, Śrīveṅkaṭeśvara Stīm Press, Bombay, no date (1890?); translated by Pargiter, Bibliotheca Indica, Calcutta, 1888-1905, .reprinted Indological Book House, Varanasi, 1969.

J. Marshall : *Mohenjo-Daro*, see under Indus Civilisation above.

Mataṅga: *Bṛhaddeśī*, ed. K. Sāmbaśiva, Trivandrum Sanskrit Series, 1928.

Mātrarāja, see Māyurāja.

Mātṛceṭa: *Varṇārhavarṇa Stotra*, ed. and translated by D. R. S. Bailey, *Bulletin of the School of Oriental and African Studies*, London, 1950, pp 671ff. and 947 ff.

: *Prasādapratibhodbhava Stotra* or *Śatapañcāśatka*, ed. and translated by D. R. S. Bailey, Cambridge University Press, 1951.

: *Mahārājakanikalekha*, ed. in Tibetan and translated by F.W. Thomas, *Indian Antiquary*, Bombay, 1903,pp.345ff.

: *Kaliyugaparikathā*, *Caturviparyayakathā* and other works available in translation in the Tibetan *Tripiṭaka*.

: extracts from another work in the *Ratnaśrī*, see under Daṇḍin.

Matsya Purāṇa, ed H. N. Apte, Ānandāśrama, Poona, 1907; translation (anon.) Sacred Books of the Hindus, Allahabad, 1916-7 in 2 volumes.

Mayūra, *The Sanskrit Poems of Mayūra*, ed. and translated by Quackenbos, Columbia University Indo-Iranian Series, New York, 1917.

Māyurāja: *Tāpasavatsarāja*, ed. Yadugiriyati, published by the editor, Bangalore, 1929.

: *Udāttarāghava*. edition promised by Professor Raghavan (MS from Kathmandu).

Meghavijaya: *Saptasandhāna*, ed. Hargovind, Jaina Vividha Sāhitya Śāstra Mālā, Benares, 1917.

Mehendale: *Historical Grammar of Inscriptional Prakrits*, Deccan College Dissertation Series, Poona, 1948.

Mīmāṃsā Sūtra, see Jaimini.

Mugdhakathā, see Chavannes (Vol. II), also Somadeva II and Kṣemendra [1254].

Mūka: *Pañcaśatī*, ed. Durgāprasād and Parab, Kāvyamālā Gucchaka V, Bombay, 2nd. edn. 1937.

Murāri: *Anargharāghava*, ed. with Rucipati's commentary by Durgāprasād and Paṇśīkar, Kāvyamālā, Bombay, 5th edn. 1937.

Nāgārjuna : *Catuḥstava*, Tucci has edited and translated the *Niraupamya* and *Paramārtha*, *Journal of the Royal Asiatic Society*, London, 1932, he has also edited Amṛtākara's commentary, Serie Orientale Roma, Rome, 1956 (in Minor Buddhist Texts, Part I), the others are available in the Tibetan Tripiṭaka.

: *Ratnāvalī*, fragments ed. and translated by Tucci, *Journal of the Royal Asiatic Society*, London, 1934 and 1936, complete text in the Tibetan *Tripiṭaka*, with Ajitamitra's commentary.

: *Suhṛllekha*, translated by Wenzel, *Journal of the Pali Text Society*, London, 1886, text in the Tibetan and Chinese (Taishō 1673) *Tripiṭakas*.

Nāgārjuna (II or III) : *Pañcakrama*, ed. La Vallée Poussin, Gand, **1896, Engelcke (Université de Gand).**

: commentary on the *Guhyasamāja*, Tibetan translation in the Tibetan *Tripiṭaka*, MS of the Sanskrit original (same ?) in Sa-skya.

Namisādhu, see under Rudraṭa.

Nārada Purāṇa, Veṅkaṭeśvara Press, Bombay, 1923.

Nārāyaṇa: *Veṇīsaṃhāra*, ed. K. N. Dravid, The Oriental Book-Supplying Agency, Poona, 1922; ed. and translated by Gajendragadkar, Āryābhūṣaṇa Press, Poona, 1922-3; ed. Parab and Māḍgāvkar with Jagaddhara's commentary, Nirṇaya Sāgara Press, Bombay, 1898.

Naṭāṅkuśa, MSS in Ceruthuruti and elsewhere in Kerala.

Nāṭyasarvasvadīpikā, MS quoted by Mankad, p. 128, in Bhandarkar Oriental Research Institute, Poona.

Nāṭyaśāstra, by 'Bharata', ed. Baṭukanāthaśarman and Baladevopādhyāya, Kashi Sanskrit Series, Benares, 1929 (referred to as 'Kāśī'); for the 'Baroda' edition see under Abhinavagupta above; the 'translation' published in the Bibliotheca Indica, Calcutta, is so inaccurate as to be practically useless, the technical terminology being for the most part lost.

Nepālamāhātmya, MS in Paris, extract ed. by Lacôte in his *Essai sur Guṇāḍhya et la Bṛhatkathā*, pp. 291ff., see under Guṇāḍhya above.

Netti, ed. Hardy, Pali Text Society, London, 1902; translated by Ñāṇamoli as *The Guide*, Pali Text Society, London, 1962.

Niddesa, ed. La Vallée Poussin, E. J. Thomas and W. Stede, Pali Text Society, London, 1916-8 in 3 volumes.

Niddesa Commentary, *Saddhammapajjotikā*, of Upasena, ed. A.P. Buddhadatta, Pali Text Society, London 1931-40 in 3 volumes.

K.A. Nilakanta (editor): *A Comprehensive History of India*, Orient **Longmans, Calcutta, 1957 in progress (Vol. II was generally more accurate and comprehensive than the work edited** by Majumdar, but Vol. V is the reverse; all Indian historical writing still falls far short of being that definitive history, free from prejudice, rhetoric and superficiality, which is so much to be desired yet undoubtedly lies many decades of discussion and research in the future).

: *The Cōḷas* (his own work), Madras University Historical Series, 2nd edn. 1955.

Nītisāra, ed. Haeberlin, *Kāvyasaṃgraha*, Thacker, Calcutta, 1847.

Nṛsiṃha, see under Dhanañjaya.

Pādalipta : *Taraṅgavatī* or *Taraṃgavaī*; *Saṃkhitta Taraṃgavaī* by Yaśas, Śrīnemivijñānagranthamālā, Jīvaṇabhāī Choṭābhāī Jhaverī, Sūriyapura (Surat), 1944; translated into German by Leumann, *Zeitschrift für Buddhismus*, Munich, 1921, pp. 193ff, and 272ff., as *Die Nonne*; Gujarati version ed. Dhīrajalāla Ṭokaraśī Śāha, Ānanda Prakāśana Bhandira, Bhāvanagara, 4th. edn. 1950.

Padma Purāṇa, ed, V. N. Mandlik (Maṇḍalīka), Ānandāśrama Press, Poona, 1893-4 in 4 volumes.

Padmagupta : *Navasāhasāṅkacarita* ed. Jitendracandra, Vidyabhavan Sanskrit Granthamala, Banaras, 1963.

Pālhaṇa : *Āburāsa*, ed. in Vajrasena, below, pp. 29-33.

: Bārahamāsa, or Nemi Rājula Bārahamāsa also reprinted with Vajrasena, below, pp. 98-100 (*Prācina*), Ahmedabad, 1975.

Pañcatantra, see 'Viṣṇuśarman'.

K. C. Pandey : *Indian Aesthetics* (Vol. I of his *Comparative Aesthetics*), Chowkhamba Sanskrit Series Studies, Varanasi, 2nd, edn. 1959.

Pāṇini : *Aṣṭādhyāyī*, ed. and translated by S. C. Vasu, (1891-8) reprinted Motilal Banarsidass, Delhi, 1962, in 2 volumes.

Pargiter, F.E. : *Ancient Indian Historical Tradition*, (1922, Oxford University Press) reprinted Motilal Banarsidass, Delhi, 1962.

: *The Purāṇa Text of the Dynasties of the Kali Age*, Oxford University Press, London, 1913.

Patañjali : *Mahābhāṣya*, ed. Kielhorn, Bombay, 1880-5 in volumes, 2nd. edn. 1892-1909 and 3rd. edn. revised by K V. Abhyankar, Bhandarkar Oriental Research Institute, Poona, 1962, in progress; ed. with Kaiyata's *Pradīpa* and Nāgeśa's *Uddyota* by Giridhara, Caukhambā Saṃskṛta Sīrija, Banārasa, 1954 in progress; ed. with Kaiyaṭa's

Pradīpa and Nāgeśa's *Uddyota* by Śivadatta, Raghunātha and Bhārgava, Nirṇaya Sāgara Press, Bombay, 1917ff., Vol. V on *Adhyāya* 6 in 1945, it is not known whether the edition has been completed; ed. with Kaiyaṭa's *Pradīpa* and Nāgeśa's *Uddyota* by Vedavrata, Harayāṇā Sāhitya Saṃsthāna, Rohtak, Vol. V on *Adhyāyas* 7 and 8 in 1962; ed. with Bhartṛhari's *Ṭīkā* by Svāmināthan, Hindū Viśvavidyālayīya Nepālarājya Saṃskṛta Granthamālā, Vārāṇasī, 1965 in progress; the best introduction is P. S. Subrahmanya's *Lectures on Patañjali's Mahābhāṣya*, published by the author, Tiruchirapalli, 1955 in progress.

Pītāmbara, see under Sātavāhana.

Po Yu King, see Chavannes (Vol. II, 1911).

Prabhācandra : *Prabhāvakacarita*, ed. Jinavijaya, Singhi Jain Series, Calcutta, 1940.

Pravarasena : *Setubandha*, ed. and translated into German by Goldschmidt, Trübner, London, 1880; ed. Śivadatta, Parab and Paṇśīkar, Kāvyamālā, Bombay, 2nd. edn. 1935 with Rāmadāsa's commentary *Rāmasetupradīpa*.

Puḷumāyi II : inscription, ed. G. Bühler in his *Die indischen Inschriften*, see above.

Purāṇas : Pargiter's books, above, offer a good synopsis of their historical contents, Hazra's work above has some useful notes on what is included in *Itihāsa*; the five most important, and on the whole most ancient as now preserved, are the *Viṣṇu*, (*Vaiṣṇava*), *Vāyu* (*Vāyavīya*), *Matsya* (*Mātsya*), *Mārkaṇḍeya* and *Padma* (*Pādma*), the others, among the classical 'eighteen' are the *Brahmāṇḍa*, *Brahman* (*Brāhma*), *Liṅga* (*Laiṅga*), *Garuḍa* (*Gāruḍa*), *Agni* (*Āgneya*), *Bhāgavata*, *Vāmana*, *Skanda* (*Skānda*), *Nārada* (*Nāradīya*), *Bhaviṣyant*, *Brahmavaivarta*, *Varāha* (*Vārāha*) and *Kūrma* (*Kaurma*), they have all been entered separately in this Bibliography; see below under *Upapurāṇas* for certain texts other than these eighteen, including the *Viṣṇudharmottara* (*Śāstra*), sometimes treated as *Purāṇas*.

Purātanaprabandhasaṃgraha, ed. Jinavijaya, Singhi Jain Series, Calcutta, 1936.

Puṣpadanta: *Mahāpurāṇa*, ed. Vaidya, Manikchand Digambara Jaina Granthamālā, Bombay, 1937-41 in 3 volumes.

Rāghavabhaṭṭa, see under Kālidāsa.

Raghavan, V.: *Bhoja's Śṛṅgāraprakāśa*, published by the author, Madras, 1963.

: *The Number of Rasas*, The Adyar Library, Madras, 1940.

: *Some Concepts of the Alaṅkāra Śāstra*, The Adyar Library, Madras, 1942.

: *Some Old Lost Rāma Plays*, Annamalai University, Annamalainagar, 1961.

: 'The Social Play in Sanskrit', *Transaction* No. 11, Indian Institute of Culture, Basavangudi, Bangalore, 1952.

Rājaśekhara : *Kāvyamīmāṃsā*, ed. Dalal and R. A. Sastry, Gaekwad's Oriental Series, Baroda, 3rd. edn. 1934; translated into French by Stchoupak and Renou, Cahiers de la Société Asiatique VIII, Paris, 1946.

: *Bālarāmāyaṇa*, ed. Jīvānanda Vidyāsāgara, Nūtana Vālmīkiyantra, Calcutta, 1884, with the editor's own commentary.

: *Karpūramañjarī*, ed. Nārāyaṇa Rāma Ācārya, Nirṇaya Sāgara Mudraṇālaya, Bombay, 4th. edn. 1949 with Vāsudeva's commentary; ed. Konow and translated by Lanman, Harvard Oriental Series, reprinted Motilal Banarsidass, Delhi, 1963.

: *Bālabhārata*, first two acts ed. with the *Karpūramañjarī* in the Nirṇaya Sāgara edn. above.

Rājaśekharasūri : *Prabandhakośa*, ed. Jina Vijaya Muni, Singhi Jaina Series, Calcutta, 1935.

Rāmacandra and Guṇacandra : *Nāṭyadarpaṇa*, ed. Shrigondekar and Gandhi, Gaekwad's Oriental Series, Baroda, 2nd. edn. 1959.

Rāmacarita, *ākhyāyikā*, see under Devavijaya.

Rāmapāṇivāda : *Uṣāniruddha*, ed. Subrahmanya and Kunhan Raja, The Adyar Library, Madras, 1943.

: *Kaṃsavaha*, ed. Upadhye, Hindī Grantha Ratnākara Kāryālaya, Hirabag, Bombay, 1940.

Rāmavarman: *Syānandūrapuravarṇana*, Trivandrum Sanskrit Series, 1920.

Rāmasetu, see under Pravarasena.

Rāmāyaṇa, see Vālmīki.

Ratnākara : *Haravijaya*, with Alaka's commentary *Viṣamapadodyota*, ed. Durgāprasād and Parab, Kāvyamālā, Bombay, 1890.

Ratnaśrījñāna, see under Daṇḍin.

Ratneśvara, see under Bhoja.

Ravivarman: *Pradyumnābhyudaya*, ed. Gaṇapati, Trivandrum Sanskrit Series, 1910

Rāy, P. : *History of Chemistry in Ancient and Medieval India*, Indian Chemical Society, Calcutta, 1956.

Renou, L. : 'Sur la structure du kāvya', *journal asiatique*, 1959, pp. 1ff.

Ṛgveda : *Saṃhitā* (Śākalya) ed. T. Aufrecht, Marcus, Bonn, 2nd. edn. 1877 in 2 volumes; translated by Griffith, reprinted, ('fourth edition') Chowkhamba Sanskrit Studies, Varanasi, 1963 in 2 volumes; ed. with Sāyaṇa's commentary by Sonaṭakke, Vaidika Saṃśodhana Maṇḍala, Poona, 1933-51 in 5 volumes; ed. with the commentaries of Skandasvāmin, Udgītha, Mādhava and Mudgala by Vishva Bandhu, Vishveshvaranand Vedic Research Institute, Hoshiarpur, 1963ff. in 8 volumes; *Aitareya Brāhmaṇa* ed. Aufrecht, Marcus, Bonn, 1879; *Kauṣītaki Brāhmaṇa* ed. Lindner, Costenoble, Jena, 1887; both *Brāhmaṇas* translated by Keith, Harvard Oriental Series, Cambridge Massachusetts, 1920; *Aitareya Brāhmaṇa* and *Āraṇyaka* with Sāyaṇa's commentary, ed. Kāśīnātha Āgāśe and Bābā Phaḍake, Ānandāśrama Saṃskṛta Granthāvali, Poona, 1896-8 (since reprinted); *Aitareya Upaniṣad* ed. with the commentaries of Śaṃkara and Vidyāraṇya by pandits, Ānandāśrama Saṃskṛta Granthāvali, Poona, 1889; *Śāṅkhāyana* (or *Kauṣītaki*) *Āraṇyaka* translated by Keith, Oriental Translation Fund, Royal Asiatic Society, London, 1908; ed. Pāṭhaka, Ānandāśrama Saṃskṛta Granthāvali, Poona, 1922; *Kauṣītaki Upaniṣad* ed. and translated by Cowell, Bibliotheca Indica, Calcutta, 1861; both *Upaniṣads* translated by R. E. Hume in *The Thirteen Principal Upaniṣads*, Oxford University Press, London, 1921.

Ṛtusaṃhāra (anon.), ed. Godabole, Paṇaśīkar and Devasthali, Nirṇaya Sāgara Press, Bombay, 1906; ed. and translated as *The Seasons* by Peiris and van Geyzel, Colombo Apothecaries, Colombo, 1961.

W. Ruben : *Kālidāsa* : *The Human Meaning of His Works* (*Kālidāsa*: *Die menschliche Bedeutung seiner Werke*), translated by J. Becker, Akademie-Verlag, Berlin, 1957.

Rudradāman I : inscription, ed. G. Bühler in his *Die indische Inschriften*, pp. 86ff., see above.

Rudraṭa : *Kāvyālaṅkāra*, ed. with Namisādhu's commentary by Durgāprasāda and Vāsudevaśarman, Kāvyamālā, Bombay, 3rd. edn. 1928.

Rūpa Gosvāmin: *Bhaktirasāmṛtasindhu*, ed. and translated by Mahārāj, Institute of Oriental Philosophy, Vrindaban, 1965 in progress.

: *Ujjvalanīlamaṇi*, ed. Durgāprasāda and Vāsudevaśarman, Kāvyamālā, Bombay, 2nd, edn. 1932.

Ruyyaka (Rucaka) : *Alaṅkārasarvasva*, ed. with Vidyācakravartin's commentary by S. S. Janaki, Meharchand Lachhmandas, Delhi, 1965; ed. with Jayaratha's commentary by Durgāprasād and Parab, Kāvyamālā, Bombay, 1893; ed. with Samudrabandha's commentary by Gaṇapati, Trivandrum Sanskrit Series, 1915.

: for Ruyyaka's commentaries see under Mahiman and Mammaṭa.

Sadāśivabrahmendra : *Gururatnamālikā*, ed. with Ātmabodhendrasarasvatī's commentary, Kumbhakonam, 1895.

Saddhammapajjotikā, see under *Niddesa*.

Saduktikarṇāmṛta, see Śrīdharadāsa.

Sāgaranandin : *Nāṭakalakṣaṇaratnakośa*, ed. Dillon, Oxford University Press, London, 1937 (referred to by line of this edition); translated by Dillon, Fowler and Raghavan, *Transactions of the American Philosophical Society*, New Series, Vol. 50, Part 9, Philadelphia, 1960.

Sāhityadarpaṇa, see Viśvanātha.

Śailālin (Śailālaka) school of actors, see p. 75 of G. Bühler's *Die indische Inschriften*, above, also *Epigraphia Indica* I 43, 1892 and Pānini IV. 3. 110.

Śaktibhadra : *Āścaryacūḍāmaṇi*, ed. Kuppusvāmin, Bālamanoramā Series, Madras, 1926; translated by C. Sankararaja, Bālamanoramā Series, Madras, 1927.

Śākyaprabha : *Prabhāvatī*, in the Tibetan *Tripiṭaka*.

Śālibhadra : *Bharateśvarabāhubalirāsa* and *Buddhirāsa*, ed. Jina Vijaya Muni, Bharatiya Vidya Research Series, Bombay, 1940.

Samantapāsādikā, see under *Vinaya Piṭaka*.

Samavāyāṅga, Āgamodaya Samiti, Bombay, 1916.

Sāmaveda: Kauthuma recension, *Saṃhitā* ed. Satyavrata

Sāmaśramin, Bibliotheca Indica, Calcutta, 1874-8 in 5 volumes with Sāyaṇa's commentary and the *Gānas*, etc.; translated by Griffith, reprinted ('fourth edition') Chowkhamba Sanskrit Studies, Varanasi, 1963; *Tāṇḍyamahābrāhmaṇa*, ed. Cinnasvāmin, Kāshī Sanskrit Series, Benares, 1935-6 in 2 volumes with Sāyaṇa's commentary; translated as *Pañcaviṃśa Brāhmaṇa* by Caland, Bibliotheca Indica, Calcutta, 1931; *Ṣaḍviṃśa Brāhmaṇa*, ed. B. R. Sharma, Kendriya Sanskrit Vidyapitha, Tirupati, 1967 with Sāyaṇa's commentary; *Sāmavidhāna Brāhmaṇa*, ed. B. R. Sharma, Kendriya Sanskrit Vidyapitha, Tirupati, 1964 with Sāyaṇa's commentary; *Ārṣeya Brāhmaṇa*, ed. B. R. Sharma, Kendriya Sanskrit Vidyapitha, Tirupati, 1967 with Sāyaṇa's commentary; *Devatādhyāya Brāhmaṇa*, ed. B. R. Sharma, Kendriya Sanskrit Vidyapitha, Tirupati, 1965 with a commentary (not Sāyaṇa's?); *Upaniṣad Brāhmaṇa* or '*Chāndogya Brāhmaṇa*', ed. Durgamohan Bhattacharyya, Calcutta Sanskrit College Research Series, 1958 with Sāyaṇa's commentary; the *Chāndogya Upaniṣad*, which is part of the *Upaniṣad Brāhmaṇa*, is ed. separately by Böhtlingk, Haessel, Leipzig, 1889, translated by Hume, see *Ṛgveda*; *Saṃhitopaniṣad Brāhmaṇa* and *Vaṃśa Brāhmaṇa*, ed. B. R. Sharma, Kendriya Sanskrit Vidyapitha, Tirupati, 1965 with Sāyaṇa's commentary; Jaiminīya recension, *Saṃhitā* ed. Caland, *Indische Forschungen*, Breslau, 1907; ed. Raghu Vira, Sarasvati Vihara Series, Lahore, 1938; *Jaiminīya Brāhmaṇa*, ed. Raghu Vīra and Lokesh Chandra, Sarasvatī Vihāra Series, Nagpur, 1954; *Jaiminīya Ārṣeya* and *Jaiminīya Upaniṣad Brāhmaṇas*, ed. B. R. Sharma, Kendriya Sanskrit Vidyapitha, Tirupati, 1967 omitting the *Talavakāra* or *Kena Upaniṣad*, which is part of the latter; the *Upaniṣad* has been ed. by Āgāśe with the commentaries of Śaṃkara and Ānandagiri in the Ānandāśrama Saṃskṛta Granthāvali, Poona, 1888, it is translated by Hume, see *Ṛgveda*.

Saṃghadāsa: *Vasudevahiṇḍi*, ed. Caturavijaya and Puṇyavijaya, Ātmānanda Jaina Grantharatnamālā, Bhāvanagara, 1930-1 in 2 volumes; on this text see the articles of Alsdorf, *Bulletin of the School of Oriental and African Studies*, vol. VIII, London, 1936, pp. 319ff., *Zeitschrift der Deutschen Morgenländischen Gesellschaft*, Leipzig, 1935, pp. 275ff., *Asiatica* :

Festschrift Friedrich Weller, Harrassowitz, Leipzig, 1954, pp.1ff.

Saṃyutta Nikāya or *Saṃyukta Āgama*, Pali recension ed. Feer, Pali Text Society, London, 1884-98 in 5 volumes, reprinted 1960; translated by C. A. F. Rhys Davids and F. L. Woodward as *Kindred Sayings*, Pali Text Society, London, 1917-30 in 5 volumes; Chinese translation of Sarvāstivādin recension ed. Takakusu and Watanabe in the *Taishō Tripiṭaka* (No. 99), Tokyo, 1924.

Saṃyutta Commentary, *Sāratthappakāsinī*, of Buddhaghosa, ed. Woodward, Pali Text Society, London, 1929-37 in 3 volumes.

Sandesara, B.V. : *The Literary Circle of Mahāmātya Vastupāla*, Shri Bahadur Singh Singhi Memoirs No. 3, Bhāratīya Vidyā Bhavan, Bombay, 1953.

Sandhinirmocana Sūtra, in the Tibetan and Chinese (T. 675-9) *Tripiṭakas*, original not available, Tibetan ed. and translated into French by Lamotte, Université de Louvain, Recueil de travaux..2e série, 34e fascicule, 1935.

Saṅgītaratnākara, see Śārṅgadeva.

Śāradātanaya: *Bhāvaprakāśana*, ed. Yadugiriyati and K. S. Ramaswami, Gaekwad's Oriental Series, Baroda, 1930.

Sāratthappakāsinī, see under *Saṃyutta* Commentary.

Saraha: *Dohākoṣa*, ed. Haraprasād in *Bauddha Gāna o Dohā*, Vaṅgīya Sāhitya Pariṣad, Calcutta, 1916.

: some of his *gītis* will be found in the collection given under Kambala above.

Śārṅgadeva: *Saṅgītaratnākara*, ed. S. Subrahmanya, with the commentaries of Kallinātha and Siṅgabhūpāla (or Siṃhabhūpāla), The Adyar Library, 1943-53 in 4 volumes.

Śārṅgadhara: *Paddhati*, ed. Peterson, Bombay Sanskrit Series, 1888.

Sarvānanda, see under Amarasiṃha.

Śatapatha Brāhmaṇa, see *Yajurveda*.

Sātavāhana : *Gāhāsattasaī*, ed. Weber in *Abhandlungen für die Kunde des Morgenlandes*, Leipzig, under the titles *Ueber das* ***Saptaçatakam*** *des Hāla*, 1870, and *Das* ***Saptaçatakam*** *des Hāla*, 1881, with a German translation and extracts from some of the commentaries; ed. with the commentary of Gaṅgādhara by Durgāprasād and Parab, Kāvyamālā, Bombay, 1889; ed. with the commentary (incomplete) of Pītāmbara by Jagdish Lāl, published by the editor, Lahore, 1942.

Sātavāhana inscriptions, see G. Bühler, *Die indischen Inschriften*, above, also Mehendale's work above.

Schlingloff, D. : *Buddhistische Stotras*, Sanskrittexte aus den Turfanfunden, Institut für Orientforschung, Deutsche Akademie der Wissenschaften, Berlin, 1955.

R. S. Sharma: *Aspects of Political Ideas and Institutions in Ancient India*, Motilal Banarsidass, Delhi, 1959, 2nd. edn. 1968.

Siddha: *Upamitibhavaprapañcā*, ed. Peterson and Jacobi, Bibliotheca Indica, Calcutta, 1899-1914.

Sīhalavatthu, see Dhammanandin.

Śīlācārya: *Caupaṇṇamahāpurisacariya*, ed. A. M. Bhojak, Prakrit Text Society Series, Varanasi, 1961.

Śiṅgabhūpāla: *Rasārṇavasudhākara*, ed. Gaṇapati, Trivandrum Sanskrit Series, 1916; ed. Sarasvatīśeṣa, Viśvanātha Press, Veṅkaṭagiri, 1895.

: See under Śārṅgadeva for his commentary on the *Saṅgītaratnākara*

D.C. Sircar: *Select Inscriptions*, Volume I, University of Calcutta, 2nd. edn. 1965.

: *The Successors of the Sātavāhanas*, University of Calcutta, 1939.

Śivasvāmin : *Kapphiṇābhyudaya*, ed. Gauri Shankar, Panjab University Oriental Publications, Lahore, 1937.

Skanda Purāṇa, Veṅkaṭeśvara Press, Bombay, 1909-11 in 7 volumes.

Soḍḍhala: *Udayasundarī*, ed. Dalal and Embar Krishnamacharya, Gaekwad's Oriental Series, Baroda, 1920.

Somadeva (I) : *Yaśastilaka Campū* or *Yaśodharamahārājacarita*, ed. Śivadatta, Paṇaśīkar and Parab, Kāvyamālā, Bombay, 1901—3 in 2 volumes, 2nd. edn. of Vol. I in 1916; see Handiqui, *Yaśastilaka and Indian Culture*, Jīvarāja Jaina Granthamālā, Sholapur, 1949.

Somadeva (II), see under Guṇāḍhya.

Somanātha: *Vyāsayogicarita*, ed. Venkoba Rao, Srinivasa Murti, Bangalore, no date (1926 or later).

M. Somasekhara: *History of the Reḍḍi Kingdoms*, Āndhra University Series, Waltair, 1948.

Someśvara: *Surathotsava*, ed. Śivadatta and Parab, Kāvyamālā, Bombay, 1902.

: *Ullāgharāghava*, ed. Puṇyavijaya and Sandesara,

Gaekwad's Oriental Series, Baroda, 1961.

Śrīdhara, see under Mammaṭa.

Śrīdharadāsa : *Saduktikarṇāmṛta*, ed. S. C. Banerji, Mukhopadhyay, Calcutta, 1965.

Śṛṅgāratilaka (anon), ed. Godabole, Paṇaśīkar and Devasthali, Nirṇaya Sāgara Press, Bombay, 1906 in the same volume as the *Ṛtusaṃhāra*; ed. and translated as *The Ornament of Love* by Peiris and van Geyzel, Colombo Apothecaries, Colombo, 1961.

Sthalapurāṇas, there are hundreds of these, dealing with the antiquities of different localities, for example the *Nepālamāhātmya*, above, the *Keralamāhātmya*, the *Nīlamata Purāṇa* (on Kaśmīra), the *Bṛhadīśvaramāhātmya* (on the great temple in Tanjore) and so on.

Sthānāṅga, ed. Suracandra, Āgamodaya Samiti, Bombay, 1918-20 in 2 volumes.

Subandhu: *Vāsavadattā*, ed. and translated by L. H. Gray, Columbia University Indo-Iranian Series, New York, 1913; ed. with his own commentary by R. V. Krishnamachariar, Srirangam, 1906-8; ed. with an anonymous commentary (by Rāmanātha?), Jñāna Suryodaya Press, Madras, 1862; ed. J. M. Shukla (Śukla), Rājasthāna Purātana Granthamālā, Jodhapura, 1966; ed. with Śivarāma's commentary by F. Hall, Bibliotheca Indica, Calcutta, 1859.

Subhāṣitāvali, see Vallabhadeva.

Śuddhānandaprakāśa, quoted by Raghavan in *Bhoja's Śṛṅgāra Prakāśa*, p. 565.

Śūdraka: *Mṛcchakaṭika*, ed. Parab and Vāsudevaśarman, with the commentary of Pṛthvīdhara, Nirṇaya Sāgara Press, Bombay, 7th edn. 1936; translated by Ryder as *The Little Clay Cart*, Harvard Oriental Series, Cambridge Massachusetts, 1905, reprinted in a Mentor Book, *The Genius of the Oriental Theater*, New York, 1966; ed. with Raṅgācārya's commentary by Paranjape, Nirṇaya Sāgara Press, Bombay, 1909; ed. with his own commentary by Śrīnivāsācārya, Oriental Press, Madras, **1907; critical edn. by Stenzler, Bonn, 1846.**

: *Viṇāvāsavadatta*, ed. K.V. Sarma in *The Journal of Oriental Research*, Kuppuswami Sastri Research Institute, Madras, Vols. XXIX-XXXI, 1963-4.

: *Padmaprābhṛtaka*, ed. and translated by J. R. A.

Loman, Uitgeverij de Driehoek, Amsterdam, 1956.
Sūktimuktāvalī, see Jalhaṇa.
Sukumāra : ***Raghuvīracarita***, **MSS in Madras (MD 12628), Trivandrum (GD 15649, TCD 1327, etc.), etc.**
Sumaṅgalavilāsinī, see under *Dīgha* Commentary.
Śūra: *Jātakamālā*, ed. Kern, Harvard Oriental Series, Cambridge Massachusetts, 1891; translated by Speyer, Pali Text Society, London, 1895.
: *Pāramitāsamāsa*, ed. and translated into Italian by A. Ferrari, *Annali Lateranensi* Vol. X, 1946.
: *Subhāṣitaratnakaraṇḍakakathā*, ed. A. C. Banerjee, Buddhist Sanskrit Texts, Mithila Institute, Darbhanga, 1959 (with Vaidya's reprint of the *Jātakamālā*).
: *Supathanirdeśa Parikathā* and other works in the Tibetan *Tripiṭaka*.
Suttanipāta, ed. Andersen and Helmer Smith, Pali Text Society, London, 1913, reprinted 1948; translated by Chalmers, Harvard Oriental Series, Cambridge Massachusetts, 1932.
Suttanta Piṭaka or *Sūtra Piṭaka* consists of the *Dīgha Nikāya* or *Dīrgha Āgama*, *Majjhima Nikāya* or *Madhyama Āgama*, *Saṃyutta Nikāya* or *Saṃyukta Āgama*, *Aṅguttara Nikāya* or *Ekottara Āgama* and *Khuddaka Nikāya* or *Kṣudraka Āgama*, which have been entered separately; the apocryphal Mahāyāna *Sūtras* include the *Gaṇḍavyūha*, *Laṅkāvatāra*, *Mañjuśrīmūlakalpa* (sometimes reckoned separately from the *Sūtra* collection in a collection of *Tantras*), *Sandhinirmocana* and *Vimalakīrtinirdeśa*, which also have been entered separately.
Sūyagaḍa, ed. Veṇīcandra Suracandra, Āgamodaya Samiti, Bombay, 1917; translated by Jacobi, Sacred Books of the East, Oxford University Press, London, 1895.
Svayaṃbhū : *Svayaṃbhūcchandas*, ed. Velankar, Rājasthāna Purātana Granthamālā, Jodhpur, 1962.
: *Paumacariu*, ed. H. C. Bhāyāṇī, Singhi Jain Series, Bombay, 1953-60 in 3 volumes.
Śyāmilaka: *Pādatāḍitaka*, ed. Schokker, Indo-Iranian Monographs, Mouton, The Hague/Paris, 1966.
Taittirīya Brāhmaṇa and *Upaniṣad*, see *Yajurveda*.
Tāranātha: *Rgya Gar Chos-ḥbyung*, translated into German by Schiefner as *Geschichte des Buddhismus in Indien*, Imperial Academy of Sciences, St. Petersburg, 1869.

Theragāthā and *Therīgāthā*, ed. Oldenberg and Pischel, Pali Text Society, London, 1883; translated by C. A. F. Rhys Davids as *Psalms of the Early Buddhists*, Pali Text Society, London, 1909 and 1913 in 2 volumes.

Tilaka, see under Udbhaṭa.

Tod, J. : *Annals and Antiquities of Rajasthan*, originally published in 1829 and 1832, reprinted Routledge and Kegan Paul, London, 1957 in 2 volumes.

Traivikrama (anon.), ed. M. Krishnamachariar in his *History of Classical Sanskrit Literature*, above, pp. 689-91 MS in Madras

Tripiṭaka, consists of *Suttanta* or *Sūtra Piṭaka*, *Vinaya Piṭaka* and *Abhidhamma* or *Abhidharma Piṭaka*.

Triratnadāsa: *Guṇāparyanta Stotra*, fragment ed. by La Vallée Poussin in the *Journal of the Royal Asiatic Society*, London, 1911; more complete edition promised by Schlingloff; translation in the Tibetan *Tripiṭaka*.

: *Bhagavacchākyamuni Stotra*, in the Tibetan *Tripiṭaka*.

Trivikrama: *Nala Campū*, ed. Nanda Kishore (Kiśora), Kashi Sanskrit Series, Benares, 1939 with Caṇḍapāla's commentary.

Udāna, ed. Steinthal, Pali Text Society. London, 1885, reprinted 1948; translated by Woodward, Pali Text Society, London, 1935.

Udbhaṭa : *Kāvyālaṅkārasārasaṅgraha*, ed. N. D. Banhatti, Bhandarkar Oriental Research Institute, Poona, 1925 with Indurāja's commentary; ed. K. S. Ramaswami, Gaekwad's Oriental Series, Baroda, 1931 with Tilaka's commentary.

Uddyotana: *Kuvalayamālā*, ed. Upadhye, Singhi Jain Series, Bombay, 1959.

Upapurāṇas, see the work of Hazra, above, for a study of this very extensive and largely unprinted literature, which supplements the 'Great' *Purāṇas* with legends and other matter, mostly religious in inspiration; by about the +8 a set of eighteen *Upapurāṇas* seems to have been recognised, just as there were eighteen 'Great' *Purāṇas*, as follows: *Ādya* or *Sanatkumārīya*, *Nārasiṃha* or *Nṛsiṃha*, *Nānda* or *Nandin*, *Śiva* or *Śaiva* or *Nandīśa*, *Daurvāsasa* or *Durvāsa*, *Nāradīya* (different from the *Purāṇa* of that name), *Kāpila*, *Mānava*, *Auśanasa*, *Brahmāṇḍa* (different from the *Purāṇa*), *Vāruṇa*, *Kālikā*, *Māheśvara* or *Vāśiṣṭha*, *Sāmba*, *Āditya* or *Saura*, *Pārāśarya*, *Mārīca* and *Bhārgava*; it is not certain that all these are extant, whilst many others have appeared; with the *Upapurāṇas* are sometimes associated a set of three or six texts which seem properly to be called simply *Śāstras*, namely the *Viṣṇudharma* and *Uttara*, *Śivadharma* and *Uttara* and *Sauradharma* and *Uttara*, of which the *Viṣṇudharmottara* is important for its sections on art and aesthetics and has been entered separately below.

Vādībhasiṃha: *Gadyacintāmaṇi*, ed. T. S. Kuppuswami and S. Subrahmanya, Sarasvati Vilasa Series, Madras. 1902, reprinted Sri Vani Vilas Press, Srirangam, 1916.

Vāgbhaṭa: *Kāvyānuśāsana*, ed. Śivadatta and Parab, Kāvyamālā, Bombay, 1915.

Vajrasena: *Bharateśvarabāhubalighora*, ed. Bhāyāṇī and Nāhaṭā, in *Prācīna Gūrjara Kāvya Sañcaya*, L. D. Series No. 40. Ahmedabad, 1975 (pp. 15-8).

Vākpatirāja: *Gauḍavaha*, ed. Pandurang, 2nd. edn. revised by Utgikar, Bombay Sanskrit and Prakrit Series, Oriental Research Institute, Poona, 1927.

Vākyapadīya, see Bhartṛhari.

Vallabhadeva: *Subhāṣitāvali*, ed. Peterson and Durgāprasāda (1886), Bombay Sanskrit and Prakrit Series, Poona, 2nd. edn. 1961.

Vālmīki : *Rāmāyaṇa*, critical edition by G. H. Bhatt and others, Oriental Institute, Baroda, 1960-1975; ed. Mudholkara, Gujarati Printing Press, Bombay, 1912-20 in 7 volumes with the commentaries of Nāgeśa, Maheśvaratīrtha and Govindarāja; translated by M. N. Dutt, Calcutta, 1892-4.

Vāmana (I) : *Kāvyālaṅkārasūtras* and *Vṛtti*, ed. Nārāyaṇa Rāma Ācārya, Nirṇaya Sāgara Press, Bombay, 4th. edn. 1953; ed. R.V. Krishnamachariar with the commentary of Tripurahara, Sri Vani Vilas Series, Srirangam, 1909; with the commentary of Subuddhimiśra, MS in the India Office Library, London, edition under preparation in Toronto; with the commentary of Sahadeva, MS in Baroda and transcript in the University Manuscripts Library, Trivandrum (No. T. 316); translated by Ganganatha Jha, 'Indian Thought' Series, Oriental Book Agency, Poona, 2nd. edn. 1928.

Vāmana (II): *Vemabhūpālacarita* or *Viranārāyaṇacarita*, ed.

R. V. Krishanamachariar, Sri Vani Vilasa Sanskrit Series, Srirangam, 1910.

Vāmana Purāṇa, critical edition by A. S. Gupta, All India Kashiraj Trust, Varanasi, 1967; translated by S. M. Mukhopadhyaya and others, ibid., 1968.

Vaṃśāvalīs of Nepal, there are several of these, of which the most important are the *Gopālarāja*, ed. Regmi in his *Medieval Nepal*, Vol. III, Mukhopadhyay, Calcutta, 1966, pp. 112ff., one from the Library of Field Marshal Kaisar, ed. Regmi in the same volume, pp. 158ff. and that written by Guvāju, of which there is a translation by Shewasankar and Wright as *History of Nepal translated from the Parbatiya*, Cambridge, 1877, reprinted 1960 (on this and other *Vaṃśāvalīs* of Nepal see Regmi, Vol I, pp. 21ff.).

Varāha Purāṇa, ed. Hṛṣīkeśa, Bibliotheca Indica, Calcutta, 1893.

Vararuci: *Vārttika*, ed. with Pāṇini's *Aṣṭādhyāyī* by Nārāyaṇa Rāma Ācārya, Nirṇaya Sāgara Press, Bombay, 1954; also incorporated in Patañjali's *Mahābhāṣya*, *q. v.*

Vararuci (II) : *Ubhayābhisārikā*, ed. and translated by T. Venkatacharya and A. K. Warder, Sambamurthy, Madras, 1967.

Vāsudeva : *Yudhiṣṭhiravijaya*, ed. Śivadatta and Parab with Ratnakaṇṭha's commentary, Kāvyamālā, Bombay, 1897.

Vasudevahiṇḍi, see Saṃghadāsa.

Vāsudevaratha : *Gaṅgavaṃśānucarita*, MS and transcript in Madras.

M. S. Vats : *Excavations at Harappā*, see under Indus Civilisation.

Vatsarāja : *Samudramathana*, ed. C. D. Dalal in *Rūpakaṣaṭka*, Gaekwad's Oriental Series, Baroda, 1918.

Vātsyāyana, see *Kāmasūtra*.

Vāyu Purāṇa, ed. Gaṅgāviṣṇu Śrīkṛṣṇadāsa, Veṅkaṭeśvara Press, Kalyāṇa/Bombay, 1933; ed. H. N. Apte, Ānandāśrama, Poona, 1905.

Veda, see *Ṛgveda*, *Sāmaveda*, *Yajurveda* and *Atharvaveda*.

Vedāṅgas or ancillaries to the *Veda*, traditionally there are six of these, namely phonetics *śikṣā*, grammar *vyākaraṇa*, lexicology *nirukta*, metrics *chandas*, astronomy *jyotiṣa* and ritual *kalpa*; see for some of their texts Pāṇini (grammar), Yāska (lexicology) and *Dharmasūtras* (considered as a branch of ritual, see under *Dharmaśāstras* above), as well as Jaimini (ritual, but strictly speaking his *mīmāṃsā* superseded the old *Kalpasūtras*, which constituted the *Vedāṅga* proper), the oldest available treatise on metrics is Piṅgala's *Chandaḥsūtra*, ed. Kedāranātha, Nirṇaya Sāgar Press, Bombay, 3rd. edn. 1938.

Veṅkaṭādhvarin : *Viśvaguṇādarśa*, ed. Surendranātha, Vidyābhavana Saṃskṛta Granthamālā, Vārāṇasī, 1963.

Vetālapañcaviṃśati, the original author seems to be unknown and there are now several versions of the work, the most important appearing to be: 1) in Book XII of the *Kathāsaritsāgara* of Somadeva II, see under Guṇāḍhya; 2) that of Śivadāsa, ed. Uhle, *Abhandlungen für die Kunde des Morgenlandes*, Leipzig, 1884, and *Berichte der Sächsischen Gesellschaft der Wissenschaften*, Leipzig, 1914; 3) that of Jambhaladatta, ed. and translated by Emeneau, American Oriental Society, New Haven, 1934; and 4) the Tibetan *Ro sgruṅ* with Sātavāhana as hero, which may be the earliest.

Vīdaēvadāta or *Vendīdād*, ed. K. F. Geldner in his edn. of the *Avesta*, Vol.III, Stuttgart, 1895; translated by J. Darmesteter, Sacred Books of the East, Clarendon Press, Oxford, 1880, reprinted Motilal Banarsidass, Delhi, 1965.

Vidyākara: *Subhāṣitaratnakoṣa*, ed. Kosambi and Gokhale, Harvard Oriental Series, Cambridge Massachusetts, 1957; translated by D. H. H. Ingalls, ibid., 1965.

Vidyānātha, ed. V. Sankaran Madras-1950

Vidyāpati: *Puruṣaparīkṣā*, ed. Rajñadatta with his own commentary, Chandraprabha Press, Benares, 1913; translated by Grierson as *The Test of a Man*, Royal Asiatic Society, London, 1935.

Vidyāraṇya: *Śaṃkaradigvijaya*, ed. with Dhanapati's commentary, Ānandāśrama Press, Poona, 1891.

Vijayā : *Kaumudīmahotsava*, ed. and translated by Sakuntala Rao, published by the editor, care of Bharatiya Vidya Bhavan, Bombay, 1952.

Vijayasena : *Revantagirirāsu*, ed. Dalal in *Prācīna Gūrjara Kāvya Saṃgraha*, see under Vinayacandra below, pp. 1-6.

Vimala: ***Paümacariya***, ed. Jacobi, Nirṇaya Sāgara Press, Bombay, 1914, revised edition by Puṇyavijaya, Prakrit Text Society, Vol. I, Varanasi, 1962, Vol. II, Ahmedabad, 1968; partial editions with translations by Chaugule and N. V.

Vaidya, published by the authors, Cantos I-IV, Belgaum, 1936, by S. C. Upadhyaya, Cantos XXVII and XXVIII, Ahmedabad, 1934, and by Laddu and Gore, Venus Book Stall, Cantos XXXIII-V, Poona, 1941.

Vimalakīrtinirdeśa, not available in Sanskrit, text from the Tibetan *Tripiṭaka* translated into French, with fragments of the Sanskrit, by Lamotte, Muséon, Louvain, 1962.

Vimānavatthu and Commentary (Dhammapāla), ed. Hardy, Pali Text Society, London, 1901; translated by Kennedy, Pali Text Society, London, 1942.

Vinaya Piṭaka, Pali recension ed. Oldenberg, Williams and Norgate, London, 1879-83 in 5 volumes, recently reprinted by the Pali Text Society; translated by I. B. Horner, Pali Text Society, London, 1938-66 in 6 volumes; Jīvaka story also translated in part in A. K. Warder, *Introduction to Pali*, Lessons 20-1 and 24-7; other recensions available of the *Vinaya* include parts of the Sanskrit Mūlasarvāstivāda text, ed. Dutt, *Gilgit Manuscripts* III, Srinagar and Calcutta, 1942-50, and Tucci and Venkatacharya, Rome, 1977-78 several recensions in the Chinese *Tripiṭaka*, such as the Mahāsaṃghika (Taishō Nos. 1425-7) and the Dharmaguptaka (Taishō Nos. 1428-31).

Vinaya Commentary, *Samantapāsādikā*, of Buddhaghosa, ed. Takakusu, Nagai and Mizuno, Pali Text Society, London, 1924-47 in 7 volumes.

Vinayacandra : *Kāvyaśikṣā*, ed. Hariprasād Śāstrī, Lālbhāī Dalpatbhāī Series, Ahmedabad, 1964.

Vinayacandra (II ?) : *Bārahamāsā*, *Nemināthacatuṣpadikā*, ed. C. D. Dalal in *Prācīna Gūrjara Kāvya Saṃgraha*, Gaekwad's Oriental Series, Baroda, 1920, pp. 8-10.

Virahāṅka : *Vṛttajātisamuccaya*, ed. Velankar, Rājasthāna Purātana Granthamālā, Jodhpur, 1962.

Vīrarāghava, see under Bhavabhūti.

Viśākhadatta : *Mudrārākṣasa*, ed. and translated by K. H. Dhruva, Oriental Book Agency, Poona, 3rd. edn. 1930; ed. with Ḍhuṇḍhirāja's commentary by K.T. Telang, Nirṇaya Sāgara Press, Bombay, 5th. edn. 1915; with Śarabha's commentary, MS in Tanjore; with Vaṭeśvara's commentary *Mudrāprakāśa*, see Aufrecht, *Catalogus Catalogorum*, II, 160, 218.

Viṣṇudharmottara, ed. Kṣemarāja Śrīkṛṣṇadāsa, Veṅkaṭesvara Press, Bombay, 1912; Third *Khaṇḍa* ed. P. Shah with a study, Gaekwad's Oriental Series, Baroda, 1958-61 in 2 volumes.

Viṣṇu Purāṇa, ed. Vāsudevācārya, Gopāla Nārāyaṇa, Bombay, 1902; translated by H. H. Wilson, London, 1840, reprinted Punthi Pustak, Calcutta, 1961.

'Viṣṇuśarman' : *Pañcatantra*, Edgerton, *The Pañcatantra Reconstructed*, with a translation, American Oriental Series, New Haven, 1924 in 2 volumes; *Tantrākhyāyikā* ed. J. Hertel, Harvard Oriental Series, Cambridge Massachusetts, 1915 (the oldest actual recension known to be extant).

Viṣṇuvardhana Yaśodharman: inscriptions, ed. Sircar in his *Select Inscriptions*, Vol. I, above, pp. 411 ff.

Viśvanātha: *Sāhityadarpaṇa*, ed. Durgāprasāda, Nirṇaya Sāgara Press, Bombay, 3rd. edn. 1915; translated by Ballantyne and Pramadādāsa Mitra, Bibliotheca Indica, Calcutta, 1865, reprinted Motilal Banarsidass, Delhi/Banaras, 1956.

Viśveśvara: *Mandāramañjarī*, ed. G. D. Pandeya, Keshava Sanskrit Granthamala, Parvatiya Pustak Prakashan Mandal, Banaras, 1939.

: *Śṛṅgāramañjarī* (*saṭṭaka*), MS *Peterson's Reports*, IV, 31.

Viṭanidrā (anon.), MS in Government Oriental Manuscripts Library, Madras (R. 3755).

Vyākhyāprajñapti, Āgamodaya Samiti, Bombay, 1918-21 in 3 volumes.

A.K. Warder : *Pali Metre*, Pali Text Society, London, 1967.

: *Introduction to Pali*, Pali Text Society, London, 1963.

: 'The Date of Bhāmaha', in *The Journal of Oriental Research*, Vol. XXVI, Kuppuswami Sastri Research Institute, Madras, 1958, pp. 93ff.

: 'Desiderata in Indian Historiography', in the *Journal of the Economic and Social History of the Orient*, Vol. II, Brill, Leiden, 1959, pp. 206ff.

: Review of Nilakanta, *A Comprehensive History of India*, in the *English Historical Review*, 1960, pp. 285ff.

: Review of the translation of the *Nāṭakalakṣaṇaratnakośa* of Sāgaranandin, in the *Journal of the Royal Asiatic Society*, 1961.

: 'The Possible Dates of Pārśva, Vasumitra (II), Caraka and Mātṛceṭa' in *Papers on the Date of Kaniṣka*, ed. A. L. Basham, Brill, Leiden, 1968, pp. 327ff.

: *Indian Buddhism*, Motilal Banarsidass, Delhi, 1970.

: *An Introduction to Indian Historiography*, Popular Prakashan, Bombay, 1971.

M. Wheeler : *The Indus Civilization*, see under Indus Civilisation.

M. Willetts: *Chinese Art*, Penguin Books, Harmondsworth, 1958 in 2 volumes.

M. Winternitz : *Geschichte der indischen Litteratur*, in the series Die Litteraturen des Ostens, Amelangs, Leipzig, 1904-20 in 3 volumes; (only) authorised English version, *A History of Indian Literature*, University of Calcutta, 1927 in progress.

Yajñaphala, ed. R. J. Kalidas, Rasashala Aushadhashram, Gondal, 1941.

Yajurveda: Taittirīya recension, *Saṃhitā* ed. Weber, *Indische Studien*, Berlin, 1871-2; translated by Keith, Harvard Oriental Series, Cambridge Massachusetts, 1914 in 2 volumes; ed. with Sāyaṇa's commentary by Āgāśe, Ānandāśrama Saṃskṛta Granthāvali, Poona, 1901-8 in 8 volumes; *Brāhmaṇa* ed. Nārāyaṇa with Sāyaṇa's commentary, ibid., 1898 in 2 volumes, 2nd. edn. 1934-8; *Āraṇyaka* ed. Phaḍake with Sāyaṇa's commentary, ibid., 1897, 2nd. edn. 1926-7 in 2 volumes; *Upaniṣad* ed. Vāmana with the commentaries of Śaṃkara and Ānandagiri, ibid., 1889-90, 5th. edn. 1929; Maitrāyaṇīya recension, *Saṃhitā* ed. von Schroeder, Leipzig, 1881, new edition by Sāṃtavalekarakulaja, Svādhyāyamaṇḍala, Aundh, 1940, with the *Āraṇyaka* or *Upaniṣad*; Kāṭhaka recension, *Saṃhitā* ed. von Schroeder, Deutsche Morgenländische Gesellschaft, Leipzig, 1900-10 in 3parts, new edition by Sāṃtavalekarakulaja, Svādhyāyamaṇḍala, Aundh, 1943; *Upaniṣad* ed. Böhtlingk, *Berichte über die Verhandlungen der Königlich Sächsischen Gesellschaft der Wissenschaften*, Philol. -histor. Klasse, Leipzig, 1890; Kapiṣṭhala-Kaṭha recension, *Saṃhitā* ed. Raghu Vira, Meharchand Lachhmandas, Delhi, 1968; Kāṇva recension, *Saṃhitā* ed. Ratnagopāla and Mādhava with Sāyaṇa's commentary, Vidya Vilas Press, Benares, 1909-15 in 2 volumes; *Śatapatha Brāhmaṇa* ed. Caland, Lahore, 1926-40; Mādhyandina recension, *Saṃhitā* ed. Ram Sakala Miśra with the commentaries of Uvvaṭa and Mahīdhara, Vidyā Vilāsa Press, Benares, 1912-3 in 3 volumes; *Saṃhitā* and *Śatapatha Brāhmaṇa* ed. Weber, Williams and Norgate, Berlin/London, 1852-9 in 3 volumes (with extracts from commentaries; there appears to be confusion between the Kāṇvīya and Mādhyandinīya recensions, which in fact are very similar as derivatives of an older Vājasaneyin school; new editions are needed of both recensions and of their various commentaries); *Saṃhitā* translated by Griffith, Lazarus, Benares, 1899; *Śatapatha Brāhmaṇa* translated by Eggeling, Sacred Books of the East, Clarendon Press, Oxford, 1882-1900, reprinted Motilal Banarsidass, Delhi, 1963, in 5 volumes; *Bṛhadāraṇyaka Upaniṣad* ed. Böhtlingk, Eggers and Glasunow/Haessel, St. Petersburg/ Leipzig, 1889; the *Upaniṣads* mentioned here have been translated by Hume, see *Ṛgveda*, along with the *Īśa Upaniṣad* or *Vājasaneyin Upaniṣad*, ed. Āgāśe, Ānandāśrama Saṃskṛta Granthāvali, Poona, 1881, with several commentaries.

Yakṣagāna, see on this G. V. Sitapati and S. Rāmakrishna in the *Annals of Oriental Research*, University of Madras, 1957.

Yāska : *Nirukta*, ed. L. Sarup, Lahore, 1927; also ed. and translated by him, with the *Nighaṇṭu*, Oxford University Press, London, 1920-1, reprinted Motilal Banarsidass, Delhi, 1967.

Yasna, ed. K. F. Geldner in his edn. of the *Avesta*, Vol. I, Stuttgart, 1886; translated by L. H. Mills, Sacred Books of the East, Clarendon Press, Oxford, 1887, reprinted Motilal Banarsidass, Delhi, 1965; see also H. Humbach, *Die Gāthās des Zarathustra*, Winter, Heidelberg, 1959 in 2 volumes.

Yaśodharman, see Viṣṇuvardhana.

Yazdani : *Ajaṇṭā*, Oxford University Press, London, 1930-55 in 8 parts, 4 of text and 4 of plates.

INDEX TO VOL. I

(The numbers refer to paragraphs)

abduction 425 427
abhidhā 271 276
ābhijātya 292
Abhijñānaśākuntala 326
abhimāna 109 111 112 115
Abhinanda 410
Abhinavagupta 34 35 37 40 44 45 52 58 75 77 78 79 81 83 85 91 92 94 96 106 117 120 132 133 134 152 153 163 165 168 170 172 174 196 313 332 334 338 341 345 347 348 352 356 357 361 362 363 364 368 375 376 377 379 380 381 382 384 385 386 387 389 390 392 393 421 495
abhinaya 180 374 390
abhūtāharaṇa 148
ability 149
accompaniment (*sahokti*) 224 259 278 279
accumulation of words 186
act (s) 124 125 126 127 154 155 158 160 281 336 349 379 384 391 394 435
acting 36 40 76 180 181 308 335 374ff 390 434
acting-dancing 375
acting time 157
action 95 122 123 124 126 127 128 130 131 138 143 146 154 166 167 405 406 408
activity of the writer 270 271 276
actor(s) 34 45 62 121 321 322 327 333 434
ādāna 149
adbhuta 53 198
addiction 100
aḍḍitā 313
adhibala 148 326
adhika 262 263
ādhikārika-itivṛtta 122
admiration 79 87 117 270 297 348
admiring 119
admonition 187
aesthetics 70 74 75 76 77 91 108 109 116
aesthetic appreciation 494
aesthetic education 73, 499
aesthetic experience (s) (*rasa*) 20 35 49 50 51 53 54 55 57 58 61 62 63 75 76 77 78 79 81 85 87 88 89 90 91 93 95 103 106 107 109 110 111 114 115 117 118 119 125 128 137 152 163 189 192 196 198 247 249 251 252 255 265 266 270 301 335 336 338 364 405 407 409 429 438 497
aesthetic plane 78
aesthetic theories 20
aesthetic truth 497
affection 96
affectionate 96 98 99 100 214 255 264 277
affectionate speech 186 214
āgama 1 12
agitation 56 107 187 348
agrāmya 202 237 405
agreement (*samaya*) 150
agreement and difference 199
Ahalyā 332
ahaṃkāra 99 109 112 113 114
āhārya 280
āhlāda 271
Ahobala 433
ākāśabhāṣita 321
ākhyāna (*s*) 187 424 443 446
ākhyānaka 175
ākhyāyikā 281 304 305 423 424
ākranda 187
akṣa 97
akṣarasaṃghāta 186
ākṣepa 207
ākṣipti 148
Alaka 356
alaṅkāra (*s*) 19 182 183 186 188 194 195 203 251 276
alaṅkāraśāstra 19 184
alaṅkārya 276
alaṅkṛti 194
alarm 56 148
ālasya 56 348
ālīḍha 359
alliteration 183 188 203 238 241 257 267 273 437
allusiveness 247
'all-self-ness' 72

altercation 149 348
Amarasiṃha 425 436 456
amarṣa 56
ambiguity 185 186 189 240 241
amiability 187
Amṛtānanda 388 394
anākula 237
analysis 494
ānanda 87 102 119 150
Ānandavardhana 61 77 90 103 168 218 247 248 249 250 251 252 255 257 260 265 267 298 299 301 411 429 441 448 449 450 451
Anaṅgavatī 454
Anantaśayana 324
ananvaya 225
ancestral pride 149
Āndhra(s) 16 324
aṅga(s) (see 'limbs') 145 393
anger 53 133 141 363
Aṅguttara Nikāya 183
anibaddha 305 417
aṅka 124
aṅkamukha 126
aṅkāvatāra 126 174
aṅkita 425
announcement 310 315 351
antarnāṭaka 104 174
anthologies 419
anticipation 149
antiquity (-ies) 3 424
anubhāvas 54 253
anugamana 348
anukaraṇa 35 82
anumāna 148 260 298
anumiti 82
anunaya 186
anuprāsa 203
anuvṛtti 382
Anuyogadvāra Sūtra 92 116
anxiety 56 363
anyāpadeśa 418 419
anyāpoha 201
anyokti 261 428
anyonya 260
Apabhraṃśa 17 357 360 366f 373 377 413 415 416 420 421 436 451 487 491 499
apahnuti 229
apakarṣa 298
aparavaktra 425 436
apasāra 384
apasārakas 379 415
apasmāra 56
apavāda 149
apology 147
apotheosis 65 67 69
apparent contradiction 263
apparent prohibition 207 279
Appayya 299
appearance 148
application 327
appreciation 22
appreciator 494
apprehensive 53 58 87 92 107 181
appropriatenesss 237 256 297
aprastutapraśaṃsā 219 264
apratipatti 348
apsaras(es) 334 343 384
ārabhaṭī 181
ārambha 127 311
arati 100
architecture 74 75 76
aroma of verse 245
arrangement of words 242 243
art 75 114 131 138
arts 23 32 75 76 77 192 479 495
artha 115 121 286 361 406 449
arthāntaranyāsa 208 419
arthāpatti 187
Arthaśāstra 424
arthaśāstra 480
arthavyakti 189 240
arthopakṣepaka 126
arthya 237 405
āryā 428 430
āryāgīti 372
Āryāvarta 470
āsakti 100
asaṃgati 262
āśaṃsā 348
āsārita 363
asatpralāpa 326
āścarya 75
ascertaining the cause 141
ascetic 71
asceticism 116
ascetic tradition 70
āsīnavādya 363
āśis 187 235 407
Aśmaka 238
Aśmakavaṃśa 238
aśoka tree 496
aspirated sounds 240
āśrāvaṇa 311
assembly (-ies) 28 408 463 466 469 471 489 494
assembly (limb) 147
associations 274
astonishment 53 75 117 348
asuras 330
asūyā 56
Aśvaghoṣa 90 91 198 238
āśvāsas 413
āśvāsana 348
ātaṅka 348
atiśaya 186 258
atiśayokti 196
attaining the fruit 127
attainment 146 186

atyukti 241
aucitya 256 297
audible *kāvya* 180 182 446
audience 79 82 85 87 88 314 315 330 463 464 471 494
aupamya 258
auspicious 67 91
auspicious ending 63 103, 329
autobiographical 430 483
autobiography 428
autpattika 337
autsukya 56
Avadhī 304
avahittha 56 348
avalagita 139 326
Avanti 12 13 239
Avantisundarī 457
avasara 260
avasthās 127
avasyandita 326
avataraṇa 311
āvega 56
āviddha 335
avivakṣitavācya 250
awaking 56

bahirgītas 311
Bahurūpamiśra 32 326 385
Bābhravya 26
balance 240 243
ballads 421
ballet(s) 180 340 342 343 356 357 361 364 365 366 370 375
Bāṇa 239 256 289 418 427 429 430 431 437 445 457 458 484 485 489
bar(s) 413 422
'bar' metre 428
bard 484
basic emotion (s) 53 54 57 80 81 82 83 87 92 93 96 99 100 101 102 111 114 117 119
battle 411
beating time 369
beautiful 280 289 293, 294 295 296
beautiful speech 194
beautiful subjects 276
beauty (-ies) 20 50 120 182 195 197 202 244 270 271 273 276 277 278 283 288 289 290 295
beguiling 133 146
benediction (s) 63 187 235 264, 277 310 315 316 407
benevolence 93
bewilderment 56
bhakti 97 118
Bhallaṭa 261 418
Bhāmaha 20 34 96 108 175 190 191 192 193 194 196 197 198 200 201 202 203 205 214 215 217 218 228 233 235 236 237 238 241 246 247 254 255 257 265 267 269 271 276 277 278 279 292 294 305 342 365 370 402 404 405 406 409 423 425 427 429 430 433 436 479
bhāṇa 319 321 375 376 381
bhāṇaka 376 377 381 385 387
bhaṅgī 271
bhāṇī (*s*) 376 383 388 474
bhāṇikā 376 377 382 383 385
bhāṇī-aṅgas 382
Bhānudatta 101 117
Bharata 45, 74 77 252 499
bharata 45
Bhārata War 9
bhāratī 181 380
Bhāravi 239 284
Bhartṛhari 75 80 270 280 418
Bhāsa 342 368
bhāṣaṇa 150
Bhāskara 351
bhāsvara 165
Bhaṭṭi 411
bhāva 49 260 364 375 389 497
Bhavabhūti 103 104 174 238 284 285 289
bhāvaka 494
bhāvanā 85 111
bhāvikatva 198
bhāvita 363
bhaya 53 141
bhayānaka 53
bheda 141 146
Bhejjala 357 421
bhitti 488
Bhoja 74 75 76 85 95 98 99 108 109 110 112 114 115 117 174 175 217 264 268 304 326 349 353 356 357 358 359 365 367 368 369 374 380 381 382 384 385 391 409 416 426 429 433 441 446 447 448 451 454
bhrānti 141
bhrāntimant 261
bhūṣaṇa 186
bībhatsa 53
bīja 123
bindu 124
Bindumatī 349
Bindusāra 347
biography(-ies) 175 252 281, 304 305 423, 424 425 426 427 428 429 430 431, 432 433 435 436 437 442 443 463 484
blackmail 349
blunder in names 141
Boar (Varāha) 381
bodhana 348
Bodhāyana 105 342 347
bold 385 387 429 442
boldness 141

Brahmā 26 42 43 44 45 73 77 181 312 316 317 333 381
brāhma 102
brahman 75
brahman (s) 73 472
Brāhmaṇas 424
Brahmanism 65
breathing 348
Bṛhatkathā 13 16 447 457
bṛhatkathā 447
brilliance 241 243
brilliant 243
'brilliant' *bhāsvara* 165
Buddha 65 90
Buddhism 65 72 73
Buddhist (s) 90 106 298 498
Buddhist *Āgama* 308
Buddhist lyrics 421
Buddhist nuns 177
Buddhist schools 86
Buddhist writers 91
building *vāstu* 75

cabinet 408
Cakravarman 378
calm 92 93
calmed 91 92 93 94 98 99 100 101 102 107 106 192 284 410
calmed *praśānta* 165
calmed (*śānta*) 87 90
Cālukyas 490
camatkāra 79 87 117 270 348
camatkārin 119
campū (*s*) 175 304 305 392, 426 432 433 435 436 446 452 463 474
canto (s) 402, 404 407 409 413 414 415 416 420 423
canto composition 305
capalatā 56
Cārāyaṇa 26 126
carcarī 359 366 367 369 370 371 415
cārī 313
cārutā 195 202
caryāpadas 421
Caturmukha 416
caturvarga 115
cause 186 196 255 259 277
cause (s) of emotion 54 57 62 81 82 84 95 111 118 119 215
censure 150
certainty of attainment of the fruit 127 133 171
Ceṭaka 456
chādana 149
chala 326
chalika 365 367 370 374 375 379 415
chālikya 342 367 368
chalina 365
chamberlain 126
chapter (s) 423 425 427 428 430 433 435 436 437 445 447 448
characters 114 115 124 125 126 177 180 336
characterisation 281 443 445 460
characteristic (s) 182 184 185 186 187 188 193 196 206 230 232 233 235 264 291
charm 297
chatter 327
check 147 382
churned 356
Churning of the Ambrosia 331 333
Cidambara 411
cintā 56
circle (s) 27 350 473 474 486
circumlocution 218 259 260 278
citation of something else 418
citra 74 141 183 198 250 257 381 391
citrakāvya 250 411 418
citrarāgakāvya 392
civilisation 498 499
clarity 189 237 238 240 241 243 244 246 292 294
class (-es) 419
classes of play 165
classical heritage 302
climax 152 260
climbing and descending of sounds 243
coercion 141
coincidence 227 264 277
colour 59
combination of several figures 234
comedy (-ies) 105 136 140 181 319 327 335 336 474 499
comic 53 58 87 95 101 105 107 163 181 330 333 336 338 348 354 358 391 393 410
commencement 127 130
compactness 240
comparative figure (s) 258 259 260 261 264
comparison 183 199
comparison as compared 222 264 279
compassion 72 93
compassionate 53 55 57 58 63 87 103 104 107 163 181 252 329 336 363 393 410 429 431 439
'complete' *samagra* play 165
complete *samasta* metaphor 188
composition 190 297
composition (s) 272 429 434 435
composition (as a whole) 174 198 237 272 276 280 283 284 409
composition of *kāvyas* 183
compounding of words 237 238 240 242 243 245 256 267 293 294 429 430
concealment 141 229 261 278 279
concentration 189 237 240 243

concentration of 'limbs' 152
concentrating 146
conciliation 141 186
conclusion 63 134 135 136 137 150
condensed expression 211 237 261 277 428
confidence 348
conflict 37 39 41 138 170 331
confusion 189 327
conjunct consonants 295
conjunction(s) 121 128 129 130 138 145 151 152 153 165 166 168 169 170 172 175 182 253 260 281 306 336 349 350 391 394 405
conjunction (reconnection with the 'seed') *sandhi* 150
connoisseur(s) 78 271 283 287 297 470 494
constructing a play 121
construction 157 475
consummation 382
consummation of the *kāvya* 150
contemporary events 79
contention 346
contentment 56 100
context(s) 174 272 280 281
contextual level 272
contextual figurativeness 174 281 282
continuance 382
continuity 124 125 166 167 171
contradiction 149 231 262 263 278 279
contrary 261
contrast 209 259 278 279
convention(s) 201 496
conversation 150
cooperation (s) 136 154 155 157 317 330 331 332 333 336 346 349
coordination theory 166 168 171 173
corroboration (s) 208 228 261 278 279 377 419
costume 95 177 181
counsel 405 408
courtiers 473
covered 262
crest 126
critic 494
critical function 43
criticism 28 300 469
cry 187
Cūḍāmaṇi 377
cūlikā 126
cultivated 290 291
cūrṇa 245
curtain 176 311 312

dainya 56
Dakṣiṇāpatha 13
dākṣiṇya 187
Damayantī 433
ḍambara 241
Dāmodaragupta 452
dāna 60
dance(s) 77 243 310 339 340 342 343 356 358 359 361 362 363 364 368 369 370 373 374 376 377 381 382 387 388 391 415 420
dancers 355
dancing 74 180 308 340 360 365 374 385
dance-*kāvya* 390
daṇḍa 141
daṇḍarāsaka 355 369
Daṇḍin 18 80 87 104 108 240 241 242 243 255 365 407 409 415 416 427 430 433 436 442 443 490
Daśarūpaka 364
Dattaka 26
day 125 160
death 67 69 126 329
deceit 187 346
decentralisation 493
deception 148 327 331
decision 150
declaration of truth 148
decoration 257
decorative 183 250
deformed and fantastic characters 352
delicacy 189 240 242 243
delicate 280 288 293 294 295 296 335 343 384 385 387 429 442
delight 20 34 35 75 76 79 87 150 192 270 271 284 298 348
delineation 276
demons 330 331 332 333
denominatives 202
denunciation 187
departure 384
depression 56
derision 149 150
description (s) 187 408
descriptive passages 253 281
descriptive topics 407
Deśī 17
despair 56
desperation 149
detached 106
devas 330
development 85 111 115 407 409
Devīmahādeva 393
devotion 97 118
Dhanañjaya 32 85 93 97 107 108 119 129 151 168 169 171 375
Dhanapāla I 437 458
Dhanapāla II 436
Dhanika 93 107 152 375 376
dharma 25 60 90 119 121 163 283 332 406
Dharmadatta 117
dharmakathā 446

Dharmakīrti 86 298
dhī 141
dhīra 99
dhṛti 56
dhruvā(s) 306 312
dhūrtas 473
dhvani 249 250 253
dialects 177
dialogue 322 357 456
Dīgha Nikāya 38
ḍima 68 317 333
Diṅnāga 198 201 202
dīpaka 188 203 223
dīpta 241
disaster 133
discontent 100
disdain 216 217 255 264 277
disguise 331
disgust 53 57
dispute 346
dissimulation 56 348
dissociation 262
diṣṭa 187
distinction 187 230 243 262 277
distinctness 243
distortion 326
divya 433
dohās 421
ḍomba company 378
ḍombī 342 376 377 382
ḍombikā(s) 361 376 377 378 379 380 389 390 415
doṣas 189
double meaning(s) 239 278 279 326 411 428
double meaning figures 258 263
doubt 56 186 233 261 248
drama(s) 14 20 28 29 34 35 36 37 39 41 42 43 44 45 51 52 62 73 74 75 76 77 83 84 85 121 126 127 180 182 252 253 281 284 285 303 305 306 307 308 309 310 313 316 317 318 319 335 364 365 375 390 408 413 420 421 426 433 463 465 466 468 475
dramatic devices 152
dramatic expression 185
dramatic stucture 175
dramaturgy 19 182 247
Drauhiṇi 165
drava 149
Dravidian languages 13 18
drawing 271 276
dream 141 363
dreaming 56
drinking 384 407
drowsiness 56
dṛṣṭānta 186 199 254 278
drum 363
duḥkha 87 100
duration of plays 155 156
durmallikā 154 349 353 474
durmilitā 349
dūta 141
duty 332
dvimūḍha 363
dvipadī 342 365 370 371 374 391
dvipadīkhaṇḍa 371
dying 56
dyuti 149 150

eagerness 56 348
East (style) 256
echo 240
edicts 183
education 34 298 476 479 481 499
effects of emotion 54 57 62 81 82 84 88 95 111 215
egoism 99 109 110 111 113 114 115
ekāvalī 260
elegance 202
elements 168
'elements' *prakṛtis* of the matter *artha* 121 122 123 129 130 166 167 169
elevated 181 245
eloquent mode 165 181 325 380 382 384
embassy 405
emboxing 347 437 458
embryo 132 133 135 136 148 151 152 171 172 326 349
embryo act 174
emotion(s) 20 42 49 51 52 53 54 55 57 59 62 75 78 79 85 96 98 107 110 111 113 114 115 119 137 152 187 253 255 288 343 348 358 361 363 364 367 375 389
emotional experience 497
empirical 62
empirical investigation 236
emptiness 348
encouragement 187
ends of life 25 26 90 115 192 390 405 406 418
energy 53
enhance(d) 240 244
enhancing 298
enigma 456
enjoyment 48
entertainment(s) 463 466 471 473
enticement 348
entrance to the stage 176 311 313
enumeration 212 259 277
envoy 141
envy 56
epic(s) 9 115 175 182 252 253 281 360 372 402 404 405 406 407 409 410 411 412 413 414 415 416 421 423 427 428 429 432 437 443 445 446 475

Epic 3 5 7 9 20 63 64 73 90 281 284 304 305 318 328 342 402 403 404 405 408 410 412 424 445 463 478
episode 446
epistemology 198
equal consequence 222 223 264 279
equanimity 93
equivocal words 143
equivocation (s) 140 248 257 263 265 325 326
error 141 261
essence (*sāra*) 260
essence of *kāvya* 184 242
essential quality of 'joy' 119
ethics 70 73
etymology 186 267
euphemism 218 260 274
evenness 189 237 240 241 243
events 125 126
evidence 199 232
exaggerated 241
exaggeration 186 196 206 262 276 278 279
exaggerative figures 258 259 260 261 262
exaltation 189 237 240 241 243
Exaltation of the Rāghava 326
exalted 98 99 137 198 216 217 255 264 277 425
example 186 199 200 254 278 279 377
exclusion 260
exclusion of what is other 201
excuse 187 196 255 259 277
exit (s) 379 384 415
expansion 107 243
expedition 405
experience 107 499
explanation 147
exposure 148
expression (s) 181 195 196 197 215 237 247 267 271 272 273 275 276 289 298
expression of something else 261 428
expressive mode of stage business 165 181 333 335 346
expressive *sāttvika* emotions 59
extension 107 146
extolling 148 186

fable (s) 261 377 381 382 452
fainting 59
fame 192 193
fancy (-ies) 213 234 239 261 276 278 279 495 496
farce 352 376 397
fashion 488
fate 346
fatigue 149
faults 183 189 200
favour 148
fear 53 141 327
ferocity 56 57
festival (s) 28 29 41 63 161 308 309 316 399 433 463 466 468
Festival of Indra's Standard 41 333
feudalism 399 474
fiction 286 304 319 337 364 425 427 430 442 443 444 445 448
fictitious 338 339
fight (s) 317 333 336
fighting 68 126
figurative expression 195 196 197 247 257 265 269 271
figurative language 182 191 213
figurative sentences 276
figurative speech 174 247 251 252 404
figurative *vakra* speech 202
figurativeness 196 198 236 237 265 272 273 276 280 281 285 286 287 289 297 298
figurativeness of a *kāvya* considered as a whole 283 284 298 409
figurativeness of the sentence 280
figure (s) 183 192 194 197 234 255 256 257 260 261 264 268 277 278 280 289
figures of meaning 258
figure (s) of speech 19 182 183 185 186 187 188 191 196 198 203 241 242 244 249 253 254 274 276
fine 296
firm 99
fitness 237
fixing 146
flowery speech 147
flute 363
folk song (s) 16 248 420 464 466
following 348
fool 30 179 434
forbearance 149 187
forgetfulness 56
forms of *kāvya* 115 191 305
former point 112
Fortune 331
freedom 493
fright 382
frustration 57 102 429
'full' *pūrṇa* 165
furious 53 58 87 95 107 181 313 336 346 367 442
future events 143

gambling 97
games 469
gāna 313
gaṇacchandas 363 370 372 413
gaṇḍa 326
Gandhāra 239

gāndhārī 363
Gāndharvanirṇaya 394
Gaṅgā 466
Gaṅgātaraṅgikā 355
gaṇikā (see 'geisha') 28
garbha 132
garbhāṅka 174
garhaṇa 187
garva 56
gāthā 417
Gauḍa(s) 238 239
Gauḍavijaya 391
gauḍīya 238 239 240 241 242 246 256 207 289 294 442
geisha(s) 28 30 466 473
general qualities 292 297
generalisation 79 88 208
genius 192 281 288 289 494
genre (see 'forms') 259 419
gentry 474
germination 146
gesture (s) 95 176 181 310 312 361 363 375 384 387 392
gesture language 159 308
geya 367
geya rūpakas 376
geyapada 363
geyāvakṛṣṭa 312
ghaṭikās 162
Ghoṭakamukha 26
gift 141
Gītagovinda 392 420 421
gītaka 312
gīti 370
gītikā 370 371
glāni 56
Gnoli 50
go-between 349
gods 312 316 330 331 332 333 343
God 66 73 77
God of War 332
Godāvarī 13
goodness 119 163
gopucchāgra 154
Gorocanā 454
goṣṭha 350
goṣṭhī 27 28 31 33 188 350 376 473 486 494
gotraskhalita 141
government 408
grace 150 189 240 241 242 243 255
grāmarāga 390
grammar 201 202
grammarians 249
grammatical figurativeness 272 275
grammatical level 272
grammatical unit 272
grathana 150 348
greediness 97 100
green-room 176
grief 53 363
grievous 103
Gujarāt 256 471 490
Gujarātī 360 421
guṇa(s) 182 186 189 198 237 442
Guṇacandra 100 162 171
Guṇāḍhya 104 444
guṇakīrtana 186
Guṇamālā 377
guṇībhūtavyaṅgya 250
Guruvāyur 392

Hāla 248 252
hallīsaka 342 365 368 376 385
happened (*vṛtta*) 425
happiness 63 64 65 67 71 72 73 78 87 100 119
hardness 296
Haribhadra 446 450 452
Haripāla 102
Harivaṃśa 28, 342 350 360 367 368
harmony 256 297
harṣa 34 52 56
Harṣa (I) 285 475 484
Harṣa (II) 456
Hastināpura 9
hāsa 53
hāsya 53
having doubt 233 261 278 279
having *rasa* 96 215 255 276
heaven 65 66 67 71
Hemacandra 116 304 348 376 377 382 384 385 386 390 441 447 448 450 451 454 455 456
hero(es) 99 122 179 283 301 304 330 405 429 436
heroic 53 55 58 59 87 91 103 104 107 116 181 284 336 346 355 367 384 410 445
heroic play(s) 136 318 328 335 336
heroine 179 358
hetu 186 196 199 254
hetvavadhāraṇa 141
highest point 110 113
Himālayas 333
Hindī 360
hint 146 196 255 259 277
historical narrative 281
history(ies) 1 3 175 304 305 318 336 338 405 423 424 427 433 436 442 443 444 482
horrific 53 58 87 107 181
horripilation 59
Hṛdayaṃgamā 367 369
humour 53 398
hundred 418
hunting 97
hyperbole 196 206
hymn 418

ideals 406 498 499
identification 204 226
identify 118
identity 279
idioms 248
īhāmṛga 317 334
illogicality 189
illusion 101 141
illustration 187 232 264 279 449 452
images 497
imagination 425
imaginary 426 436
imaginative reproduction 495
imitation 35 42 82 83 87 495
immortality 331
implication(s) 187 249 431
implied meaning 218 247 250 251 252 260 265 279 289 298 464
importunity 187
imposed 280
impulse 123
incidents 153
incongruity 260
independent verse (s) 305 417 418
indifference 56 102
indignation 56
indirect meanings 247 249
individual variation among writers 291
indivisible utterances 270
Indra 41 308 316 332 381
Indra's elephant 331
Indra's standard 310 312 313
Indulekhā 326
inference 82 83 84 148 186 201 260 298
injection of subsidiary matter 143
innocence 348
inscriptions 305
insinuation(s) 207 248
instruction 34 35 43 44 293 286 452
instrumental music 381 387
intention 260
intermediate state 110
intermediate style 290 293
intervention 122 169 171
intonation 182 268
intoxication 56 141
introduction to the (next) act 126
introductory scene(s) 126 174 336 344
invented 281 286 337 346 350 364 425 436
investigating 150
invocation 407
ironical flattery 326
irrelevance 189
Islam 493
Īśvarakṛṣṇa 85
itihāsa 1 423 424 478
itivṛtta 121 449
jaḍatā 56
Jaimini 318
Jaina 88 92
Jaina school 87
Jainism 116 446 491
Jāmbavant 350
Jāmbavatī 380
jarjara 310
Jātakamālā 433 435
Jātaka Commentary 161
jāti(s) 259 306 363 389 419
Javanese 18
Jayadeva II 261 299 III 350
Jāyasī 304
Jayasiṃha 156
jealousy 56
jester 30 31 159 179 322 324 326 349 353 355 357 371 383 434
Jīvānanda 365
Jīvandhara 432
joke 147 326
joy 34 52 56 85 102 111 119
judgment 146 152
jugupsā 53
jumping in 327
justice 60
Kādambarī 448
kaḍavaka(s) 416 417 420 421
kaiśikī 181
kāku 268
Kalhaṇa 378 470
Kālidāsa 288 343 367 371
Kaliṅga 299
kalpanā 425
kalpavallī 354
Kalyāṇa 470
kāma 42 115
Kāma 23 351 406
Kāmadattā 382
kāmaśāstra 24
Kāmasūtra 23 25 26 27 164 183 342 426
Kambala 421
kampa 348
Kanakavatīmādhava 348
Kāñcī 241 490
Kannaḍa 18 324
kānti 189 240 255
Kānyakubja 470
kapaṭa 187
karaṇa 146
Karṇa 216
kārpaṇya 101
karuṇa 53 380
kārya 122 253 284
Kāśī 393
Kaśmīra 77 378 470
kathā(s) 305 425 436 441 445 446 447 448
kathakali 392

kathānaka 451
kathodghāta 139
Kātyāyana 423
Kauṭalya 183 423
kavi 6 270 271 400 476 ff.
Kavikarṇapūra 119
kāvya 1 6 11 12 22 33 36 74 75 76 84 121 150 250 271 376 389 391
kāvya composition 183 184 185
kāvyakriyā 183
kāvyakriyākalpa 19 183
kāvyālaṅkāra 183 184
Kāvyamīmāṃsā 496
Kāvyānuśāsana 352
kāvyasaṃhāra 150
Keliraivataka 368
Kerala 158 159 161 303 316 324 392 426 434 435
khaṇḍa 370
khaṇḍakathā 439 449 451
khaṇḍakāvya 305 417
kheda 149
Kirātārjunīya 427
kīrti 192
knotting 348
knotting (getting the problem'tied up') *grathana* 150
knowing 348
knowledge 201
Kohala 164 341 356 374 375 376 389 426
komala 237
Koṅkaṇa 470
krama 148
krīḍanīyaka 34
Krīḍārasātala 380
Krishnamacharya 432
kriyākalpa 183
krodha 53 141
Kṛṣṇa 118 324 334 350 357 360 368 380 420 432
Kṛṣṇācārya 421
Kṛṣṇaśarman 101
Kṛtyārāvaṇa 285 326
kṣamā 187
kṣatriya 481
Kṣemendra 452
Kṣīrasvāmin 425 436
kṣobha 107 187
kṣudra kāvya 439
Kumāra 332
Kunjunni Rāja 104 158 434
Kunhan Rāja 50
Kuntaka 174 215 236 269 270 271 272 276 277 278 279 280 282 286 287 289 291 293 294 297 298 301 409 495
Kuṣāṇa 14
kūttu(s) 4 26 434

lakṣaṇas 182 184 193
Lakṣmī 331
Lakṣmīdhara 408
lalita 99 165
lamenting 348
lamp 176 188 203 259 278 279,
language(s) 7 120 194 201 202 238 241 249 253 436
language of the drama 182
language of *kāvya* 184 191
lāsikā 388
lassitude 56 57 348
lāsya 340 341 342 358 360 362 363 364 365 367 374 375 383 387 388 391 393
lāṭīyā 256
Lāṭa 256
Laughing Fish (Fish Laugh) 455
laughing off 147
laulya 97
lāvaṇya 292 297
leading into (the play) 139 314 326
legend 304
leitmotivs 306
lekha 141
length of an act 155 162
length of a play 154 162
leśa 187 196
letter 141
lexical level 272
lexical figurativeness 274
lexical unit 272
liberation 90 93 115 192 286 446
libraries 471
light play ('little play') 339
life 127 138
life of a poet or writer 483
Līlāvatī 448
limbs of the *bhāṇikā* 382
limbs of comedy 327
limbs of the conjunctions 145 151 152 153 164 165 171 173 184
limbs of the *lāsya* 358 362 363 383 387
limbs of the *śilpaka* 393 394
limbs of the street play 140 325 326 330 357
liquor 141
literal 247 248 249 250 251
Literary Criticism 190
literature 1 269 270 271 291 298
little play 339
logic 198 199 298
lokadharma 62
Lokānanda 91
Lokanātha 119
Lokāyata 24 329
Lollaṭa 81 87 95 108
love *rati* 53 57 75 80 110 111 115
lucidity 189 240 241 243
luptopamā 183

luxuriant 245
lyric(s) 252 253 305 360 366 417 418 419 420 421 422 465
lyric verse(s) 176

mada 56 141
Madanikākāmuka 357
Mādhava 380
Mādhavabhaṭṭa 411
mādhurya 189 237 240
madhyama 290
madhyamāvasthā 110
madness 56
Madurā 324
Māgha 252 284
Magadha 9 26 190 238 484
Magadhan Empire 11 13 178
Māgadhī 8 10 13 14 487
magnanimity 60 116 217
magnanimous 91
Mahābhārata 3 90
mahācārī 313
Mahādeva 117
mahākathā 436 437 448
mahākāvya 305
Mahāmallapura 490
13 16 190 238
Mahārāṣṭra 13 16 190 238
Māhārāṣṭrī 13 15 16 178 344 359 413 415 436 454
Māhārāṣṭrī lyrics 248 252 414
Mahendrapāla 486
Mahendrasūri 457
Mahiman 84 298
main action 122 123 126 128 130 135 143
maitrī 93
make-up 177
Maladhārin Hemacandra 116
Mālatikā 322 326
Malayālam 18 159 392 434
Malayasundarī 457
Mallanāga Vātsyāyana 25 26 73
mallikā 353
Mammaṭa 94 299 429 442
Mānaveda 392
manifestation of meaning 189
maṇikulyā(s) 353 455 458
Māṇikyavallikā 354
Mañjīra 290
Maṅkha 470
Mankad 352 386
manner of performance 325
manoratha 186
manthulli(kā) 454
mantra 405
Mānyakheṭa 491
maraṇa 56
mārga 148 240 442
mārgāsārita 363
Mārīcavadha 390
marked 425 433
marking 427
marvelling 150
marvellous 53 58 63 75 87 103 107 117 137 181 189 198 445
masṛṇa 296 429
matallikā 454 474
Mataṅga 75 389
Mathurā 14 178
mati 56
Mātrarāja 283
Mātṛgupta 95 129 166 167 171 290 336
Matsyahasita 455
matter 121 122 123 124 126 127 133 134 153 171 199 215 237 272 298
mature 461
mauḍhya 348
maugdhya 348
māyā 101 141
Māyākāpālika 346
Māyāpuṣpaka 285
Mayūra 418
Māyurāja 283 285 290
meaning (s) 189 194 195 196 200 237 239 241 242 243 247 249 259 263 271 276 280
meaningful 405
meaninglessness 189
means 348
mechanical devices 176
Medhāvin 190 191
meditation 93
Meghavijaya 411
melody 243
members of discourse 200
Menakāhita 357
Meṇṭha 252 285
merchant class 471
messenger 141 349
metamorphosis 67
metaphor 183 188 203 204 221 226 234 240 261 264 274 278 279
method of composition 183 191
metre (s) 404 407 409 413 414 415 420 422
metrical structure 370 391
middle term 199 254
mīlita 260
milkmaids 350 368
Mīmāṃsā 66 80 318
mime 176
miming 388
mingling 260
minstrels 9
miracle 210 262 278 279
misery 56
miserliness 101
misunderstood word 326
mithyādhyavasāya 187

mithyājñāna 101
mixed figures 280
mixture 234
mode of stage business 165 181 249 253 333 335 346 348 380 382 384 391
mode(s) (musical) 306 363 389 420
mode-*kāvya* 389
models 176
moha 56
mokṣa 90 406
moment 403
monologue 321 426
Moon 331
moral causation 65 329
moral purpose 405 409
mṛdava 326
mṛgayā 97
muditā 93
Mudrārākṣasa 286
Mugdhakathā 452
muhūrta 154 162
mukha 128
muktaka 417

music 27 40 74 75 76 306 307 310 480
musical metre(s) 413 414 422
musical modes (see 'modes') 389
musical play 343
musicians 176 311
mystery(-ies) 455 458 460
mystery story 353
myths 330 331 332 334 343
mythology 317 497

nāda 75
nāḍikā(s) 154 155 162 349
Nāgānanda 91
nāgaraka(s) 27 28 29 30 31 33 321 337 349 350 466 471 473 474
Nahuṣa 357
nālikā 326
Nāmaliṅgānuśāsana 426
namaskriyā 407
Namisādhu 437 440 441 449
nāndī 310 312
Nandin 26
Nārāyaṇa (I) 284
Nārāyaṇa (II) 117
narmadyuti 147
narman 147
Narmavatī 358
narrating 426
narration 176 187 403
narrative 402 404 437 443 464
narrative metres 422
narrative verse 424
nartanaka 365 374 376
nāṭaka(s) 63 128 156 157 161 165 175 181 318 335 336 338 340 343 347 365 367 368 427
Naṭāṅkuśa 104 307
naṭas 45
nāṭī 339
nāṭikā 324 339 344 345 359 371 373
naṭkuṭaka 313 363
natural 280 288 290 291
naturalism 495
naturalistic description 197 259 276
nature 95 114 419 497
nāṭya 36 305 348 364 375 390
Nāṭyadarpaṇa 129 153 325 326 334 337 338 349 350 351 356 367 368 374 380 381 382 384 391
nāṭyadhārā 347 *dharma* 62
nāṭyarāsaka 342 354 358 359 360 365 366 367 376 415
Nāṭyasarvasvadīpikā 352 386
Nāṭyaśāstra 19 35 36 37 39 45 47 48 52 54 57 62 63 73 74 75 76 77 83 85 89 92 95 99 106 107 119 121 124 126 129 130 135 137 138 140 145 151 152 153 154 164 176 181 182 183 184 185 186 188 189 192 203 254 306 434 494
nāṭyaśāstra 19 34
nāṭyāyita 174
Nāyaka 84 85 93 106 107 108 111 265 298
Nepal 323
news 196
nidarśana 187 232 264 279 450 451 452 454 474
nidrā 56
nirṇaya 150
nirodha 147
nirukta 186
Nirvāṇa 69 71 72 90
nirvahaṇa 134
nirveda 56 102
niṣedhanā 149
nīti 418 421 452
niyatā phalaprāpti 127
nobility 282 296
nonsensical speech 326
North (style) 256
Northern (writers) 239
novel(s) 6 18 115 175 182 240 252 286 303 304 305 337 353 412 425 426 427 433 436 437 438 440 442 443 444 445 446 447 448 451 454 456 457 458 460 461 465 474 490
Nṛsiṃha (Viṣṇu) 351 381
Nṛsiṃha 107
nṛtta 361 364
nṛttakāvya 390
nṛttavāra 347
nṛtya(s) 342 343 361 363 364 365 375 376 421

Nyāya 82
nyāyya 237
nymph (s) 334 343 357

object (s) 201 240 243 280
objective 63 122 127 138 253 284 285 364
objective figures 258 259 260
obstacle 133 135 136 149 170 171 172 346 349
obstinacy 187
off stage 126 351
ojas 141 189 237 240 241 294
open speech 326
opening 107 128 130 136 146 152
opening to the act 126
opening benediction 351
opening proceedings 309 361
opera 394
opportunity 260
opposition 262
oratory 411
order 425
Origin of Kumāra 332
originality 243 301
Orissa 299 350
ornament (s) 184 194 195 196 276 277 409
ornaments of a play 185
ornamentation 186 194 195
orthodoxy 493
osaras 415
other conjunctions 141
outburst 148
outlines 271
outwitting 148 326
overtones 247
overture 306 315

Pādalipta 446
padapūrvārdha 272
padārtha 280
padoccaya 186
painted scene 176
painting (s) 27 74 76 141 176 271 324 363
Paiśācī 13 16 436 444 447
pāka 461
Pālha a 421
Pali 12 183 190 414
Pallava 490
Pañcāla 26 239
Pañcāla Empire 9
pāñcāla 239 246
pāñcālī 242 256 267 290
pāñcapāṇi 363
Pañcatantra 452
Pandey, K. C. 74 75
panegyric 63 305 348 495
panegyric (the final benediction) *praśasti* 150
panic 148 346
Pāṇini 7 10 45 47 178 202
paradox 230
parā koṭiḥ 110
parallelism 139 326 327
parallel-simile 279
paralysis 59
paramparā 426
paramā kāṣṭhā 113
paraphrase 218
parasite 27 30 179 321 349 353 362 378 383 384 391 473
paribhāṣaṇa 150
paribhāvanā 146
paridhānaka 363
pārijātalatā 355
parikara 146
parikathā 441 443 449
parinyāsa 146
parisaṃkhyā 260
parisarpa 147
parivartinī 312
parivṛtti 228
parokṣa 88
partial fancy 234
particular qualities 292
partridge 496
parts of a *kāvya* 281
Pārvatī 313 362
paryāya 259
paryāyokta 218
paryupāsana 147
pasaṃta 92
pāṣaṇḍa 346
paścāttapana 187
patākā 122 135 163 166
patākāsthānaka 143
Patañjali 202 423
pathetic 380
pathetic play 318 329 335
patron 163
patronage 466 471 472 484 490 491 492
Paurava Dynasty 9
pause 133 170
perceived 425
performance 154 158 161 163 181 307 309 426 436 466 484
performed 434 435
performing 146 433
perplexity 348
perseverance 149
personification 213 274 275 497
perspiring 59
perversity 348
phalayoga 127

philosophical character of an epic 406
philosophy 410
phoneme(s) 272 273 295
phonetic(s) 272 295
phonetic figurativeness 273
pihita 262
piṇḍībandhas 356 361
pīṭhamarda 32 (Additional note : Śāradātanaya, p. 94, describes the tutor as settling on his stool in front of her and acting on behalf of the hero and others to induce trust and propitiate an angry woman. Vallabhadeva on Māgha I. 59: by the arts, music, etc., he makes angry women eager for love.)
play 147
play on words 326
play within a play 174 281
playful *lalita* 99 165 245
pleasure 23 24 25 27 28 34 42 63 70 73 115 142 192 286 390 406 426 446 479
plot 130 138 165 460
poetic words 195
poetics 19 21 182 183 184 191 247
policy 418 452
politics 405 480
popular background 373
popular traditions of dramatic dance and song 395
possessed 56
possibility of attainment 127
poverty 419
prabandha(*s*) 237 272 276 409 435
prabandhālaṅkāra 174
prabandham kūttu 434
pracchedaka 363
pradāna 141
praharṣa 348
prahasana 319 327
prahelikās 352
praise 186
praise of *kavis* 428
praise of what is not the subject 219 261 264 278 377
praising great writers 430
prakāra 276
prakaraṇa 128 175 181 319 335 336 337 338 427 474
prakaraṇavakratā 174
prakaraṇī 345
prakarī 122
prakhyāta 336
Prakrit(s) 3, 8 13 14 17 126 177 341 344 366 367 372 373 415 420 451 487
prakṛtis 121
pralobha 348
pramada 348
pramāda 348
prapañca 326
prāpti 146 186
prāptisambhava 127
prārambha 127
prarocanā 149 314 348 351
prārthanā 148
prasāda 150 189 237 240
prāsāda 74
praśamana 147
prasaṅga 149
prāsaṅgika 122
praśānta 165
praśasti 150 305 348
prasthāna (*s*) 376 377 384 385 387
pratibhā 192 494
pratīcya 256
pratijñā 199
pratimā 74
pratimukha 131
pratīpa 261
pratiṣedha 187
prativastūpamā 279
pratīyamāna 247 251 289
Pratyabhijñā ('Recognition') school 77
pratyāhāra 311
pratyaya 272
pratyutpannamati 141
pravahlikā 456
Pravarasena 372
praveśaka 126
pravṛttaka 139
prayatna 127 348
prayoga 335
prayogātiśaya 139
pṛcchā 186
predicate 199
prekṣaṇaka 342 351
prekṣya (*s*) 365 366 374 376
preman 111
preraṇa 352 376 377 385
presence of mind 141
presentation 153
prevention 149
preyas 96 214 264
pride 56 99 113 141 217
printing 488
prīti 20 34 79 192 271
private and lower class life 337
priyokti 186
probability 198
producer 121 139 307 312 314 351 357
production 306
profundity of meaning 410
progress 148
prohibition 187
prologue 139 174 310 314 315 325 326
promise 199
proposal 147 382
proposition 199 200

props 176 181
prose 6 240 241 245 252 304 306 424 425 427 429 430 432 433 435 436 437 438 442 443 448 454 461 462
protsāhana 187
proud 99 264
pun 226 234 257 263
punning 240
Purāṇa (s) 3 304 424 478 484
pūrṇa 165
pūrvā koṭiḥ 113
pūrvaraṅga 309 310 314 325 326 333 361
pūrvavākya 150
puṣpa 147
Puṣpadanta 416 491
puṣpagandhikā 363
puṣṭārtha 237

quality (-ies) 119 182 183 186 189 196 198 237 238 240 241 242 243 244 246 252 255 256 273 287 288 292 293 297 299 409 442
quality of that 262
quantity 414
quantitative metres 422
quatrain 404 415 417
quatrain metres 422

Rādhā 357
Rādhā 326
rāga (s) 306 389 390 391 392 420
(*rāga*) *kāvya* 341 342 376 389 390 391 392 394 420
Raghavan, V. 19 102 117 326 341 349 369 392 425 433 454 455
Rāghavabhaṭṭa 95
Rāghavavijaya 390
Rāhula 91
Raivataka 368
Raivatamadanikā 350
Rājapurī 470
Rājaśekhara 4 18 108 190 266 267 268 285 289 307 344 369 469 479 485 486 487 488 494 496
Rāma 217 283 432 433
Rāmacandra 151 162 171
Rāmacandra and Guṇacandra 87 100
rāmākrīḍa 376 386
rāmākrīḍaka 385
Rāmānanda 380
Rāmaśarman 238
Rāmavarman 433
Rāmāyaṇa 463
Rambhā 367
Rāṇaka 377 379
raṅgadvāra 313
Raṅganātha 343
rape (s) 317 334 336 343
rasa (s) 20 35 36 40 48 49 50 51 52 55 75 79 81 82 83 84 85 87 88 89 91 92 95 96 97 98 99 100 101 102 103 104 105 106 107 108 110 111 112 113 114 116 117 118 119 196 198 214 215 216 217 240 243 247 249 251 253 255 256 264 270 276 281 284 297 301 306 336 346 348 360 363 364 365 367 375 389 391 393 405 410 442 445 449 486 494 497
rāsa (s) 360 421 499
rasa sūtra 54 81 82
rasa theory 62 76 80 182 191
rāsaka (s) 341 342 356 357 358 365 366 368 370 376 377 385 415 421
rāsakāṅka 356 357
Rasātala 380
rasavant 96 215 276
rascals 473
rashness 56
rasika 494
rati 53 75 110
Ratnākara 356 488
Ratnaprabhā 447
Ratnaśrījñāna 19 183 365 415 425 427 433 447
raudra 53
Rāvaṇa 283
reader 494
reading 180 436
real 192
realism 198 235 237 304 443 445 464 495
realistic 405 429 452
reality 276 496 497
reason (s) 198 199 200 254
reasoning 348
reassuring 348
reciprocity 260
recitation 426
recited narrative 321
Recognition School 77
reducing 298
redundancy 189
reflection 56 99
refrain 359 367 415
release 406
religion 70 71 73 77 94 318 332 445 452
religious basis of theory (Rūpa) 118
religious function 316
religious play (s) 317 330 334 335
remembrance 56
reminded 261
reminding 150
remorse 147 187 348
rendezvous 363
renunciation 64 65 73 91 101 102 418
re-opening 131 136 147 172 346
repetition of sounds 188 203 273
reply 260
reported 126
reporting 426 495

representation 180
reproach 149 382
reproduction of life 318 495
republics 399
resignation 382
resumption 149 171
revolution 228 259 279
rhetorical question 186
rhyme(-d) 188 203 250 257 273 411 416
rhythm(s) 359 362 363 364 368 376 381 387 420 422
rhythm and tempo 180 358 384
riddle (s) 326 352 456
ripe 461
rīti (*s*) 240 242 256 442
ritual 308 309 310 311 313 484 486
ṛju 237
Rudradāman 178
Rudraṭa 96 108 214 255 256 257 259 260 261 262 264 265 266 268 276 278 325 409 428 430 437 438 439 448 451
rūpa 148
Rūpa Gosvāmin 97 118
rūpaka (*s*) 183 203 320
Ruyyaka 429 442 470

sabhā 469 470
sādhana 348
sādhvasa 382
Sāgaranandin 61 91 94 126 152 166 172 185 322 326 332 343 344 346 348 349 350 351 357 358 359 362 368 380 382 383 384 388 391 393 394
sahaja 280
sāhasa 141
Sāhityadarpaṇa 346 350 357 358 380 382 384 388 394
Sāhityavidyā 190
sahokti 224 259
sahṛdaya 494
Śailālika school 178
Śailālin 178
Saindhava 17 341 357 363 377 421
saindhava 363
Śaiva philosophers 77
Śaka 178
sakalakathā 450 451
Śakra 332
Śakrānanda 332
śakti 149
Śaktibhadra 104
Śakuntalā 357
Śālibhadra 421
sallāpa 342 346
sally 260
salutation 407 428 429 430 437
śama 92
samādhāna 146
samādhi 189 240
samagra 165 347
samāhita 227 277
samāja (*s*) 28 408 463 469 471 473 475 494
sāman 141
samarpaṇa 382
samāsokti 211 277
samasta 188 204
samatā 189 240
samavakāra 317 330
samaya (*s*) 150 201 496
sambhoga 57
Saṃghadāsa 450
saṃhāra 382
Sāṃkhya 85 99 109 119
sampheṭa 149 348
saṃśaya 186 261 348
saṃsṛṣṭi 234
samuccaya 260
saṃvaraṇa (concealment) 141
saṃvṛti 274
śamyā 342 355 365 369 374
sandhi (as limb of conclusion) 150
sandhis 121 128 182 281 306 420
sandhi (canto) 416
sandhyantaras 141
Saṅgītaratnākara 75 363
saṅgraha 148
śaṅkā 56
saṅketa 363
Śaṅkuka 82 88 172
Sanskrit 7 9 14 177 178 425 429 436 438 451 487
śānta 87 90 92 99
santoṣa 100
sāra 260
Śāradātanaya 91 94 164 165 171 268 336 343 344 346 347 348 349 350 351 353 354 355 356 357 358 359 368 376 377 378 381 382 383 384 385 386 391 394
Saraha 421
Sarasvatī 28 190 308 316 470
sargas 402 413
sargabandha (s) 305 415
Śārṅgadeva 75 76
sārūpya 186
Sarvānanda 426
Sarvasena 288 372
sarvātmatā 72
śāsana 183
sasandeha 233
śāstra (*s*) 1 4 272 298
śataka 418
Sātavāhana 16 248 444
satire 327 397 398 433 451 452 454
satirical stories or novels (see

nidarśana, etc.) 465
satirical monologue (s) 30 319 321 322 327 335 337 340 362 375 388 473 474
saṭṭaka 341 344 359 369 373
sattva 119 163
sāttvatī 181
sāttvika 59
Satyabhāmā 380
Satyabhāmā 350
saubhāgya 297
saukumārya 189
Śaurasenī 14 177 178
sauśabdya 194
scattering 107
scene (s) 176 177 344 379 382 384 415
scenes 'hinting at the matter' 126
scenery 176
sculpture 74 76 176 271
seasons 386 407 419 487 496 497
secondary meaning 260
secondary sense (s) 240 267 274
secular character of the heritage of *kāvya* 317
seed 123 124 125 127 128 130 131 133 134 138 166 167 169 171 330
self-assertion 109 110 111 112 113 115
self-consciousness 99 109 112 114
self-respect 99 109 113 114
semi-musical metres 313
sensation 201
sensitive 53 55 57 58 75 80 87 88 95 102 103 107 108 109 110 111 112 113 115 118 163 181 189 252 284 313 330 333 336 350 354 355 358 362 367 383 386 391 393 410 418 421 429 438 439 445
sensuous beauty 292 295 297
sentences (s) 200 272 280 375
sentence level 272 276
series 260 347
servant 391
seven-day plays 161
sham praise 220 264 278
shame 56
shameful 92
short story (-ies) 304 305 439 441 443 449 451
shows 365
showiness 241
showiness of sounds 239
showing 433
sickness 56
Siddha 450
siddhi 186
ṣidga 385
ṣidgaka 348 376 385 387
significance 497
Śīlā 475
śilpaka 348 385 394
śiṃgaka 348
similarity 186
simile 183 188 203 204 229 261 264 278
simile-metaphor 221 264 277
simplicity 243
Sindhu 17 341 377 421
Śiṅgabhūpāla 32 75 94 151 171 327
singers 311
singing 74 385
Sinhalese 18
Śiśunāga 190
Śiśupālavadha 284
situations (s) 125 127 180 403
Śiva 66 77 312 313 316 317 332 333 361 381
Śivasvāmin 407
skandhaka (*s*) 342 365 372 415
skandhakabandha 413
slave 384
slaying 141
sleeping 56
śleṣa 189 240 241 257 258 278 411
slip of the tongue 326
śliṣṭa 226 240
śloka 417
smaraṇa 261
smṛti 56
sneha 96
śobhā 186 277
social background 23
social criticism 261 400 443 465 495
social function 29 463
social harmony 499
social life 473
social obligation 28
social regression 499
society 37 38 40 43 71 72 73 94 330 399 489 498
Soddhala 304 433 436
softness 189 237 240 241 242 243 293 296
śoka 53
soliloquy 362
solo 375 383
solo actor 434
solo dance 361 362
solo dancer 367 387
Somanātha 433
Someśvara 156
song(s) 176 339 343 363 367 373 375 387 393 394 414 416 417 420
song cycle (s) 390 420 421
songs linked by narrative 392
soul 112 114
sound (s) 75 189 242 243 249 257 263 295 297
sound effects 273
South 238 303 304
South style 256

Southern writers 239 241
space 176
special arrangement of words 242
spectacle 351
spectator 78
speech 75 95 181 194 195 198 201 271 276
speech in space 321
split 141 146
spṛhā 101
spurning 147 207 261 278 279
śrama 56
śravya 425
śrīgadita 376 380 385
śṛṅgāra 53 418
Śṛṅgāraprakāśa (see 'Bhoja') 350 351 455 456
Śṛṅgāratilaka 384
stage 176 311 312
stage business 165 181
stage directions 307
stages of the action 121 127 129 130 133 138 166 168 169 172
stages of love 142
stammering 327
status of *kavi* 475
sthāpanā 314
Sthaviravāda school of Buddhism 12 13
sthāyibhāvas 53
sthitapāṭhya 363
sthitavādya 363
stick dance 369
story(-ies) 121 128 130 133 134 138 171 280 281 284 285 301 336 337 338 436 437
stotra 418
street 351
street play(s) 140 176 181 318 322 323 324 325 326 328 335
strength 141 189 237 238 240 241 242 243 244 246 294
strophe(s) 370 404 415
structure 243 405 437 458
stupidity 56
style (s) 181 182 183 196 237 238 239 240 241 242 243 246 249 252 253 255 256 268 273 280 287 288 289 290 291 292 293 294 295 410 429 442 461
stylistic analysis 268
stylistics 182 254 265 267
Subandhu 165 343 347 457 461
subject(s) 199 251 252 277 304 367 415
subject matter 35 48 121ff 124 215 249 265 276 277 280
sub-plot 122 135 164 166 167 169 171
subsidiary action (s) 122 128 135
Subuddhimiśra 276
success 186
succession 426
Śuddhānandaprakāśa 369
śūdra 40 327
Śūdraka 243
suggested sense 251 (revealed)
suggestion 249
Sugrīvakelana 391
sukha 100
sūkṣma 196
sukumāra 288 335 442
sukumāratā 240
Sun 381
śūnyatā 348
supporting scene 126
suppression 229
supreme 102
supta 56
surpassing 262 263
surprise 146
śuṣkāpakṛṣṭā 312
sūtras of the actors 45
sūtradhāra 307
svabhāva 95
svabhāvokti 197 259 276
svapna 141
Svayambhū 370 371 416
Śvetaketu 26
sweetness 189 237 240 241 242 243 246 292 293
syllables 437
sympathetic joy 93
synonyms 274
tablets 488
tadguṇa 262
Taittirīya Upaniṣad 75
tāla 359 362 420
tālalaya 180
Tamil 18
Tamil country 324
tāṇḍava 312 333 361 365 367 376 381 387 390
Tañjanagara 324
Tanjore 324
tāpa 348
tāpana 147
Tāpasavatsarāja 286
Taraṅgavatī 457
tarka 348
taste(s) 50 51 52 53 55 303 419
tasting 79 119
tautness of language 240
tears 59
technology 445
Tejahpāla 471
Telugu 18 324
tender 165 181 296 335 382 384
terror 56 57
terse 245

theatre (s) 19 49 52 55 76 78 79 85 87 106 159 176 303 307 316 322 340 361 373 434 466 468 494
theme (s) 176 310 312 313
theory of knowledge 298
thesis 199
thought-types 107
thunderbolt (outspoken statement) 147
Tibet 488
time 154 176 437
timetable for the *kavi* 486
time for performance 163
tolerance 493
topics in anthologies 419
toṭaka 148 341 343 359 371 373
totality of objects 408
tracing 147
tracts 449
Tradition 1 3 9 38 73 90 298 304 318 324 328 329 332 335 336 338 351 402 405 412 423 424 425 431 433 463 464 466 478 482 484
tragedy 65 90 329
tragic 64 103 122
tragic play (s) 181 336
tragic spirit 493
transaction 327
transfer 267 268 274 279
transferred senses 243 267
transient emotions 54 56 57 59 82 110 111 348
transmigration 64 65 79 90 329 459
trāsa 56
treatises 272
trembling 59
trigata 314 325 326
trimūḍha 363
Tripiṭaka 2 5 38 435
Tripura 351
Tripuradāha 333
Trivandrum 324
Trivikrama 433
troṭaka 343
tulyayogitā 223
Turks 471
turn 347
tutor (s) 32 349 354 358 383 385 473 (see '*pīṭhamarda*')
types 301
types of play (*rūpaka*) 164 317 318 319 320 339 340
typical 497

ucchvāsa 348 423
udāharaṇa 148 186
udāratā 189
udāratva 240
udātta 99 137 198 217 255 264 425
Udāttakuñjara 394
udaya 425
Udayana 283
Udbhaṭa 92 133 152 172 205 214 254 255 256 264 266 278 279
udbheda 146
uddhata 99 264 442
Uddyotana 359 436 446 454
udghātyaka 139 326
udīcya 239
udvega 148 348
ugratā 56
Ujjayinī 178
uktapratyukta 363
ukti 267
ullāpyaka 393 394
ullopyaka 393 394
ultimate point 110 113
ultimate reality 75
Umā 332
understanding 141 192
undertaking 127 348
Underworld 380
ungrammatical construction 189
unhappiness 87 100
union 57 102 103 189 240 241 243 295
unity of action 122
unity of an epic 407
universal 78
universality 410
universe 71
unmāda 56
unseen 88
untruth 327
upacāra 267 268 274 279
upādhis 119
upadiṣṭa 187
upagūhana 150
upakathā 446
upākhyāna 446
upakṣepa 146
upalabdha 425
upamā 183 203
upamārūpaka 221
upameyopamā 222
upanyāsa 147 382
upekṣā 93
upohana 363
ūrjasvin 98 99 216 217 255 264
usage 274
utkalikā 245
utkaṇṭhā 348
Utkaṇṭhitamādhava 391
utkarṣa 87 298
utmost limit 113
utpādya 337 425
utprekṣā 213
utprekṣāvayava 234
utsāha 53
utsṛṣṭikāṅka 318 329
uttamottamaka 363

uttara 260
uttarā koṭiḥ 110
Uttaratantra 341
utthāpanī 312

vācya 247 251
vadha 141
Vāgbhaṭa 376
vaicakṣaṇya 34
vaicitrya 270 271 277
vaidarbha style 190 238 239 240 241 246 256 442
vaidarbhī 242 267 288
vairāgya 418
vaiśāradya 348
vaiśyas 471 481
vajra 147
Vajrasena 421
Vākāṭaka Empire 190 238
vākkelī 326
Vākpatirāja 413 488
vakra 195 202 257 263
vakratā 271 276 280
vakrokti 195 197 236 247 257 265 269 271 325
vaktra 103 404 424 425 436
vākya 272
vākyavādins 270
Valayakarambaka 415
Vālin 351
Vālmiki 103 252
Vāmana 34 76 108 240 242 243 244 245 254 255 264 265 267 276 287 442 461
vāmya 348
vanities 473
vāra 342 347
Vararuci 423 444
variable qualities 119 292
variety 493
varṇa 272
varṇasaṃkara 147
vārttā 196
vāsakasajjā 358
Vāsavadattā 347 425
Vāsavadattā 433
vāstava 258
vastu(s) 251 276 280 336 367 370 379 382 415
vastu structure 387
vāstu 75
vastukas 370
vastunirdeśa 407
Vastupāla 471
Vasubandhu 198
Vāsudeva 411
Vāsudevaratha 433
Vāsuki 91
Vatsagulma 190 238
Vatsarāja 155
Vāyu Purāṇa 38 484
Veda 2 5 7 298 308 318 424 435
Vedic 8 432
Vedic metres 332
Vedic tradition 317
velaṇaa 92
Veṅkaṭādhvarin 433
verisimilitude 198
verse(s) 6 241 306 402 404 417 435 436
Vetālapañcaviṃśati 451
vibhāvanā 210
vibhāvas 54 253
vibodha 56
vicchitti 271 276
vice 100
vicitra 289
vicitrapada 363
viḍambi 377
Vidarbha 190 238
vidhāna 146
vidhūta 147
vidrava 148 346
vidūṣaka 30 179
vidyādharas 445
Vidyākara 419
Vidyānātha 151 171
Vidyāpati 304
Vijayanagara 493
Vijayasena 421
Vijñānavāda 86
vikāsa 107
vikaṭa 429
vikṣepa 107
vilāpa 348
vilāsa 147
Vilāsavatī 358
vilāsikā 388
villages 466
village life 464
vilobhana 146
vilopa 348
vimarśa 133
Vinayacandra 421
Vīṇāvatī 383
vinoda 34
vinyāsa 382
violent 165 181 333 335 336 343 346
vipralambha 57
vīra 53
Virahāṅka 366 369 370
Vīrarāghava 103
virodha 150 231 263 382
virodhābhāsa 263
virodhana 149
virtue 25 40 42 44 63 65 73 90 115 163 192 283 286 406 446
Virūpākṣa 351
viṣāda 56
Viśākhadatta 285

viṣama 260
visarga 295
viśeṣaṇa 187 230
viśeṣokti 230 277
visible *kāvya* 182 446
visible representation 180
viṣkambhaka 126
vismaya 53 75 117 348
Viṣṇu 181 317 331 381
Viṣṇudharmottara 74 76
viśrāma 34
vistara 107
Viśvāmitra 357
Viśvanātha 117 151 171 309
Viśveśvara 304
viṭa 27 179 321
vitarka 56
vīthī 318 322 324
vīthyaṅgas 140
vivakṣitānyaparavācya 250
vocabulary 274
voice 59
vrīḍā 56
vrīḍanaka 92
vṛtta 425
vṛttagandhi 245
vṛtti (*s*) 165 181 249 253
vyabhicāribhāvas 54
vyādhi 56
vyāghāta 262
vyāhāra 326
vyājastuti 220
vyaṅgya 247 260 265
vyasana 100
vyatireka 209 259
vyavasāya 149
vyāyoga 318 328
uyutpatti 298

want of agreement 225 264 279
war 60 405
watches 162
water clocks 163
ways of the world 62 198
wealth 25 40 42 63 73 115 192 286 405 406 446 480
weariness 56
well-known 336 337 346
Western (style) 256
Westerners 239
whole work 198 237 272 276 283 284 285 286 (see 'composition')
wisdom 418
wish 148 151 186
wishing 348
wizards 445
words 201 295 375 376
'world' *loka* 62, 198
writing materials 488
wrong cognition 101

yācñā 187
yakṣagāna 324
yamaka 188 203
yāmas 162
Yaśovarman 165 285 475
Yāska 19 183 190
yathāsaṅkhya 212
yearning 101
yogavṛtti 267
yuddha 60
Yudhiṣṭhira 90
yukti 146 348

zones of the stage 176

APPENDIX

(the numbers refer to the relevant paragraphs)

1. Rājaśekhara (*Kāvyamīmāṃsā* pp. 2-5) first divides speech (*vāṅmaya*, 'made of speech', this may mean fixed in books, oral or written) into *kāvya* (literature) and *śāstra* (learning). Then he subdivides the latter into 'non-human' (i.e. *Veda* or *āgama*) and 'human'. The latter again consists of *purāṇa* (including *itihāsa* according to 'some', which seems better, but according to others *itihāsa* is non-human, revealed *āgama*), *mīmāṃsā* (interpretation of the *Veda*, a *śāstra*), *smṛti* (*dharmaśāstra*) and *ānvīkṣikī* (treatises on analytical philosophy). He adds indirectly that all the other *śāstras* (economics, pleasure, crafts, commentaries, etc.) belong here (cf. [477] and A.K. Warder: 'The Description of Indian Philosophy'). Nāyaka (quoted by Abhinavagupta II p. 298) had three categories: *śāstra* (including *Veda*) as mainly speech (words), *ākhyāna* (Epic, i.e. tradition *itihāsa*) as mainly meaning and *kāvya* in which both speech and meaning are equal but the activity of the author dominates. But earlier writers had long taken this twofold (literature and learning), threefold (with tradition), fourfold (with treatises distinct from canonical works), and the further subdivisions of each, for granted. Drama is included in literature or even identical with it (almost all literature was 'performed'; *Nāṭyaśāstra* passim, see Chapter II).

29. It may be of interest to give an Indian calendar with the principal festivals. The year usually begins in March = spring at new Moon. In the medieval period the month starts at new Moon and the full Moon day is in the middle, dividing it into 'light' (first) and 'dark' (second) halves. The months are named after the constellations (some named after single stars) where the Moon becomes full.

Season.	Month.	Festival.
Vasanta	Caitra	*Suvasantaka* (spring, New Year)
spring	Spica	*Madanotsava/trayodaśī* (Pleasure,
	(Mar. - Apr.)	Kāmadeva)

		Sahakārabhañjikā (breaking the mango shoots)
	Vaiśākha Libra	*Āndolanacaturthī* (swing) = *Yavacaturthī*
		Vaiśākhī (the Buddha)
Grīṣma summer	Jyeṣṭha Antares	*Vaṭasāvitrī* = *Bhūtamātṛkā* (Sāvitrī)
	Āṣāḍha Sagittarius	*Navāmbudābhyudaya* (celebration of new clouds)
Varṣa rains	Śrāvaṇa Altair	*Navodakābhyudgama* (rising of the new waters)
	Proṣṭhapada Pegasus	*Navapatrikā* (new leaves at end of rains)
		(*Bisakhādikā* seems to be the same: eating lotus stalks)
Śarat autumn	Āśvayuja Aries	*Kaumudī* (*jāgara*) (Moon viewing)
	Kārttika Pleiades	*Indrotsava* (Indra) *Yakṣarātri* (Sprites, = *Dipotsava*, lamps)
		Abhyūṣakhādikā (eating a kind of cake)
Hemanta winter	Mārgaśīrṣa Orion (part)	*Navekṣubhakṣikā* (drinking new sugarcane) (= *Saṅkrānti*, winter solstice)
		— (nothing important in Pauṣa = the Crab)
Śiśira cold season	Māgha Regulus	*Kundacaturthī* (jasmine, Sarasvatī)
	Phālguna Leo (part)	*Holākā* (squirting with water coloured with pollen)

Besides the festivals proper a number of amusements or diversions *vinodas* are described in the *Kāmasūtra*, a lost book of Rājaśekhara's *Kāvyamīmāṃsā*, by Bhoja and so on. The distinction is vague, but the following seem more pastimes than religious events, though often appropriate for a particular season. Several became 'occasions' for description in *kāvyas*.

Usual Month.	Diversion.
Caitra	*Aṣṭamīcandraka* (Moon honoured by women on the eighth for love)
	Damanabhañjikā (breaking off *damana* flowers for ear ornaments)
	Vanavihāra (amusement in the woods)
	Aśokottaṃsikā (wearing *aśoka* flowers on the head)
	Kuralāliṅgana (embracing *kurala* trees)
	Bakulavihāra (amusement with *bakula* flowers)
	Puṣpāvacāyikā (gathering flowers)
Vaiśākha	*Ekaśālmali* (dancing round a great *śālmali* tree)
	Udakakṣveḍikā (squirting water with syringes)
Jyeṣṭha	*Udyānayātrā* (excursion to a park)
	Jalakrīḍā (water sports)
	Śikhaṇḍilāsya (peacock dance anticipating rains)
Śrāvaṇa	*Kadambayuddhāni* (battles with *kadamba* shoots)
	Krīḍāparvatavihāra (amusement on a miniature mountain)
	Ālolacaturthī (lightning on the fourth)
Kārttika	*Śaratpulinakeli* (pleasure of autumn sandbanks)
	Haṃsalīlāvalokana (watching the play of geese)
	Pānagoṣṭhī (drinking party)
Māgha	*Prekṣodīkṣaṇa* (seeing shows at the theatre)
	Goṣṭhīvihāra (amusement in the 'circle')

27, 30. 'Parasite' is not a good translation of *viṭa*, but nothing more precise seems to be available. 'Agent' might be nearer, but does not suggest his sophistication.

40. On the *Upavedas* see the Bibliography to Vol. VI.

42, 53ff. 'Emotion' though usually satisfactory is a narrower term than *bhāva*. One might try something less specific like '*mouvement*' (in its +18 sense) or 'impulse', but this would be restrictive in another way. *Śṛṅgāra* means etymologically 'pointed' and in ordinary usage 'brilliant' (as of dress). See *ALB* 1980-1, p. 630.

47. On the conjectural development of the *Nāṭyaśāstra* text, we find that Abhinavagupta (I p. 264 on VI. 10) mentions there were five parts *aṅgas* (originally?): *sāttvika abhinaya*, *āṅgika abhinaya*, *vācika abhinaya*, *gīta* and *ātodya* (respectively expression-acting, gesture-acting, speech-acting, song and musical instruments). Thus we have three kinds of acting *abhinayatraya* only, a term found elsewhere, and two kinds of music. 'Expression-acting' seems obscure if taken in some narrow sense as later, but may originally have meant acting of characters or living beings or even acting of emotions (in general, not just those few eventually called *sāttvikabhāvas*). The *Nāṭyaśāstra* VIII.11 says that *sāttvikābhinaya* has been described above with the *bhāvas* (i.e. in the previous chapter). If the five parts covered the essential topics one might expect that both the preceding chapters were originally intended, in other words *sāttvika* acting comprehended aesthetic experience *rasa* and emotion *bhāva*. Gesture is now covered by chapters Kāśī VIII-XIV and XXVI. Speech is now Kāśī XV-XXII. Song would be XXIX and XXXII and musical instruments XXVIII, XXX-XXXI and XXXIII. There is no evidence how far the *sūtras* known to Pāṇini in the -4 [45] covered these topics, but we can conjecture that the essentials were included and gradually extended and perhaps that a *bhāṣya*, commentary, was added in about the –2 and the verses *kārikās* and etymologies *nirukta* separately elaborated later. Then Abhinavagupta (I p. 264) says the *saṅgraha* with eleven parts was made according to Kohala's doctrine, apparently a synthetic handbook collecting these *sūtra* and commentary, verses and etymologies, later (+2?). The eleven are: aesthetic experience *rasa* (VI), emotion *bhāva* (VII), acting *abhinaya* (of four kinds including XXIII on costume and props *āhārya*; thus this topic covers most of chapters VIII-XXVI, with 'universal' *sāmānya* acting in XXIV as a combination of the original three [3729]), *dharmi* (ways of the world and of drama, now part of XXIII), modes *vṛtti* (now part of XXII, here *sāttvatī* appears again as the expressive or elevated), customs *pravṛtti* (local geography, dress, dialects, etc., now part of XIV), success *siddhi* (now XXVII), notes *svara* (now XXVIII), musical instruments *ātodya*, song *gāna* (XXXII) and the stage *raṅga* (now part of XIV and possibly II). Still later the

present text was finalised by adding chapters I-V on the mythical origins of drama and related matters such as the opening ritual and other chapters at the end including the descent of the theatre to Earth. Other smaller changes may have been made elsewhere, the biggest of which may have been the account of 'basic emotions' at the beginning of chapter VII. As they are not to be acted directly but only as described in the *rasa* chapter preceding (through their causes and effects but to produce *rasa*, not *bhāva*), this seems redundant: the idea perhaps is to describe the inferior stage of *rasa* and the descriptions are in fact very similar, but this is doubly superfluous because the actors are aiming at *rasa*, not an inferior degree of it. The *Nāṭyaśāstra* text itself (XXXVI.65 Kāśī) says that Kohala will (future) add a supplement *Uttaratantra* on the 'rest' *śeṣa*. This is not now available: judging from quotations by Abhinavagupta and others it described new forms of dramatic performance [341]. We may hazard a guess that all this organisation of drama conjectured to be going on in the +2 had something to do with the establishment of the theatre in Mathurā, the Eastern capital of the Kuṣāṇa Empire in that period [14, 178]. It may have been patronised by the Emperor Vāsudeva mentioned by Rājaśekhara [662], but this also is an uncertain identification. Cf. now our article 'The Origins of the Technical Senses of the Word *Rasa*'.

62. On *nāṭyadharmi* cf. [3681, 3886].

82. Kṣīrasvāmin (+11) on Amara (p. 51) similarly says *rasas* are imitations of *bhāvas*, but that they are so called because they are primarily tastable (when combined with the causes and effects and the transients).

126, 176. The curtain is held by two stage hands and is about a man's height. 'Entrance' is thus made front-stage near the lamp [3421] (and can be sitting or lying down), the curtain being gradually lowered to reveal a crest, etc. It may be grabbed and dragged by the actor to reveal character.

146. The bare statement that the limbs are of the conjunctions in the main action indicates that they all belong to this. The brief definitions in the *Nāṭyaśāstra* connect these opening limbs with the 'seed' or more often with the 'matter', or with both together, except for 'beguiling' and 'surprise' where probably the 'matter' is to be understood from the

preceding lines. Thus all these 'limbs' or 'parts' are aspects of the 'matter' of the plot, the seed of which, suggesting the objective, is being represented as that conjunction.

147. But in the re-opening the connection is not made clear and it seems the plot develops more freely and, as indicated earlier, the seed may be lost track of. One might say the matter 'opens up' and anything seems possible, the seed being largely forgotten.

148. In the embryo too the connection is usually not stated, except for the 'exposure', which is the 'breaking out' of the embryo. Nevertheless by implication 'deception' and the rest appear to bear on the main action as it develops.

149. In the obstacle again many limbs are not explicitly connected with the main action, but 'prevention' is of the 'matter' or objective desired and then 'resumption' is of the objective *kārya* of the seed; then the remaining 'forbearance' and 'anticipation' relate to the objective and the matter.

150. Some of the conclusion limbs are referred to the objective or the matter, but as the objective has already essentially been attained the rest also are evidently the celebration of this.

174. Examples of the play within a play, always of crucial significance for the main action, will be found in Harṣa [1772-3, 1775], Bhavabhūti [2372-6], Rājaśekhara [3661-8] and Kṣemīśvara [3843, 3869-75].

186. *Udāharaṇa* [1786], *hetu* [1786, 1842], *nirukta* [2828], *siddhi* [2493], *atiśaya* [1788], *anunaya* [1863], *guṇakirtana* [1789], *priyokti* [2557].

187. *Viśeṣaṇa* [2215], *garhaṇa* [1852], *leśa* [1846], *ākranda* [2222], *yācñā* [2279], *kṣamā* [2369].

266. Rājaśekhara seems to have invented the idea of figures of both sound and meaning, though otherwise following Rudraṭa. Since this book (XII) of his *Kāvyamīmāṃsā* seems to be lost we do not know what these were, though Bhoja has such a class.

268. For Bhoja, literature is an extension of language and criticism of grammar. In the *Śṛṅgāraprakāśa*, starting from Bhāmaha's definition of literature as speech and meaning combined [194], he sets out twelve aspects of this 'combination' *sāhitya*, which ascend from the grammatical to the aesthetic.

Thus having discussed questions of grammar in chapters I-VI he then proposes in chapter VII four aspects of the powers of speech units (words) taken singly to carry meanings: 1) expression *abhidhā* [2410] has three functions *vṛttis*, primary *mukhyā*, secondary *gauṇī* (transfer, etc.) and tertiary *lakṣaṇā* (totally different) [2243] ; 2) the wish of the speaker *vivakṣā* (shown by intonation, etc.) [2446, 2887] ; 3) intention *tātparya* (the meaning is that of another speech unit, such as the 'revealed' or implied meaning) [3341] ; 4) analysis *pravibhāga* by the method of agreement and difference (synonyms, etc.). The next four aspects (chapter VIII) concern speech units when connected with other speech units: 5) mutual expectancy *vyapekṣā* of meanings between speech units [2338] ; 6) capability *sāmarthya* which is the power of meanings of words to combine in another meaning; 7) a series *anvaya* of words in a sentence has a meaning; 8) unity of meaning *ekārthībhāva* is the combination of a whole work in a 'great sentence' having a single meaning [2191]. The last four aspects cover the main topics of criticism. But first from the principles of Vedic interpretation, Mīmāṃsā, and from grammar, especially Bhartṛhari's *Vākyapadīya*, Bhoja derives a set of forty-eight 'qualities of a sentence' *vākyadharmas*, such as secondary meaning [2338], 'induction' *ūha* [2269], supersession [4820], system [1916, 1963, 2885], extension [1873, 2240, 2263], competence [2280] and breaking of order [2974]. With these he introduces his chapter (IX) on avoiding faults and acquiring qualities: 9) faults *doṣas* are avoided in good literature; 10) qualities *guṇas* are found; 11) (chapter X) figures of speech *alaṃkāras* (of sound, meaning and both, twenty-four of each); 12) (chapters XI and following to the end of the work) aesthetic experience *rasa*. Bhoja considers especially three linguistic levels, namely word, sentence and entire composition. Aspects 1-8 concern the word and sentence levels. Aspects 9-12 are applied first at the sentence level and afterwards at the level of entire composition. Thus at the sentence level we find the faults, qualities and figures usually defined by earlier critics. At the compositional level we have the avoiding of faults in a story and the qualities and ornaments *alaṃkāras* of entire compositions. The qualities are that a composition relates to the four ends of life, is constructed with the conjunctions and so on, uses appropriate metres [1551]. The ornaments are the descriptions of places, times, pleasures and so on [1267, 1520-1]. Bhoja's theory of the aesthetic experience is set out at the sentence level, since every sentence in a good work should contribute to it, as sketched above [98-9, 108-14]. But at the compositional level Bhoja defines forty-eight literary types or genres in relation to *rasa* never being absent from them and in relation to the qualities and ornaments of compositions which these genres may have and which serve as causes for aesthetic experience never being absent [115, 409].

298-9. Śobhākaramitra (+12) should be noted for his excellent analysis of the (about one hundred) figures of speech, criticising Mammaṭa and Ruyyaka. The anonymous *Sāhitya-mīmāṃsā* attempts to combine Kuntaka and Bhoja but reduces the figures to ten only (+13?). Appayya's unfinished *Citramīmāṃsā* begins an exceedingly thorough analysis of the figures and their definitions to ensure that each is logically distinct.

348. Eagerness [2226], knotting [2209], wishing [2226], doubt [3727] remorse [2102], affliction (alarm? *udvega)* [1716], lassitude [1136, 2206], perplexity [2099], perversity [2109], following [3905], astonishment [2100], emptiness [2212], confidence [2403], reassuring [2099], terror *ātaṅka* [2233], pleasure *pramada* [2344], aberration *pramāda* [2229]. Example of a *śilpaka*: *Rāmavijaya* (Vema: *Sāhityacintāmaṇi*).

363. *Geyapada* [1757], *sthitavādya* [1783], *āsinavādya* [1791], *pracchedaka* [2507], *trimūḍha* [1789], *dvimūḍha* [1787, 3915], *uttamottamaka* [1793].

367. The verse quoted by Bhoja is also quoted, for its metre *duvahaa* [3260], by Svayambhū (*Chandas* p. 79), on which see the editor's notes "90.1" on p. 224.

375-6. Uddyotana (+8) mentions (in Prakrit) *bhâṇaya*, *ḍombilliya* and *siggaḍāiya* (p. 150) [2729] (with *giya* and *vāiya*).

382. Rūpa's *Dānakelikaumudi* (+16) is a *bhāṇikā* with the seven limbs.

402. Gopīnātha (+18) in his *Kavicintāmaṇi* (chapter IV) says that an epic should not have fewer then eight cantos.

435. The meaning of the word *campū* is obscure, but a Buddhist commentary, Jayarakṣita's undated *Śrighanācārasaṃgraha Ṭikā*, says that *campū* means comic *hāsya* (p. 74), though this is hardly true of such Buddhist *campūs* as Śūra's *Jātakamālā*

[903-32]. But we have just noted the tradition of *campūs* being presented by a 'fool' *vidūṣaka*, which harmonises with this in that the actor would add plenty of comedy.

449. Jaṭāsiṃhanandin (+7) seems to refer to his Jaina *Varāṅgacarita* as a *parikathā* (XX.91, XXXI.114-5) and it is a fairly bare narrative (plus Jaina lectures), nevertheless it is a long work [1934].

451 and 456. The *Vetālapañcaviṃśati* [4477, 4480] might be considered a *pravahlikā* in a very broad sense because its stories end with a question to be decided or a judgment to be passed by the hero, though the 'correct' answer is to say nothing and the work as a whole is not of this type. Some *Jātaka* stories are of the type where the hero has to solve a problem. A version of the *Ceṭaka* may be found in Hemavijaya's *Kathāratnākara* (the Silent Princess) [4480]. It would seem natural that these types of short story should overlap and not be severely distinguished and separated. On the short story see the Preface to Vol. VI.

80. Udbhaṭa (late + 8) has *rasa* an increase or excess of the basic emotion (IV. 4).

86. Saṃgharakkhita's Pali *Subodhālaṅkāra* (+12) should have been mentioned here. He says the basic emotions, including calm *śama*, when increased or enhanced, become *rasa*, including the calmed *śānta*, even in experience which appear unhappy [6250, 6253, 7308]. His interpretation of Bhāmaha is important (see our article 'Saṅgharakkhita's Poetics' *in Studies in Buddhism and Culture*, Tokyo, Sankibo Busshorin, 1991.)

154. [See 160].

176. The curtain *yavanikā* (perhaps the original word was *javanikā* from *jū*, 'move quickly', 'impel', falsely Sanskritised by substituting *y* for *j*) is held by two stage hands by means of strings attached to the top of it, near the front of the stage. It is opposite the main oil lamp, which is on a stand at the centre. An actor 'entering' from the green room first salutes the musicians at the rear of the stage, then takes up a position screened by the curtain, so that when it is lowered his face will appear opposite the lamp, his expression clearly visible. The actual lowering or 'entrance' may take some time and varies according to the character, the actor first showing only facial expressions, then gestures, which may include grasping the top of the curtain, before speaking. Since the actor does not change his position during the entrance we often find

such stage directions as 'enters sitting' or 'enters asleep', etc. Afterwards the stage hands remain motionless in the background, one of them holding the folded curtain, until it has to be raised again for another entrance. In between it may also be used to screen actors who have nothing to say for some time, are in a separate zone whilst others occupy the central zone and speak. In general, whichever actor is speaking should be at the centre of the stage in front of the lamp, so that his expressions can be seen clearly. Those previously on stage are therefore displaced to one side, another zone, and are as a rule understood to be as yet out of sight of the new arrival, who likewise may be unseen by them for some time. Occasionally an actor may rush in urgently to another without touching the curtain *apatīkṣepeṇa.* For more details see Vol. V, especially [3398ff.].

318. The *Mahābhārata* claims to be the fifth *Veda* (I. LVII. 74). This is mentioned also in an ancient Pali text (D.I. 88).

329. Śāradātanaya (p. 251) says that according to Kohala an *utsṛṣṭikāṅka* may have two acts.

352. cf. the *Nṛttaratnāvalī* of Jayā Senāpati, Raghavan's Introduction pp. 138-39.

369. A *śamyā* may be (originally?) the 'yoke-pin' of a chariot 32 *aṅgulas* long (*Kātyāyana Śulva Sūtra* II.5). Bhoja (II. 468, 3 lines from the bottom) describes striking a stick with sticks in a *rāsaka.*

377f. *Ḍomba* > *roma* = 'gypsy'.

404. In a *kāvya* epic the metre usually varies from canto to canto and sometimes (later) every canto may be in a different metre.

ADDITIONAL BIBLIOGRAPHY

(Relevant for Vols. I-III; see separately for IV and V)

Ājñāsundara: *Śilavati*, MS in Jaisalmeru.

Anādimiśra : *Rāsagoṣṭhirūpaka*, MS in Bhuvaneśvara State Museum, L.319, edn. in press.

Appayya Dīkṣita : *Citramīmāṃsā*, ed. Śivadatta and Paṇaśīkara, Nirṇaya Sāgara Yantrālaya/Aṅkanālaya, Mumbayī, 2nd edn, 1907.

Arjunadāsa : *Kalpalatā*, MS in Bhuvaneśvara State Museum.

Cāritrasundara : *Mahīpālacaritra*, ed. Hīrālāl Haṃsarāj, Jamnagar, 1909.

Devakavi : *Kusumāvali*.

Gopīnātha : *Kavicintāmaṇi*, MSS in Orissa State Museum, Bhuvaneśvara.

Guṇāḍhya : *Utayaṇakumārakāviyam* (modern abridgment of Kongu-Vēḷir), ed. V. Swaminatha Iyer, Mylapore, 1935; there is still another abridgment in MS in the V. Swaminatha Library, Madras.

Guṇasamṛddhi : *Añjanāsundari*, ed. N. J. Śāha and A. M. Bhojak, supplement to *Sambodhi*, Vol. I No. 2, 1972, separately paginated.

Gopālabhaṭṭa Drāviḍa : *Halliśaka nṛtya*, MS in Vārāṇasī Sanskrit University.

Hemavijaya : *Kathāratnākara*, ed. Haṃsarāja, Jamnagar, 1911; incomplete translation by Hertel, Müller, Munich, 1920.

Jayadeva III : *Vaiṣṇavāmṛtagoṣṭhirūpaka*, *Kaliṅga Historical Research Journal*, Kalākurdi State; Bhuvaneśvara Orissa State Museum has a MS.

Jayarakṣita : *Śrighanācārasaṃgraha Ṭīkā*, ed. Sanghasena, Tibetan Sanskrit Works Series, K. P. Jayaswal Research Institute, Patna, 1960.

Jinaharṣa : *Rayaṇasehari*, MS in BORI, Poona.

Kālidāsa : *Raghuvaṃśa* with Aruṇagirinātha's commentary and Nārāyaṇa's, Sri Ravivarma Sanskrit Series, Sanskrit College, Trippūnitthura, 3 vols., 1959.

Kṣemīśvara : *Naiṣadhānanda*, ed. K. K. Raja and A.K. Warder, Adyar Library Series, Madras, 1986.

Narasiṃhasena : *Parimalā*, MS in Bhuvaneśvara.

Nārāyaṇa (Melputtūr) : *Matsyāvatāra*, University Manuscripts Library, Trivandrum, 1945.

Nemicandra : *Līlāvati*, Karṇāṭaka Kāvyamañjarī, Mysore, 1898.

Pādalipta, the *Saṁkhittā Taraṃgavaī* has been reedited by H.C. Bhāyāṇī, along with another abridgment by Bhadreśvara, and a Gujarati translation, L. D. Institute, Ahmedabad, 1979

Ratnaśekhara : *Śrīśīpālanarendrakathā* (Rayaṇasehara : Sirisirivālakahā): Mumbai, Devacaṇda Lālabhāī Pustakoddhāra, 1923. First 400 verses ed. and tr. by V.J. Chauksi Ahmedabad, 1932. Florence Ms. 782; Śrīpālamahārājakathā;

Rūpa (Gosvāmin) : *Dānakelikaumudī*, printed in *bengali* script, Radharaman Press, Berhampur, Murshidabad, 1926; MS in Bhuvaneśvara Orissa State Museum, L. 526.

Sāhityamīmāṃsā (anon.), ed. K. Sāmbaśiva, Trivandrum Sanskrit Series, Government of Travancore, Trivandrum, 1934.

Śobhākaramitra : *Alaṅkāraratnākara*, ed. C.R. Devadhar, Poona Oriental Series, Oriental Book Agency, Poona, 1942.

Sūranna : *Kalāpūrṇodayamu*.

Timmakavi : *Sujanamanaḥkumudacandrikā*, MSS in Waltair, Andhra University (32647 and 37387), transcript prepared in 1977.

Upendrabhañja : *Lāvaṇyavatī* MSS in Calcutta (RASB) and London.

Vāsudevaratha : *Gaṅgavaṃśānucarita*, ed. Pramila Mishra, Directorate of Tourism and Cultural Affairs, Orissan Oriental Text Series No. 12, Bhubaneswar, 1979.

Vema (bhūpāla) : *Sāhityacintāmaṇi*, MS in Trivandrum, University of Kerala. Adyar 175.

Vidarbharāja (presumably not Bhoja Mālavarāja) : *Rāmāyaṇa Campū*, ed. with Bālacandra's commentary, Nirṇaya Sāgara Press, Bombay, 1924.

Warder A. K. : 'The Description of Indian Philosophy', in the *Journal of Indian Philosophy*, Reidel, Dordrecht, Vol. I, pp. 4-12, 1970.

__________ : 'Classical Literature', in *A Cultural History of India*, ed. A.L. Basham, Clarendon Press, Oxford, pp. 170-96, 1975.

__________ : 'Indian Kāvya Literature', in the *Journal of Oriental Research*, Kuppuswami Sastri Research Institute, Mylapore, Madras, Vol. XXXIX, pp. 56-64 (1972 Address, correct misprint in footnote, see p. 94), 1976

__________ : *The Science of Criticism in India*, Adyar Library and Research Centre, Madras, 1978.

__________ : 'The Origins of the Technical Senses of the Word Rasa', in *The Adyar Library Bulletin*, Vols. 44-5, Adyar Library, Madras, pp. 614-34, 1980-81

__________ : 'Tantrā and Shīrāzād (the 360 and the 1001 Nights)', in *Sambodhi*, L. D. Institute of Indology, Ahmedabad, 1982-3, pp. 113-20.

__________ : see Kṣemīśvara, unfortunately there are very many misprints as this joint editor was sent only one round of proofs and could make no corections at all to the Introduction; this was due to the work being rushed out for the Centenary of the Library.

__________ : 'Feudalism and Mahāyāna Buddhism' in *Indian Society: Historical probings*, ed. R.S. Sharma, New Delhi, People's Publishing House, 1974, p.p. 156 ff.

__________ : 'Jaina Aesthetics' in *Approaches to Jaina Studies*, ed. N.K. Wagle and and O. Qvarnström, Toronto, Centre for South Asian Studies, 1999, pp. 342 ff.

__________ : 'Science Fiction in India' in *Lex et Litterae*, ed. S. Lienhard and I. Piovano, Torino, Edizione dell' Osso,' 1997, pp. 555 ff.

__________ : 'Saṅgharakkhita's Poetics', in *Studies in Buddhism and Culture*, Tokyo, Sankibo Busshorin, 1991, pp. 13-22.

__________ : 'Merutuṅga and Vikrama' in *Anusandhāna* 18, *Ahmadābāda*, 2001. pp. 16 f.